SPECTRUM

SPECTRUM

◆

PERRY ANDERSON

VERSO
London • New York

First published by Verso 2005
© Perry Anderson 2005

1 3 5 7 9 10 8 6 4 2

Verso
UK: 6 Meard Street, London W1F 0EG
USA: 180 Varick Street, New York, NY 10014-4606
www.versobooks.com

Verso is the imprint of New Left Books

ISBN 1-85984-527-4

British Library Cataloguing in Publication Data
A catalogue record for this book is available from the British Library

Library of Congress Cataloging-in-Publication Data
A catalog record for this book is available from the Library of Congress

Typeset in Monotype Sabon
Printed in the United Kingdom by Bath Press

For Tom Mertes
in friendship

CONTENTS

ACKNOWLEDGEMENTS

The first versions of part or all of the following essays were published in the *London Review of Books*: 'The Intransigent Right', 24 September 1992; 'Constitutional Theatre', 22 October 1992; 'Dreams of Central Europe', 25 November 1999; 'In Memoriam', 21 October 1993; 'Civil War, Global Distemper', 4 November 1993; 'Philologist Extraordinary', 10 May 2001; 'The Vanquished Left', 3 October and 17 October 2002; 'An Anglo-Irishman in China', 30 July 1998 and 20 August 1998. 'Designing Consensus' was originally published in *Dissent*, Winter 1994; 'Plotting Values' and 'Arms and Rights', in *New Left Review*, I/231, September–October 1998, and No. 32, January–February 2005. 'Tropical Recall' and 'An Atlas of the Family' appeared in *The Nation*, 26 January 2004 and 30 May 2005; the first appendix as a 'Reader's Note' in *London Review of Books: An Anthology*, London 1996. Most of these texts have undergone correction or amendment. 'Norming Facts' is hitherto unpublished. Postscript expansions are indicated by date at the end of the text.

I would like to thank my editors at the *LRB* and *NLR*, Mary-Kay Wilmers and Susan Watkins, and my brother Benedict Anderson for their comments on different parts of this book; and Tom Mertes, Choi Sung-eun and Zhang Xiaohong for all the help they gave me in preparing it.

FOREWORD

This book is an exercise in the history of contemporary ideas. It can be viewed as a panning shot, moving from right to left, of a particular intellectual landscape. The thinkers and writers it looks at belong to a political world in which the categories of Right, Centre and Left visibly still retain their meaning, even if – this is one of the questions raised along the way – the locations and boundaries of each are far from fixed. This is the spectrum to which the title alludes. The existence of such a gamut of conceptions and convictions is familiar enough. Yet a passage through it remains relatively rare, as an analytic venture. There are two good reasons for that. The first is the natural tendency of each political family to take a greater interest in its own kin than in aliens or adversaries. Polemical zeal can produce an fixation on the other side, or sides, of purely hostile intent. The Cold War was full of that kind of literature, as ephemeral as it was instrumental. But at a more serious intellectual level, minds tend to divide according to sympathies, in a scholarly version of the attraction of like for like. The impulse to study, first of all, the sources – proximate or remote – of one's own loyalties is perfectly proper and productive. Yet it can evidently also lead to a narrowing of horizon. Ideas are rarely absolute values: their worth is always relative to what other notions are in play across the field, knowledge of which alone affords a measure of them. Intra-mural absorption can never deliver this.

The second reason for the paucity of comparative work here has to do with the nature of the domain itself. Politics is not a self-enclosed activity, organically generating a body of concepts internal to it. What counts as a set of ideas with a bearing on the political conflicts of a time varies according to epoch and region. Today it stretches far beyond the purview of political science, traditionally conceived. Philosophy, economics, history, sociology, psychology, not to speak of the earth and life sciences, and the arts, all intersect at different points with terrain of politics, in its classic definition.

Formal political theory, though far from extinct, occupies only a part of the resulting space. This is an expansion, however, subject to the iron laws of specialization. The wider the span of disciplines with potential purchase on political outlooks at any one time, the more difficult it becomes to achieve an appropriate sense of the range of ideas about power and society – the domain of politics proper – that make up the inventory of the time. Specialist restriction reinforces partisan introspection in inhibiting exploration of the field as a whole.

In attempting, nevertheless, a step in this direction, I have followed methods set out in *A Zone of Engagement*, a previous volume to which this can be regarded as a sequel. It would be otiose to repeat them at length here. All that need be said is that a premise of this book, too, is that ideas of any complexity are best studied in the detailed work of the particular writers who produce them, as texts inseparable from, but not reducible to, historical contexts that are always at once social and conceptual. The option, in other words, is to treat them neither as timeless motifs, nor as generic discourses, nor as specialized languages, the three most popular alternatives on offer. On the other hand, this volume is not a simple pendant to the earlier work, because its design involves an alteration of range. In the latter I explained that since my primary impulse in engaging with a body of work was usually a critical admiration, I found it difficult to write about authors to whom I felt myself personally too close. In constructing a volume dealing with thinkers covering the span from the extreme right through the moderate centre to the radical left, I have tried to overcome this limitation. *A Zone of Engagement* mentions three thinkers of the Left about whom I would liked to have written at that time, but felt unable to. Two of these, Eric Hobsbawm and Sebastiano Timpanaro, feature in this book; the third, Fredric Jameson, is the focus of another study, *The Origins of Postmodernity*. This is a widening at one end of the spectrum. At the other, I consider here a group of thinkers who, unlike any treated earlier, were not liberals of more or less conservative persuasion – Max Weber and Francis Fukuyama, who feature largely in *A Zone of Engagement*, were certainly that – but theorists of a more uncompromising Right, enemies of any liberal consensus.

The result is a book more systematic in conception than its predecessor. Any selection of figures picked from each segment of a political hemisphere is, of course, bound to be somewhat arbitrary, answering to the accidents of personal interest. Reflection on those included in this collection was in any case not always premeditated, but answered to different solicitations. But the intention of a survey with the structure below was formed early on, and guided the ensuing set of choices. The political spectrum, giving the general coordinates of the book, has also largely determined its topical range. Right, Centre and Left have not invested equally in the same subjects or disciplines. The classical legacies of political thought, from Plato to Nietzsche, and the immediate tasks of running the world, at home and abroad, have been of most concern to the Right. Normative philosophical constructions have become a specialty of the Centre. Economic, social and cultural investigations – of past and present – dominate the output of the Left. Any attempt to come to grips with all three outlooks is thus obliged to traverse quite variegated ground. In this book, among the topics to be encountered are theories of law, of the state, of the economy, of the family, of international relations, of the lessons of antiquity and of the twentieth century, of memory and mortality. Clearly, each of these is best handled by a specialist in the matter. But something can still be said about them, however partially, where they enter the general stock of political culture as resources for a particular front of opinion. My own attempt to do so is based not on any polymathic competence, but comes more mundanely from the necessities of editorial practice, now getting on for half a century, in a generalist journal that imposes a certain diversity of reading and – at any rate in principle – criticism, as a technical requirement.[1] The limitations that also implies are plain enough.

No pretence is made that the collection of topics reviewed below, in each case through the prism of a particular body of work, is remotely comprehensive. Some of the gaps are intellectual systems I have dealt with elsewhere: notably French post-structuralism, whose most active political thinker, Jean-François Lyotard, I have discussed in *The Origins of Postmodernity*. Figures in other fields have been so well captured by close colleagues that addition would be superfluous. These include the two most significant theorists of inter-state relations today, of very different stamp, John Mearsheimer and Philip Bobbitt.[2] The world-systems theory of Immanuel Wallerstein and his school has yet to receive assessment of this quality, but has attracted

---

1. *New Left Review* was founded in 1960. I became editorially involved with it in 1962. The connection defines, of course, my own position along the political spectrum.

2. See Peter Gowan, 'A Calculus of Power', *New Left Review* 16, July–August 2002, pp. 47–67; and Gopal Balakrishnan, 'Algorithms of War', *New Left Review* 23, September–October 2003, pp. 5–33.

a large literature. The same could be said of the cultural politics of Edward Said, whose influence today is no less. Other lacunae have more to do with the lack of any one figure or body of work so far central enough to represent an obvious point of entry into the terrain concerned. This is typically the case with issues that make up a good part of the emergent agenda of politics in the new century, but have yet to generate a literature equal to their importance. Ecology and biotechnology are the obvious examples. Feminism is a different case, its now considerable history offering a puzzling pattern of intellectual stops and starts. If the current period is one of relative lull – there is no *Second Sex* in view – that is unlikely to last. The world of political ideas remains a much more male affair than that of political careers, but sooner or later the one will catch up with the other.

The lay-out of the book follows the parade of the time. Since the end of the Cold War, when *A Zone of Engagement* was published, the ideas of the Right have gained further ground; the Centre has increasingly adapted to them; the Left remains, globally speaking, in retreat. The scale of the intellectual restoration that has occurred – the term 'neo-liberalism', taken seriously in its historical reference, captures something of it – is habitually repressed on the Left in a variety of ways. Defeat is a hard experience to master: the temptation is always to sublimate it. But if it is eventually to be overcome, it is necessary to be able to look theoretical adversaries in the face, without either indulgence or self-deception. That requires a culture of curiosity and critique that is not content to rest within the traditions of the Left itself, where the general inclination of political tendencies to self-absorption has typically been intensified by the siege mentality of any minority formation, as the intellectual universe of the Left – in the West, at any rate, with fleeting exceptions in post-war France and Italy – has always been; never more so than today. One of the aims of this collection is to resist this involution.

The first part of the book considers bodies of writing that belong in one way or another to the literature of the Right. Dominating this landscape are the four thinkers, each in his own fashion of outstanding gifts, discussed in the opening essay: Michael Oakeshott, Carl Schmitt, Leo Strauss, Friedrich von Hayek. Since this text was written, the secondary literature on each, as an individual thinker, has been enriched.[3] But it is the complex inter-relations between these

---

3. The most notable contribution to this literature is Gopal Balakrishnan, *The Enemy: An Intellectual Portrait of Carl Schmitt*, London 2000. Paul Franco, *Michael*

minds, as they reacted to the arrival of mass democracy, that remains
the key to an understanding of their political impact. This is the
theme of the chapter devoted to them here. The rest of this section
looks at two writers from subsequent levies, each prominent in
English public life, who illustrate something of the way democracy
has been conceived downstream from that moment: Ferdinand
Mount bringing the legacy of Oakeshott to bear on the internal
structures of British state and society; Timothy Garton Ash concerned with the external replication of Western models, detoxified of
the hazards that alarmed the inter-war quartet, in Eastern Europe
and the world beyond. The title of this section, 'Politics', is to be
understood in the narrower sense of the term – that is, the devising
of forms and policies for managing a state, as distinct from broader
issues of the nature and structure of power in a society, or in French
usage *la politique* as opposed to *le politique*. It is logical that writing
in this area should fall predominantly to the Right, since that is how
the way of the world has gone in this period.

The second part of book looks at three leading political philosophers at the turn of the century, all of whom are widely regarded –
and have regarded themselves – as figures of a moderate Left: John
Rawls, Jürgen Habermas and Norberto Bobbio. Here they are
treated, without any particular polemical emphasis, as thinkers who,
at any rate by this time, are better considered figures of the Centre. In
the case of Rawls and Habermas, the justification comes from the
ideal that unites the domestic political theory of their later work:
'consensus'. If this is not a quintessential value of the Centre, it is
difficult to know what would be. Bobbio, who had a longer and more
committed record as a figure of the Left, never subscribed to it:
indeed he sought with no little eloquence to re-draw clear-cut lines of
division between Right and Left that allow only a space of evasion to
the Centre. In his case, more clearly even than with Habermas or
Rawls, political classification is a function of historical conjuncture
rather than essential identity. I have written elsewhere of the earlier
work of Habermas and Bobbio, when they were unambiguously of
the Left.[4] If one compares the domestic political theory of the three

---

Oakeshott, Yale 2004, and *Daniel Tanguy, Leo Strauss: une biographie intellectuelle*,
Paris 2003, are both of interest. *Alan Ebenstein, Friedrich Hayek. A Biography*, New
York 2001, and Hans Jorg, *Friedrich August von Hayek. Die Tradition der Freiheit*,
Dusseldorf 2000, are fair, but limited first steps.

4. For Habermas, see *In the Tracks of Historical Materialism*, London 1982,
pp. 57–67; *A Zone of Engagement*, London 1992, pp. 327–331; *The Origins of*

thinkers, as reviewed below, Bobbio remained to the end more radical
in sensibility than Rawls or Habermas. But if we look at the writing
on international relations of the trio, the topic of the middle essay of
this book, their convergence on the principles of military intervention
that have justified successive imperial wars situates all three at the still
centre of conventional wisdom today.

The third section of the book moves to the terrain of the Left,
where all those under review can be regarded as more overtly concerned with history as the record of the past, distinct from any
deontology, than any of the figures of the Right or Centre considered
here. This goes without saying, of course, for such famous modern
historians as Edward Thompson, Robert Brenner or Eric Hobsbawm.
But it holds good of Sebastiano Timpanaro too, a historian of nineteenth-century ideas as well as a classical philologist; of Göran
Therborn, by profession a sociologist, but whose principal work is by
any standards a major historical synthesis; and even in his own style
of Gabriel García Márquez, whose fiction has never taken the contemporary world as its object. Is this a common disposition on the
Left because its active life as a movement to change the world now lies
behind it? That would be too easy a conclusion, and not only because
none of these figures ever ceased to be engaged in contemporary
politics. What this historical-mindedness indicates is rather shared
connexions with what was until recently the *Leitkultur* of the international Left, which its founders after all termed historical materialism.

That a Marxism capable of informing works of such obvious
magnitude as Therborn's or Brenner's or Hobsbawm's – dealing with
such world-encompassing topics as the history of the modern family,
the dynamics of the global economy, the periodization of the twentieth century – can scarcely be pronounced dead, is self-evident. My
treatment of the different figures of this Left varies in part as a
function of the occasions on which I was asked, or wanted, to write
about them. Two of these texts were composed on the death of their
subjects, Edward Thompson and Sebastiano Timpanaro, and strike
a more personal note. Two others deal only with a single work by the
author, one on Göran Therborn, the other on Gabriel García
Márquez, whose inclusion here, as the most generally admired

Postmodernity, London 1998, pp. 36–44; for Bobbio, *A Zone of Engagement*,
pp. 87–129. Bobbio replied both to the latter, and to the essay on him in this volume.
For our exchanges on each, see *Teoria Politica*, Nos 2–3, 1989, pp. 293–308, and *New
Left Review* I/231, pp. 82–93.

novelist in the world today, is less strange than it may seem at first sight – what chrestomathy of the Left could really exclude him? Two, finally, look at their subjects at greater length, each in dual focus: Robert Brenner in his work on the English Civil War and on the Long Downturn, Eric Hobsbawm in his tetralogy of the world since the French Revolution, and his memoirs. This last essay, in keeping with the way its author has himself written of *Age of Extremes*, as with the reality of the period, is entitled 'The Vanquished Left'. But to be defeated and to be bowed are not the same. None of these writers has lowered his head before the victors. If a dividing line is wanted between what has become the Centre and remains the Left, it would lie here.

Essays about others, practised as a form, often tacitly pose questions about the essayist. Cultural studies have made 'self-positioning' fashionable, as an often laboured exordium to matters in hand. Here I have preferred simply to indicate two of the debts I owe as a writer. The first is to the *London Review of Books*, in which many of these essays were first published. Coming from a political background quite distant from the general tenor of the paper, I learnt from it how to write – also therefore think – in ways that were new to me. The description I attempt of the *LRB* tries to capture the peculiar alchemy of the journal, and can be read as a sign of what these pages owe to its education. Periodicals are difficult to write about, and not much writing is done on them. The reflections below, critical as well as admiring, are written from the standpoint of a contributor on the far left of the journal's band-width. The book ends with an account of my father's life in Republican China. What one generation owes another varies a good deal historically. The circumstances I describe separated me from this past, but when I discovered it, rather late, I realized in a complicated way something of what had gone into my own make-up. But the story itself, of an individual and an institution, stands as a piece of history on its own.

I. POLITICS

THE INTRANSIGENT RIGHT:

Michael Oakeshott, Leo Strauss, Carl Schmitt, Friedrich von Hayek

A few months after the fall of Margaret Thatcher, the most original thinker of post-war Conservativism died. Perhaps partly because of the commotion caused by the change of national leadership, the passing of Michael Oakeshott did not attract much public notice. Even *The Spectator,* which might have been expected to mark the event with a full salute, ignored it for half a year, before carrying a curiously distracted piece by its editor, reporting strange losses in the philosopher's papers, without so much as mentioning his political ideas.[1] The remoteness of Oakeshott's intellectual origins from the contemporary landscape was perhaps another element in the muted reaction. Anglo-Scottish Idealism of the early years of this century, its other lights long since extinguished, has become one of the least re-collected episodes of the native past. Oakeshott was always held difficult to place. Although he was an exemplary patriot of British institutions, a superficial glance might lead one think he was latterly more regarded in the United States than at home. His last book, *The Voice of Liberal Learning*, was edited from Colorado. The first posthumous collection, an enlarged version of *Rationalism in Politics*, now appears from Indianapolis.[2] The only extended survey of his work is an admiring monograph from Chicago.[3] But his profile, on either side of the Atlantic, continues to be elusive.

---

1. See Charles Moore's 'Another Voice', *The Spectator*, 15 June 1991.
2. Both volumes have been edited by Timothy Fuller, of Colorado College.
3. Paul Franco, *The Political Philosophy of Michael Oakeshott*, New Haven 1990: a lucid and careful study, originally conducted at the University of Chicago, that never moves far from its subject's own positions.

Oakeshott has most frequently been taken as the wayward voice of an archetypical English conservatism: empirical, habitual, traditional, the adversary of all systematic politics, of reaction no less than reform; a thinker who preferred writing about the Derby to expounding the Constitution, and found even Burke too doctrinaire. The amiably careless, comfortable image is misleading. To set Oakeshott in his real context, a comparative angle of vision is needed. For he was, in fact, one of the quartet of outstanding European theorists of the intransigent Right whose ideas now shape – however much, or little, leading practitioners are aware of it – a large part of the mental world of end-of-the-century Western politics. It is alongside Carl Schmitt, Leo Strauss and Friedrich von Hayek that Michael Oakeshott is most appropriately seen. The relations between these four figures await documentation from future biographers. But whatever the circumstantial contacts or conflicts – some more visible than others – the lattice of intellectual connections between them forms a striking pattern. By generation, three were virtually exact contemporaries – Strauss (1899–1973), Hayek (1899–1991), Oakeshott (1901–1990). Older by a decade, Schmitt (1888–1985) overlapped with them, living like Hayek into his nineties, a longevity approached by Oakeshott too. They came from different disciplines – economics (Hayek), law (Schmitt), philosophy (Strauss) and history (Oakeshott) – but politics drew their concerns into a common field. There, they were divided by marked contrasts of character and outlook, and by the respective situations they confronted. The interweaving of themes and outcomes, across such differences, is all the more striking.

The formative experience of all these thinkers was the crisis of European society in the inter-war years, as the established order came under increasing pressure from economic dislocation, labour revolt and middle-class backlash, and then proceeded to buckle at its weakest points. In the Weimar Republic, the Westphalian Schmitt began his career as the most original Catholic adversary of socialism and of liberalism. In polemics of electric intensity, whose charge was increasingly aimed at the precarious parliamentarism of post-Versailles Germany, he treated their ideas as dilute theologies, which were bound to prove weaker than the force of national myth.[4] His own

---

4. The three decisive texts are: *Politische Theologie* (1922); *Römische Katholizismus und politische Form* (1923); *Die geistesgeschichtliche Lage des heutigen Parlamentarismus* (1923).

positive doctrine became a neo-Hobbesian theory of politics. Its critical twist was to project the state of nature depicted in *Leviathan*, the war of all against all in which individual agents are pitted against each other, onto the plane of modern collective conflicts: thereby transforming civil society itself into a second state of nature. For Schmitt, the act of sovereign power then becomes not so much the institution of mutual peace as the decision fixing the nature and frontier of any community, by dividing friend from foe – the opposition that defines the nature of the political as such.[5] This stark 'decisionist' vision came out of a regional background in which the choices seemed, to many others as well as Schmitt, to be revolution or counter-revolution. 'We in Central Europe live *sous l'œil des Russes*', he wrote.[6] His own option for the second term – he was an admirer of De Maistre and Donoso Cortés – was never in doubt.

In England, where Schmitt's incandescent early manifesto for the Roman Church was edited in a Catholic series of *Essays in Order*,[7] polarities were not so acute. The Cambridge of the twenties was a sheltered place, and Oakeshott's concerns were not initially so political. Anglican rather than Catholic in background, his first publication was a tract on Religion and the Moral Life whose theme was the necessary completion of ethical choice by religious wisdom, and thus the substantive unity between civilization and Christianity.[8] Oakeshott's personal piety seems to have declined over the years, yet the contrary accents of religious tradition and of radical choice remained: a combination recalling the early Schmitt, with the difference that Oakeshott's decisionism was always moral rather than political in register. But he had studied theology at Marburg and Tübingen, and was familiar with *Political Theology*, Schmitt's famous application of religious categories to secular doctrines.[9] When he turned to politics, Oakeshott's intellectual allegiance proved to be

---

5. The classic statement is *Der Begriff des Politischen* (1932), originally published as an essay in the *Archiv für Sozialwissenschaft und Sozialpolitik* in September 1927, pp. 1–33.

6. 'Das Zeitalter der Neutralisierung und Entpolitisierung' – Schmitt's visionary address to the European Cultural Union in Barcelona, delivered in October 1929, and collected in *Positionen und Begriffe im Kampf mit Weimar–Genf–Versailles*, Hamburg 1940: see p. 120.

7. Under the title *The Necessity of Politics*, Sheed and Ward, London 1931, with an introduction by Christopher Dawson; other works in the series included texts by Maritain and Berdyaev.

8. 'D' Society Pamphlet, Cambridge 1927, pp. 10–13.

9. See his note in 'Thomas Hobbes', *Scrutiny*, IV (1935–36), p. 264.

the same. It was on Hobbes that he set out to build a theory of the state. For both men, *Leviathan* – 'the greatest, perhaps the sole, masterpiece of political philosophy written in the English language', as Oakeshott termed it[10] – was to be the permanent touchstone for any modern account of civil authority.

Nor was this the only parallel in their outlook. When he ventured political opinions in these years, Oakeshott's scorn for liberalism and democracy was scarcely less incendiary than Schmitt's. Giving his verdict on the other English philosopher usually held for a classic, he spoke with the authentic voice of the radical Right. 'Locke was the apostle of the liberalism which is more conservative than conservatism itself, the liberalism characterised, not by insensitiveness, but by a sinister and destructive sensitiveness to the influx of the new, the liberalism which is sure of its limits, which has a horror of extremes, which lays its paralysing hand of respectability upon whatever is dangerous and revolutionary ... He was meek, and until recently he inherited the earth.'[11] Fortunately, that legacy was now passing into other hands. 'Democracy, parliamentary government, progress, discussion, and "the plausible ethics of productivity" are notions – all of them inseparable from the Lockian liberalism – which fail now to arouse even opposition,' Oakeshott scoffed: 'they are not merely absurd and exploded, they are uninteresting.'[12] These lines were written in the autumn of 1932, on the eve of the Nazi victory in Germany. A few months later, Schmitt – who had been adviser to Brüning and then to Schleicher – went over to Hitler. Looking at the new regime from England, Oakeshott by the end of the decade had decided that, compared with available alternatives, representative democracy, however incoherent as a doctrine, had something to be said for it after all. Catholicism, however, was the repository of another tradition of profound importance, authoritarian without caprice, 'an inheritance we have neglected': 'so far as this country is concerned,' he went on, 'I venture to suggest that many of the principles which belong to the historic doctrine of Conservatism are to be found in this Catholic doctrine'[13] – which had been given constitutional shape in the Austria of Dollfuss and the Portugal of Salazar. In

---

10. 'Introduction to *Leviathan*' (1946), collected in *Hobbes on Civil Association*, Oxford 1975, p. 3.

11. 'John Locke', *Cambridge Review*, 4 November 1932, p. 73.

12. Ibid.

13. *The Social and Political Doctrines of Contemporary Europe*, Cambridge 1939, pp. xix–xx.

April 1940, the month France fell, he was still dismissing 'clap-trap about government by consent'.[14]

Leo Strauss, meanwhile, from an Orthodox background in Hessen, had made his debut in the Zionist movement with texts on Jewish religion and politics – his first significant piece was on *Das Heilige*[15] – before moving to the study of Spinoza's biblical criticism, and thence to research on Hobbes. This brought him into contact with Schmitt, with whom he enjoyed friendly relations in Berlin. Before leaving Germany in 1932 he devoted his last publication – in the same months as Oakeshott was pronouncing his sentence on Locke – to the most arresting of Schmitt's works, *The Concept of the Political*. In a critique that was both admiring and admonitory, Strauss argued that Schmitt's laudable rejection of liberalism had mistaken its philosophical bearings. For Hobbes's theory of the state was not an antidote to modern liberalism, but its very foundation. In radicalizing Hobbes's matter-of-fact view of the human passions and their resolution in civil society into a tacit exaltation of enmity as the necessary signature of any political life, Schmitt had only produced a 'liberalism with a minus sign'.[16] What was needed was a 'horizon beyond liberalism', of which intimations could nevertheless be found in Schmitt's text, when he spoke of an 'order of human things' that could only be found in the return to an undefiled nature. It was this natural order, Strauss remarked, which the liberal conception of culture had forgotten.[17] Schmitt took these objections in his stride, making a few quiet adjustments in subsequent editions of his work to accentuate the hints of a religious background that Strauss had noted.[18] He also helped Strauss get to France before Hitler came to power. Six months after

---

14. 'Democratic Socialism', *Cambridge Review*, 19 April 1940, p. 348.

15. See *Der Jude*, No. 7, 1923, pp. 240–242.

16. 'Anmerkungen zu Carl Schmitt: Der Begriff des Politischen', *Archiv für Sozialwissenschaft und Sozialpolitik*, August–September 1932, p. 748. Publication of the text in the same journal in which Schmitt's own essay had originally appeared was not a coincidence: Schmitt had personally recommended it to the editor. Strauss's critique is included in the English edition of *The Concept of the Political* (a translation of the main body of the 1932 version of the work), introduced by George Schwab, New Brunswick 1976: see p. 103.

17. 'Anmerkungen', pp. 736, 739, 749; 'Comments' in *The Concept of the Political*, pp. 86, 90, 104–105.

18. The significance of these emendations is traced with a delicate precision by Heinrich Meier in his outstanding study, *Carl Schmitt, Leo Strauss und 'Der Begriff des Politischen'*, Stuttgart 1988 – the central work on the relationship between the thought of the two men.

the installation of the Third Reich – on the day Goering elevated Schmitt to the Prussian State Council – Strauss was writing to him from Paris, asking for an introduction to Maurras. In 1934 Strauss moved to London, where he complained that Schmitt's latest publication, his first development in legal theory under the new order, had incorporated Strauss's proposals for an advance beyond decisionism without acknowledgement.[19]

It was in England that Strauss now undertook the demonstration that Hobbes was indeed the theoretical fount of a levelling modern individualism. Appearing in 1936, *The Political Philosophy of Hobbes* argued that the revolution wrought by Hobbes was to replace the classical vision of a political order founded on philosophical reason and shaped by aristocratic honour, with a doctrine of sovereign power motivated by fear and fabricated from will: a construction built on the marshlands of 'his denial of any gradation in mankind' because he could conceive of 'no order – that is, no gradation in nature'.[20] Commended to the English reader by the impeccably liberal Ernest Barker (who performed the same service for Oakeshott's survey of contemporary political doctrines soon after, forming an incongruous *trait d'union* between the two), Strauss's book was on the whole well received by Oakeshott, as the most original study on Hobbes to have appeared in many years. But whereas for Strauss the remedy to Hobbes's defiled naturalism lay intact in the ancient wisdom set forth by Plato, for Oakeshott the incoherence of Hobbes's naturalistic doctrine of will was only to be overcome in the modern re-union of reason and volition in Hegel and Bosanquet – even if their synthesis remained to be completed.[21] Oakeshott was also, as he later made clear, unwilling to accept that Hobbes had relinquished the heroic values of pride as an ingredient of civil peace: he had merely, in his realism, confined these to a select few, 'because of the dearth of noble characters'.[22]

In 1938 Strauss moved to the United States, where after the war he occupied a chair at Chicago in the same period that Oakeshott was at

---

19. For Strauss's letters to Schmitt of 10 July 1933, and to Jakob Klein of 10 October 1934, see Meier's documentation in *Carl Schmitt, Leo Strauss und der Begriff des Politischen*, pp. 134–138.

20. *The Political Philosophy of Hobbes – Its Basis and Genesis*, Oxford 1936, p. 167.

21. 'Dr Leo Strauss on Hobbes', originally published in *Politica*, II, 1937, and collected in *Hobbes on Civil Assocation*, pp. 132–149.

22. 'The Moral Life in the Writing of Thomas Hobbes' (1960), first published in *Rationalism in Politics*, London 1962: p. 292.

the LSE. There he produced the remarkable series of works, in form an oracular retrospect of the history of philosophy from Socrates to Nietzsche, in effect a systematic political doctrine, which has since nurtured the most distinctive and strong-minded school of American conservatism. There were two principal themes in this oeuvre. A just political order must be grounded in immutable demands of natural right. Nature, however, is inherently unequal. The capacity to discover truth is restricted to a few, and to endure it exhibited by scarcely more. The best regime will therefore reflect differences in human excellence, and be led by an appropriate elite. But although the highest virtue is philosophical contemplation of the truth, this does not mean – contrary to a superficial reading of the *Republic* – that the just city will be ruled by philosophers. For philosophy gazes without faltering not only at the necessary conditions of political order, discomfiting as these may be to demotic prejudice, but at the far more terrible realities of cosmic disorder: the absence of any divine authority, the delusion of any common morality, the transience of the earth and its species – every insight that religion must deny and society cannot survive. Unfolded at large, these truths would destroy the protective atmosphere of any civilization and with it all stable conditions for the pursuit of philosophy itself. Esoteric wisdom and exoteric opinion must therefore remain distinct, on pain of mutual destruction. Leisured gentlemen instructed in rule – but not raised to truth – by philosophers should uphold a rational order of political stability against levelling temptations. In this regime, theoretical knowledge could find institutional shelter, without dangerous side-effects on civic practice. In keeping with his teaching, which now enjoined such prudence on the philosopher, during the Cold War Strauss made the concession – earlier unthinkable – of describing these views as a contribution to liberalism, albeit 'in the original sense' understood by the ancients, of a 'liberality' that was another name for 'excellence'.[23] In the campus emergency of 1968 he even publicly endorsed Richard Nixon. In general, however, Strauss eschewed official bromide or partisan pronouncement; that was the role not of the teacher but of the taught.

The veiled pole star of Strauss's journey through the past was Nietzsche, the one modern thinker who – he believed – had grasped the full depth of the crisis of modernity, once philosophy had abandoned propriety with Hobbes, by setting out to relieve man's estate

---

23. *Liberalism Ancient and Modern*, New York 1968, pp. vii, 28.

rather than pursue eternal truth, and social forms became detached from natural order.[24] The equivalent authority for Oakeshott was Burckhardt. Characteristically, he liked to compare the two to the advantage of the Swiss seer, as a friend who shared Nietzsche's abhorrence of mass society and contempt for democracy, but displayed a cool equanimity rather than an 'erratic and pathological sensitivity' towards them, and disdained to offer any cure for the times.[25] These were, in fact, largely imaginary virtues: Burckhardt's venomous anti-Semitism and often deranged political small talk have no counterpart in Nietzsche.[26] Nor did Oakeshott's own record in these years live up to the contrast he sought to make. The war left him a nationalist, and the post-war election an alarmist. Forgetting earlier dicta, he now announced that 'there is nothing whatever in common between British Conservatism and any of the categories of continental politics. Loose talk of this sort about British politics merely liberates a fog of unreality.'[27] The Labour Party was another matter. Recent German experience was all too ominously germane to its enterprise, even if 'the absence of a *coup d'état*' in its accession to power had misled observers at first. But 'established tyranny cannot forever conceal its character except from willing slaves', and it was now clear (1947) that 'the Labour Party has an *incentive* to become despotic, the *means* to become despotic, and that it has the *intention* of becoming despotic.' Indeed Oakeshott could already detect 'a simple plot to establish, not by force but by subterfuge, a single-party system and the slavery from which it is inseparable'.[28] Strauss would probably have found such parochial diatribes overwrought.

But the Burckhardtian standpoint still yielded a position close to the Nietzschean, if with its own twist. Whereas for Strauss, modern political democracy rested on a denial of the inequality of man as a permanent gradation within nature, for Oakeshott this inequality was the outcome of a historical differentiation. In the late Middle Ages, a

24. See 'The Three Waves of Modernity', collected *in Political Philosophy: Ten Essays by Leo Strauss*, edited by Hilail Gildin, New York 1989, pp. 95ff; and 'Note on the Plan of Nietzsche's *Beyond Good and Evil*' (1973), collected in *Studies in Platonic Political Philosophy*, edited by Thomas Pangle, Chicago 1983, pp. 174–191.

25. 'The Detached Vision', *Encounter*, June 1954, pp. 69–74.

26. See, for example, *Jakob Burckhardts Briefe an seinen Freund Friedrich von Preen 1864–1893*, Stuttgart and Berlin 1922, pp. 137, 189, 203.

27. 'Contemporary British Politics', *The Cambridge Journal*, I, 1947–48, pp. 479–480 – a key text.

28. 'Contemporary British Politics', pp. 485, 483.

new character emerged on the scene, as Burckhardt had shown, the *uomo singulare* who was an autonomous moral individual freed from the shackles of community, capable of choosing his own way of life. The spread of this kind of individuality, the pre-eminent event of European history, gradually gave rise to institutions expressing its freedom. These achieved their climax with the parliamentary government that emerged in England in the late eighteenth and early nineteenth centuries. But the salutary dissolution of traditional communities had also released a dangerous multitude of opposite bent. These Oakeshott called individuals *manqués* – all those left behind in the new conditions because they were unwilling to accept the responsibility of personal independence, a swarm of moral and social failures consumed with 'envy, jealousy and resentment'.[29] By the late nineteenth century, this inferior mass had pressed towards a dire change: the gradual transformation of 'parliamentary' into 'popular government', whose 'first great enterprise was the establishment of universal adult suffrage'. For, Oakeshott went on, 'the power of the "mass man" lay in his numbers, and this power could be brought to bear upon government by means of the "vote"' – that is, a regime based on 'the authority of mere numbers'.[30] Modern democracy in this sense defied not the hierarchy of natural gifts, as in Strauss's view, but of existential choices. For the anti-individual behind universal suffrage, Oakeshott explained, 'is specified by a moral, not an intellectual, inadequacy'.[31]

The nuance here is reproduced in their respective conceptions of the vocation of philosophy. For both men, this was the supreme endeavour of human understanding, and one so uncompromisingly radical that it could never consort directly with politics, which required a customary stability philosophy's ruthless quest for the truth must subvert. For philosophy, in Oakeshott's formula, was 'experience without presupposition, reservation, arrest or modification'[32] – a phrase to make Burke shudder. The practice of politics by contrast, necessarily involved all four of the conditions that philosophy as theory precluded. 'Philosophy is the attempt to dissolve the element in which society breathes, and thus it *endangers* society,'

29. 'The Masses in Representative Democracy' (1957), in A. Hunold (ed.), *Freedom and Serfdom: An Anthology of Western Thought*, Dordrecht 1961, pp. 152–160 – an essay now collected in the enlarged edition of *Rationalism in Politics*, edited by Timothy Fuller, Indianapolis 1991.
30. 'The Masses in Representative Democracy', p. 166.
31. Ibid., p. 168.
32. *Experience and its Modes*, Cambridge 1933, p. 2.

wrote Strauss.[33] Oakeshott was if anything even more outspoken. 'Philosophy is not the enhancement of life, it is the denial of life ... there is something perhaps decadent, even depraved, in an attempt to achieve a completely coherent world of experience; for such a pursuit requires us to renounce for the time being everything which can be called good or evil, everything which can be valued or rejected as valueless.'[34] The tension between the two poles common to the pathos of each – a metaphysics of scandal and a pragmatics of convention – found differing resolution, however. For Strauss philosophical knowledge could not disclose itself to the vulgar, but might shape the forms of civic life from afar, so long as the barriers between esoteric and exoteric truth were maintained. For Oakeshott, however, philosophy and politics were categorically separate. Politics was a second-rate activity that inherently involved 'mental vulgarity, unreal loyalties, delusive aims, false significances'[35]; but on the other hand it was proof against improvement by philosophy, which could shed no light even on the worth of particular political projects.[36] The belief that it might do so, indeed, could lead to the worst of all practical delusions: the notion that institutional forms were amenable to intelligent design, rather than the outcome of traditional growth. That was the characteristic idiocy of 'rationalism in politics'.[37]

Here paths inevitably parted. Strauss's ideal remained what Oakeshott abjured: the deliberate forethought for a well-governed city that had been the aim of the line from Socrates to Cicero which he described and admired as 'classical political rationalism', and reproached Burke – whatever his other merits – for abandoning.[38] Behind the opposite prescriptions lay contrasted intellectual starting-points: normative origins located alternatively in the late medieval and the ancient worlds. This was a sharp division. Oakeshott could dismiss the *polis* as irrelevant to modern government: Strauss take the pogrom as an epitome of the Middle Ages.[39] But beyond this basic

---

33. 'On a Forgotten Kind of Writing' (1954), in *What Is Political Philosophy?*, Chicago 1964, p. 221.

34. *Experience and its Modes*, pp. 355–356.

35. 'The Claims of Politics', *Scrutiny*, VIII, 1939–1940, p. 148.

36. 'Political Education' (1951), in *Rationalism in Politics*, p. 132.

37. For this central theme, see the keynote essay that gives its title to *Rationalism in Politics*: pp. 1–36.

38. *Natural Right and History*, Chicago 1953, pp. 311–314ff.

39. See Oakeshott, 'The Masses in Representative Democracy', p. 156; Strauss, 'Preface to the English Translation' of *Spinoza's Critique of Religion*, New York 1965, p. 3.

difference of historical horizon, there was a contemporary reason for the divergence of emphases at this fork. The peculiar vehemence of Oakeshott's refusal of any idea of 'political engineering', no matter how piecemeal, as a malignant dream that could only be coercive and abortive, came from the ordeal of Labour rule and (talk of) Labour planning. These were less urgent concerns in Chicago than in London.

They were to be conveyed there, however, by the thinker who had preceded Oakeshott in the indictment of economic planning in particular, and of social 'constructivism' in general. Hayek had arrived at the LSE in 1931. His intellectual background in Austria was quite unlike that of Strauss, Oakeshott or Schmitt: thoroughly secular, positively liberal, exempt from any supra-sensible temptation – Mach was his first philosophical enthusiasm. His political mentor was Ludwig von Mises, famous for arguing against the very possibility of a socialist economy, and for an uncompromising defence of a pure model of free-market capitalism. There was no more outspoken champion of classical liberalism in the German-speaking world of the twenties. Yet the Austrian political scene left little room for this outlook, dominated as it was by the conflict between a social-democratic Left and a clerical Right. Here Mises had no hesitation. In the struggle against the labour movement, authoritarian rule might be required. Looking across the border, he could see the virtues of Mussolini: the black-shirts had for the moment saved European civilization for the principle of private property – 'the merit that Fascism has thereby won will live on eternally in history.'[40] Adviser to Monsignor Seipel, the prelate who ran the country in the late twenties, Mises approved Dollfuss's crushing of Austrian labour in the thirties, blaming the repression of 1934 which installed his clerical dictatorship on the folly of the Social Democrats in contesting his alliance with Italy.[41]

Hayek was in close touch with Mises in this period, when his own energies were devoted to pursuing the arguments against socialist economic calculation, and to upholding his variant of the Austrian theory of the business cycle against Keynes. There is no record of his view of the Dollfuss regime – certainly of any protest against Austro-Fascism – but it seems likely that he shared Mises's attitude towards

---

40. *Liberalismus*, Jena 1927, p. 45; English edition, *Liberalism: A Socio-Economic Exposition*, Kansas City 1962, p. 51.

41. *Erinnerungen von Ludwig v. Mises* (with a foreword by Margit v. Mises and introduction by Friedrich v. Hayek), Stuttgart and New York 1978, pp. 51, 89–90.

it. At any rate, there was to be a striking coincidence in their subsequent political interventions, once the Second World War had broken out. Evacuated to Cambridge Hayek produced in 1944 the impassioned cry of alarm against the totalitarian logic of collective planning – *The Road to Serfdom* – that made him famous. Among its leading themes was the fundamental continuity between socialism and Nazism, as malignant products of specifically German origin – whatever their later capacity for general contagion.[42] This was precisely the argument, developed on a more extensive scale, of Mises's *Omnipotent Government*, completed in America a month later, but based on a manuscript written in Switzerland just after the Anschluss, four years earlier. Here the motive for totalised incrimination of Germany lies on the surface, serving all too visibly as an exculpation of Austria, the land of 'the *only* people on the European continent who' – in the days of the Heimwehr – 'seriously resisted Hitler'.[43]

After a decade in Great Britain, this was not a claim Hayek, whose *Road to Serfdom* avoids all reference to his native country, would have made. His polemic was aimed at the terms of English political debate. There it found a ready resonance in the Conservative Party, and may have stirred Churchill to his prediction of a British Gestapo should Labour win the forthcoming elections. But its vehemence left Hayek somewhat isolated in the post-war climate of opinion, when the Attlee Government failed to live up to his billing. Still, however unpopular in the Labour consensus, his intervention might have been expected to earn all the more honour from those set upon resisting it. Oakeshott, however, was not among them, dismissing *The Road to Serfdom* as just another example of doctrinaire rationalism, little more than a plan to oppose planning.[44] Discouraged by this atmosphere, Hayek left for the US in 1950, as Oakeshott was invested at the LSE.

At Chicago, Hayek put aside his more technical economic work for the development of a social and political theory that became in time the most ambitious and complete synthesis to emerge from the ranks of the post-war Right. Among its themes – the overriding significance of the rule of law, the need for social inequality, the function of unreflective tradition, the value of a leisured class – were many cultivated by Strauss across the campus. Neither thinker, however, ever referred

---

42. *The Road to Serfdom*, London 1944, pp. 16–17, 124–134, etc.
43. *Erinnerungen*, p. 91.
44. *Rationalism in Politics*, p. 21.

to the other. Did temperamental antagonism, or intellectual indifference, dictate the silence? Whatever the case, latent tensions of
outlook between them were to find expression in due course. Schmitt,
on the other hand, was never far from Hayek's mind – standing for the
prime example of a skilled jurist whose sophistry helped to destroy
the rule of law in Germany, yet a political theorist whose stark defini-
tions of the nature of sovereignty and the logic of party, at any rate,
had to be accepted.[45]

But it is Hayek's relationship with Oakeshott that is of most significance for understanding each. In *The Constitution of Liberty* (1960),
published just before *Rationalism in Politics* (1962), Hayek distinguished two intellectual lines of thought about freedom, of radically
opposite upshot. The first was an empiricist, essentially British tradition descending from Hume, Smith and Ferguson, seconded by Burke
and Tucker, which understood political development as an involuntary process of gradual institutional improvement, comparable to the
workings of a market economy or the evolution of common law. The
second was a rationalist, typically French lineage descending from
Descartes through Condorcet to Comte, with a horde of modern
successors, who saw social institutions as fit for premeditated construction, in the spirit of polytechnic engineering. The former line
alone led to real liberty; the latter inevitably destroyed it. Thus far the
distinction looks all but identical to Oakeshott's. But in Hayek's
account, Locke becomes central to the authentic tradition of freedom,
while Hobbes is cast as the political rationalist *par excellence* – a mind
out of national character, progenitor of what were later to be the
lethal fallacies of legal positivism.[46]

Social constructivism was not the only threat to genuine liberalism:
it also faced potential dangers from another quarter – the rise of
modern democracy. Equality before the law, Hayek continued, might
seem to lead naturally to equality in making the law. But the two were
in reality absolutely distinct principles, and the latter could undo the
former. For the idea of popular sovereignty contained the assumption
that declarative public law – what legislative majorities might at will
decree – could override the inherited wisdoms of private common law,
transgressing the inviolable limits that a liberal order placed around

---

45. See *The Road to Serfdom*, pp. 59, 139; *The Constitution of Liberty*, Chicago
1960, p. 485; *Law, Legislation and Liberty*, Vol. I, *Rules and Order*, London 1973,
pp. 71, 139; Vol. II, *The Mirage of Social Justice*, London 1976, p. 144, 167; Vol. III,
The Political Order of a Free People, London 1979, pp. 125, 192, 194.
46. *The Constitution of Liberty*, pp. 54–62ff, 170–171.

individual property and person. In this sense, Hayek remarked, an authoritarian regime that repressed popular suffrage but respected the rule of law could be a better guardian of liberty than a democratic regime liable to the temptations of economic intervention or social redistribution. Still, that was an extreme hypothesis. So far, at any rate, democracy could be justified as the most peaceful form of change and the best means of educating the masses to greater maturity.[47] But these were technical and provisional advantages, which did not make democracy a value in itself.

A decade later, Hayek was more pessimistic. *Law, Legislation and Liberty* opened with the avowal that his political ideals had not attracted the support they merited, and that he had failed to bring home that 'the predominant model of liberal democratic institutions' in the Western world 'necessarily leads to a gradual transformation of the spontaneous order of a free society into a totalitarian system'.[48] To avert this fatal propensity, which Hayek remarked that Schmitt had in his time understood – but also encouraged – more than any other observer, three truths urgently needed to be understood. The first was the fundamental difference between a spontaneous order and a purposive organization, or what Hayek now termed a *cosmos* and a *taxis* – the one an unintended yet coherent web of relations within which individual agents pursued their different ends, regulated only by common procedural rules; the other a willed enterprise seeking to realize substantive collective goals. The rule of law could be preserved only so long as the structure of government reflected a principled separation of the two, according an absolute priority to the maintenance of the first, as the condition of a market economy in a free society, and confining the second to strictly delimited, subordinate functions in the public interest. All current democracies confused these requirements, permitting the reckless trespass of *taxis* onto the proper ground of *cosmos*, with the intrusion of macro-economic steering and the erection of a welfare state, in the name of an imaginary 'social justice' – a notion without meaning. For the spontaneous order of the market not only precludes equality, it necessarily ignores desert: success within it is undeniably often a mere matter of chance.[49] The social hierarchy it generates is thus, unlike Strauss's, not founded on a cultural gradation in nature. Hayek confessed that this was perhaps

---

47. *The Constitution of Liberty*, pp. 103ff.
48. *Law, Legislation and Liberty*, Vol. I, *Rules and Order*, p. 2.
49. *Law, Legislation and Liberty*, Vol. II, *The Mirage of Social Justice*, p. 74.

too uncomfortable a truth to be widely proclaimed, and – in a move now recalling Strauss – concluded that religion might after all be a necessary dummy to assure social cohesion, against dangers from the disappointed in the run of chance.

Yet whatever the need for such individual consolations, there was a general rationale for the *cosmos* of the market. It was the evolutionary product of historical competition between rival economic practices, which had proved its worth in the superior overall growth of production and population it had assured.[50] Here Hayek's doctrine took a concluding utilitarian turn. The yardstick of a desirable order was not philosophical truth but practical well-being. In its own terms, this was a perfectly coherent conclusion. But his theory still faced an awkward difficulty in the apparent institutional outcome of the spontaneous social mechanisms it celebrated. For was not the steady erosion of the division between *taxis* and *cosmos*, with the seemingly inexorable growth of the welfare state, itself pre-eminently an evolutionary process? To roll it back required – according to Hayek's new prescriptions – drastic redesigning of the structure of the state. Indeed, what he now proposed was nothing less than a dismantling of every known legislature into two novel bodies with different competences and disparate electorates, to correspond to the two ontological kinds of order – the more powerful chamber, guardian of the rule of law as such, striking anyone under the age of forty-five off the voting-roll.[51] This, as even sympathizers could not fail to notice, was a violent attack of the very constructivism his theory had set out to purge. Hayek was unmoved. Such was the price of preserving *nomos*, or the law of liberty, from the logic of popular sovereignty. Assemblies had to be stripped of their powers of general meddling, in order to secure the limited government – based on the rigour of law, not the licence of consent – which was the only guarantee of freedom. The correct formula, Hayek explained, was demarchy without democracy.[52]

Two years after the first volume of *Law, Legislation and Liberty* appeared, Oakeshott published his own culminating work, *On Human Conduct*. Its leading theme was the fundamental distinction to be made between the idea of a 'civil association', articulated by procedural

---

50. For the significance of population growth, see *The Fatal Conceit*, London 1988, pp. 120ff; for the functional role of religion, pp. 135–140, 157.

51. *Law, Legislation and Liberty*, Vol. III, pp. 112–114.

52. Ibid., p. 40.

rules, and an 'enterprise association', devoted to the attainment of substantive goals. Government conceived as an engagement in keeping with the first was a 'nomocracy', and in pursuit of the second a 'teleocracy'. The correspondence between this dichotomy and Hayek's was plainly intimate. Hayek was aware of Oakeshott's couplet (developed in lectures, and perhaps first employed in print in praise of Geoffrey Howe in 1967) and had typically acknowledged it.[53] The courtesy was not returned. Obituarists have stressed Oakeshott's charm of character, but his virtues did not include conspicuous generosity in intellectual matters. Withal, however, his construction was distinguished from Hayek's by two essential differences. Oakeshott did not place the superiority of civil over enterprise association as a conception of government on any evolutionary foundation, as the necessary political form of spontaneous economic progress. Instead, he again sketched a particular history, presenting the emergence of the modern European state as from the outset drawn towards the opposite ideals of – in medieval terminology – *societas* and *universitas*: rule envisaged in juridical or in managerial terms.

Each of these dispositions derived from a miscellany of contingencies, without ulterior logic. But though they had co-existed from the start, they were structurally irreconcilable. The state could take the form either of a civil association, or of a managerial enterprise, but there could be no legitimate combination of the two.[54] In other words, although Oakeshott's dichotomy has a seemingly more casual genesis, in the mere relative happenstance of the European past, it actually acquires a far more absolute – even fanatical – force than Hayek's. Where *Law, Legislation and Liberty* allows for a necessary, if tightly circumscribed exercise of *taxis* by the liberal state, the antithesis of *societas* and *universitas* in *On Human Conduct* is unappeasable. Behind the idea of government performing calculable tasks, Oakeshott wrote, lay a '*canaille* recently emancipated from one idiom of servility and not able to afford to be repulsed by the smell of another' – among whose worst current aromas was 'the vile expression, "social choice"'.[55]

---

53. See Hayek, 'The Confusion of Language in Political Thought' (1967), in *New Studies in Philosophy, Politics, Economics and the History of Ideas*, London 1978, p. 89. Oakeshott seems to have introduced his terms to the public for the first time in his favourable notice of *The Conservative Opportunity*, a collection of Bow Group essays on 'Tomorrow's Toryism', in *New Society*, 15 July 1965, pp. 26–27.

54. The two forms are 'irreconcilably opposed one to another' – 'they deny one another': *On Human Conduct*, Oxford 1975, pp. 319, 323.

55. *On Human Conduct*, pp. 303, 87.

Government as civil association, based on pride of free individuality, excluded collective purpose, categorically.

But if this was so, what could motivate the compact of civil association itself? Hayek's answer had been anticipated and dismissed early on, as no more than 'the plausible ethics of "productivity"': in Oakeshott's eyes, any justification of *societas* in terms of the satisfaction of material wants was to be deplored as the 'saddest of all misunderstandings'.[56] This was the kind of concern, indeed, that had typically moved teleocratic projectors, from Bacon's ominous dream of forcing nature to yield up her secrets onwards. Even if he never expressed it with quite such eloquence, Oakeshott shared Strauss's hostility to technological lordship over the natural world.[57] This was a basic dividing-line separating them from Hayek, who remained to the end resistant to even moderate ecological arguments. But Strauss's alternative rationale for the best regime, as the shield of philosophers, was not available to Oakeshott either. He was left, on his own terms, with an acute problem of justification. For if their association was void of purpose, why should individual agents ever accept a public authority at all? In Oakeshott's construction, government without goal yields what looks very much like an *état gratuit*. His famous image of politics – a vessel endlessly ploughing the sea, without port or destination[58] – is all too apt. For why then should any passengers want to board the ship in the first place?

Oakeshott attempted to answer the question with another analogy, formally more developed, actually yet more extravagant, in *On Human Conduct*. Subscription to civil association was entirely non-instrumental. But a non-instrumental practice – acts performed for their own sake, not for ulterior ends – was the definition of moral conduct.[59] It might seem from this as if Oakeshott, having dismissed any prudential case for the civil condition, was going to give his will-less state an ethical foundation. But this would be an illusion. For

---

56. 'John Locke', p. 73; 'Talking Politics', *National Review*, 5 December 1975, p. 1427, now collected in *Rationalism in Politics and other essays*, Indianapolis 1991, p. 457.

57. For Oakeshott, see *On Human Conduct*, pp. 288–292; for Strauss, see *inter alia* his introduction to *The City and Man*, Chicago 1964.

58. 'In political activity, then, men sail a boundless and bottomless sea; there is neither harbour for shelter nor floor for anchorage, neither starting-place nor appointed destination' – nor 'even a detectable strand of progress': *Rationalism in Politics*, pp. 127, 133.

59. *On Human Conduct*, pp. 62–64, 122–124.

what Oakeshott proceeds to identify as a morality is a 'colloquial idiom' of conduct, spoken with varying degrees of skill and verbal style by different speakers. Civil association, in other words, is actually modelled on language rather than dictated by virtue.

There was a logic to this move. It was Carl Menger, founder of Austrian economics, who first made a general theoretical case for the beneficence of social institutions that were the product of spontaneous growth as opposed to intentional design.[60] To illustrate the merits of the market, he compared it to two other human inventions, that were equally unplanned: law and language – whose slow crescence had been the themes of the great figures of German romantic scholarship, Savigny and Grimm. What Hayek and Oakeshott did, each in their own way, was to extend the same reasoning to the state – a move Menger too had anticipated. But whereas Hayek took the market and common law as his paradigms for a political constitution, Oakeshott chose language as the enabling metaphor. The two options have a quite distinct logic. Economic transactions satisfy human wants – the market exists only as a clearing-house of utilities; legal rules too reflect social exigencies, and are regularly altered to further practical ends. From these background analogies, a plausible conception of 'the political order of a free people', in the form of the Hayekian state, could be projected, as answering to the same aims. Language, however, is not generally amenable to deliberate change, and is notoriously other than merely instrumental in function. It offers a much more radical metaphor for a state divested of active sovereignty.

On the other hand, of course, it provides no appropriate emblem of morality either. The second half of the twentieth century has seen many attempts to use language as an all-purpose key to the understanding of human affairs – the 'linguistic turn' still retaining, even at this late date, a blowsy appeal for those who live predominantly by words. Oakeshott's version is in this sense no more, or less, simple-minded than those of Heidegger, Lévi-Strauss, Wittgenstein, Lacan, Habermas, Derrida or others. But it has its own specific syllogism. Civil association is non-instrumental; practice that is not instrumental is moral; morality is a language of conduct; so political order can be conceived as a vernacular of civil intercourse. In this chain of forced analogies, the significant elision is the second one. For there is

---

60. *Gesammelte Werke*, Bd II, *Untersuchungen über die Methode der Sozialwissenschaften und der politischen Ökonomie insbesondere*, Tübingen 1969, pp. 161–163ff.

a much more familiar and unambiguous kind of practice performed for its own sake than the moral – and it is this which actually supplies the silent support of the whole construction. The real gist of *On Human Conduct* is a conception of politics taken from aesthetics. This becomes visible whenever Oakeshott seeks to illustrate his claim that moral conduct or civil association is a language: 'an instrument which may be played upon with varying degrees of sensibility' by so many 'flute-players', all nevertheless 'concerned with the same skill'; a vernacular which can be 'spoken pedantically or loosely, slavishly or masterfully', which 'the ill-educated speak vulgarly, the purists inflexibly', leaving 'the connoisseurs of moral style' to 'delight in the small perfection of those flashes of felicity which redeem the dullness of commonplace moral utterance'.[61] The controlling imagery is of literary taste or musical skill.

This way of seeing politics, as the occasion for aesthetic performance, has a considerable history. By a nice irony, the sharpest critique of it was written by Carl Schmitt, whose *Political Romanticism* (1919) had already captured this strain in the outlook of the author of *Rationalism in Politics* (1962) – indeed even singling out for demolition the phrase that became its most famous slogan, the notion of politics as an 'endless conversation'.[62] Oakeshott's romanticism, however, was of a paradoxical kind. For it continued to be encased within a formal allegiance to Hobbes. It would be difficult to think of a more incongruous authority for any 'non-instrumental', let alone quasi-aesthetic understanding of the state. The pact of civil association between individuals in *Leviathan* is supremely an instrument to secure common ends – the aims of security and prosperity, 'mutual peace' and 'commodious living'. Thereafter, the sovereign power it institutes can override any private claim, save that to life itself, in the collective interest. The 'mortal god' lacks no managerial prerogatives in his care of the community. Hobbes indeed flatly declares, in a formula to make monetarist hair stand on end, that state expenditure must be in principle without limit: 'commonwealths can endure no diet.'[63] Cambridge scholars like to complain about Strauss's wayward use of classical texts, but compared with Oakeshott, about whom they have had little to say, he was philological loyalty itself.

---

61. *On Human Conduct*, pp. 65–66, 121.

62. See *Politische Romantik*, Munich and Leipzig 1919, pp. 129–130; English edition, *Political Romanticism*, Cambridge, Mass., 1986, p. 139.

63. *Leviathan*, Part II, Chapter 24.

The question that is posed, of course, is why Oakeshott should have selected Hobbes, of all unlikely patrons, for his theory of *societas*? The answer lies in what Hobbes excludes. There is no place for rights in his scheme of things. Once the sovereign is constituted, subjects have only obligations. Here indeed, there is no cant about consent: just a limpid statement of duty – obedience to civil authority. It was this that drew Oakeshott. Scorning 'the absurd device of a Bill of Rights' and 'drivel about something called "society"', he dismissed – as he once put it to an American audience – 'the fanciful doctrine of the Declaration of Independence, in which governments are said to exist merely to secure rights that they have not themselves the authority to prescribe, and where the "consent" of subjects can legitimize nothing more than the apparatus of power which is necessary to provide that security.'[64] The merit of the Hobbesian state was to leave no ground for the typical claims of modern democracy.

There still remained a difficulty. Due subjection to the conditions of civil association, Oakeshott insisted, was not dependent on any approval of them (which might then be withheld): it was an unconditional obligation. But if obedience to civil authority was, as Hobbes had laid down, the rule of just conduct, did that mean any law it decreed was therefore justice? Here the formalism of Oakeshott's account of *societas*, association without aim or approbation, risked an unacceptable conclusion that might sanction the vagaries of rationalism. To avoid this, there had to be some other principle to lend it colourable substance. Here his background in English Idealism, otherwise recessive in his work since the war, came to his help. Oakeshott found the supplement he needed in a weak echo from Hegel: law should not conflict with the 'educated moral sensibility' of the time.[65] Where he had once looked forward to a theory of Rational Will as the necessary corrective to Hobbes, he now fell back on a merely consensual *Sittlichkeit* – convention clear of reason. Like some uncomfortable, half-forgotten visitor from the past, Hegel is still received in *On Human Conduct*, but he is out of place. Oakeshott's effort to make the supreme theorist of the state as a substantive, goal-directed community – *universitas* raised to the highest power – into a humble clerk of civil association is a whim even by the measure of his Hobbes. For Hegel, the ethical life realized by the modern state was a

---

    64. 'Talking Politics', pp. 1424, 1427; *Rationalism in Politics and Other Essays*, pp. 448, 450.
    65. 'The Rule of Law', in *On History and Other Essays*, Oxford 1983, p. 160.

rational pattern of social forms reflecting the immanent development of a universal history. In Oakeshott's version, the husk of political order harbours no more than a pulp of random custom – for each moral language is as contingent as the past of the people that speaks it, and the world is divided among unrelated vernaculars.[66] Of course, even on these terms, the filling disintegrates, since no modern community has ever contained just one 'educated sensibility'. The collision of moral codes within the same state is the stuff of the political life which the dream of civil association represses.

Nearly all of Oakeshott's obituarists stressed his unworldliness, typified by his indifference to the official honours his achievement might have been expected to deserve. There is no reason to doubt that this was an appealing trait of the man. But it also tells something about him as a thinker. Although Oakeshott was trained as a historian, and in one compartment of his mind always knew more about the actual detail of the European past than Hayek, Strauss or Schmitt, his normative theory of the state takes leave of its realities as a historical structure more completely than anything they ever proposed. For, as the slightest glance at its record shows, from the outset the overwhelming *raison d'être* of the European state was warfare, the most 'managerial' and 'instrumental' of all collective activities. Oakeshott could never afford to register the logic of military competition for state construction: his vision of public authority is purely domestic. War was simply a period of exception, when the proper role of the state as the watch of civil peace was temporarily 'suspended'.[67] So determined, indeed, was Oakeshott to exclude any trace of common enterprise from the idea of government that he was even driven to deny all existence to the nation-state. Politically, his own outlook was thoroughly nationalist. Who could doubt the superiority of English institutions to 'the five futile "republics" of France', the fake unification of Italy, the anarchy of Spain and the banditry of Greece: indeed to the 'conspicuous failure of most modern European states (and all the imitation states elsewhere in the world)'?[68] But philosophically, the conjunction of nation with state left ajar an unacceptable suggestion of collective agency, which had to be closed.

---

66. *On Human Conduct*, pp. 80–81, where 'the modest mortal with a self to disclose and a soul to make' is 'disinclined to be unnerved because there are other such languages to which he cannot readily relate his own'.

67. *On Human Conduct*, p. 147.

68. *On Human Conduct*, pp. 188, 191.

Oakeshott lamented that the European state had come to be predominantly shaped as an enterprise association, but his theory left him with no historical explanation for why this aberration should have occurred. All he could offer was a psychic diagnosis. Within the individual there were two contrary bents, one towards a sturdy spiritual 'self-employment' in a life of adventure, the other towards a menial 'partnership' for the reception of benefits – and such were the springs of the two types of government, which could not be reconciled.[69] All of Oakeshott's imposing erudition ends in the bathos of this small parable of the divided soul of economic man. The laws of rule – the social realities of the accumulation of power and property in the history of the West – were so forgotten in the mists of the rule of law – the ideal habitat of the self-employed man – that Oakeshott could actually write with boyish enthusiasm that the Romans and the Normans were the two great donors of civil association to Europe.[70] That their states were among the most ruthlessly single-minded and successful 'enterprise associations' of all time, machines of conquest and colonization without peer, could be forgotten.

It was the theorist of political decision, not of conversation, who understood what such examples meant for any realist jurisprudence. In his last tour de force, published under the Federal Republic, *Der Nomos der Erde* ('The Law of the Earth'), Schmitt showed that the very term fetishized by Oakeshott and Hayek to bespeak the transcendence of abstract procedural rules, exempt from all specific social directives, in its origins actually signified the opposite: and that none other than Thomas Hobbes had been the first to make this clear. 'Seeing therefore the Introduction of Property is an effect of Common-wealth ... it is the act only of the Sovereign; and consisteth in the Laws, which none can make which have not the Sovereign Power. And this they knew well of old, who called that *Nomos* (that is to say, *Distribution*), which we call Law; and defined Justice, by *distributing* to every man *his own*. In this Distribution, the First Law, is for Division of the Land itself.'[71] For Schmitt, such original distribution presupposed a founding appropriation, what he called a

---

69. *On Human Conduct*, pp. 323–325.

70. 'The Rule of Law', p. 164.

71. *Leviathan*, Part II, Chapter 24: 'Of the Nutrition and Procreation of a Commonwealth'. On this theme, see Schmitt's remarkable essay 'Nehmen / Teilen / Weiden' (1953), collected in *Verfassungsrechtliche Aufsätze*, Berlin 1985, pp. 489–504.

Landnahme:[72] the occupation of territory that necessarily preceded any division of it, and which English soil had known as memorably as any, under Roman boot and Norman stirrup. The 'radical title' (the term used by Locke) underlying any law lay in such taking and allocating, as the etymological linkage of *nomos* with *nemein* (to take) suggested. Here, conceptually and historically, the oppositions between rule and goal, law and legislation, the civil and the managerial, dissolve. *Nomos* and *telos* are one.

Schmitt's exploration of the spatial logic behind any legal regulation did not lead to a metaphysic of origins. He drew from Weber, whom he had known and in many ways resembled in cast of mind, a ready grasp of social and historical variation. He had no difficulty in seeing the kind of distinction that Oakeshott wanted. Towards the end of the Weimar period, he had noted the difference between the ideals of a *Regierungsstaat* and a *Gesetzgebungsstaat* – a governing as opposed to a law-giving state, and the greater approximation in the nineteenth century of the English state to the first and the Continental to the second, while stressing that neither had ever existed as a pure type. In the twentieth century, however, with the massive increase in economic regulation, welfare provision, cultural supervision by public authorities – he pointed out that by 1928 over half of national income was controlled by the Weimar Government – a 'structural change' had occurred. The *Gesetzgebungsstaat* not merely everywhere predominated, but was now moving towards a new configuration, in which the state was increasingly becoming something like 'the self-organization of society'.[73] If we ask what was the common anxiety that lent imaginative energy to the work of all these thinkers, this is an expression that suggests its nerve-centre.

After the debacle of the First World War, and the victory of Bolshevism in Russia, the old political world of landed rulers and limited electorates, modest budgets and stable currencies, had crumbled away. A new kind of mass enfranchisement and expectation gripped Europe, the arrival of a democracy capable of brushing aside, in the pursuit of security or equality, traditional barriers between the tasks of government and the affairs of business – a semi-oligarchic state and a still-hierarchic civil society. Where would popular sovereignty

---

72. *Der Nomos der Erde im Völkerrecht des Jus Publicum Europaeum*, Berlin 1950, pp. 15–20ff.
73. 'Die Wendung zum totalen Staat' (1931), in *Positionen und Begriffe*, pp. 148–152.

without social liability lead? Communism was, of course, the first
and greatest danger. Fascism, which looked to some as if it might be
an antidote, proved little better – indeed, in German guise at least, all
but identical. But even when these were seen off, there was still the
welfare state, a creeping version of the same disease. In the course of
six decades, political judgements of this changing scene varied.
Strauss and Oakeshott, scornful of liberalism before Hitler came to
power, were more circumspect after the war; Hayek, who described
himself as a classical liberal during the war, repudiated the term as
compromised beyond recovery when he got to America; Schmitt, who
never had any truck with liberalism, moved from Catholic authoritarianism to National Socialism, before ending as an informal doyen of
the most respectable post-war constitutionalism. But beyond the
discrepant local sympathies of these careers – with their splay of
temporary identities: Conservative, Zionist, Nazi, Old Whig – they
reflected a common theoretical calling.

It was Schmitt who found the symbol for it. His later work is
haunted by a theological image. Again and again, he alluded to one
of the most enigmatic of all apocalyptic texts, the second letter to
the Thessalonians, without ever quoting it. What does Paul say there?
'The mystery of lawlessness doth already work; only there is one that
restraineth now, until he be taken out of the way; and then shall be
revealed the lawless one, whom the Lord Jesus will slay with the
breath of his mouth, and bring to nought with the manifestation of
his coming'. It was the second clause that mattered. Who was the
Restrainer – the *katechon* who holds back the prowl of evil on earth,
until the arrival of the Redeemer? Learned speculation has debated
the cryptic identity of the *katechon* (this is its sole scriptural appearance) since the time of Tertullian. In Schmitt's own writing, the
obscure figure assumes various – typically oblique – historical guises,
as political or juridical *Aufhalter* in different epochs.[74] But the Stygian
cap fits the collective effort of this cluster of thinkers. For these were
indeed constructions designed to hold something back. What they all
in the end sought to restrain was the risks of democracy – seen and
feared through the prisms of their theories of law, as the abyss of its
absence: *to misterion tes anomias*, the mystery of lawlessness.

---

74. Byzantium for *Land und Meer*, Berlin 1944, p. 12 (perhaps also later Rudolf
II: p. 56); Carolingian, Saxon and Salian Emperors for *Der Nomos der Erde*,
pp. 28–34; Savigny and Hegel, for 'Die Lage der europäischen Rechtswissenschaft'
(1943/44), *Verfassungsrechtliche Aufsätze*, pp. 428–429; wanting by the time of
Tocqueville, for *Ex Captivitate Salus*, Cologne 1950, p. 31.

Each put up their own barriers against the danger. The dichotomies which are the signature of their work – the esoteric and the exoteric, the civil and the managerial, the friend and the foe, the lawful and the legislative – are so many cordons. Their function is to hold popular sovereignty at bay. The different gifts displayed in this enterprise, whatever view is taken of it, were remarkable. For all his later tendency to textual dressage, Strauss's range and subtlety as a master of the canon of political philosophy had no equal in his generation. Schmitt's moral instability never impaired an extraordinary capacity to fuse conceptual insight and metaphoric imagination in lightning flashes of illumination around the state. Hayek could seem tactically ingenuous, but he fashioned a theoretical synthesis out of his epistemology and economics whose scope and strength has yet to be supplanted.

Oakeshott was the literary artist in this gallery. His writing varies considerably in quality, and can be whimsically arch at one moment and curiously crude at another, disconcertingly close to *Punch* or Cross-Bencher. But at its best, when it moves into high register, it can rise to a lyrical beauty. Oakeshott was a stranger to argument, which he anyway largely disavowed: his expositions have nothing of it. Nor, despite his prescriptions, do they have the least character of conversation: Oakeshott's declamations bear no relation to the tentative rhythm of a conversational style, such as one finds in Hume. What they are is rhetoric – a sustained exercise in the art of seduction, not of interlocution. There is a touch of Edwardian lushness in this prose. But to understand its spell, it is only necessary to consult – the most apposite example – the excursus on religion in *On Human Conduct*.[75] The continuing claims of such writing are no surprise.

If we compare the general fortune of these thinkers of the radical Right to that of more conventional eminences of the Centre, there is a pregnant contrast. The work of just one theorist, John Rawls, may have accumulated more scholarly commentary than that of all four put together. Yet this veritable academic industry has had virtually no impact on the world of Western politics. The reticence of its subject, who has never risked his reputation with express commitments, is no doubt part of the reason. But it is also to do with the distance between a discourse of justice, however Olympian, and the realities of a society driven by power and profit. The quartet considered here had the political courage of their convictions. But these also went, more largely,

---

75. To be found at pp. 81–86.

with the grain of the social order. So although they could often appear marginal, even eccentric figures to their colleagues, their voice was heard in the chancelleries. Schmitt counselled Papen and received Kiesinger; Straussians thronged the National Security Council under Reagan, and surround Quayle; Hayek earned formal homage from Thatcher on the floor of the Commons; and Oakeshott, under the anaesthetic Major, has entered the official breviary. Even arcane teaching can reach gentlemen. They are the heirs.

1992

2

CONSTITUTIONAL THEATRE:

Ferdinand Mount

'Constitutional theorists who wish to hold our attention must charm as well as instruct; this is not so, I think, in other countries,' writes Ferdinand Mount.[1] Who better to illustrate the claim? Few figures in the world of English letters possess such a combination of engaging credentials. Author of a number of accomplished novels, with more than an echo of his uncle Anthony Powell; popular columnist or leader-writer for half of the nation's press, with a record of service from the *Sketch* to *The Spectator*; debonair advocate of the iconoclastic values of the family; hard-headed political counsellor at Downing Street; the editor of the *Times Literary Supplement* seems the ideal candidate for the task in hand. Nor is the success of *The British Constitution Now* in fulfilling the first part of the requirement in doubt. Mount's account of the framework of the United Kingdom, and what repair it may call for, has beguiled its readers across the political spectrum. Commentators on Right and Left alike have lauded its wit and acumen. If few have seen eye to eye with every proposal it makes, virtually all have agreed that this is the work of an enlightened reformer, of liberal temper, within the party of tradition. Here, so it would appear, is a rare conservative who might even be regarded as an ally, in his own fashion, of the radical *franc-tireurs* around Charter 88.

The admiration *The British Constitution Now* has won is not misplaced. It is, indeed, a graceful and intelligent book. But it has attracted a misapprehension. The charm of the image has, so to speak, obscured the instruction of the text. There are a number of ways of approaching this, but the best is probably to begin with its dedication.

---

1. *The British Constitution Now*, London 1992, p. 65. Henceforward *BCN*.

The book is devoted to the memory of Michael Oakeshott – whose thought, Mount tells us, has left its traces, 'no doubt sadly smudged', on many of its pages.[2] At first glance, the affinity between author and authority here seems straightforward enough, for Oakeshott was widely held to be the most civilized conservative thinker of his time, a philosopher above party or prejudice, admired on occasion as far afield as the early *New Left Review*.[3] But it has more political charge to it than might be thought. To see this, we need to look back at the original occasion on which Mount paid tribute to his mentor.

On 17 November 1975, Oakeshott delivered a public lecture in New York, 'Talking Politics', in honour of the twentieth anniversary of *The National Review*, the journal of the American far Right. In the issue of 21 November, Mount – a regular contributor – toasted the appearance of Oakeshott's 'majestic work' *On Human Conduct*, whose 'fresh and memorable definition of political liberty' was cause for 'gratitude and celebration'. This was a representative number of the magazine. Mount's homage was accompanied by two tributes, from James Burnham and F.R. Buckley, to 'our century's most successful ruler', Generalissimo Franco – 'a giant who will be truly mourned by Spain', giving 'the lie to cant about "fascism"'. Fronting the journal was an admiring interview with General Somoza, 'long the best friend the United States has in Central America', as he set about the reconstruction of his country in the aftermath of the Nicaraguan earthquake. Winding it up came a warning from Robert Bork against the menace of the 'clerisy of power' now (under the Ford Presidency) steering the nation towards the shoals of equality and uniformity.[4]

The following bumper issue of *The National Review*, on 5 December, was mainly taken up with the text of Oakeshott's lecture, accompanied by 'a pictorial essay' on the banquet commemorating the journal's twentieth year in the Grand Ballroom of the Plaza Hotel – a *Tatler*-style spread awash with tuxedo and chalice, whose stars were Barry Goldwater ('regarded more than any other living American with almost universal affection') and Ronald Reagan ('about to engage in a great enterprise – indeed this occasion is at once his last, and unlikeliest chance to back out'). Peering out elf-like from the convivial flux was Oakeshott. Perhaps we should imagine the young Mount too, somewhere off-camera, hovering respectfully in

2. BCN, p. ix.
3. See Colin Falck, 'Romanticism in Politics', *New Left Review*, I/18, January–February 1963, pp. 60–72.
4. 'Oakeshott's Distinction', *National Review*, 21 November 1975.

outlying eddies. At all events, this is the constellation from which a
consideration of *The British Constitution Now* – for that matter, the
current *Times Literary Supplement* – can most usefully start.

Mount's book opens with a skilful salvo against reigning compla-
cencies and canonical authorities, calculated to win the sympathy of
every radical reader. The vanities of British exceptionalism – the
unique political wisdom of Westminster – and the illusions of
seamless continuity in our constitutional development, are lightly dispatched. Then, at greater length, the received doctrines of Bagehot,
Dicey and Jennings are dismissed, as so many crude or mischievous
simplifications of the subtler, more surprising reality of Britain's
heritage. Having demolished these, Mount proceeds to pass in review
the actual shape of the country's Constitution – an edifice rather than
an engine, he stresses, in Oakeshottian idiom. Surveying its principal
parts in turn, he finds fault not only with the way they are understood, but also how some of them in fact operate. There has been, he
concludes, a falling away from the original virtues of the British
Constitution, that still lie dormant within it. Mount's proposals for
reform seek to reawaken its 'old spirit', with a set of candid yet
moderate changes, that would also help it adjust to the 'incoming
tides' of the world outside the UK. Entrenchment of existing constitutional conventions, incorporation of the European Convention on
Human Rights, fixed-term Parliaments, some kind of Scottish
Assembly, are the main items of this agenda. Not far enough, sup-
porters of Charter 88 might say, but moving in the right direction.

The drift of the enterprise, however, is not to be caught so readily.
The feature of Mount's book that has perhaps most caught the fancy
of the Left is its disposal of 'the three great simplifiers', which clears
the decks for his own view of the Constitution. The caning given
Bagehot and Dicey, in particular, has aroused more than one pleasur-
able *frisson*. Greater attention should have been paid to Mount's own
classification of his trio. 'By coincidence', he remarks, 'the three
most noted constitutional analysts represent each of the three main
political tendencies – Bagehot the Liberal, Dicey the Unionist,
Jennings the Fabian'.[5] A critic of all three, the reader can deduce, will
not be pleading from any narrow standpoint of party. The description is, however, a feint. Dicey was indeed a 'Unionist', but he was
never a Conservative, remaining a Liberal of Whig persuasion
throughout his career. One of the 'main political tendencies' is tacitly

---

5. *BCN*, p. 80.

exempt from stricture here, and forms the real basis for the critique of the other two.

For on inspection, the substance of Mount's objections to the standard authorities turns out to be not their coinage of conventional pieties, but subversion of them. Bagehot, to begin with – otherwise the epitome of 'manly common sense' – had the bad taste to treat the monarchy as if it were a mere charade to gull the masses, rather than a 'heart-touching symbol' of the culture they shared with the educated classes – and so in truth 'the legitimate authority which was entitled to demand their obedience'.[6] It was C.H. Sisson, from a Maurrassian background, who first vehemently lodged this complaint,[7] which Mount now repeats in more decorous terms, regretting that Bagehot should have been so distrustful of the broadening of the electorate.

Dicey, on the other hand, was guilty of something worse. Behind his high doctrine of the sovereignty of Parliament, unencumbered by rival power or binding precedent, 'lurks the menacing, insatiable sovereign will of the people – the id to Westminster's ego'.[8] The tenets of Diceyan constitutionalism, despite appearances, amount in the end to little more than a formula for 'mob-rule' – as his own conduct during the long Irish crisis, when he appealed for popular resistance to parliamentary decisions, showed. Here the affront is not to royalist *pudeur*, but to the rule of law itself. Mount affects to be shocked that Dicey could have contemplated insurrection to preserve the Union – as if this was not a widespread option among the political establishment of the time, entertained by Bonar Law and many others: indeed a famous episode in the modern history of his own party. Like Bagehot's opinions of the Second Reform Act, Dicey's interventions against Home Rule form a tactically convenient stick for Mount to beat authors whose real offence lies elsewhere – tarnishing the aura of monarchy, and opening the door to popular sovereignty. Jennings, by contrast, requires no side-gambit. Mount taxes him without further ado for 'unashamed bureaucratic slurring' of the constitution, by treating bodies like the trade unions as if they had some relevance to it.[9] That was the road to a calamitous corporatism, swelling the opretensions and corrupting the integrity of government.

If such are the defects of the accepted authorities, what has been the practical effect of their doctrines – did they simply reflect or actually

---

6. BCN, pp. 39, 43.
7. *The Case of Walter Bagehot*, London 1972, pp. 64–77, 127–129.
8. BCN, p. 52.
9. BCN, p. 68.

promote dangerous trends in the body politic? 'Are Bagehot, Dicey and Jennings merely unwitting agents of an intellectual degeneration which was inbuilt?'[10] That would imply structural faults in our constitutional heritage itself. This is delicate ground, where his natural constituency has strong convictions, and here Mount treads carefully. His solution is an equivocation. Essentially, the problem is our 'understanding' of the Constitution, rather than the reality of it. If certain strains in it have appeared over time, the ancient structure contains the remedies for them – strengths that have been long neglected, under the distorting influence of official misinterpretations. The pragmatism of the past century is a 'symptom of decadence'.[11] The need today is to return to the principles that informed our original institutions – to recover the 'old spirit' of the Constitution, as Mount puts it.[12]

The convenience of the notion lies, of course, in the absence of any letter to correspond to – even contradict – it. The 'British Constitution' is, in any comparative meaning, *just* spirit. Indeed, one might say, any number of them, in the table-turning sense. Mount's own seance is rather desultory, and after a few erratic results, he abandons the board. The ghosts that briefly appear include Bracton, Grattan, inevitably Burke. The ideal past summoned up oscillates mistily between Angevin and Hanoverian times. Without lingering on either period, Mount passes to the safer task of 'summarizing' the genie in general. Naturally it includes the rule of law, as a horizon superior to all legislators. Beyond this, in Mount's retrospect, the old spirit of the Constitution turns out to be what Montesquieu had supposed, but few English have believed – the separation of powers peculiar to our kingdom. Colported home by Leo Amery, the judgement of *De l'esprit de lois* re-emerges as the deeper truth of our institutions after all, whatever historians may say.[13] This departure from the verdict of modern scholarship is not, however, pursued in any detail. For what Mount really wishes to stress is not the separation, but the *multiplication*, of powers in the national past. The term he uses to deplore the modern decline of the Constitution is significant. When he describes the trend of the twentieth century, he always speaks of the 'thinning' of British institutions:[14] not 'fusing'. What he means by this is essentially the process whereby first the monarchy

10. *BCN*, p. 71.
11. *BCN*, pp. 31, 265.
12. *BCN*, pp. 81ff.
13. *BCN*, pp. 88–89.
14. *BCN*, pp. 21, 33, 36, 79.

lost the substance of its prerogatives within the King-in-Parliament, and then the Lords lost most of theirs to the Commons, leaving the latter in something perilously close to full control of the state. In short, what is normally accounted the emergence of democracy.

Just this process, of course, has remained incomplete. For in Ukania the supremacy of Parliament is not the sovereignty of the people, either in theory or in practice. The step from one to the other, which Mount reproaches Dicey with having paved, was never made. The historical reasons why the forms of the new-old settlement of 1689 have survived three centuries are best set out in Tom Nairn's *Enchanted Glass*, a study Mount consigns to a nervous footnote. But it is the appropriate gauge for measuring his own. For what a comparison of their work shows is that a critique of what both writers call 'parliamentary monotheism' can move in two, diametrically opposite directions. It can either point out all the ways in which Westminster remains a pre-modern assembly, without even pretence of equitable representation of electoral opinion, let alone democratic control of executive power; or it can lament the lack of modern impediments to legislation in the name of a popular mandate, of the kind that palace and peers once provided. Mount's dislike of parliamentary sovereignty, twentieth-century-style, is of the latter kind. It is not adjacent to a radical rejection of the present system, as a somewhat more moderate variant along the spectrum, but lies at the opposite pole.

This is why, of course, Michael Oakeshott is the garden god of its intellectual landscape. For his theory of the state was designed precisely to rope off popular government and purposive legislation from the proper conduct of rule. 'Civil association', as the framework of order, debarred collective aims or common consent from the structure of government. These were the features of another kind of activity, 'enterprise association', which had nothing to do with true governance. The confusion of enterprise association with civil association, when rulers undertook 'managerial' tasks – intervening in economic life or meddling in social affairs: in short, any programme for public welfare – was the path to servitude. Mount, closer to day-to-day realities, can see the difficulties of this stark dichotomy for the practical politician, and assures us that the two kinds of association are not mutually exclusive, and were 'not really intended to be so'.[15] The pious gloss is without consequence. For the burden of Mount's argument is that the Constitution should indeed be seen, not in the way Bagehot envisaged

---

15. *BCN*, p. 75

it – as an 'engine' for purposeful government, or the dire image of an enterprise association – but as a civil association: a form of living, he writes, as exempt from wilful shape or aim as South Kensington.[16]

This flourish was probably penned while the author was still a columnist for the *Daily Telegraph* – one can think of London boroughs whose name would give a less poetic effect. But the reassuring ring of SW3 does not mean that the idea it is intended to suggest is of simply local import. It was civil association that Oakeshott expounded to *The National Review*, and celebrated in the Grand Plaza. Goldwater and Reagan were fighting for it before anyone had heard of Thatcher. So too, at his own station, was Mount, excoriating Macmillan's collusion with planning and Heath's retreat from the market as early as 1972, when the MP for Finchley was just another corporatist.[17] In those days, the American hard Right was well ahead of the British. But from the Atlantic cameraderie between the two, lasting ties developed – Mount's connections with the world of Bork and Burnham among them.

If, today, prime ideological occasions in the *Times Literary Supplement* often feature the talents of American neo-conservatism – Alan Bloom, Harvey Mansfield, Joseph Epstein, Hilton Kramer, Charles Murray, Paul Craig Roberts, Irving Kristol, even such names for the connoisseur as Richard Cornuelle – these are among the fruits of a mutually beneficial association. For on the one side, there are limits to local supply – the efforts of Conor Cruise O'Brien, Paul Johnson or Norman Stone, however infallible, will only go so far; while on the other, the lights of *New Criterion* or *Public Interest* shine brighter in the antique British mirror than they do at home. The result is a formula that makes for a livelier mixture than before, in which liberals otherwise remain perfectly presentable, under an editor who has managed a turn without drawing unnecessary attention to it, or intrusive personal signature.

Behind the affinity visible here, however, lies a deeper attraction for the American polity as such. It is striking how often, when Mount turns for a foreign example from which the UK would do well to learn, it is to the US he looks. His zest here is such that Thatcher herself stands revealed, through the happy chance of underlinings in a tattered paperback she gave the author, as – at any rate once – a secret believer in the superiority of American to British constitutional

---

16. BCN, p. 46.
17. *The Theatre of Politics*, London 1972, 'Fashions in Planning', pp. 204ff.

arrangements, as a 'system of fortifications for liberty and justice'.[18] Wherein does such superiority lie? Not in a written constitution, or republican government, or separation of church and state, or rights to freedom of information. What fortifies liberty and justice is the sort of thing Oakeshott had in mind – 'a stately, even somnolent tenor of non-political life and the extreme conservatism of attitudes and practices which belies the conventional view of American addiction to novelty', a 'kind of procedural stateliness' and 'constitutional steadiness' that has 'impeded the advance of the enterprise-association conception of politics'.[19] In other words: a state that is strong and stable, but with less ability to pass legislation, less expenditure on welfare, and less interfering turn-out at the polls.

How does the British Constitution today look, set against an Oakeshottian ideal? Mount proceeds to a stock-taking, for which he is exceptionally well equipped – combining, as he does, experience of the partisan think tank, the modern mass media, and the *arcana imperii* of the premier's office itself. He begins his account of the executive, rather solemnly, with the monarchy, which he complains has not been given its proper precedence before all other elements of government in recent textbooks. Any problems here? Only in received underestimates, stemming from Bagehot, of its vital role as the guardian of the constitution. The culture of deference is imaginary, and the idea of citizenship redundant – subjects enjoy immemorial rights under the Queen. In fact, the monarchy is blossoming in prestige as members of the royal family enjoy a new freedom of speech themselves. He even commits himself to the view that the monarchy has a more secure sense of its future than Parliament. Here the readers of the *Sun* seem to have deserted him.

Next comes the Prime Minister. Has there developed an undue concentration of power in Downing Street, at the expense of the Cabinet as a whole, as Crossman and so many others have thought? Not at all. Mrs Thatcher, often frustrated, presided over neo-baronial government as her predecessors had to do – ministers taking no direct orders from Number 10. But then what about collective responsibility – don't *ad hoc* coteries confidentially summoned by the PM often bypass the full Cabinet on important decisions altogether? Yes, and a very good thing too: strong executive government absolutely requires this. 'The calling or non-calling of meetings, together with the

---

18. *BCN*, pp. 27–28.
19. *BCN*, pp. 178, 76.

inclusion or omission of items on the agenda, remains an important instrument of power' – indeed 'an indispensable weapon for the effective dispatch of business'.[20] But does even the Budget have to be decided behind the back of ministers? Certainly – 'iron secrecy' necessarily 'ensures the impotence of the Cabinet in budgetary matters'.[21] In fact, Mount informs us from experience, not even long-term strategy is a suitable topic for discussion by the body nominally responsible for governing the land.

What of the civil servants that staff the departments below each minister – do they exercise more actual power, as is popularly supposed, than their status officially warrants? Well, they have the advantages that naturally accrue to continuity and numbers, as against the transient politicians, with their few aides, above them; and they could benefit from business experience in, say, a tobacco company before serving public welfare at large. But the loyalty and integrity of this incomparable band is assured by their allegiance to the monarchy – 'a concrete reality and not mere sentimental memorabilia', that is 'a matter of the head as well as the heart', with 'practical as well as emotional implications'.[22] Still, there is room for improvement in the organization of the Service: the Prime Minister is stupidly deprived of direct control of the Cabinet Office – the green baize door separating it from Number 10 is even locked – on the old-fashioned grounds that functionaries should maintain neutrality by distance from formation of policy. This is an anachronism: more command by Downing Street, not less, is the answer here.

Freedom of information? 'The problem of open government seems a great deal less real once one has had even a modicum of experience of life inside government' – for example, 'Cabinets meet *in private* – a less contentious and misleading word than "secret"'.[23] But mightn't the late Press Secretary have overdone news management a bit? On the contrary – in an affectionate salute to his old colleague, Mount has told readers of the *TLS* that the only shortcoming of Bernard Ingham's stalwart service was that 'he performed his office too faithfully and modestly, was insufficiently manipulative and viewy and did not actively help his mistress to conspire with the winds and tides of politics'.[24] In short, what we get here is government observed from the fastness of the Policy

---

20. *BCN*, p. 119.
21. *BCN*, p. 122.
22. *BCN*, p. 104.
23. *BCN*, p. 114.
24. 'National Articulators', *Times Literary Supplement*, 21–27 December 1990.

Unit in Number 10 – a Plumbers' View of the executive. At every point, the imperatives are centralized authority, efficacy, secrecy. These are the values Mount served then and upholds today. Whatever one's attitude towards them, his report of their machinery is a compelling description that forms the most vivid part of the book.

Moving on to the legislature, Mount contends that Parliament has three possible functions: remonstration, scrutiny and control. The first of these, redress of the grievances of constituents, he thinks the contemporary House of Commons performs excellently. The second, inspection or improvement of prospective bills, it does very poorly. The third, monitoring of actions by the executive, it pursues only lamely. His own suggestions for reform concentrate on scrutiny, for which he thinks Special Standing Committees of the House, able to take evidence on bills as well as read them, are the solution. The significant feature of this account of the role of Parliament, however, is the function it is *not* accorded – the capacity actually to make laws, rather than merely ratify or refine them. This is a 'legislature', in other words, that does not legislate. Mount approvingly cites his preferred modern authority to make the point. 'The main task of Parliament', declared Leo Amery, 'is still what it was when first summoned, not to legislate or govern'. Or, as Mount puts it: 'we have to recognise the intrinsic limits on the capabilities of Parliament, perhaps of all parliaments'.[25] But this is no reluctant acceptance of imperfection. On the contrary, such limits are a salutary safeguard and need to be, not regretted, but reinforced. The purpose of his new committees, he explains, would be to reduce the amount of law-making, by slowing the whole process down and making it more laborious.

Mount's depiction of current realities is, of course, accurate enough. A long-standing lobby correspondent before he was a policy adviser, his knowledge of Westminster is as close as that of Whitehall. But if we ask why the House of Commons is not a legislature, in the sense intended by the classical theorists of representative government in the last century – Guizot or Mill or Dicey – the answer has long been plain. Laws are not made on the floor of the House, but are determined by party leadership, and whipped through by party discipline. Debate is incidental. This is the central reality of the political process. What does Mount have to say about it? Nothing. There is simply no discussion of the role of parties within British constitutional democracy in *The British Constitution Now*. The enormity of this omission can be

---

25. *BCN*, p. 179.

seen by a glance at any modern commentary on the subject. When Crossman wrote his introduction to Bagehot – still the best reflection on *The English Constitution* – his essential theme was the political transformation wrought by the rise of organized parties, which Bagehot never really grasped. A generation later, Dicey was well aware of the change, which he roundly attacked from the standpoint of an intransigent liberal individualism that held the independence of the MP in the Commons to be an indefeasible value. By the inter-war period, the situation was such that Jennings could simply write, 'A realistic survey of the British Constitution must begin and end with parties and discuss them at length in the middle .'[26] So it must continue to do – and in how much greater measure – today.

The fade-out that party suddenly undergoes in *The British Constitution Now* is thus a startling regression. It seems to compromise any claim Mount's account could otherwise make to realism. What explains the absence? Certainly not inadvertence. A veteran of the Conservative Research Department and the Centre for Policy Studies, not to speak of the tabloid amplifiers of Tory opinion, of all his vantage points Mount knows the perspective from Smith Square perhaps best. The reason why parties are nevertheless screened out from his analysis of the constitution is that consideration of them fatally poses the question his design is conceived to repress. What is the substance of *democracy* in Britain? The word does not appear in the index of Mount's book. This is not an oversight. The indexer has been thorough. The term is not there because the idea does not animate the text. There is no surprise in this. For it was against the logic of democracy, as the exercise of popular will, that the theoretical scheme of civil association was devised, whose hope was to put the pattern of wealth and power beyond it. The modern political life of Western societies has never, of course, corresponded to this dream. The reality has been a continual contest over social ends, between organized parties competing against each other, as vehicles of the popular will. This is the form of the democracy we possess.

Its substance therefore inevitably turns on the ways in which the parties themselves are constituted and elected – in other words, how far their organization is free, their funding fair and their representation equitable. Distortion in any of these three conditions means, straightforwardly, diminution of the chances of democratic self-determination. In Britain, the block vote in the Labour Party exhibits

---

26. *The British Constitution*, Cambridge 1945, p. 31. The book was completed in 1940.

a notorious example of the first; the corporate finance and tycoon press of the Conservative Party a flagrant example of the second. But uniting the two parties is their exploitation of our gross national illustration of the third – a voting system that regularly disenfranchises up to a quarter of the electorate. It is the ending of this mortmain that is the real test of constitutional reform in Britain. Mount, aware that the first-past-the-post system is no longer quite so untouchable, goes through the motions of considering changes to it, but naturally rejects them. Even by unexacting local standards, the arguments he puts up are nugatory. But they should not be unduly held against him, since the role of parties and the nature of their representation have been excluded from his agenda in the first place. For these, we are given to understand, belong to the order of mere 'facts' of the political landscape, which have nothing to do with the 'structures' of the constitution. Jennings's great mistake, Mount explains, was to confuse these two quite distinct orders of reality.[27]

This is not the sum of what Mount has to say about the legislature. For there remains the other chamber. How does he view the Lords? He would like to see it gain more authority, and to this end is willing to concede some 'reduction' – but not abolition – of its hereditary element: we are referred to Lord Home's Conservative Party Report to Mrs Thatcher (1978) for appropriate details. It is the aim rather than the means that is significant. For the role for the Lords that Mount would like to see enhanced is judicial – ideally, the emergence within it of a supreme court to rule on the constitutionality of laws passed by the Commons, or actions taken by the executive. This evolution would cap a wider change. For in Mount's conception of reform, the judiciary is the branch of government with a future. It is not below, in the emancipation of political choice among the electorate, but above, in the higher deliberations of the bench, that liberty can be enlarged.

Political temperaments without any mixed impulses or traces of ambiguity are rare. The diversity of Mount's gifts and avocations makes him unlikely to be an exception. There are good reasons for wishing to entrench civic rights in law against executive abuses in Britain, and Mount gives forceful expression to some of them. If there is one note struck in his book that has understandably attracted the reformers of Charter 88, it is this. Here, at least, one definitely libertarian thread in his argument, leading to a plea for incorporation of the European Convention on Human Rights in British law, can be detected.

---

27. *BCN*, pp. 70–71.

It would be wrong to minimize it. But the generous note struck on these pages must still find its place within the score as a whole. There, the logic of doctrine determines the selection of attention. For, alongside the general plea for greater protection of the rights of the subject, silence falls over every specific oppression of them. In a discourse of civil liberties, one can search for those landmarks of British justice – Birmingham, Guilford, Gibraltar – in vain. GCHQ or Spycatcher might have never happened. There is only one case that comes to mind, Ponting. What is to be said of him? 'It was generally agreed that, rather than leaking or going public,' Mount writes, 'he should have taken his anxieties to his Permanent Secretary and rested content with the advice given him by that dignitary.'[28] Generally agreed? A pity about the jury. What matters is the good sense of the judge.

Here the sensibility of *The British Constitution Now* is all of a piece. Mount's generally cool prose flushes into rubicund enthusiasm whenever judges are mentioned. There is the inestimable service to the nation of Lords Hewart, Radcliffe, Denning; the stout performance of Lord Lane, traduced by journalists and demagogues; the veritable 'revolution' in our courts, as increased judicial review brings the vital breath of natural justice to them.[29] The suggestion that the composition of the British judiciary might harbour any dangers for the freedom of the ordinary citizen is 'little more than a cheap attempt to arouse popular paranoia'.[30] Mount's particular admiration goes to former Chief Justice Denning, whose 'noble' efforts more than any other 'kept alive in the minds of Englishmen an idea of law which is broader and higher and more enduring than the ever fattening annual volumes of Acts of Parliament'.[31] It is well to remind ourselves of those efforts. This was the judge who said of the Birmingham Six: 'If the six men win, it will mean that the police were guilty of violence and threats, that the confessions were involuntary and were improperly admitted in evidence: and that the convictions were erroneous. That would mean the Home Secretary would either have to recommend they be pardoned or he would have to remit the case to the Court of Appeal. This is such an appalling vista that every sensible person in the land would say: it cannot be right that these actions should go any further.'[32] Sentiments worthy of that other great West Country Justice, George Jeffreys. If

---

28. *BCN*, p. 104.
29. *BCN*, pp. 24–28, 209–210, 261.
30. *BCN*, p. 212.
31. *BCN*, pp. 266, 209.
32. Judgment issued as Master of the Rolls, 17 January 1980.

these count for so little in Mount's scale of things, we may assume it is
because he is thinking of Denning's higher services. His hero might on
occasion be 'erratic', but he led the way on the real battle-front of
liberty – moves to curb the trade unions, who have been 'wrecking
Britain's industrial prospects for most of this century'.[33]

Confidence in the judiciary allows, in Mount's conception, for a
kind of semi-inscription of the wisdom of the Constitution. This
would not amount to any written instrument as formal as a fundamental charter, which might raise awkward questions of philosophical
principle or architectural coherence, but would simply take the form
of a parliamentary bill enumerating certain rights and procedures that
could only be altered by a two-thirds majority in any successor
Parliament. Interpretation of this act would be entrusted to the
courts, extended by a final tier of specifically constitutional judges
seconded from the Lords. For the credentials of this solution, we are
referred to cousinly arrangements in New Zealand (an example that
has presumably become less congenial since Mount wrote – its
citizens having just voted by a majority of over 80 per cent to abolish
first-past-the-post). An appeal to reassuring precedent in the former
White Dominions is now a common move in moderate reforming literature. In Rodney Brazier's *Constitutional Reform*, for example,
which appeared shortly before Mount's work, it is Australia that
affords inspiration for improvements at home.

The contrast between the two books, however, is revealing of the
limits of Mount's approach. In a quiet and unshowy way, Brazier's
apparently more conventional study is consistently more radical. It
puts the realities of party at the centre of its analysis of the constitution, and of prospects for changing it; argues for electoral reform, if
only the alternative vote; envisages popular recall of MPs to make
them more accountable; requires reduction in Prime Ministerial
powers and collective control of the budget; notes the 'dismal catalogue' of affronts to civil liberty under Thatcher's rule, and the 'record
number of cases for any state represented in the Council of Europe'
decided against the UK in the European Court of Human Rights;
points out that 'the entire judiciary in England and Wales owes its
appointment to one, and occasionally to two, politicians', and calls
for a Supreme Court that would 'not be composed only of men, drawn
from a small pool, unrepresentative of the general population'.[34]

---

33. *BCN*, p. 266.
34. Rodney Brazier, *Constitutional Reform*, Oxford 1991, pp. 60–62, 52–53,
100–102, 126–127, 153, 162.

Brazier's work, for all its merits, is still in many ways quite cautious. For a more comprehensive programme of reform, we must turn to James Cornford's impressive plan for a democratized British state, the detailed draft of a written *Constitution of the United Kingdom*[35] that was published by the Institute for Public Policy Research last year. There the issues of popular sovereignty and of equitable representation, the core of meaningful political reform in Britain, acquire their fitting relief. Mount's otherwise abundant references to current constitutional writings, perhaps unsurprisingly, include no mention of it.

What do the different elements of his own package amount to? Greater reverence for the monarchy; unchanging Prime Ministerial authority; no ventilation of the bureaucracy; less legislation by Parliament; wider powers for the courts. There is a rights dimension to this, but it is a very modest one: entrenchment of an existing minimum, not development towards any optimum. Consecrated executive, inhibited legislature, fortified judiciary. It might be said that Mount, rather than overthrowing Bagehot, has merely refurbished him – with a schedule of works whose formula is: redecorate the dignified and pre-stress the efficient parts of the constitution. But there is a difference, to which Mount is entitled to draw our attention. The efficiency of the renovated structure is not to be conceived in dynamic fashion. The state as civil association requires the abandonment of its misguided ventures into enterprise association. The genuinely radical element in Mount's programme lies not so much in its astygmatic concern for civil liberties, as in its off-hand proposal to abolish entire ministries to slim down the state. The Departments of Energy, Agriculture and Employment head the list, but there seems no reason why Industry should not follow. Here, there is a first touch of the drastic Hayekian spirit, in an otherwise Oakeshottian scheme.

Hayek himself, of course, had too forthright a view of the shortcomings of the Ukanian Constitution to be a comfortable guide otherwise. British government represented a 'monstrosity and caricature of the ideal of the separation of powers', he wrote – adding that Parliament could even theoretically send him to the Tower for saying so.[36] His own remedy for the ills of parliamentary supremacy was to reconstitute the legislature into a superior chamber, based on electors of mature age only (over forty-five), to invigilate strict constitutional

---

35. Institute for Public Policy Research, 1991.

36. *Law, Legislation and Liberty* , Vol. III, *The Political Order of a Free People*, London 1979, pp. 126, 179.

rules, and an inferior one, based on universal suffrage, allowed to pass limited particular statutes within them. Mount's realism naturally precludes reception of this idea. But the general sense of his scheme moves in the same direction: conversion of the upper house into *garde-fou* of the lower, to keep down improper legislation. In tune with Oakeshott's prescriptions, however, here institutional changes are not advanced in any rationalist spirit, as blueprints of improvement, but as intimations of so many 'shapes to come' latent in the course of things itself. Recapitulated at the end of the book, such reforms unfold in succession as those 'becoming visible', 'likely soon', and discernible 'in the longer term'.[37]

The alterations envisaged are 'plausible', Mount explains, in the happy sense of being both desirable and probable. But, from a Conservative standpoint, there is still the question: why make any changes at all? Mount readily concedes that 'the case for the status quo is a powerful one'.[38] What then has caused him to consider amending it? At first glance, the answer would seem to be a reaction against the corporatist extensions, or illiberal intrusions, of the post-war state into civil society. That certainly looks like the underlying concern of his introductory theme, summoning up the diversity of powers in the old spirit of the Constitution, against the dangerous presumptions of an overmighty Commons in the new. In this tenor, Oakeshott's way of justifying reform – as the 'correction' of an 'accumulated mass of maladjustment' due only to the 'negligence of past generations' – is also reproduced. 'It is important to appreciate how much we have forgotten', Mount insists, reminding us of the origins of British freedom in the 'dappled world' of the Middle Ages, as his mentor liked to do.[39]

But such gestures prove less of a guide to the pressure of the book than might be imagined. It is noticeable that, intellectually, Mount himself scarcely presses them. After first describing the original form of the Constitution, since fallen into neglect, as 'a magnificent structure, delicately yet powerfully stressed and balanced', he forgets himself, to the point of writing on virtually the next page, of 'a set of arrangements so notoriously fluid and imprecise' that 'even to outline firmly anything which can be dignified by the name of structure is to invite attempts to subject its girders to stresses which they were not designed to withstand'![40] Politically, moreover, the traditional dangers

37. *BCN*, pp. 260–267.
38. *BCN*, p. 215.
39. *BCN*, p. 79.
40. *BCN*, pp. 79–81.

that have exercised critics of governmental corporatism, or for that matter authoritarianism, do not loom large in what follows. The reasons for that are fairly clear. Thatcher's rule, after all, has beaten back the first; while Mount seems content with most time-honoured manifestations of the second. It is certainly not any failure to sell British Rail, or success in neutering the Cabinet, that has prompted *The British Constitution Now*.

The real spurs to reform lie elsewhere. Mount moves on to them at the end of his book. They correspond to a set of problems that were left unresolved for British Conservatism by the Thatcher years. The first of these is the position of Scotland within the United Kingdom. The difficult position of the party north of the Border, in country now permanently in opposition to it, and potentially capable of slipping the leash altogether, has long counselled some accommodation to national feeling. Here Mount ingeniously turns Tory prejudice against logic or symmetry into an argument for a Scottish Assembly inserted below Westminster, without reduction of Scots representation in London – or substantial autonomy in Edinburgh. 'So long as it is carefully constructed along minimalist lines',[41] such an untidy arrangement would help to preserve rather than weaken the Union.

A second and graver problem is posed by the fate of local government under Thatcher. Within Conservative ranks, Mount was a prescient critic of the poll tax from the start, and his hostility to it – 'one of the worst and most obviously doomed innovations in British political history'[42] – has not abated. But he goes out of his way to stress that the restless record of previous Labour and Conservative administrations was not much better. The root of the evil lies in an excessive parliamentary centralism that has led to frivolous disdain for municipal independence and county tradition alike. It is unlikely he now regards the council tax, already exposing the party to further strains, as much of an improvement. The solution lies rather in a clear and stable demarcation of the powers and revenues of local authorities, to ensure 'responsible housekeeping', by a constitutional settlement that should, wherever possible, restore 'historic loyalties' on the ground.[43]

Here, as it happens, a significant bifurcation in Conservative retrospect has occurred. For alongside Mount's book, we now have another Oakeshottian study, Shirley Letwin's *Anatomy of Thatcherism*, which

---

41. *BCN*, p. 263.
42. *BCN*, p. 205.
43. *BCN*, p. 205.

draws the opposite lesson from the poll tax. The two authors were associates together in the Centre for Policy Studies, and share much the same theoretical commitments. Where Mount expressly keys his work to Oakeshott's distinction between civil and enterprise association, Letwin tacitly organizes hers around Oakeshott's contrast between the spiritually 'self-employed' individual and the 'dependent' anti-individual. The real thrust of Thatcherism, she contends, was to revive the 'vigorous virtues' characteristic of the former – not simply those of Lords Hanson and King, but also of Dr Johnson and Edward Elgar, of Baden-Powell and Edith Cavell – among a population long inured to the vices of the latter.[44] Letwin's account of these years, the doughtiest defence of the late Prime Minister to date, is nevertheless not uncritical of her record. Higher education, where Thatcherism betrayed Oakeshott's ideals of liberal learning for the misplaced targets of an enterprise association, was certainly a black spot – one that left Mount, removed from academic life, more indifferent. On the other hand Letwin, trouncing critics of the poll tax, treats reverence for imaginary 'traditions of local autonomy'[45] in Britain in the brisk spirit of Churchill's *mot* on the customs of the Navy. The major failure of Thatcher's third administration did not lie in local government, but in its failure to keep control of inflation. The technical means of doing so, however, necessarily vary over time, and this defeat meant no burial of the Thatcherite cause of reviving the morality of vigorous virtues in British society. Simply, the battle-front has changed, as the major adversary has become the bureaucratic ethos of European federalism.

Europe is, in the end, the decisive issue for Mount too. In the deepening quarrel within British Conservatism today, the two theorists take opposite sides. For Letwin, authentic British individualism has never had any counterpart on the Continent, and the 'ever closer union' promised by the Treaty of Rome spells the extinction of our national independence. Her book, which simply takes the Constitution for granted, ends with a none-too-coded warning against those who could prove to be the usurpers of Thatcherism. For Mount, on the other hand, the institutions of the Community are now facts of life in Britain, to which timely adjustment must be made. By the end of his book, the central argument for taking the step towards something like a written constitution becomes the fact that the legal obligations of the European Community have in effect already imposed one on us, which

44. *The Anatomy of Thatcherism*, London 1992, pp. 32–48.
45. Ibid., pp. 159–162ff.

we might as well 'patriate' into a proper English version we have designed by ourselves. In this logic, if – in Lord Denning's phrase – the incoming tides of the Treaty of Rome cannot be halted, then let us dike and polder them into some fruitful landscape of our own.

This is an argument from necessity. Mount, however, goes beyond it. The Community is a modern project, yet one linked to the old idea of Christendom. It stands for human rights, and shares ecological concerns. There is an unmistakeable whiff of what *The Spectator* would condemn as 'Euro-enthusiasm' in these pages – Mount at moments even uses the suspect jargon of Brussels, extolling subsidiarity ('foreign clap-trap' in Doughty Street). Behind this sense for Europe, there is an attractive width of personal culture, free of any sour insularity. But it would be an error to take Mount's vision of the Community as – so to speak – an amiable streak of wetness in an otherwise bone-dry political outlook. The great merit of the EC is to form a vast space of free trade. Monetary union is no threat to a deregulated capitalism, but its best insurance. For a European Central Bank whose independence of political pressures was constitutionally entrenched – that is, of just the kind foreseen at Maastricht – would be a far tougher policeman of a sound currency than any national set of politicians could be, subject as they are to electoral temptations. Turning Nicholas Ridley's arguments against him, Mount remarks that the only practical reason for opting out of the ERM would be to resort once again to the discredited tool of devaluation. 'The powers which are liable to be surrendered in Europan economic union are the very powers to do things which most robust free-marketeers abhor. By contrast, constitutional entrenchment of the economic principles they hold most dear can, it seems, be achieved, if at all, only at European level.'[46]

There is a history to this argument. Oakeshott, whose technical theory afforded no space for the nation-state, since collective solidarity was not a principle of civil association, had – as might be expected – nothing to say about the problems of a supra-national one. Asked his view of Britain's entry into the EEC in the early sixties, Noel Annan reports, he replied: 'I do not find it necessary to hold opinions on such matters.'[47] Hayek, on the other hand, held firm and far-seeing ones. As early as 1939, he argued in his prophetic essay 'The Economic Conditions of Inter-State Federalism' that transcendence of national sovereignty in a supra-national framework should be of

---

46. *BCN*, p. 245.
47. Noel Annan, *Our Age*, London 1990, p. 400.

natural advantage to a free economy, since the higher the plane on which its structural parameters were set – that is, the remoter from local faction and interest – the more insulated they would be from popular passion.[48] In other words: the less immediately democratic the machinery of decision, the safer it was likely to be for the reproduction of capital. Of course, this was less a logical deduction than an empirical wager – that the task of constructing a supra-national popular sovereignty, capable of determining the social path of a supra-national economy, would prove impossible. That calculation has yet to be confounded, as the terms of union agreed at Maastricht – a central monetary authority for Europe, without any commensurate elected assembly – show.

In making it his own, Mount is not a heretic in the ranks of the radical Right, but faithful to his origins. *The British Constitution Now* does not seek to enlarge democracy, but to circumscribe it, in the interest of older liberties. It does so with a light touch and a good-humoured air, that deserve the compliments they have received. Mount's first book on public life was called *The Theatre of Politics*. The trope was eminently Oakeshottian. Politics was not a battle of interests, or a quest for truth, or a voyage of progress – it was an aesthetic performance, to captivate an audience. But it was not high theatre (Oakeshott had also insisted that politics was a second-rate activity). It was more like commercial theatre, the drama of the boulevards that plays to our emotions or embarrassments – Rattigan rather than Racine, he explained. On this stage, Mount has certainly given us a stylish production. We might call it the comedy of reform.

1992

---

48. *Individualism and Economic Order*, Chicago 1998, pp. 255–271.

Postscript

A decade later, there has been a startling change of set. Mount's new book, *Mind the Gap*, offers us not an urbane renovation of Britain's constitutional heritage, but an impassioned indictment of its social polarization. In tones closer to Cobbett than Burke, Mount excoriates the arrogance and irresponsibility of a New Corruption, and its demoralization of the least well-off. An aide to Thatcher has become an elegist of the working class. The metamorphosis is not to be mocked. But the particulars of its message bear examination.

Mind the Gap is divided into three parts. In the first, Mount sketches a bitter portrait of a polarized country. Notwithstanding myths of classlessness, in which he says till recently he believed, Britain is a society divided into two utterly disparate fates. Above are the Uppers, those in possession of wealth, education and mobility. Below are the Downers, those performing menial tasks in dead-end jobs, some without work, all without hope. The former correspond to what were once distinct upper, upper middle and middle classes, but today have become a single union of self-indulgent privilege. The latter consist of what was once a working class, but is now increasingly reduced to a brutalized underclass. The gap that separates them, far from diminishing, is steadily widening. Economic inequality continues to increase. Life-styles may have have altered, but remain as stratified as ever. Education reinforces inherited advantage. Poverty is branded as personal failure. Between the two worlds, moreover, there is little or no human contact of the kind that softened class relations in the past. Only at night do Downers invade the homes of Uppers, as the lurid protagonists of the dramas of violent crime and sordid domestic strife that swamp the small screen.

Mount does not deny the material conditions of life in the lowest layers of society are much better than half a century ago. But these are ruined lives, nonetheless, because 'cultural impoverishment blots out any modest material improvement'. In this, most fundamental of senses, 'Downers today are *much* worse off than the Downers of 1970 or even the 1930s.'[49] They are also – perhaps a yet more unexpected argument, coming from this author – the most wretched among all the lower classes of the West. Again and again, *Mind the Gap* points to a better popular experience, not just in the United States, which

---

49. *Mind the Gap*, London 2004, p. 262: henceforward *MG*.

has nearly always been a positive reference for Mount, but in Europe – where historically industrialization was less harsh, schools have been egalitarian, and a sense of civic commonality is stronger. France, in particular, becomes a pole of comparison just as attractive as America, with which it is often paired for purposes of effect, in passages stressing the special British misery.[50] Such foreign lands act as background markers in what follows. The foreground is occupied by a set of contrasts between the past and present of manual labour within the nation, as Mount looks back at the culture of the British working class in its heroic age.

Here, he insists, there was no question of widespread anomie or disintegration. In the mills and slums of the early nineteenth century, the industrial revolution did not undermine a traditional morality, as contemporary critics feared, but rather created a new popular determination to keep the family together at all costs. Such moral tenacity was sustained by the religious faith displayed in a vast network of Dissenting churches, to which working-class families thronged, and from which their children received education on Sundays. 'Throughout the nineteenth century, far from being untouched by religion, the great majority of the lower classes were cradled in a complex hammock of religious education, controversy and ritual, more intensely so than perhaps ever before or since.'[51] Out of this sturdy Nonconformity came in turn a series of deeply impressive working-class institutions – chapels and day schools; mechanics' institutes and friendly societies; in their way, too, trade unions. This was a self-standing and self-respecting culture of enormous ethical strength. 'It is not too much to say that the lower classes in Britain between 1800 and 1940 had created a remarkable civilization of their own which is hard to parallel in human history: narrow-minded perhaps, prudish certainly, occasionally pharisaical, but steadfast, industrious, honourable, idealistic, peaceable and purposeful.'[52]

What then reduced this proud Victorian edifice to the rubble of today's 'abodes of desolation', as Mount calls them – the wilderness of run-down council estates, chapels transformed into bingo halls, sink schools, beer-sodden louts and tattooed slatterns, conjured up in

---

50. *MG*, pp. 10, 111–112, 140, 243–244, 271, 316. Mount even allows himself to treat the protests of French farmers, blockading roads with their tractors – actions that would no doubt leave him speechless in Britain – as expressions of a healthy spirit of independence.

51. *MG*, p. 173.

52. *MG*, p. 198.

Mind the Gap? For Mount, two forces were responsible for garotting the self-confidence of the working class. The first was the intellectual elite of the nation, which from early Victorian times onwards consistently jeered at Nonconformity, filling literature with slanderous representations of Dissenting preachers and even Evangelical ministers – Dickens was an especial culprit, Trollope not far behind – born of snobbery and ignorance. Worse, an unholy alliance of thinkers from across the political spectrum – Disraeli and Marx are singled out – insisted that where there had once existed a subtle gradation of stations in society, Britain was now irretrievably divided into just two opposing classes; and that the inferior of these was in an alarming state of moral dissolution. By late Victorian and Edwardian times, Mount argues, this dual dogma – class simplification and lower-class degradation – had become an *idée fixe* in the British intelligentsia, spawning the nightmare visions of stupefied, brutish masses that populate the writings of Gissing, Welles, Woolf, Lawrence, Eliot and their like. In the end, this mountain of misprision could not but affect those who were the object of such contempt.

Graver still, however, was the impact of these myths on the elites obsessed by them, who came to believe that the lower classes, at once helpless and dangerous, desperately needed redemption. If left in their state of darkness, they might one day rise up and bring the temple of society down with them. It was therefore the duty of the state to step in and improve their conditions of life. Thus after a long and relentless intellectual bombardment, undermining the confidence and self-respect of the working class, a regiment of bureaucratic panzers now advanced against weakened defences, pushing aside or levelling the popular institutions that it had created. Church schools were sideswiped by rate-supported alternatives run by the state. Friendly societies were swallowed up by compulsory insurance schemes. Charitable hospitals were annexed by a National Health Service. Traditional slums, wretched enough but not *ungemütlich* in their way, were cleared for council estates that soon became bleaker and more anomic than the warrens they replaced. Religion was exposed to the winds of derision. Even marriage has ceased to be sacred, as perverse divorce and tax legislation all but incite family breakdown among the worst-off. Insecurity and deskilling of jobs at the bottom end of modern capitalism have also damaged the poor, but the principal author of their disinheritance is plain. By the end of the twentieth century, the British working class had been drained of its substance by an all-meddling state. In today's Downers, we are looking at the end result of a century of condescension and expropriation.

Such is the plot of *Mind the Gap*. It tells an affecting story, with real feeling. But what sort of narrative is it? Billed as an essay by its author, it would be unfair to treat it as a history. Its basic gesture is rather that of 'once upon a time'. But to say that there is something fabular about what ensues is insufficiently specific. It would be more accurate to say that *Mind the Gap* belongs to a genre associated with the theatre. Staged in this case, however, is not comedy but melodrama. For among other traits, the melodramatic as a form is always characterized by an uncomplicated binary of good and evil. Here this dichotomy takes the shape of a stark temporal contrast: the flowering, and the wreckage, of a once admirable way of life. Conventionally, that might be described – no doubt has been – as a tragedy. But Mount's script not only lacks the moral complexity of a tragedy; what is missing even more pointedly is any realistic sense of agency, without which the tragic cannot exist. That we are in the realm of melodrama instead can be seen, already, in the way that Mount has reproduced his own complaint of the Victorians. After a spirited philippic against the 'class simplification' of the proponents of One Nation and of Communism alike, Mount reduces contemporary Britain to a still more elemental version of the same dualism – Uppers and Downers *sans phrases*. Significantly, in his depiction of the latter, immigrants are missing.[53]

More revealing still is the role that politics plays – or fails to play – in the journey from good to evil. Mount is an eminently political writer – who more so? – yet *Mind the Gap* tells a story of the British working class in which all trace of its political trajectory is virtually expunged. There are a few nervous references to Edward Thompson's history of its early years, deploring his mischievous account of Methodism. The culture of popular radicalism that is the central concern of *The Making of the English Working Class*, and bears directly on Mount's theme of the 'hidden civilization' of the labourers of the time, is simply ignored. All that work like Thompson's shows is that 'this industrial working class was conceived of not for its own sake, but as a weapon in the political battle' by Communist historians and their kind, dreaming of a 'great pulsating, protesting collective', that 'would lead to a social upturning' – an idea quite alien to flesh-and-blood workers themselves.[54] Giving fancies of this sort a wide berth, British labour chose instead the sensible path of peaceful reforms through Parliament. In virtually the only comment on the

---

53. Similarly, he writes of the preferable condition of the worst-off in America as if black ghettoes did not exist.

54. *MG*, pp. 110, 249.

politics of the next hundred years of its history, Mount writes: 'Anything less headstrong and erratic than the British Labour movement would be hard to imagine. These are people soaked in traditions of democratic debate and parliamentary procedure. When they came to sit at Westminster, they took to the life of the Commons as though they had been born to it and found no greater difficulty in heading a government ministry than in acting as general secretary or even a branch secretary in the trade unions that sent them there'. Mount did not always take so kindly a view of unions, as we have seen – he is better known, even now, for fulminating against them as veritable wrecking-balls of British industry. Here, however even the undoubted damage their restrictive practices did to the economy is treated with leniency, as the *faux-frais* of their better selves. For 'the political *manners* of British trade unionism have always owed more to the friendly society than to the revolutionary mob'.[55] In other words, since gaining entry to the seats of power, the British labour movement has, all told, behaved extremely well.

But why, in that case, have things turned out so badly for the people it has represented? In Mount's account of the disaster that has overtaken the British working class, a curious anonymity surrounds the political actors responsible for it. Intellectuals are named and arraigned, of course. But scandalous as their attitude to the lower orders may have been, no one has ever attributed practical power to E.M. Forster or Virginia Woolf. Must not some weightier forces – not to put too fine a point on it: governments – have taken the actual measures that cut down a honourable culture of independence? If so, what parties were in office when they did so? Mount's story skirts the question. Its construction depends on an extended ellipse. What happened between the halcyon days and the sinister present is left blank. Certainly, 'elites' were guilty and 'errors' were made on both sides of the House of Commons. But Mount's allusions to these are scattered and vague. In this nebulous haze, there is, to be sure, a villain of the drama, but it remains a pure abstraction, to which Mount resorts without further specification – 'the state'.

The actual history was a more painful one for the purposes of any polemic, and undoes the tale he wishes to tell. For the obvious fact, which virtually follows from the contradictory logic of his own characterizations of them, is that it was just the political traits of British labour he extols that ultimately led to the social results he decries. The beginning and end of the story have a much closer

---

55. *MG*, pp. 191–192.

connection than he would have us think, and one that might more properly be called tragic, the heroes themselves encompassing their own downfall. Moderate and respectable it certainly was, but far from being steeped in democratic practice, the Labour Party was from the start built on more bureaucratic lines than any other social-democratic party in Europe, resting on block votes controlled by a handful of trade union bosses. The political culture that generated this inherently authoritarian structure found no difficulty in accepting the crippled version of representative democracy offered by Westminster, complete with pre-modern electoral system and hereditary second chamber, not to speak of an imposing colonial empire. The very idea of constitutional change scarcely occurred to it. This was the reality of the excellent 'steadiness' and 'political maturity' Mount applauds. But, of course, the subsequent reforms it introduced had the same cast. Without the slightest feel for the values of popular participation, let alone rebellion, Labour presided over the construction of a welfare state, technocratic in design and bureaucratic in delivery, that is the consistent object of Mount's dislike. If 'statism' is the enemy, here was the prime architect of it. As for Labour's attachment to culture, in any sense of the term, the less said the better.

It is not, of course, that the scenes which now disturb Mount are merely an outcome of the genetic code of Labourism. Historically, capital always set the field to which it adjusted. But the relations between the two were the opposite of the way they notionally figure in *Mind the Gap*. The rulers of the country remained on their guard, but from the second half of the nineteenth century onwards they did not, and with reason, on the whole regard the working class as either tremendously dangerous or particularly helpless. When Labourism materialized as its principal political expression in the twentieth century, they by and large greeted it, with no less reason, as essentially safe and potentially helpful – as in 1914, it hastened to show it was. For real independence of spirit was just what the instinctively deferential, respectable mainstream of this political culture lacked. The reforms that eventually produced the kind of state and society that exists today were thus rarely, if ever, simply the fruit of its initiative. Typically, they were either compromises that the privileged classes accepted because they had secured concessions or opt-outs from their provisions, or measures of prophlyaxis, seasoned or otherwise with compassion, taken by the party representing them. So educational reforms never created a common school system, the most fundamental of all sources of cultural division. The health system left private practice to flourish at the expense of public service. State pensions became the poor relation of schemes of commercial speculation. Historically, in the hybrid arrangements that resulted – bureaucratic conceptions proposing, market considerations disposing – Liberals and Conservatives met Labour half-way. But if we take Mount's view of the political virtues of British labour, on the one hand, and the ugliness of todays's social landscape, on the other, the conclusion is inescapable that to a large extent the working class dug its own grave.

In fact, of course, the labour movement in Britain was always more complex than Mount's oleograph of it, containing many a strand at variance with the conformism of its dominant culture, which did not just fade away over time. These had to be broken, in tough struggles to root out rebellious impulses in the bottom layers of society. In the general strike of 1926, in the dock strike of 1949, in the seamen's strike of 1963, it fell to Labour to extinguish such flare-ups of insurgency. In the miners' strike of 1982, it was the task of a Conservative government to crush resistance to the requirements of the time. New Labour is heir to that final clean sweep, in which Mount was himself a participant. Twenty years later, a question that is obviously posed by the argument of *Mind the Gap* is how he sees this succession, and the regime under which the book has been written.

However long he has served the Conservative cause – in his time, he has worked for party, press and Prime Minister alike – Mount has never lost his independence of mind.[56] When Blair took over Thatcher's policies and ran with them, he was the last person to begrudge him credit for realizing so many of her objectives. Anyway dismayed by the back-stabbing of Major in his own party, he was more than ready to

---

56. For comparative side-lights on those he served: 'I do not hero-worship Margaret Thatcher. For one thing, as Montaigne first observed, no man or woman is a hero to his or her valet and I was her political valet for a couple of years. She could be petty, obtuse, vindictive. Like almost all successful politicians, she never shrank from repeating herself. She was a stranger to irony. Yet far outweighing these minor weaknesses, she radiated a sense of possibility. She always believed that something could be done. And she was determined to see that it was done, if necessary – in fact preferably – by herself alone, if nobody else could be bothered to see it through to the end' ('Britain and the Intellectuals – In Thrall to Bad Old Times', *The National Interest*, summer 2001, p. 91). In less flattering terms, he once described Thatcher as the Evita of the Tory Party. By contrast: 'Keith Joseph must have been the most serious politician I ever met. Sometimes I think he was the only serious politician I ever met. To me he remains the most bewitching character I have met in British politics and the most crucial single influence in the thought and policy of the Conservative Party since the War – and since the Conservative Party has been in power for so much of that period, the most crucial influence on domestic policy-making in the nation as whole' (the Fourth Keith Joseph Memorial Lecture, 23 March 2000).

take a benevolent view of New Labour. There were plenty of grounds
for satisfaction, which he did not hesitate to express. The unions were
now more effectively emasculated than under Thatcher. Fees were at
last introduced into higher education. The mail service was no longer
sacrosanct. Above all, Blair had the courage to lead the nation into just
battle in the Balkans and Iraq. Even where New Labour departed from
Thatcher's legacy, it was often in the right direction: more open to a
prudent measure of devolution at home, less prejudiced and hostile
towards the EU abroad. As with any government, there were less
attractive sides: stealth taxes, excessive spin, bullying attitudes to
teenagers. But all found, the balance-sheet was on the face of it thoroughly positive. Around the millennium, Mount gave exuberant voice
to his elation at the national turn-around of what, in a revealing
reversal, he now called 'the Blair–Thatcher years'.[57]

What then accounts for such an abrupt darkening of his vision of
Britain, a couple of years later? His own explanation of the black-
and-white contrast between what he was writing in 2001 and in 2003
is remarkably lame, and out of character – he tenders the postmodern
vacuity that British society is so complex that it can be looked at from
any number of different angles, no matter how contradictory.
Elsewhere he writes, not much more convincingly, as if there were a
virtually Pauline moment at which the scales of class-blindness
suddenly fell from his eyes. Only guesswork is possible here, but part
of what could be involved might lie simply in Mount's penchant for
the theatrical, with its requirements for dramatic changes of scene
and heart. In his political writing, vivid and intelligent as it usually
has been, there is often also something slightly stagey – the sense of a
performance, not always taken too seriously by the performer himself.
Yet in *Mind the Gap* there is no doubting the strength of Mount's
feelings about the gulf between Uppers and Downers, depicted with
gifts of observation and imaginative sympathy that belong to the
novelist rather than the publicist in him. He seems never to have
written with quite this passion before.

That still leaves unresolved why a writer as observant as this failed
for so long to register what he now sees as clear as day. But a surmise
can be made of at least one politically enabling condition.[58] Ironically,

---

57. 'Britain and the Intellectuals', p. 86. For an earlier contribution in this eupeptic
vein, see 'Farewell to Pudding Island', *Times Literary Supplement*, 28 April 2000.

58. In the remark that 'anyone who is compelled to watch television continuously,
when laid up in a hospital, can only wonder how any viewer can survive without
having their brain irreparably addled', there might be a hint of a more personal experience that changed his mind about some of the blessings of the country: *MG*, p. 234.

though he has applauded much of what New Labour has done, and expressed distaste for the tone of latter-day Conservatism, it is likely that Blair's regime has liberated critical impulses that might, had his own party been in power, have lain repressed. It is difficult to imagine him uncorking the same bitter jet of outrage under Thatcher or Major, though the landscape then, as he virtually admits, was little different. Blairism itself, if now and then a bit off in style, is fine. Clustered around the Prime Minister, indeed, its cadre of 'progressive reformers' – above all, the upright trio of Mandelson, Byers and Milburn, singled out for praise – offer hope of fresh ideas for the problems of the underclass.[59] But inhibited by no personal ties to New Labour, Mount is now free to point to long-running sores all governments have neglected, if not actively created, including this one.

Mind the Gap ends with his own prescriptions for the plight of the Downers. He begins on an apparently incendiary note: 'By now it ought to be obvious that only a more robust proactive daring is likely to efface this bleeding shame. Only a whole-hearted, even reckless opening up of substantial power to the bottom classes is likely to improve either their self-esteem or the view which the managing classes take of them.'[60] A friendly critic, describing this as one of Mount's 'engaging Mao-meets-Oakeshott moments' has pointed out that the British political system is so designed that any such empowerment is inconceivable.[61] Though true enough, this is a misunderstanding of Mount, whose allegiance to the most restrictive interpretation of democratic arrangements has not significantly altered since *The British Constitution Now*. In such matters the only change is that he has belatedly come round to the alternative vote, the slightest of all possible tweaks to first past the post, out of fear that without it New Labour might perpetuate itself in office more or less indefinitely. For the rest, the last thing he envisages is tampering with Westminster in the name of electoral equity or popular sovereignty.

The power that Mount wishes to extend to the lower depths is of another sort altogether. It is the power, not of the citizen or the voter, but of the owner and consumer. The spirit of his injunction is familiar to anyone with a smattering of Conservative history. It is Churchill's slogan of the 1950s: 'Set the people free' – that is, free to buy and sell without interfering state controls. Half a century later, Mount's case

---

59. *MG*, pp. 13, 53–54, 304.
60. *MG*, p. 283.
61. John Lanchester, *London Review of Books*, 21 October 2004.

against the cumulative insolences of the state is far more sweeping than would have made sense to Conservatives in the time of Eden or Butler. His programme of liberation from them is correspondingly more radical too. It contains a small redistributive element: perhaps some increase in the minimum wage, certainly tax cuts for the least well off. But it is not by depredations on the rich that the morale of the poor can be uplifted. The solution lies elsewhere. On the social side, the priorities are school vouchers, bounties for marriage, tithes to help churches, independent hospitals. On the economic side, firms could offer employees a modest proportion of new share issues at a discount, and councils give tenants the chance to buy their flats. But above all – the *pièce de resistance* of Mount's vision of a better future – green-belt regulations should be scrapped, and allotments in the countryside made available, by grant of public or sale of private land, to dwellers in the abodes of urban desolation to plant or build on them what they will.

This is the agenda, Mount explains, of an updated 'property-owning democracy', the time-honoured ideal of many a Conservative manifesto.[62] But his version of it is less English than the term itself suggests. Tacitly, the inspiration behind most of these proposals comes from the United States. School vouchers, faith-based initiatives, legislation to protect marriage: we are in the neighbourhood of Karl Rove. More fundamentally, the whole idea of installing a class of self-reliant tillers and builders on rural allotments is a transposition into the more cabined English scene of the historic American dream of a 'fee-simple empire', a society of sturdy farmers prospering on homesteads across an ever-receding frontier, all the way to the Pacific. Mount's scheme is a reduction of Jefferson's vision to suburban scale, given the want of prairies in Hampshire or Kent. Its lack of realism as a prescription for the *bas fonds* in Britain has drawn comment. But that it has something of the fantastic quality of an agrarian experiment from the other side of world, the exodus once planned to Birobidjan in the USSR, is less significant than its logic in Mount's scheme of redemption.

For the alternative Mount offers to the world of Uppers and Downers still bears the stamp of his distinctive mentor. As a political philosopher, Oakeshott gave an absolutist turn to two contrary strands of English conservative sensibility, taking each of them to an extreme in a way no other thinker has ever quite done. In a single unyielding outlook he combined a caustic individualism with a mystical traditionalism. Oakeshott had little time for American

---

62. Mount dates the phrase to Eden's period as Conservative leader: *MG*, p. 285.

political culture, in his eyes compromised by rationalist notions of rights that had the brand-mark of the Enlightenment on them. But as a society, the United States embodied in action, more than any other, something like the fusion of opposites he represented in thought: on the one hand, an extreme individualism of economic life, on the other, an extreme traditionalism of religious life. Mount, free of the residual prejudices of Oakeshott's generation against the upstarts of 1776, could see this conjugation more clearly. He has always looked admiringly at 'the great, sleepy republic' across the water, more tradition-bound, in the best sense, than England itself. *Mind the Gap* contains, among other things, a glowing description of the vitality of Methodist and Baptist churches in the US, contrasted with their decrepitude in the UK. To be sure, revivalism itself cannot easily be reimported into Britain. But as a sense of the transcendent, inspiring faith and loyalty, and creating a collective identity, royalism will do instead. The monarchy, if only intellectuals were not still running it down, could become once more the symbol of our national unity and continuity, and indispensable focus of patriotic feeling, as it latently remains among the lower classes (immigrants, once again, presumably excluded). Meanwhile, any restoration of the social fabric in zones of deprivation must go hand in hand with a return of the churches, to whom the administration of welfare might once again well be entrusted. Attracted equally to the values of the libertarian and the devotional strands of the American Right, Mount has put the two together in a colourful package for local consumption, with a brio that leaves the Cato Institute and the Heritage Foundation standing.

Still, the vision of a callous inequality and complacency at the core of contemporary Britain remains. Intellectually less coherent than *The British Constitution Now*, which was a cooler production, *Mind The Gap* is politically more troubled and generous. Each work is a kind of dramaturgy. But who could withhold some applause? In the desert of ideas that has surrounded the regimes of Major and Blair, they make a pair of original compositions – on the state, on society – that no other writer of the British establishment, Right or Left, has matched. The juxtaposition of the 'magnificent structure' of our constitutional order, celebrated in the first, and the 'unexpiated curse' of our class system, denounced in the second, may seem jarring. But the underlying prescriptions, of economic liberty and spiritual commonality, are the same.

2005

3

DREAMS OF CENTRAL EUROPE:
Timothy Garton Ash

Western curiosity about other lands, as a literary phenomenon, has a long history – its fashionable origins generally dated to the *Grand Siècle*, the time of the voyages to Mughal India of François Bernier or Thomas Coryate. Distinctions between the more advanced European cultures in the volume, or quality, of travellers' tales would be difficult to make for most of the modern period. In the Enlightenment, for every Cook there was a Bougainville or Forster; at a higher level, a little later, Humboldt or Custine. But in the twentieth century, the tradition seems to have forked, one society outproducing all others, across the genres. Between the wars, there was a strong strain of exoticism in French writing, variously surfacing in Gide, Morand, Saint-Exupéry, Michaux, Leiris, Malraux, and others, to which Lévi-Strauss's *Tristes Tropiques* can be seen as a melancholy quietus. Little comparable followed. On this side of the Channel, where the tradition was always less philosophical, no such break is visible. Looking back at the cumulative record, the literature of travel appears to have become something like a British speciality.

Why this should be so is not at first glance clear. But two powerful – opposite, yet not unrelated – impulses may supply much of the explanation. On the one hand, the stifling parochialism and puritanism of an insular middle-class culture, with all its weight of boredom and repression, made escape abroad an instinctively attractive option for restless spirits: a motive that can be traced back to early Victorian times, when George Borrow's fascination with Spanish or Gypsy low life was bred of detestation for native 'gentility'. On the other hand, Britain's imperial primacy – whose memory long outlasted its reality – inevitably encouraged dreams of daring exploits in remote lands, stirring encounters with alien peoples, without necessarily unsettling loyalty to the values of the Home Counties. The horizon of Empire habituated Englishmen to the idea of overseas adventures.

Within these two banks an abundant stream of writing poured forth, with any number of undertows, eddies and cross-currents (even a side-swamp in the recent multiplication of 'professional' travel writers, churning out commissions on one area after another, in underlying ignorance and indifference to any of them – the world of *Granta* at its worst). Confining ourselves to the first half of the century, a number of features are noticeable. Geographically, there were long three privileged zones: the Middle East, the Mediterranean and the Danubian basin. These were, famously, the terrains of St John Philby or Robert Byron, of Norman Douglas or Patrick Leigh-Fermor, of R.W. Seton-Watson and Rebecca West. Sorties farther afield – like Peter Fleming's expeditions to the Gobi or Matto Grosso – were fewer. Paradoxically, the vast expanse of the Empire itself was not fertile soil for this kind of writing. There, British power was too close at hand. It generated another set of forms altogether: memoirs, morose or nostalgic, of colonial functionaries like Orwell or Woolf, or avowedly scientific monographs of anthropologists like Firth or Evans-Pritchard.

Division of the field by the role of the subject is less clear-cut than in the case of the object. In principle, three types of author were professionally distinguishable – the journalist, the writer, the scholar. In practice, as a glance at the names above indicates, there were originally few practicioners who did not combine aspects of more than one such role, sometimes all three. Seton-Watson, most unambiguously a scholar – chairs in History at London and Oxford – first made his name as a periodical correspondent in Eastern Europe. Leigh-Fermor, by any definition a writer, was as interested in the distant past of his obscure finger of the Peloponnese as its life in the present. Evelyn Waugh, on the other hand, set out for Horn and Levant as a mercenary for Northcliffe, but who imagines he ceased to observe or write as a novelist? As for the post-war period, the enormous growth of the media and dwindling number of authors 'with independent means' have made resort to journalism of one kind or another a virtual necessity, even for relatively successful writers; encouraging journalists, in turn, to think of themselves as writers, if not – on receipt of institutional grants – as interim scholars. Lines of distinction between these callings, still relevant, have become more than ever blurred.

Another kind of taxonomy would take as its focus neither local subject nor alien object but the relationship between them. Here the range of possible aims and attitudes behind a literary engagement with unfamiliar cultures is much wider. It is interesting that systematic hostility should be rare (exceptions often light-hearted), in contrast to the notorious ambivalences of biography as a project, as if to demonstrate that it is more difficult to turn against a society than an individual. For the most part, the stances adopted have not been those of the critic, still less the foe. They are rather those of the adventurer, the admirer and the advocate. These typical positions might be combined, but should not be confused – though, of course, there are no watertight divisions between them. An advocate is likely, though not certain, to be an admirer. An admirer may easily also be an adventurer. An adventurer – this is much more unusual, but possible: Malraux in Indochina – can be an advocate, without being an admirer.

Yet not only do quite pure cases of each type exist. Where they blend in any given individual, it is rarely hard to see which is the dominant. Evelyn Waugh in Ethiopia was an adventurer *sans phrases*. Wilfred Thesiger, although unquestionably adventurous, was an admirer. In 1916, at the age of six, watching Ras Tafari's triumphal entry into Addis Ababa, his enemies hauled in an atrocious train after him, he later recorded: 'I believe that day implanted in me a life-long craving for barbaric splendour, for savagery and colour and the throb of drums, and that it gave me a lasting veneration of long-established custom and ritual'.[1] In 1930, watching Ras Tafari's coronation as Emperor Haile Selasse, Thesiger regretted that Waugh, 'the one person present with a gift for writing, was blind to the historical significance of the occasion, impercipient of this last manifestation of Abyssinia's traditional pageantry'. His vision of Waugh is a violent declaration of distance between the two species. 'I disapproved of his grey suede shoes, his floppy bow tie and the excessive width of his trousers; he struck me as flaccid and petulant and I disliked him on sight. Later he asked me, at second hand, if he could accompany me into the Danakil country, where I planned to travel. I refused. Had he come, I suspect only one of us would have returned.'[2]

Thesiger, passionately attached to Ethiopian feudatories, Arabian bedouin, dwellers in the Iraqi marshes, saw the worlds he admired dissolve in his lifetime: Haile Selasse deposed by the Dergue, Nuri al-Said felled in his palace, the imam of the Yemen – for whose slave-holding tyranny Thesiger fought in old age – defeated in his bid

1. *The Life of My Choice*, London 1987, p. 56.
2. Ibid., pp. 91–92.

for a counter-revolution. But his books contain little or no advocacy; they are virtually pre-political. Philby, his senior in exploring the Empty Quarter, offers an ironic contrast. An outspoken enemy of British imperialism after the First World War, who encouraged Ibn Saud to cut deals with American oil companies to assure Saudi independence of London, he died a self-declared socialist – who never hesitated to advocate unpopular causes in his own country – under secure Saudi protection.

The figure of the British enthusiast for the cause of an oppressed people abroad goes back, of course, to Byron in Greece. Lawrence and Philby, espousing rival dynasties in the break-up of the Ottoman Empire, brought it to the Middle East. But its more natural stage was always Mediterranean or Balkan, where buried identities or ancient unities of European civilization could more readily be invoked. Rebecca West's massively idiosyncratic *Black Lamb and Grey Falcon*, an emotive cry for the Serbs as the Wehrmacht swept through Yugoslavia, belongs in this tradition. Its greatest representative, however, was the elder Seton-Watson, who not only wrote the first modern histories in English of the Czechs, Slovaks and Romanians – he did not live to complete a companion study on the South Slavs – but played a key role in the wartime ideology and diplomacy that led to the creation of all three states of the Little Entente. This was advocacy at its highest – historically most effective – level.

After the Second World War, conditions changed. The figure of the explorer, still significant in the inter-war literature – Fleming, Thesiger, Saint-Exupéry – soon became defunct, as the inventory of the globe closed. Distance was banalized by television and mass tourism. 'Primitive' societies were enrolled in modern markets. The world became a universal political battleground. In this setting, the heroic strain in the earlier literature – so to speak its Foreign Legion side – was more difficult to sustain. Not that drama was missing. But it was now typically modern and political, calling for professional skills of a different kind. The representative figure became the journalist with specialist knowledge of a given country or region, reporting or analysing the events of the day, from some longer historical or cultural perspective. The literature of overseas engagement is now dominated by this form.

Among its most fluent practitioners are the three Anglo-musketeers regularly featured in the *New York Review of Books* – Neal Ascherson, Timothy Garton Ash and Ian Buruma: spurs won respectively in Eastern Europe and East Asia. United by common liberal convictions, the profiles of the trio are otherwise quite distinct.

Garton Ash, a generation younger than Ascherson, followed his path
from Germany to Poland as lands of primary reportage. In 1982–83,
both wrote passionately committed books about Solidarity.
Thereafter, Garton Ash immersed himself much more deeply and
single-mindedly than Ascherson in the politics of Eastern Europe
during the final years of the Cold War. The period may have something to do with the difference. As the eighties unfolded, the East
European oppositions to Communism were steadily drawn into the
magnetic field of the dominant ideology in the West – the doctrines of
the hard Right proclaimed by Reagan and Thatcher. For Garton Ash,
contributor and editor at *The Spectator* at the time, this was a perfectly natural and desirable evolution. For Ascherson, a sharp critic of
Thatcherism, it must have posed more difficulties. Probably, too,
domestic considerations weighed in their own right. Ascherson and
Buruma mix Scottish and Dutch with Jewish origins; both have
expressed sharp dislike of standard British identities and their customary supports – leading, in Ascherson's case, to direct involvement
in Scottish radical politics. The English credentials of Garton Ash, by
contrast, appear to be unalloyed. When he set out in 1978 for Berlin
in his blue Alfa Romeo, Britain was not in question. Undistracted by
doubts about the home country, he could throw himself more completely into patriotic causes beyond the Elbe.

The result has been an impressive oeuvre, widening over two
decades. After initial reportage on life in East Germany based on his
time as a post-graduate there, serialized in *Der Spiegel*, and a detailed
account of the rise of Solidarity in *The Polish Revolution*, came *The
Uses of Adversity* – subtitled 'Essays on the Fate of Central Europe' –
in the spring of 1989, extending his range of testimony to Hungary
and Czechoslovakia. In these years, slipping from one underground to
another, he developed an incomparable set of friendships with dissident intellectuals in the last three countries (by now he was banned
from the DDR), that enabled him to chart the erosion of Communism
in the region more intrepidly and acutely than any other journalist of
the time: a process he expected to take the form of a prolonged
'Ottomanization' – loosening and decay – of Soviet power in Eastern
Europe.

When, a few months later, sudden collapse came instead, he was
perfectly placed to provide the best snapshots of the victors. *We the
People* (1990) offers a slide-show of the heroes of the hour, caught in
dazzling close-up: Michnik, Kuron, Balcerowicz, Geremek in
Warsaw; Göncz and Orbán in Budapest; in Berlin, 'the greatest street-
party in the history of the world'; and finally, the climax in Prague

with Havel – 'it was extraordinary the degree to which everything ultimately revolved around this one man' – which Garton Ash observed
as a participant alongside Klaus or Dienstbier in the headquarters of
the Civic Forum, 'the very heart of the revolution', as the old order
disintegrated around it.[3] Adventurer and admirer have seldom been so
dramatically or effectively at one.

After this triumph as a reporter, Garton Ash went back to his
intended starting point as a scholar, with a major historical study of
the origins and outcome of German *Ostpolitik*. Based on careful
archival research, as well as extensive interview material, *In Europe's
Name* (1993) traced Bonn's often camouflaged and oblique path to
German unification – a goal relished neither by France nor Britain,
pursued by ambiguous invocation of the unity of Europe, and tenacious cultivation of relations with Russia. Garton Ash's own
reservations about the process, as might be expected, attach to actors
or episodes judged culpable of backsliding from Western values in
dealing with Communist rule in Eastern Europe: principally, Social
Democrats from the time of Schmidt's coolness to Solidarity onwards.
But the book, his most substantial achievement to date, is scrupulously
balanced and fair in its overall judgement of the upshot of West
German strategy towards the East. *The File* (1997) can be read as a
personal coda – Garton Ash's quest for those who spied on or informed
against him as a student in East Berlin in 1980, whose identity now
stood revealed by Stasi dossiers. What could easily have been a formu-
laic inquest becomes, as autobiographical memory is startled into life
by the disturbing encounters, the most self-questioning and humane of
all his writings.

Historically, Garton Ash belongs to the last levy of the Cold War, a
youthful cohort fired by an uncomplicated anti-Communism. His
staunchness made him a natural candidate for recruitment to MI6,
which propositioned him early on, as it had Ascherson in his time.
Though not unattracted by the idea of clandestine work for British
espionage, he eventually decided against it on the grounds that he did
not want to be controlled from above: it was better to be a freebooter
than a functionary in the battle against totalitarianism. After his
book on Solidarity came out, he was invited to become deputy director
of Radio Free Europe in Munich; again he declined. Repeated
approaches of this kind were logical enough. Politically, his credentials as a Cold Warrior of the liberal Right were impeccable. By the

---

3. *We the People*, London 1990, pp. 85, 89.

mid-eighties he could be counted, according to the best inside source, among the select group of academics – Hugh Thomas, Brian Crozier, Norman Stone, Leonard Schapiro and others – lending extra-mural advice and assistance to Mrs Thatcher.

But George Urban's refreshingly forthright memoir, *Diplomacy and Disillusion at the Court of Margaret Thatcher*, also makes clear that Garton Ash was a courtier with quirks of his own. Looking round the table at Chequers, with the Prime Minister at its head, Urban noted of his neighbour: 'Tim is an excellent analyst; he is young and has already made a name for himself. I can see in him a future R.W. Seton-Watson or a politician of the first water. He is rational, can think on his feet and his heart is in the right place – with one or two exceptions: he made misjudgements about Nicaragua and has a soft streak in him when it comes to the Third World, but on Eastern Europe he is sound and has written some excellent stuff.'[4]

Doubts about the Contras proved to be less of an anomaly than they might have seemed. A sceptical, empirical side of Garton Ash – he identifies it with the best native traditions – was always capable of checking doctrinal enthusiasm. The overthrow of Communism in Eastern Europe, he concluded in 1990, brought no new ideas into the world, even if it recalled West Europeans to moral and intellectual values they had often forgotten. It was – simply and decisively – the World Turned Rightside Up: that is, the arrival of a familiar order of elected parliaments and free markets, civil rights and private property, in which there was only one kind of democracy, legality and economics. Still, in the first flush of enthusiasm, it was possible that some of the new converts would overdo things. Among intellectuals in the forefront of the transition to capitalism, Garton Ash detected 'an opposite danger: that of regarding the free market as a cure for all ills, social and political as well as economic. Hence the popularity of Hayek. One might almost say that the free market is the latest Central European utopia.'[5]

The essays and dispatches brought together in *History of the Present* record Garton Ash's responses to what has happened since this was written. The collection opens with various German themes, later amplified – Kohl's electoral triumphs with unification in 1990 and 1994, and his downfall over its consequences in 1998; vignettes of

---

4. *Diplomacy and Disillusion at the Court of Margaret Thatcher*, London 1996, pp. 121–122.

5. *We the People*, p. 152.

Honecker in prison, Markus Wolf on trial, and reflections on the Gauck Office as catharsis for the legacy of the Stasi. Moving to Poland, there is a critical sketch of the beginning of Walesa's presidency – sadly, the former leaders of Solidarity 'belabouring each other with rusty clubs', amidst potentially hopeful signs of a Thatcherite economy under his authoritarian rule. There follows an account of its unthinkable sequel, the victory of the post-Communist Kwasniecki in 1995 – under whom, nevertheless, such changes as the evolution of Solidarity's *Gazeta Wyborcza* into a Murdoch-style media conglomerate offer wry confirmation of Polish entry into Western consumer normalcy. The different meanings of the Hungarian Revolt, for contemporaries and posterity, are revisited. In the Czech Republic, a set-piece – one of the pivots of the book – recounts a public clash between Havel and Klaus, President and Prime Minister, in which the author also had his say.

Returning to the lands of his choice, Garton Ash is generally alert and measured. The predominant note is one of rueful satisfaction. Walesa and Havel may have been disappointments in office, hopes of a higher regional ethos all but extinguished in a common rush for humdrum consumption, yet – however unseemly some of its former nomenklatura ornaments – the foundations of a democratic capitalism have been secured. The principal interest of the new collection, however, lies elsewhere. From 1995 onwards, Garton Ash started to go beyond his traditional beat, travelling into what was once Yugoslavia. His sorties into this unfamiliar landscape produce the best sketches and essays in the book. Here, as if freed from conventional attachments, he has reached more radical and original conclusions.

These give little comfort to the semi-official liberal consensus about the region. Garton Ash's coverage opens with a chilling description of the Krajina just after the Croatian sweep had emptied it of 150,000 Serbs, and of European indifference to their fate. When he comes to Bosnia, the complexities of the tripartite war between communities are given their due, without diminishing Serb responsibility for ethnic savagery, or the enormity of European moral default in face of the disaster. In Kosovo, Garton Ash argued for independence before there was talk of any Western intervention, and expressed pointed reservations about the aerial assault on Serbia when it came – as he had about the potemkin polity set up in Bosnia.

Informing his treatment of these issues is an unpopular conviction, or perhaps it would be better to say, divulgation of what the Western consensus (voices in the bars of Tuzla) would prefer to leave unsaid.

Stable European democracies, he argues, require fairly homogeneous populations – an ethnic majority of at least 80 per cent.[6] Here a background outside the Balkans was perhaps a condition of breaking ranks. Although tact forbids him to mention it directly, Garton Ash's favourite lands are states founded on far the largest two ethnic cleansings in Europe since the Second World War, Poland and the Czech Republic. There is no hint of condonation in his account of the repetition of these processes by the Adriatic, only horror – and the prediction that out of them may come liberal democracy as we know it. The example he gives is the abluted Croatia of tomorrow. This is an argument first made by Tom Nairn about Bosnia, in much the same tension of grief and realism.[7]

The extension of Garton Ash's range to the Balkans thus involves more than a geographical move. It represents an intellectual and moral enlargement. But by the same stroke, it throws into sharp relief the limitations of his earlier work. For if there was a single leitmotiv of his writing down to the mid-nineties, it was the special character of the countries of Central Europe in the spectrum of captive nations, and their quite particular call on the sympathies and resources of Western Europe. The notion of 'Central Europe' – as expounded by spokesmen like Kundera or Milosz – designated Czechoslovakia, Hungary and Poland, extending on occasion to Lithuania. Its function was essentially twofold. On the one side, it drew a cultural line demarcating this zone from such truly East European (viz: backward) countries as Romania or Yugoslavia – let alone from perpetually barbarian, totalitarian Russia; on the other side, it linked this region to the homelands of liberty and prosperity in Western Europe – from which, on Kundera's showing, only malign fate had wrenched it, as a cradle of political tolerance and high culture, away.[8]

The naively ideological character of this construct was transparent from the outset. If Bohemia and Western Hungary could reasonably be described as Central European, the idea that Bialystok or Vilnius were situated in the middle of the continent and Belgrade or Timisoara to the east of them was always ridiculous. The notion that 'Central' Europe so construed, lands where serfdom persisted down to the late eighteenth or nineteenth centuries, was culturally or socially closer to Western than Eastern patterns of historical experience does not

6. *History of the Present*, London 1999, pp. 365–366. Henceforward *HP*.
7. 'All Bosnians Now', *Dissent* 40: 4, 1993, pp. 403–410.
8. 'The Tragedy of Central Europe', *New York Review of Books*, 26 April 1984.

withstand serious scrutiny. Essentially, the function of the term was the kind of redescription to be read in the brochures of estate agents – the upgrading of some disregarded quarter by metonymy to a more fashionable district (its glamour typically exaggerated): Harringay promoted to East Highgate.

In one part of his mind – the historian's – Garton Ash always knew that this version of Central Europe was a self-interested myth; apart from anything else, as he pointed out, what of the contributions of the region to the most violent forms of modern racism and nationalism?[9] But in another part of his mind, he needed the myth, and cultivated it. For by the mid-eighties, were not the PCH trio – Poland, Czechoslovakia, Hungary – genuinely set apart from their COMECON neighbours by the vigour of their democratic oppositions, and the longing of their populations to join the Western comity of nations? If the past did not offer any very firm foundation to the current idea of Central Europe, the future might do so, for here surely lay the Achilles heel of the Soviet empire. In this sense, the definition of Central Europe was political: it designated the front line against Communism, wherever that might be – Garton Ash even ventured the thought that we might now say George Orwell was a Central European, and if so, he himself 'would apply for citizenship'.[10] His was a pragmatic usage, he explained. The British do not like splitting hairs.

In itself, such a conception – just because it was so unabashedly designed to render the PCH trio *salonfähig* in the West – could be dismissed as a harmless ideological fancy of the hour. Garton Ash had no resort to it in his earlier book on Solidarity, which locates Poland straightforwardly in Eastern Europe,[11] and repudiated its most obvious danger – the pale it drew between civil and uncivil nations in the region – when he later turned to the Balkans. *History of the Present* rejects such 'cultural determinism'. Indeed, Garton Ash now writes that he is appalled at the way the idea of Central Europe has been 'recruited into the service of politics of relativism and exclusion'.[12] The failure of the European Union to prevent disaster in Yugoslavia he condemns in the strongest possible terms. Preoccupation with the misbegotten project of a single currency was

---

9. See *The Uses of Adversity*, Cambridge 1989, pp. 165–167.
10. *The Uses of Adversity*, p. 191.
11. *The Polish Revolution: Solidarity 1980–1983*, London 1983, pp. 4, 8, etc.
12. *HP*, pp. 209, 392–393.

responsible: the fiddlers at Maastricht were blind to the fires about to explode in Sarajevo.

The sincerity of this verdict on the Western record in the Balkans is beyond question. But there is something wanting in it. Absent is any hint of self-criticism. Yet, if ever there were a case of the pot calling the kettle black, Garton Ash's complaints of the indifference of Brussels to the fate of the Balkans would be it. For the cult of 'Central' Europe – which he still defends as 'a good cause', and continues to manipulate (with lurid descriptions of why Ukraine doesn't belong, though happily Slovakia is rejoining) – was not just a matter of whimsical definition. It had a hard policy edge. In adopting it, Garton Ash moved from admirer to advocate in a quite precise sense. Warmth of sympathy for Polish, Czech or Hungarian dissidents as they fought their regimes was one matter. Urging privileged treatment of the PCH trio after the fall of Communism, at the expense of other East European nations, was quite another. In October 1990, Garton Ash was demanding that 'a clear and very high priority' – both of economic assistance and political welcome into the European Union – be given to Poland, Hungary and Czechoslovakia. 'If German, European and Western help is spread more or less indiscriminately across this whole vast region', any transition to liberal capitalism would be compromised, and the 'the region could indeed become Europe's Near East'.[13] Since everything could not be done at once, discrimination was essential. The Visegrad countries, whose Western Christianity and pre-war legacies anyway made them natural partners, should get fast-track access into the EU, In fact, Garton Ash soon came to insist, they deserved entry forthwith.

Although this last demand was plainly impracticable, it served to ratchet up the rhetorical pressure for special PCH treatment, in a campaign that was otherwise thoroughly successful – in large part because it coincided so closely with German foreign policy objectives, aiming for a security and investment *glacis* round the Federal Republic. French proposals for equitable treatment of all former Communist states in the region, in a confederation linking them to the EU, were indignantly scuttled – not least by the Czechs, Havel at their head, furious at the prospect of being put on the same footing as Bulgars or Romanians. At Kohl's behest, the PCH states were promised first claims on the EU, and promptly received the lion's share of Western assistance. Hungary, with a per capita income four

---

13. *HP*, p. 62.

times that of Macedonia, got twelve times as much aid. Central Europe had found its economic rationale: to him that hath shall be given.

Garton Ash's justification of this biblical wisdom was consistent: it alone could prevent disaster befalling the region as a whole, since the success of democratic capitalism in the PCH trio was the condition of peace and stability in the rest of ex-Communist Europe – all that stood between it and the squalid destiny of the Levant. As late as 1993, he was still writing: 'Once again, the Central European question bids fair to be the central European one.'[14] As these lines were printed, Sarajevo had already been under siege for a year, and the main 'Central European' contribution to peace in the Balkans had been the clandestine sale by Hungarian democracy of 36,000 Kalashnikovs to the Croat paramilitaries.

The historical reality is that not only was an 'all favour to PCH' strategy morally objectionable, it was also politically blind. At its centre lay a colossal astigmatism. In his conclusion to We the People in early 1990, Garton Ash complained angrily of commentators in the West who warned of the dangers of nationalist revival in Eastern Europe. 'What on earth does this mean?' he exclaimed. 'The historical record must show that 1989 was not a year of acute national and ethnic conflict in Eastern Europe west of the Soviet frontier. Quite the reverse: it was a year of solidarity both within and between nations.'[15] For the pen that could write that, the Balkans had been erased from history. Banished from 'the central European question', they effectively vanished from sight.

The truth, of course, was that nationalist conflicts had reached fever pitch in Yugoslavia already by the spring of 1987, when Milosevic made his bid for power on Kosovo Polje. With Slovene complicity, Serbia tore up the autonomy of Kosovo a year later, before the two dominant republics entered on a collision course themselves. In 1989 – the year of 'no acute ethnic conflicts' – massive Albanian demonstrations in Kosovo led to violent clashes with the police: a full-scale state of emergency was declared, jets and tanks enforcing a virtual occupation of the province, while Croat and Slovene leaders prepared for secession. These were not obscure or peripheral events. They clearly presaged the break-up of Yugoslavia, a country with a larger population than Hungary and Czechoslavkia combined. For

---

14. *In Europe's Name*, London 1993, p. 409.
15. *We the People*, pp. 143, 145.

democrats, they involved violations of human rights that far exceeded any in 'Central Europe', and had done for some time, as a glance at Amnesty reports would have shown. A disaster was plainly in the making.

To blame the Treaty of Maastricht for West European failure to perceive what was at stake in Yugoslavia, as Garton Ash now wishes, will not do. Long before it was conceived, the powder keg in the Balkans was evident. Nor did the project for a single currency ever distract the EU from the East. 'Enlargement' – confined to the PCH trio – was officially endorsed as a goal at Maastricht itself. Thereafter, preparations for the euro were managed by central banks and finance ministries. Policy towards the East was determined in the European Council and the officialdom of assorted foreign ministries, now on autopilot towards Warsaw, Prague and Budapest. To make the single currency the whipping-boy for Sarajevo, however convenient for a conservative British sensibility, is displacement – as Freud understood it – with a vengeance. The Western leader most responsible for forcing through monetary union, François Mitterrand, was actually the only one with a unitary vision for Eastern Europe as a whole – exactly what Garton Ash opposed. Oblivious to the Balkan crisis, a tireless lobbyist for aid and attention to be concentrated on 'Central' Europe, if any individual voice bears responsibility for the tragic inversion of priorities as Yugoslavia slid towards the abyss, it would be his.

Of course, he was not alone. From the eighties onwards, well before it was marketed as such, 'Central Europe' was a magnet for many good reporters and enquiring intellectuals. Its attraction was two-fold. Poland, Czechoslavakia and Hungary were both the scene of the most vigorous and interesting movements against Communism, and the zone readiest to claim kinship with the West itself. Yugoslavia – still more, its neigbours – lacked either of these elements of affective investment. However complex or turbulent Balkan politics might be, they could not easily be dramatized (yet) as a straightforward battle of good against evil. Culturally, too, they offered few of the *images d'Epinal* – the Black Madonna of Czestochowa, the Square of St Wenceslas, the Crown of St Stephen; the liberator pope, the philosopher President, the Nobel electrician – with which the media could uplift audiences in the West. Kadaré might be a better writer than Havel, but apart from a few readers in France, who cared? No Montenegrin estate lay waiting to be reclaimed by English lords; but in Bohemia, Garton Ash can introduce us to Diana Phipps (née Sternberg) recovering her ancestral domain, with its seven thousand acres, boar-filled woodlands and venerable castle ('restored with rare taste and imagination'), and find 'this not just fabulous, in the original sense of the word, but also moving'.[16]

In the literature of foreign engagement, advocacy has an honourable record. Comparisons with R.W. Seton-Watson, as such, do Garton Ash credit. But there is a general rule here. Such advocacy is best when purest of any inclination to find likenesses to the self in the championed other. Colonial history is too rich in versions of that: the 'Martial Races' in India as so many subcontinental Highlanders. The trope of Central Europe was blind in part because it was so self-regarding: the cousins of Orwell in the mirror.

So Poland was forgiven half its foreign debt, while the same Western creditors squeezed Yugoslavia dry, forcing one draconian stabilization plan after another on the country, while unemployment rocketed and federal government was undermined. The immediate background to the disintegration of Yugoslavia was economic breakdown. The myth of Central Europe was not just a negative condition of the unfolding of this crisis; it was an active catalyst of it. As Susan Woodward's *Balkan Tragedy*, the commanding scholarly work on the break-up of Yugoslavia, puts it: 'As early as 1989 Western governments began to declare that the central European countries were better prepared to make the economic and political transition from socialism to capitalism than those in southeastern Europe. But this historico-cultural criterion, largely of Mitteleuropa, Roman Catholicism and Habsburg tradition, cut straight through the centre of Yugoslavia. It left a great gash undefined where the military border of mixed populations between Habsburg and Ottoman rule had been, and it reinforced the separatist arguments already being made by Slovene and Croat nationalists. These intellectuals began to talk about the existence of "two worlds" in Yugoslavia, and both groups proclaimed their greater preparedness for European membership as central Europeans'.[17] The supposed precondition of civil peace in the East proved, not unexpectedly, to be an incitement to ethnic war.

History of the Present avoids any acknowledgement of this fatal link, separating use – the 'good cause' – and misuse – the 'appalling exclusion' – of the cult of Central Europe as if they were unrelated. Yet its condemnation of Croat *Flur-und-Feldbereinigung* and Western indifference to it, and the breadth of its sympathy for all the victims of ethnic violence and hatred in former Yugoslavia, still stand among

---

16. *HP*, pp. 116–117.
17. *Balkan Tragedy*, Washington, DC, 1995, pp. 104–105.

the most powerful commentaries on the region in the later nineties. In face of such decency, why recall its troubling antecedents? There are two answers to this, one intellectual and the other political. They take us to the way the collection is framed as a whole.

The book, in a new twist in the spiral of contemporary hype, takes its title from a fulsome encomium in the *New York Review of Books* of one of Garton Ash's earlier works, in which George Kennan compared him to Tocqueville as 'historian of the present'. This sobriquet the author now unblushingly appropriates to describe his new work – which helpfully displays Kennan's full *laudatio* on the back, beneath a heroic representation of the writer, posed against a bleakly peeling wall, gazing sombrely into the distance with the garb and air of a Scott of the moral Antarctic. It must be hoped that this was dreamt up by Penguin's publicity department, rather than Garton Ash himself, who has hitherto given signs of modesty and dislike of such pretensions even among friends (lamenting Vaclav Havel's adoption of a 'gruesome imperial stare' – what now of his own?).[18]

If so, however, the packagers have induced him to more than lapses of taste in presentation. For his introduction to the book sets out to justify its title with a set of claims about contemporary history. Today, so Garton Ash argues, actors in great events no longer commit their thoughts or deeds to paper as they did in the past; they talk or telephone or issue electronic instructions. Documents dwindle in importance. On the other hand, statesmen and others have never been so eager to give their version of events 'live', in the real time of television interviews or speeches. The result is that 'what you can know soon after the event has increased, and what you can know long after the event has diminished'.[19] This affords opportunities for a quite new kind of history – one capable of transcending the retrospective illusions of a cloistered archival scholarship, by direct reports of 'what it was really like at the time', as Garton Ash puts it, that is, conveyed by the informed eyewitness. Here television – not only many scholars, but viewers will be taken aback to learn – becomes of inestimable help in capturing the truth of the world: 'it brings you closer than any other medium to how things really were'. Best of all, however, is the writer on the spot himself, as Garton Ash has so often been: 'there is nothing to compare with being there'.[20]

---

18. *HP*, p. 20.
19. *HP*, p. xii.
20. *HP*, pp. xvi, xiv.

The innocence of this discovery recalls, irresistibly, Peter Sellers's bewildered presence in the White House. The notion that personal presence affords a special access to reality, or that a television interview is a higher vehicle of truth, belongs to the world of the magazine racks at the check-out counter, not an Oxford college. To try to elevate even the best journalism to supra-Rankean status in this way can only discredit it. The distance between a real history of the present, necessarily only a preliminary version, and *History of the Present* can seen by looking at Woodward's *Balkan Tragedy*. It is not just the scale of narrative, or level of detail and documentation, that separate the two. It is above all the difference between an enterprise that consistently holds to a chain of causality, however difficult that may be, tracing the complexities of major processes from their remote origins through to their ultimate consequences, and one that essentially offers a series of episodes and vignettes, without responsibility for any deeper understanding of the interconnections between them. For study of these, the frisson of the bystander is no more than a lure. No amount of time in the Magic Lantern will ever tell us what was the role of the secret police in the student demonstration of 17 November that set off the Velvet Revolution: historians are still arguing about it. Garton Ash, the author of *In Europe's Name*, knows this perfectly well. His actual work as a historian is sufficient reply to the title of this volume.

Not that its credo is that of just any reporter. In Garton Ash's case, the illusions of immediacy come from something else as well. He is best known as a writer for the intimacy of his knowledge of the leading dissidents of Eastern Europe. These were the friends in whose company he witnessed historic events. When they became rulers, he did not hesitate to criticize them or argue with them, when he thought necessary. This was not simply a question of temperament, it was also one of belief. In his famous disagreement with Havel, Garton Ash held to a radical distinction between the roles of intellectual and politician. The task of the intellectual was, in the phrase Havel coined as a dissident, to 'live in truth'. The job of the elected politician, Garton Ash then rejoined, was to 'work in half-truth' – the best that can be hoped for in a competitive party system based on 'limited adversarial mendacity'.[21] Each was a honourable calling. But to try to combine the two, power and truth, was to serve neither. In a liberal state, a division of labour between independent intellectuals and professional

---

21. *HP*, p. 22.

politicians was essential. Having become President, Havel – his friend put it very politely – risked ceasing to be a serious intellectual.

Havel naturally rejected the antithesis, not only as too absolute in itself, but as tantamount to denying that purity of intentions could be of any effect in practical government. Why should not intellectuals try to raise the standards of public office? For Neal Ascherson, seconding Havel, this is just what sterling figures like Geremek and Balcerowicz – architects of military integration and shock therapy in Poland – have been doing in Eastern Europe. Garton Ash would no doubt reply that as ministers they are no longer the thinkers they once had been. In this strange debate, two features are striking. Garton Ash's definition of an intellectual derives from a coinage of Havel's – 'living in truth' – originally of quite general application, as a term for moral integrity under totalitarian rule. There was always a somewhat sententious pathos to the phrase, since truth is not an abode but at best an aim, variable and missable, in life. But if clandestine literature has its licence, argument overground needs to be more exact. Garton Ash's conversion of the term into a talisman of the intellectual rests on a confusion. Integrity can be found (or lost) in any occupation. Intellectuality is something else: its field is ideas.

Values – ethical, epistemological, aesthetic – figure in the contests over this field, but they do not define it. Intellectuals are judged not by their morals, but by the quality of their ideas, which are rarely reducible to simple verdicts of truth or falsity, if only because banalities are by definition accurate. As bearers or originators of ideas, intellectuals have quite naturally participated in politics – with roles both in opposition and in power – ever since they first emerged as modern types, in the epoch of the American and French Revolutions. Legitimately invoking De Gaulle for his case, Havel could just as well have cited Jefferson. Indeed, Garton Ash's exemplars of intellectuals who lived in moral independence, free from the blandishments of political power, tell the same story, less gloriously. 'We have Orwell. We have Raymond Aron':[22] the one supplying officialdom with a secret list of suspect acquaintances, the other keeping silent about the Algerian War in Le Figaro, not to displease his employers. To seek to insulate intellectuals, even such cynosures, from the grime of politics is vain.

Although it was his prescription for intellectuals that has attracted debate, perhaps the more significant aspect of Garton Ash's dichotomy

---

22. *HP*, p. 155.

lay on its other side, which passed virtually undiscussed. Politicians could not be expected to speak the unvarnished truth; lies were part of their professional equipment, functional necessities of a successful career in any parliamentary democracy, where competition between parties typically requires the skills of advertising, rather than the pursuit of ideas or exercise of reflection. In other words, if norms for intellectuals are set at improbably high – unworldly – levels, expectations of politicians appear to be geared to indulgently low – all too worldly – standards, as if mediocrity and chicanery were more or less inherent in the trade as practised in the West. This is not, however, as Garton Ash sees it. On the contrary, while at times scathing about the collective default of Western leaders in Eastern Europe, he is remarkably respectful about most of the individual statesmen who feature in his pages.

Here the illusions of immediacy seem to come from too close a proximity to power – regular briefings by senior officials, discussions at semi-diplomatic conclaves, intimate conversations with Top People. The tone of his references to the latter can become stuffily reverential to a degree difficult to imagine, for example, in the more unconventional and free-spoken Buruma. Although Garton Ash finds himself longing for Mrs Thatcher in Yugoslavia, it is the German Chancellor who receives his abundant accolades. 'Helmut Kohl is the most formidable politician – and statesman – in Europe. He will not lightly be deflected from the last great task he has set himself,' he writes. 'As the twentieth century draws to its close, we can safely say that Helmut Kohl is its last great European statesman. Watching him leave the stage, I thought of a memorable conversation we had a few years ago ... This amazing sally encapsulated several ingredients of Kohl's greatness: his acute instinct for power, his historical vision, and the bold simplicity of his strategic thinking'.[23] If Gerhard Schroeder is not, alas, of the same calibre, there is consolation in the higher values of his counterparts in Britain and America; 'Someone who knows him quite well told me that, unlike Clinton or Blair, he does not have any religious attachments. So he's a sort of Clinton without the principles'[24] (sic).

Best of all, however, is the pope himself. 'Philosopher, poet and playwright as well as pastor,' Garton Ash declares, 'John Paul II is simply the greatest world leader of our times.' Commensal witness to the

---

23. *HP*, pp. 144, 331.
24. *HP*, p. 338.

planetary vision of the pontiff – 'When I once had dinner with him, in a circle of Polish friends, speaking Polish. I was struck by … his global experience, faith and mission' – he has no doubt that among historical giants, the pope overtops all. 'I have had the chance to talk to several credible candidates for the title of "great man" or "great woman" – Mikhail Gorbachev, Helmut Kohl, Václav Havel, Lech Walesa, Margaret Thatcher – but none matches Karol Wojtyla's unique combination of concentrated strength, intellectual consistency, human warmth and simple goodness.'[25] Too many dinners of this kind are unlikely to produce the sort of intellectual Garton Ash recommends.

But in his case the principal danger lies not so much in a seduction by power, effusive though his idiom on occasion becomes, as in a distortion of perspective. The sense of face-to-face contact, 'being there' with the regents of the world, risks telescoping history into edifying fables. He concludes his homage to John Paul II by claiming that the pope was the prime mover in the fall of Communism, from Berlin to Vladivostok – Gorbachev himself to be seen as little more than a by-product of the forces Wojtyla set in motion, when the Holy Father's return to Poland stirred his people thaumaturgically to action in Solidarity. 'Here' – he exclaims – 'is the specific chain of causation that goes from the election of the Polish pope in 1978 to the end of communism, and hence of the Cold War, in 1989.'[26] What this amounts to is something like a parodic inversion of Stalin's legendary question – how many divisions has the pope? *Perestroika* demoted to a side-show, the pious may now ask: how many masses had the Kremlin?

With this, however, we reach the other reason why the late reinvention of Central Europe continues to mortgage Garton Ash's understanding of the time. The idea was constructed as a barrier to dissociate Poland, Hungary and Czechoslovakia from Russia. When Communism fell, myth logically required that it be the work of their oppositions, overthrowing the old order from below. In fact, of course, the historically decisive change came in the hegemonic power itself. After the invasion of Czechoslovakia in 1968, the East German dissident Rudolf Bahro wrote in his book *The Alternative* that the politbureaucratic system would come to an end when – he thought this inevitable – a Dubcek appeared in Moscow.[27] His prediction was accurate. Nothing fundamental could change in Eastern Europe so

---

25. *HP*, pp. 344–345.
26. *HP*, p. 347.
27. *The Alternative*, London 1978, p. 333.

long as the Red Army remained ready to fire. Everything was possible
once fundamental change started in Russia itself. Bahro, in fact,
foresaw better than he knew. Gorbachev's figure and fate eventually
came to resemble Dubcek's: the puzzled, well-meaning *naif*, uncere-
moniously bamboozled and bundled to his ruin by those he still
imagined were his friends – now as much in the West as in the East.

Russia is to all intents and purposes absent from *History of the
Present*, as it was in Garton Ash's scenarios of 1989. But if it remains
the limit to his imagination, the reason is no doubt the same as for the
pope's pre-eminence within it. Garton Ash orchestrates his European
themes on a generous scale; but in the scoring, there is always a ripple
of the *Polonaise* in the background. Within Central Europe, one
country was his first love – by tradition, the most passionately anti-
Russian – and still commands his prospect. In this, of course, he was
not alone. For different reasons, Poland has in recent years held a
special position in the calculus of Western capitals. In the United
States, the Polish vote that worried Roosevelt at Yalta was a powerful
support of Reagan, and remains a broad domestic force. In Germany,
the desire to have a firm political and military buffer against Russia
gave diplomatic priority to relations with Warsaw. Sentimental and
cultural memories linked France to Poland. With much the largest
population and most strategic location of the PCH trio, not to speak
of its seniority in the loosening of Communism, Poland was bound to
be the centrepiece of Western *Drang nach Osten* after the Cold War.

Repeatedly deploring the failure of the European Union to extend
an immediate welcome to the Visegrad states, Garton Ash is more
discreet about the success of NATO in absorbing them. He expresses
regret that Britain did not take a lead in the process, as he would have
wished it to do, but otherwise essentially confines himself to a passive
impersonal phrase: 'the NATO argument has been won'.[28] The practical implications are left unspoken. Today Western command-
and-control systems camp on the edge of White Russia. The confidential assurances Gorbachev received (but characteristically never
thought to secure on paper) that NATO would not expand to the East
if he would dismantle the Warsaw Pact, are scattered to the winds.
Three months after digesting Central Europe, the Atlantic Pact – still
'defensive' – uncorked a full-scale military offensive in the Balkans.

Honourably troubled by an aerial assault from stratospheric
distance on the supports of civilian life in Serbia, Garton Ash passes

---

28. *HP*, p. 412.

over in silence the evolution of strategic purposes behind it. His book ends by stating once again its case for a 'liberal order' in Europe – a free-trade zone that would avoid a common currency and shun any federal unity, but embrace the lands that were once Communist, admitted in their appropriate sequence. Eschewing any attempt to be a single actor on the world stage, this European order would yet possess 'a degree of power-projection, including a coordinated use of military power in adjacent areas of vital interest to us, such as North Africa and the Middle East'.[29] Such could be the viewpoint of any mildly Euro-sceptic, enlightened British conservative. As a prospectus for the continent, its principal interest lies in what it leaves out.

For just as when he writes of Eastern Europe, a roller-blind falls across Russia, when he turns to Western Europe – the Community and the Union that has developed out of it – a more delicate veil falls over the United States. References of any substance to Washington are few and fleeting. At most, Garton Ash discreetly notes that even in a 'liberal order that is by design non-hegemonic', a 'benign external hegemon' may be necessary.[30] From this standpoint – harshly translated: traditional British servility to America, imagined as a special affinity – it is clear why the notion of Europe as a single actor, and so capable of challenging America, is anathema; while at the same time local 'power-projections', in which British forces can continue to act as the most reliable dobermans of American will, remain indispensable. But this is at most a negative deduction. The positive structure of American dominion in Europe is not so much as skirted in these pages.

Yet, as the founders of the Community were well aware, if the continent was to be united, it would ultimately have to be at the expense of the United States as a global power – no matter how benevolent Washington's assistance in helping to jump-start the process of integration. Mountains of unctuous rhetoric to the contrary, such remains the unspoken truth of European construction to this day. A common identity in the Old World can only be realized in tension with the New, that has been its fifty-year master. That American ascendancy is not just practical or institutional. In proper Hegelian fashion it continues to be theoretical too. If we want to understand contemporary Europe, it is to the United States – still producer of much the largest and often sharpest academic literature on the Community, as well as commander of its military and diplomatic

---

29. *HP*, p. 327.
30. *HP*, pp. 323, 326.

field – that sooner or later we have to turn. To adapt a famous dictum of Adorno and Horkheimer: he who would not speak of America should be silent about Europe.

So if we want to see the reasons why NATO so swiftly overtook the EU in the drive to the East, it is to debates in Washington and Boston that we should look. After the collapse of the Soviet Union, two schools of thought contended over Western policy towards post-Communist Russia. One camp, including some of the most conservative as well as 'liberal' minds in the country, argued that the overriding priority was to shore up Yeltsin's new Russia against any risks of a Weimar-style descent into social chaos and embittered nationalism, by supplying generous material assistance, and avoiding unnecessary humiliation of the country. The expansion of NATO to Russia's doorstep would be an unwise provocation, pushing Moscow into an resentful isolation, without really strengthening the Alliance. This standpoint, common among Russianists in the universities, also enjoyed a good hearing in the media: Richard Pipes and Thomas Friedman were not unrepresentative.

Ranged against it was the camp of those who argued that Russia remained a dangerous potential foe, a semi-barbarous imperial power that would not readily change its spots, and should be fenced in forthwith, while the going was still good in Eastern Europe. For this viewpoint, the rapid expansion of NATO was a priority, to deter Russia from any temptation to think it could regain great-power standing, by bringing home to the Federation its reduced circumstances in the world. Rather than cosseting status susceptibilities or national nostalgia in Moscow, the West should build a strong set of fortifications on former Tsarist soil – independent states firmly integrated into the Western Alliance, capable of checking any resurgence of Russian ambitions. The pivot of such a system of containment would inevitably be Poland. In due course, however, it should extend to the Baltic states in the north and the Ukraine in the east. Henry Kissinger was among those favouring this option.

But – not by accident – its leading exponent was another Polonist, Carter's National Security adviser Zbigniew Brzezinski. It was the trenchancy and clarity of his case that carried the day. NATO expansion to Eastern Europe, from which Bush had vowed to refrain, was espoused by the Clinton administration, and pushed through by Brzezinski's dim former pupil and side-kick on the NSC, now promoted to Secretary of State, Madeleine Albright (suitably enough, of Czech origins). To understand the political thinking behind the advance of NATO to the marches of Belorussia and Ruthenia, we need only turn to Brzezinski's recent manifesto *The Grand Chessboard*. Here are laid out, with impressive candour, the foundations of a long-term American design for Europe. Confidently and consistently, it spells out what Garton Ash prefers to leave unsaid, or not to confront. Not that Brzezinski can be treated simply as the truth of Garton Ash between the lines. There is at least one element in his argument that would make painful reading for the latter. But by and large, this is the outer frame of the landscape sketched in *History of the Present*, in the real world.

Brzezinski starts by noting that today 'America stands supreme in the four decisive domains of global power'.[31] Militarily, it is without rival; economically, it is the locomotive of world growth; technologically, it leads in all areas of innovation; culturally, its appeal is universal among youth. The result is a global hegemony without precedent in history. But if its scope is wide, its depth is in some respects shallow, since it stretches across a far more extensive space than any of the empires of the past, but unlike them does not rest on direct control of territory. Imagination and vigilance will be necessary to preserve US power. *The Grand Chessboard* sets out the requirements for maintaining American primacy for another half century.

Here one battlefield will be decisive. 'For America the chief geopolitical prize is Eurasia.' There, where three-quarters of the world's population and resources are located, for the first time in history 'a non-Eurasian power is preeminent'.[32] This is the great chessboard on which the United States must play to win, all the way from the Atlantic to the Indian to the Pacific Oceans. Brzezinski has much to say about the Far East, the Middle East and Central Asia. But his survey starts uncompromisingly in the West. 'Europe is America's essential geopolitical bridgehead on the Eurasian continent. America's geostrategic stake in Europe is enormous. Unlike America's links with Japan, the Atlantic alliance entrenches American military power and political influence directly on the Eurasian mainland.'[33] In Europe itself, there is a common market in the Western half of the continent, but so far no political unity, and signs of a decline in economic vitality.

In these conditions, not altogether healthy, 'a truly European "Europe" as such does not exist'. Brzezinski draws the consequences without euphemism. 'The brutal fact is that Western Europe, and

---

31. *The Grand Chessboard. American Primacy and its Geostrategic Imperatives*, New York 1997, p. 24.
32. Ibid., p. 30.
33. Ibid., p. 59.

increasingly also Central Europe, remains largely an American protectorate, with its allied states reminiscent of ancient vassals and
tributaries.'[34] Nevertheless, European unity should be encouraged by
the United States, which ought to engage constructively with its
leading actors to guide the process in a mutually desirable direction.
These actors – here Garton Ash might wince – do not include the
United Kingdom. 'Great Britain is not a geostrategic player.'
Entertaining no bold vision of Europe's future, clinging to the illusions of the special relationship, the country has lost continental
relevance. 'It is America's key supporter, a very loyal ally, a vital
military base, and a close partner in critically important intelligence
activities. Its friendship needs to be nourished, but its policies do not
call for sustained attention.'[35]

By contrast, France and Germany – the axis historically central to
the Community – each have ambitious agendas for Europe, derived
respectively from an imperial past and a unified present, whose directions may now increasingly diverge. Given French coolness towards
American primacy, the US should support German leadership in the
EU in the short run, working together for common goals such as
NATO expansion. But in the longer run, once the right security framework has been established, it should be willing to make concessions to
French sensibilities. For in time France will become a useful partner for
Poland to balance against Germany. These three states might then
form the backbone of a unified Europe of the future.[36] America,
meanwhile, should quietly dissuade Germany from any unwise commitments to Russia, coaxing it towards the extension of NATO to
Riga and Kiev. A map displays the combined might of France,
Germany, Poland and Ukraine in 2010. As for Russia, the test of its
democratic credentials will be acceptance of European arrangements
like these, and the shedding of its residual pretensions in the Caucasus
and Central Asia. Perhaps, Brzezinski has speculated elsewhere, it
might break up altogether into a number of more manageable units.

It is not difficult to discern visionary features in this prospectus.
Brzezinski himself expresses misgivings about the future of the
Ukraine, as liable to be reabsorbed by Russia if America fails to
anchor it to the West. But what is most striking is something else.
Official rhetoric in Europe, and to a large extent in America too – not

34. Ibid., p. 59.
35. Ibid., pp. 42–43.
36. Ibid., p. 78.

just the lofty communiqués of G7, but the pious editorials of count-less *bien-pensant* columnists – continually stresses the need to treat Russian patriotism with dignity, the danger of fostering a revanchist reaction against the West, the risks inherent in a loose nuclear stock-pile and the urgency of conciliating the country's fledgling democracy. What more reckless contradiction of this chorus of commonplaces than the game-plan of *The Grand Chessboard*?

Yet its calculation has so far proved more realistic. Practice says more than any amount of preaching. America – Western Europe in its tow – has expanded NATO to once Soviet borders without a flicker of real resistance in Moscow. The new NATO has since unleashed the first war of 'post-war' Europe, against the last state supposedly close to Russia, not only without any serious opposition from Moscow (dire warnings of which filled a loyal Western press), but ultimately with its willing collaboration – Russian diplomats and soldiers proffering the necessary fig-leaf behind which Milošević could more decently surren-der. A free hand in Chechnya is small return for such services. Behind the clouds of canting solicitude, a lucidly contemptuous judgement has been reached. The Russian elites are so corrupted and supine, from the presidential family down to all but the lowest deputy in the Duma, that – whatever the bluster – they will in practice take anything from the West, provided the taps of the IMF are not turned off.

How long that will continue is, of course, another matter. Precedents here say little. For the moment this is the reality of the con-tinent, in which derisory entities like the 'Organization for the Security and Cooperation of Europe' are mere phantoms. At the end of *History of the Present*, Garton Ash expresses his disappointment with the current state of things – rather like R.W. Seton-Watson, who felt after Versailles that his cause had won the war, but lost the peace. 'Whatever its name,' Garton Ash writes, 'this is not the order I hoped for.'[37] Torn between continuing Cold War attachments and humane impulses that have long ceased to square with them, he has chosen to blame Brussels. But he has got the address wrong: the problem lies not in the Charlemagne Building, but the Boulevard Léopold. Garton Ash's last words enjoin Britons to 'see Europe plain and to see it whole'.[38] But the whole is wider than he allows; and to see it we need a different travel card.

1999

---

37. *HP*, p. 412.
38. *HP*, p. 417.

Postscript

With the publication of *Free World*, his most recent book, Garton Ash has broadened his angle of vision. No one could reproach this work, subtitled 'Why the Crisis of the West Reveals the Opportunity of Our Time', with a bashful reluctance to touch on the role of America in Europe. The cover could not be more direct. On it, two pieces of a jigsaw wait to be joined. The United States extends a fraternal arm from one towards the outstretched arm of the European Union on the other: beneath is the Union Jack, sustaining both sides. The 'Opportunity of Our Time' will be seized when the two pieces fit snugly into each other. The 'Crisis of the West' is the unfortunate interval that still keeps them apart. *Free World* will show how to make the puzzle whole.

Below the image and subtitle, Vaclav Havel proclaims the book a 'compelling manifesto for the enlargement of freedom and a new era of world politics'. Prearranged puffs of this sort – celebrities sponsoring mental sportswear – have become such a standard feature of contemporary publishing that it would perhaps be unfair to single out the former President for this one, however pompous or vacuous. But there is some irony in it. For what has occasioned *Free World* is the war in Iraq, an enlargement of freedom warmly supported by Havel, yet causing the unfortunate rift in the West represented on the cover. In writing his book, Garton Ash's first concern is to show that this has no deep basis. Confronted with the Baath dictatorship in Baghdad, the Western powers could and should have presented a common front. But lack of statesmanship led to wrangling rather than unity in the Security Council, and then to recriminations within the Atlantic alliance. 'The diplomacy of the Iraq crisis of 2002/3 was a case study, on all sides in how not to run a world,' he writes.[39] That the West runs the world, and for the time being ought to do so, is not in question. Things will go awry, however, if it fails to show a sense of collective purpose. In *Free World* Garton Ash is careful to avoid judgement of the war itself, of the sort that might perpetuate the frictions he seeks to overcome. But a glance at the way he describes the leading actors in the recent *déboire* leaves little doubt which parties were most to blame for the falling-out within the Atlantic Alliance. There was 'the unprecedented spectacle of France actively canvassing for votes against the United States in the Security Council of the

---

39. *Free World*, London 2004, p. 44. Henceforward *FW*.

United Nations, on a question of war and peace that the United States considered vital to its own national security', and the 'political opportunism' of Schroeder in allowing 'even the basic tenets of a nation's foreign policy to be abandoned in the cause of re-election'.[40] These were fundamental desertions of principle. By comparison, the blunders of Bush and oversights of Blair may be treated as less culpable, if making their own contribution to a calamitous display of Western disunity.

Still, these were after all no more than a quartet of politicians, capable as individuals of either learning or leaving the scene. If Blair, for example, showed 'occasional callowness', it was because like many democratic politicians he was an expert in the techniques of winning power at home, but on entering office an amateur in the exercise of power abroad. So 'he had to learn on the job', which 'was difficult even when you had first-rate diplomatic advisers sitting just down the corridor in No 10 Downing Street'.[41] Another such learner was Bush, who by the autumn of 2003 had matured remarkably, now endorsing multilateralism in a 'return to the great continuity of those eleven Presidents since Roosevelt'.[42] Chirac and Schroeder, more incorrigible, are now happily on their way out, and we can look forward to successors like Sarkozy and Merkel, who will be distinctly preferable. Too much should therefore not be made of the diplomatic mishaps surrounding the toppling of Saddam Hussein.

Of greater concern are intellectual trends that have used the war in Iraq as a sounding-board for constructions designed to imply major contrasts between America and Europe. These tendencies have ensnared even hitherto responsible thinkers like Habermas, whose joint manifesto with Derrida, on the occasion of protests against the war, propounded a set of value-differences supposedly separating Europe from America, and capable of forming the basis for a common European identity: secularism, the welfare state, social solidarity, refusal of capital punishment, limitation of national sovereignty. Such schemas lead to the notion that Europe is not only different from the United States, but somehow better than it. This is a divisive idea, based on a false dichotomy. Europe is not a single social or political model, but a diverse set of communities, in which features of local life

---

40. *FW*, pp. 8, 70.
41. *FW*, p. 43.
42. *FW*, p. 129.

are often closer to American norms than to those of neighbouring states, let alone a continental standard. Nor does America offer a homogeneous scene, let alone resemble fashionable caricatures of it. England has a state religion, which the US does not; Irish and Poles are more ardent patriots than Americans; in the Ukraine and Moldova there are as many handguns as in Kansas or Oklahoma; public spending on Medicaid is proportionately higher than on the NHS; Indian immigrants prefer the welcome of Silicon Valley to that of the Rhineland. The United States and the various countries of Europe belong to a wider family of liberal democracies, and show far more similarities than differences. What differences there are, moreover, cannot be generalized into any contrasting overall valuation. America is better in some respects, Europe in others. The important thing is that they stick together.

The unilateralism of the Bush administration, after the attacks of September 11, put this unity at risk. Overwhelming military power created the temptation to act alone, first in Afghanistan and then, in an access of hubris, in Iraq. Yet however clumsily executed, American goals have remained admirable, in the best Wilsonian tradition of spreading democracy and human rights. The real danger would be not US activism, but US disengagement from the trouble spots of the world, 'leaving the job half done' in Iraq and elsewhere.[43] For the United States continues to be the indispensable nation, with a combination of military, political, economic and cultural power that the European Union cannot hope to match. This is not always grasped in the EU itself, where Garton Ash warns of the illusions of 'Euro-Gaullism' – the idea that Europe could act as a power independent of the United States, even in potential rivalry with it. The seat of this hazardous conception is obviously France, but it has a wider constituency among European elites, and is encouraged by notions like that of Habermas. Its dangers are obvious. 'The line between Europe as Not-America and Europe as Anti-America', Garton Ash observes ominously, 'is not clearly marked on any map'.[44] Fortunately, ranged against such Euro-Gaullism is a healthier Euro-Atlanticism, represented not only by opinion in Britain, but above all in the new democracies of Central and Eastern Europe, particularly Poland, whose leaders were 'Blairite long before Blair'.[45]

---

43. *FW*, p. 133.
44. *FW*, p. 64.
45. *FW*, p. 87.

Chirac-style notions of a European superpower in a multipolar
world are doomed to failure. But if Euro-Gaullism is a 'hiding to
nowhere',[46] Euro-Atlanticism remains a project still to be accomplished
in the twenty-first century. Here Britain's role becomes critical. An
island with a glorious past, hence also some residual insular traits, it
is also a crossroads of the world, whose capital is now as multiracial
and multicultural as New York itself, if not more so. Bound to Europe
by membership of the EU, as well as a long history, the UK is also the
colonial ancestor of America, to whom it has given its language, legal
traditions and founding political ideas. Who better than this 'four-
headed Janus' to bring both sides of the Atlantic, even North and
South of the planet, together? 'These islands are anything but
ordinary; for five centuries, until the American and French
Revolutions, we were pioneers of freedom in the West', and still today,
wherever Westerners are trying to change things for the better, 'the
British are always to be found among these world-shapers.'[47]

They have, moreover, produced a Prime Minister in tune with the
times. Blair's strategic vision of Euro-Atlantic unity, and what it can
give the world, sets him apart from his peers in NATO. He alone,
unlike Bush, Chirac or Schroeder, sought to prevent a disastrous split
in the ranks of the West by obtaining common endorsement of a
tough American policy on Iraq in the Security Council. If this
outcome foundered on Franco-German intransigence and American
indifference, the burden of blame lies elsewhere. Not that his own
performance during the crisis, or for that matter before it, was
perfect. Blair instinctively understood that the very nature of Britain
as a country required concord between Europe and America, and
spoke with an unrivalled clarity and authority of what the two continents could do together. But he was too inclined to depict the UK as
a bridge between the US and EU, an image with exclusive connotations, rather than as one lane in an inclusive highway; and convinced
European though he was, in the delicate balances of discourse and
diplomacy leant too far towards America at the expense of Europe.
The reason for that, however, was less any personal failing, or greater
ease in the Anglosphere, than the blackmail of Europsceptic tabloids,
to which he was in some degree electorally beholden. But his basic
outlook remains the right one. The worldwide interests of America

---

46. *FW*, p. 93.
47. *FW*, pp. 207–208.

and Europe are one. Together, the US and the EU can deliver global public goods the world most needs.

The second part of *Free World* addresses this larger scene. The West faces what Garton Ash describes as four 'New Red Armies' today: turmoil in the Near East, the rise of China in the Far East, poverty in the South, damage to the environment everywhere. But if it pulls itself together, it will discover a landscape of unprecedented opportunity. For freedom is already on the march, mustering no less than a billion citizens in democratic states around the world, and the role of the West must be to help spread it to all corners of the earth. To play its part in this mission, Garton Ash argues the EU should expand to 40 states, embracing not only the southern Balkans and Ukraine, but Turkey too. At home, its economies need to be less regulated, its immigrants better integrated, and symbols created to bond its people together, such as an anthem all could sing. The alternative, if something like this prospect fails to come about, could be a relapse into European barbarism, as tendencies to evil in human nature itself reassert themselves. In America, less change is in order. But out of respect for the sensibility of others, the US should not only act as if it had somewhat less power than it really has, but accept Europe as a benign corrective to its executive prerogatives in the world. Americans must also cut their emissions of carbon dioxide.

So reformed and reunited, the West could take on today's Red Armies. In the Middle East, where Europe has a special responsibility for joint action with the US – for this is its 'near abroad' – the task is democratic modernization, to drain the swamp that breeds terrorism. In the policing job required, there can be a 'division of labour between a European "soft cop" and an American "hard cop"'.[48] Economically, the EU has a duty to create a Mediterranean Free Trade Area, to assist American development strategy for the region. For geographical and historical reasons, the Far East is a more strictly American bailiwick, but there too the US and the EU share the same interests, and their joint economic power can be used to lever China towards democracy. For the remaining Red Armies, poverty and ecological risk, what is needed is essentially 'globalization with a human face' – more aid and freer trade. Europe should abolish CAP and America accept Kyoto. The statesman who embodies the necessary spirit of practical generosity and environmental responsibility is the British Prime Minister. Whatever people may say of his bias towards Washington, on matters

---

48. *FW*, p. 154.

to do with climate change, he has been 'every centimetre the European'.[49] Garton Ash ends his book by calling on the one billion citizens of today's democracies to rally behind the programme he has outlined, and join him in conversations about it on his website.

Such is *Free World*. What relation does it bear to Garton Ash's previous work? The most striking aspect of the book is the time warp of its framework. In the eighties, when he was formed as a young Cold Warrior, the unity of the United States and Western Europe in the struggle against Communism went without saying, to a point where once the war was won, America represented such a natural background for 'seeing Europe whole' that it scarcely needed to be mentioned in his *History of the Present*. For a political sensibility of this vintage, the outbreak of disputes over Iraq was bound to come as a shock, requiring remedial action to ensure that Europe remained anchored firmly within the Atlantic Alliance, and that the latter was retooled to meet what out-of-area challenges now arise. To that end, Garton Ash offers not simply gestures of repair, but ambitious proposals for rejuvenation. These, however, remain frozen within a conceptual ice cap dating from the Cold War. The 'West' – a notion to which he devotes a first few ardent pages – remains the absolute origin and horizon of contemporary political reference. Beyond it lies, in future, the empyrean of a 'Free World' – distinguished, he explains, from its compromised predecessor in the days of the Dulles brothers, by the crucial substitution of an indefinite for a definite article. The enemies whose menace can galvanize the West into victorious battle once again? Reincarnations of the Red Army – the T-52s of the poor, the SAM-9s of the ozone layer, the SS-20s of the jihadis, the Sukhoi of Chinese growth, apparently.

The conceit is not to be dismissed as a mere trick of journalistic presentation. For at the centre of Garton Ash's book lies a proposition that says everything about the Free World it envisages. The 'old Atlantic-centred West which has been shaping the world since about 1500, probably has no more than twenty years left in which it will still be the main world-shaper. That's another reason why it's so stupid for Europeans and Americans to waste any more time squabbling with each other. In a longer historical perspective, this may be our last chance to set the agenda of world politics'.[50] The message is: the hegemony of the

---

49. *FW*, p. 181.
50. *FW*, p. 192.

West must prevail, while still it may. For the foreseeable future – since beyond twenty years, not much can be realistically predicted – the guide-lines for humanity are to be laid down by Washington and Brussels. Or rather, he hastens to add, by all one billion of us, the free citizens not just of North America and Europe, but also Japan and Australasia, topped up by the rich of Russia, the Middle East and Latin America, who can be counted as honorary members of the West for the purposes of the 'opportunity of our time'.

What is the opportunity? To extend their kind of freedom to the rest of the world – democracy and prosperity for all. There is a decent impulse in this, but not a glimmer of self-critical irony. The growing comity of democratic states, as graded and catalogued by Freedom House in Washington, is the signpost to an auspicious future. The spread of democracy as we know it is what the West must now work for in the rest of the world. At no point does it occur to Garton Ash that there might be anything wanting in the models he seeks to export. That scarcely more than than half the population – often less – vote in American presidential elections; that the incumbency rate in con-gressional contests is now over 90 per cent; that the cost of a senatorial race in even the smallest US state runs into millions; that the current British government rests on the votes of not much more than a fifth of the electorate; that turn-out for elections to the European Parliament has sunk with each successive poll – all such facts, in a book replete with figures on every other matter, are con-signed to an oubliette. An entire chapter is devoted to the prospects of an EU engorged with forty members, without a line on how popular control of any kind is to be assured in this desirable entity. On the last pages of his book, Garton Ash finally recollects an anomaly. 'One of the oddest features of our age of unparalleled democracy is that so many people feel so disillusioned with conventional politics that they don't even bother to vote.'[51] It is not an oddity that detains him. The idea that there might be a connection between the spread of this sort of democracy and the growing indifference of people to it is beyond his imagining.

The reality is that democracy has extended across the world *pari passu* with a decline in the range of choices it offers. Once the world has been made safe for capitalism – a term largely banished from *Free World* – elections in even the least stable societies can be afforded. With no alternatives to the narrowest span of 'market-friendly'

---

51. *FW*, p. 249.

policies on offer, expressions of the popular will have become riskless in a way that in the days of Mossadegh, Arbenz or Allende they were not. Should there be any danger of reversion, the West can see to it that the results come out right all the same: witness the rescue of Yeltsin. Unwittingly, Garton Ash's own language tells the truth of the story. Describing the ways his billion free citizens can influence the rest of humanity, he writes enthusiastically: 'That's a lot of people with a lot of money, a lot of votes, a lot of voices.'[52] Such is the order of attributes that matters in the Free World, updated. The image that occurs to him to conjure up the prospect of democracy a eventually arriving in China belongs to the same vocabulary: 'the greatest pay-out in the history of freedom' – cash tumbling from the tote or the fruit-machine. Even when Garton Ash appeals for greater aid and less restricted trade for the South, the same political calculation is at work. During the Cold War, he explains, 'most of us' believed that fighting 'dictatorships and the wars they cause' was the priority; today the front has shifted, and we must do battle against 'extreme poverty'.[53] Translated: now that socialism has been seen off, we can get around to thinking about misery.

Not that the good cause can be confined to the use of our economic wealth to promote liberty and distribute charity abroad. Force is still needed to usher in a better world. The West, Garton Ash insists, must institutionalize the doctrine of 'just wars' that has been such a major step forward since the collapse of the Soviet bloc. Military interventions around the world continue to be needed, if not to oust dictatorships, certainly wherever barbaric states commit genocide or risk acquiring weapons of mass destruction. The two criteria are not unwarrantably restrictive. 'What qualifies as genocide is a matter for the most serious debate', while how 'we establish whether there is a real and present danger' of WMD is 'something we will all have to wrestle with'.[54] Since, according to Garton Ash, there was genocide in Kosovo – 5,000 out of 1.7 million Albanians dead – there is little risk of disallowing operations like NATO's war on Yugoslavia. If it was illegal – though thoroughly legitimate – the answer is to change international law to give future such actions the stamp of legality.

As for weapons of mass destruction, who can blame Blair for believing in their existence in Iraq? He had the right intentions and, as invasion approached, he was after all Prime Minister of his country –

---

52. *FW*, p. 194.
53. *FW*, p. 241.
54. *FW*, p. 243: for further on the need for just wars, pp. 184–185, 221.

'He has to decide. He has to lead.' If the intelligence on which he based his decision was wrong, that was not his fault, but the responsibility of the functionary who provided it.[55] Garton Ash doubted the wisdom of the invasion from the start, but his opposition was not one of principle. He simply feared, as US and British tanks rolled into Iraq, that the war might prove 'not grotesquely, criminally wrong, but prudentially, politically wrong'.[56] Once launched, he was soon praying for its success and worrying mainly that the America might withdraw too soon, a danger of which he has since repeatedly warned. Today Europe should be pulling its weight on the Tigris alongside the United States. 'In Iraq, where we did not have to intervene, we none the less have promises to keep, and Europe has an even more vital interest than America in the outcome.'[57]

Reactions of this kind to the war in Iraq have been typical enough. Garton Ash can claim he foresaw the difficulties of holding down Iraq earlier than many, and deplores the quagmire which has since developed there. But, like his predecessors in the time of Vietnam, he still urges the need to see the job through. Behind this commonplace response, however, is a larger blindness – or rather, complaisance – at the core of *Free World*. The book ends with a series of maps intended to supply graphic illustrations of the uneven distribution of income per capita, spending on arms, population, 'values' and freedom in the world. Suppressed is what would be still more striking, because asymmetrical, than any of these – a map of foreign military bases around the globe. The armed forces of the United States are currently camped in over 100 countries, far more than during the Cold War itself. This immense grid of poised violence is the armature of the Free World that Garton Ash proposes to the unhappy five billion who do not yet enjoy its benefits. That he does not mention it once is sufficient to define the quality of the freedom he offers. The empire of bases is the unspoken basis of the human liberty to come.

The author of *Free World* has changed. The principal question the book poses is how and why that alteration has occurred. The most immediate reason clearly lies in the arrival of New Labour in Britain. In the

---

55. Compare 'In Defence of the Fence', *Guardian*, 6 February 2003, and 'Scarlett Must Go', *Guardian*, 14 October 2004.

56. 'America on Probation', *Guardian*, 17 April 2003.

57. *FW*, p. 244. As early as April 2003, he was writing: 'There's a lot of talk these days about America's new empire. But the biggest danger is not American imperialism; it's American inconstancy': *Guardian*, 17 April 2003.

eighties, when Garton Ash was reporting from Eastern Europe for *The Spectator*, he belonged for a time to an informal brains trust on foreign policy around Thatcher, whose anti-Communism – no less resolute, but more alert than Reagan's – he naturally admired. But without any strong feelings about domestic politics, beyond the belief that private property and the market were the foundation of a free society, he was not a Conservative loyalist. Where he did have strong feelings, moreover, they were mixed with regard to Thatcher. She was certainly a gallant enemy of the Soviet Union. But regrettably she was also anti-European – to the point of not even much welcoming the reunification of Germany.

By the time Blair was preparing himself for office, and Garton Ash was summoned to meet him in Islington along with other academic and diplomatic insiders,[58] he was thus more than ready to offer advice. Once Blair was in power, Garton Ash seems to have quite soon decided that here at last was a leader who combined pro-Americanism and pro-Europeanism, the two conditions of a sane British foreign policy, in almost perfect measure. 'Tony Blair has grasped and articulated this British national interest, role and chance better than any of his predecessors. In setting the strategic direction for Britain in the world, he has been bold, consistent and sometimes brave.'[59] If the wider impulse behind the writing of *Free World* came from a pressing need to reunite Europe with America, the narrower – on the evidence, perhaps originating – motive seems to have been a desire to shore up Blair's position in Britain, at a jumpy moment for New Labour. Garton Ash declares it strange that, while Blair's foreign policy is the only sensible course for the UK, 'it is the one least represented in the British media', dominated by a Euro-sceptic press, with the eloquent exceptions of the *Financial Times* and *The Economist* – presumably out of modesty, he omits the *Guardian*, where he expresses himself. *Free World* seeks to make good this lack of support. In an avowal that suggests the extent of his identification with the ruler of the country, and candidly delivers the rationale of his book, he writes: 'To ask "why did Blair's bridge fall down in 2003?" is thus a way of asking, "how, if at all, could those who share his strategic vision of partnership between Europe and America do better in future?"'[60]

---

58. See John Kampfner, *Blair's Wars*, London 2003, p. 10.
59. *FW*, pp. 198–199.
60. *FW*, p. 42. Even domestically, this is the right formula. 'Being so intimate with Europe and America, we have the chance to take the best of both. In many ways this is what the New Labour government has tried to do': p. 205.

The tone, of mingled intimacy and *engouement*, is not altogether new. Earlier, however, there was typically more geographical distance between the admirer and the objects of his utmost admiration, giants like Kohl or Woytila. Cheer-leading for a regime at home, week after week, is something else. 'As Blair said in his magnificent speech to the House of Commons on Tuesday ...'; 'I am totally convinced the Blairite vision of a new postwar order of world politics is the best one available ...'; 'Not since Churchill has a British leader had such a magnetic resonance across the Channel ...'; 'Long live Blairismo ...'; 'Blairism is the answer to Europe's ills ...' – and so on, *ad libitum*.[61] The stream of gushing phrases is periodically interrupted with a few scraps of critical flotsam, the token of any self-respecting intellectual. But the condition of mind is all too clear. One of its signs is the depths of silliness to which Garton Ash can descend in this rapt condition. Calling for a 'historic compromise' between Britain and France under the sign of Blair's Euro-Atlanticism, he tells us not only that Britain would have the stronger position in such an arrangement – since 'the British are winners', thanks to 'the hegemonic succession from the British Empire to the United States' – but that De Gaulle himself would have been delighted to accept this.[62]

Topping and tailing *Free World* is a famous egalitarian declaration of Thomas Rainsborough, supposedly delivered in St Mary the Virgin's church in the Putney debates of 1647, and presented here as expressing not just the spirit of Garton Ash's own endeavour, but a *genius loci* displayed in the lively mosaic of multicultural facilities in the nearby High Street – McDonald's, Benetton, Starbucks, Hot Wok Express are among those mentioned – and reincarnate, above all, in Blairism. 'The Blair bridge project is, so to speak, Putney made policy.'[63] That Rainsborough never spoke in the church described, though Garton Ash has done so, almost goes without saying.[64] Why should anyone be surprised that a republican revolutionary assassinated by royalists, in the cause of an institution of which Blair remains a fulsome admirer, is served up for ideological consumption

---

61. *Guardian*, 20 March 2003; 16 September 2004; 2 June 2005.

62. *FW*, pp. 200–201.

63. *FW*, p. 52.

64. The debate of 29 October 1647, at which Rainsborough and others argued with Ireton and Cromwell over the Leveller *Agreement of the People*, was held in the lodgings of the quartermaster-general of the Army. Three hundred and fifty years later, of course, the Levellers' demand for a written constitution, entrenching basic rights, remains unrealized in the 'no ordinary island' celebrated by Garton Ash.

in this stew along with Big Macs and United Colours? Not since Thatcher claimed St Francis of Assisi on the doorstep of Downing Street has there been such a grotesque misappropriation of a historical figure for a political kitchen-sink.

Such moments form a specifically British nadir of *Free World*. But it would be unfair to judge the book simply by the clammy imprint of New Labour on it. More personal proclivities have been at work. Garton Ash's attraction to congenial power-holders, always strong, has been increasing over the years. In this volume, we are conducted into the presence of Bush in the White House, Blair in Downing Street, Fischer in former East Berlin, Havel in the Hradcany Castle. The epithets that garland these politicians are consistent. We have seen quite a few in the case of Blair, but Garton Ash distributes them more widely. Bush, showing an appealing humility – 'the meeting is to prepare the president, still new in office, for his first trip to Europe' – tells him 'wryly' that he is still learning his job. When the President has learnt something, Garton Ash marvels at the 'extraordinary change' for the better that has come over him. Clinton makes 'an amazing statement of commitment' to Europe, and delivers 'a brilliant speech' to the Democratic Convention. Fischer, 'in a memorable conversation' over a café table, says 'wise and mature things'. Rumsfeld 'twinkles' to him as they stroll together to a banquet with Havel. Powell gives 'a riveting performance' in the Security Council. Rice's vision is 'breath-takingly ambitious'. Wrestling with the problem of whether Western values are the same as universal values, Garton Ash comes upon the philosopher's stone. What sage discovered it? Why, James Baker, who 'saves the day' with the deft phrase 'democratic values' when Bush senior and Gorbachev, 'bobbing up and down in stormy seas off Malta', were puzzling over the right formulations to end the Cold War. The general tone is: 'Stepping out of the famous front door of No 10, on a red carpet that had appeared for the Premier of Serbia, I reckoned ...'[65]

This downpour of hyperbole and cliché could simply be taken as the natural language of a political counter-jumper. It belongs with the decorations lovingly enumerated on Garton Ash's website: 'What the Papers Say' Award, Imre Nagy Memorial Plaque, the Hoffman von Fallersleben Prize, Polish, Czech and German Orders of Merit, Premio Napoli, Companion of the Most Distinguished Order of St

---

65. *FW*, pp. 93, 129, 112, 237; *Guardian*, 28 November 2002, 6 February 2003, 20 January 2005, 10 February 2005.

Michael and St George. Can the Medal of Freedom be far off? Garton Ash was once better than such vanities. He has become a victim of his own success, and that of a cause he originally served well. The freshness of observation and warmth of sympathy he brought to the still half-hidden world of East European dissidence, in his adventures as a reporter, depended in part on a youthful defiance of much conventional Western opinion about détente – vindicated when he became the leading witness of popular revolutions against the revolution. He was not, of course, isolated in his outlook, as Thatcher settled into power, but at the beginning he was not exactly in a European mainstream either. When, however, complete victory in the Cold War was followed by the consolidation of a neo-liberal order across the advanced and most of the developing world, not least in his lands of choice in Eastern Europe itself, what he had once stood for, as a kind of Western dissident, became a universally received wisdom, typically the death sentence on an idea. But rather than any questioning of his assumptions, Garton Ash has only sunk deeper into them. Attempting to project his formative convictions outwards, from Eastern Europe to the planet at large, without any of the direct experience that originally gave them life, has merely led to the inanity of the New Red Armies. The world after the Cold War cannot be analogized in this fashion. Trying to turn the mental clock back has yielded a book that, intellectually speaking, rises only occasionally above smugness and uplift. In a vacuum of virtually any contact with movements from below of the sort he once drew strength from, his universe has increasingly narrowed to convivial audiences with a banal clutch of office-holders.

Occupational changes have played their part in this transformation. The freelance reporter has become a syndicated pundit, and a pillar of two academic institutions, each closely connected to the foreign policy establishments of their country, first St Antony's at Oxford and now – the element of *translatio imperii* is clear – at the Hoover Institute, dedicated to the struggle against Communism from its inception in the thirties. *Free World* is in large measure – not all: there is Blair – the view from Palo Alto. The more consequential of these new roles, however, is the first. The relentless demands of a newspaper column always risk exposing the weaknesses in a writer. Garton Ash's platform in the *Guardian*, extensively used to sell his book, has not just been a vehicle of his current political allegiance. More disastrously, it has highlighted and accentuated the strain of glibness in his writing even at its best, a penchant for the cute jingle and deafness to bathos and *poshlost*. Here is his description of a conclave orchestrated

by Havel in Prague: 'Now it was about his fellow presidents, and
whether they would stay for the amazing after-dinner hymn to
freedom, combining Beethoven's Ode to Joy, the Marseillaise and
John Lennon's Power to the People, that he had specially commissioned for the NATO summit – and for his own farewell ... We sit in
the conference centre, looking across the river to the castle, illumi-
nated, imposing and lovely, above central Europe's most beautiful city.
But this evening, above the castle itself, there is a huge, crimson, neon
heart, slowly pulsating. The heart is Havel's symbol – he puts it next
to his signature in letter to friends – and this is his farewell gesture.
Some Czechs mutter that it's kitsch and undignified, especially since
in Czech lands a red neon heart is usually the sign of a brothel. But
Havel doesn't give a damn, and I think he's right. Against the night
sky, it looks magical'.[66] Orlando on the Vltava.

Or, here in a related mode, is how he finishes a chapter on Britain:
'We must have a national strategy that engages fully, on all fronts,
with the world. The task is daunting, but given luck and the right
allies, not impossible – like Churchill's promise of eventual victory in
1940. Writing that same year, Orwell concluded *The Lion and
Unicorn* with these words: "I believe in England, and I believe we
shall go forward". We still can. The only obstacle is ourselves.'[67] What
satire of vapid bombast could improve on it? At the end of the book,
we are told: 'The recipe for human happiness is mysterious and
cannot be purchased at Wal-Mart.'[68] Written by a Professor of
European History at Oxford.

Le style, c'est l'homme is not an infallible maxim. There is too
often variance between them. But the style of *Free World* is, in this
case, the proper verdict on its content. Flaubert would have fallen on
it with delight, as an incomparable *Dictionnaire des idées reçues* of
our times. It contains scarcely a single idea that cannot be found,
virtually any day of the week, in the editorial columns of the mainstream press in the West – the *Financial Times*, the *Guardian*, *Die
Zeit*, the *International Herald Tribune*, *La Repubblica*, the *New
York Times*, *The Economist*, *El País* and the rest. What the book
really supplies is a compendium of the conventional opinions endlessly repeated in this universe, laced only with a special partiality
for Blair and boosterism for Britain. Without fully realizing what he

---

66. *Guardian*, 31 January 2003.
67. FW, p. 208.
68. FW, p. 247.

is saying, Garton Ash lets out as much himself. As he puts it, once Saddam was overthrown, 'The chorus of American and European voices calling for the transatlantic relationship to be "repaired", "renewed" or "reborn" rose to the fortissimi of the last movement of Beethoven's Ninth Symphony. Not a day passed without at least one op-ed commentary, open letter, speech, conference, workshop, think-tank meeting, high-level group or task force devoted to putting the West together again. Often these meetings or initiatives were financed by a German-owned American company, or an American-owned British company, or one of the hundreds of other businesses with a direct stake in the transatlantic economy. The Atlantic community which has grown over sixty years – and in a larger but weaker sense, over four hundred years – defended itself like a human body fighting off a virus'. Listening to this 'chorus of fellow-spirits on both sides of the Atlantic', who together with him have been 'arguing against the stupidity of Europe and America quarrelling while the world burns', has been 'very heartening'.[69] No political writer should want to be original, he explains. That is for poets or novelists. What matters is how many other people are saying the same thing as yourself, and to multiply them.

As a credo of conformism, this has the merit of candour. *Free World* tirelessly repeats the message that 'A Europe that likes the idea of America is a better Europe', just as 'an America that likes the idea of the new Europe is, in turn, supporting another version of itself'. Or, in Thomas Friedman's 'punchy' dictum, which Garton Ash cites with approval: 'I support united Europe, because I believe two United States are better than one.'[70] Indeed. Today's Garton Ash risks becoming a pallid British version of his American counterpart, less crass and truculent, but also less iconoclastic and forthright. He has little appetite for the brutal truths relished by Friedman. Where the style of the American is to *épater*, the instinct of the Englishman is to *adoucir*, in the accents of the Foreign Office. Garton Ash once indignantly denied he could be associated with another US plain-talker, Zbigniew Brzezinski.[71] A little later, he explained that he always found him 'lucid, incisive, far-reaching and stimulating', and was hard put to disagree with his 'analysis and policy recommendations,

---

69. *FW*, pp. 127, 250.
70. *FW*, p. 232.
71. *London Review of Books*, 3 December 1999, replying to remarks made above on *The History of the Present*.

especially those on NATO and EU enlargement'.[72] But one point still stuck in the craw. Brzezinski should not say that Europe is a military protectorate of the US. That was not only inaccurate, but 'unhelpful'. The adjective speaks worlds: a euphemism to protect euphemisms, from the catacombs of the civil service.

2005

---

72. Symposium on 'Living with a New Europe', *The National Interest*, summer 2001, p. 32.

II. PHILOSOPHY

4

DESIGNING CONSENSUS:

John Rawls

No work of modern political philosophy, in any language, has generated such an enormous output of learned commentary as John Rawls's *Theory of Justice*. After some twenty years of uninterrupted critical flow, Rawls's new book is billed as a correction of the original, in the light of subsequent discussion. *Political Liberalism* offers abundant – even super-abundant – evidence of careful response to the reception of *A Theory of Justice*, in a forest of footnotes to different readings of it. But the attention proves selective, and the result disconcerting. Rawls's pristine theory argued for two fundamental principles of justice: first in order – equal political rights and liberties for all, and second – only such social or economic inequalities as are compatible with equal opportunity, and yield most benefit to the least well off. These principles, Rawls maintained, would infallibly be chosen by us if we were to imagine ourselves deciding the form of a just society from the hypothetical standpoint of an 'original position', without any knowledge of what might be our particular lot within it. Around this core doctrine, conceived as an updated variant of Kantian constructivism to supersede all latter-day forms of utilitarian calculus, Rawls developed a capacious intellectual edifice, culminating in ethical reflections of noble scope.

Out of the huge literature set off by this construction, what were to be the most pregnant objections to it? Four stand out as most significant. Firstly, the device of the original position was widely convicted of circularity. In order to get the parties in the original position to produce his principles of justice, Rawls had surreptitiously to endow them with sympathies that only the principles themselves could induce. The logical circle betrays the historical *petitio principi*. In effect, far from being a genuinely aboriginal condition, like the state of nature posed in earlier social-contract theory, Rawls's position originates in assumptions possible only with the advent of developed industrial capitalism. The 'veil of ignorance' draped around his actors is all too diaphanous: beyond lies the familiar landscape of an established – if not enacted – morality. Among the most obvious signs of the restrictive context of Rawls's theory is the 'lexical' ordering of the principles of justice themselves, object of the second common criticism of it. Why should equal liberties always have priority over equal sufficiencies? Material subsistence is a condition of any juridical existence, and its demands have for most of human experience been overriding.

In the advanced capitalist countries of today, the claims of absolute need are rarer than those of relative deprivation. How satisfactory is Rawls's formula for meeting these? The 'difference principle' – warranting only those inequalities which are to the greatest benefit of the least advantaged – is the most memorable single thesis of *A Theory of Justice*. But what is its actual import? The massive ambiguity of the Rawlsian theory of justice lies at precisely this point. Is the difference principle a powerful call for an all but socialist redistribution of income – since, on one reading, so little of the glaring disparities of wealth that surround us contributes to the well-being of the poor? Or is it, on another reading, simply a sensible defence of the normal operation of capitalism – whose constant increase of productivity, raising general living standards, requires precisely the incentive structures, tried and tested by experience, we have today? To grasp the full depth of the indeterminacy at the crux of Rawls's construction, it is enough to note that it can be applauded imperturbably at one extreme by John Roemer on the Left, and at another by Friedrich Hayek on the Right, each contending that its message coincides with their own.[1] Clearly, both cannot be right. But Rawls's *Theory*, in which the legitimacy of socialism can be mooted on one page and American society held 'nearly just' on the next, leaves space for either view. It might be said that, within its framework, the difference principle is politically indifferent.

Outside the framework altogether lie the problems of justice conceived on an international scale. The last of the major criticisms of Rawls's work has always been the anachronism of its territorial assumptions. Not just the West, but the nation-state formed the boundary of its imagination.

---

1. Compare Hayek, *Law, Legislation and Liberty*, Vol. 2, *The Mirage of Solid Justice*, London 1976, pp. xx, 100, 185, with Roemer, *A Future for Socialism*, Cambridge, Mass., 1994, pp. 26–27.

Twenty years on, what does Rawls have to say about these issues? On the whole, very little. The idea of the original position, he reiterates, is a device of representation – its outcome thus 'hypothetical and nonhistorical'. Yet the parties to it 'must take organizational requirements and economic efficiency into account' – in other words, have internalized modern capitalist imperatives ('thus it is unreasonable to stop at equal division') of an eminently historical kind.[2] On the other hand, the priority of civic liberty over social equality, Rawls now concedes, is 'not required under all conditions', but presumes 'reasonably favourable circumstances' of prosperity and literacy.[3] The principle of liberty, however, 'can easily be preceded by a lexically prior principle that citizens' basic needs be met' – without, apparently, further need of adjustment to his scheme.[4] What, then, of the difference principle? Unlike the principle of liberty, it is unsuitable for constitutional codification, for its interpretation is nearly always contestable, resting on 'complicated inferences and intuitive judgements that require us to assess complex social and economic information about topics poorly understood'.[5] That is all the reader gets – in effect, a keep-off sign to the curious. Treatment of international relations is even more clipped. These are merely 'problems of extension', which Rawls 'leaves aside' to concentrate on 'the fundamental question of political justice'.[6]

Political Liberalism, in other words, deflects or ignores all the classical difficulties raised by *A Theory of Justice*. It addresses instead a less obvious one. In his original work, Rawls argued that stable realization of the principles of justice required a well-ordered society, in which citizens shared a certain moral outlook – a sense of the good complementing a sense of the right. The latter third of the book, entitled 'Ends', explored the shape of such a vision. It is this conclusion, Rawls has decided, that was misguided. For it amounted to a 'comprehensive philosophical doctrine' whose effect was not, as he had earlier believed, to fortify the principles of justice, but to jeopardise them. Why should this be so? Because, he now argues, in a modern society there will always be a variety of comprehensive doctrines that are reasonable, if incompatible. Any attempt to make one of them the basis of public reason must therefore be divisive and

---

2. *Political Liberalism*, New York 1993, pp. 24, 281–282. Henceforward *PL*.
3. *PL*, pp. 297.
4. *PL*, p. 7.
5. *PL*, pp. 229–230.
6. *PL*, pp. 20–21.

sectarian – a project that could only succeed by an intolerant use of state power, cancelling the first principle of justice itself.

The cure is to be found in the title of the new book. What does the formula *Political Liberalism* denote? The antonym of 'political' here is not – as it once would have been – 'economic', a liberalism never mentioned in these pages, but 'metaphysical'. By this Rawls means the larger account of values taught by Kant or Mill, and sketched in their spirit by *A Theory of Justice*. In a strict sense, Rawls's new book is thus not a development of his earlier work: it is an amputation of it. The burden of *Political Liberalism* is an intellectual renunciation, rather than any substantive addition. For Rawls this is no real loss. He believes his basic theory becomes the stronger for this sacrifice. For in the new version the principles of justice require only a loose 'overlapping consensus' between the various contending doctrines in society, rather than any deeper sense of ultimate ends shared by its citizens. The more modest aim is a gain in realism, as well as a check against temptation.

How persuasive is this change of mind? It is not hard to resist it. Contrary to his hopes, Rawls's new construction is more fragile than the old. *A Theory of Justice* presupposed a historical time and a national space, but abstracted from them to generate ostensibly timeless principles. *Political Liberalism* introduces history and sociology directly into its justificatory structure, but in a way that exposes rather than heals the original contradiction. For the whole book depends on the thesis that a plurality of incompatible – but reasonable – comprehensive doctrines is a permanent feature of modern societies. But Rawls offers no evidence for this claim, which he seems to think so obvious as to require none. He simply alludes to the religious conflicts of the sixteenth and seventeenth centuries, notes the growth of toleration that followed them, and then concludes that nevertheless 'the fact of religious division remains'.[7] Given the relentless advance of secularization in all European societies, the fate of supernatural beliefs today tells, of course, against rather than for Rawls's assumption. Perhaps American anachronism here has misled him. More likely, however, would seem to be a certain philosophical innocence. The large body of social theory, from many different standpoints, that insists on increasing cultural homogenization as the trend-line of historical development – it includes names all the way from Kant and Hegel to Parsons and Gellner, not to speak of Bell or Fukuyama or

---

7. *PL*, p. xxiv.

any number of others – appears scarcely to have registered. The point is not that this tradition of thought is necessarily right, but that serious historical evidence and argument is needed to prove it wrong. For this purpose, appeal to theological survivals is futile.

Is it unfair to Rawls to tax this illustration too heavily? It would be good to think so. But his only other examples of the doctrinal plurality prompting the revision of his theory suggest otherwise. What are the comprehensive doctrines whose conflict disables the conclusions of *A Theory of Justice*? In his 'model case', they number a tolerant Protestantism in the spirit of Locke, and 'liberal moral doctrines such as those of Kant or Mill' – elsewhere subdivided into 'Kant's moral philosophy' versus 'the utilitarianism of Bentham and Sidgwick'.[8] It is enough to consider this list to see how trifling the claim of grand incompatibilities actually is. Locke's brand of Calvinism, which did not even give birth to a sect, is long forgotten. Who imagines Kant's imperative is a significant civic inspiration? Where is Bentham's calculus respected? How many recollect so much as Sidgwick's name? The reality is that *comprehensive* philosophical doctrines, of the kind of which Rawls repents, have all but vanished from the contemporary scene. His own retraction is just one more instance of the process he has failed to see, which undermines his grounds for it. One might say that the history he has let into his theory, like air into a sealed tomb, tends to disintegrate rather than preserve it. The only real candidates left for the role of all-purpose visions are, in fact, religious; and to give force to the idea of an 'overlapping consensus' as the suitable support for the principles of justice, Rawls is obliged – though not without a tremor of compunction – to declare all major world faiths 'reasonable' doctrines that are capable of accepting them.[9] Here distance from reality becomes all but absolute: as if the office of the philosopher was neither to interpret the world nor to change it, but simply to change its interpretations.

Paradoxically, however, Rawls himself is unable to live up to his own self-denying ordinance. For the political liberalism that is supposed to exclude metaphysical vision rests, as he explains, on a 'conception of the person' that is a quite traditional species of ontological construct. This is a figure endowed with 'two moral powers' (and two only): the capacity for a sense of 'justice' as what is 'reasonable', and for an idea of the 'good' as what is 'rational', which together make possible a

---

8. *PL*, p. 145, 169.
9. *PL*, p. 170.

society conceived as 'fair cooperation'.[10] Where does Rawls find this
person? Not, he confesses, in any 'account of human nature as given
by natural science and social theory'. Rather, it is a 'normative conception'.[11] Where do the norms, then, come from? Not from any
comprehensive philosophical doctrine, but from 'plain truths now
widely accepted, or available, to citizens generally'.[12] What guarantees
these truths? They are 'the conceptions of the person and of social
cooperation most likely to be congenial to the public culture of a democratic society'.[13] In other words, where older doctrines grounded their
ideas of identity or value in principled argument, the new dispensation
simply appeals to the status quo of our democratic culture – or what
purports to be such. In actual fact, of course, most citizens would be
bemused by Rawls's shortlist of their moral powers, which is essentially a residue of what was once a coherent ethical vision, like one of
the broken shards of *After Virtue*. Extracted from their metaphysical
seat, they are now assigned inappropriate lodging in the sprawl of
public opinion, where they do not belong.

Beyond the fiction of their domicile, however, there is a more
serious effect of Rawls's move. What was a latent and subtle circularity in *A Theory of Justice* becomes a gross and explicit one in *Political
Liberalism*. For Rawls simultaneously appeals to the natural outlook
of a democratic society to found his conception of the person, and to
his conception of the person to found the basic structure of a democratic society. The warrant of the doctrine of two moral powers is that
it 'suits' a society in which justice is conceived as fairness; and the
warrant of justice as fairness, with its schedule of fundamental principles and primary goods, is that it 'protects' the exercise of the two
moral powers. The attenuated idea of a person is the theoretical
plinth of a desirable constitution, determining what count as primary
goods 'in advance' of any further requirements of social life[14] – yet is
also no more than an ideological reflex of the culture it is supposed to
generate. In a vicious circle, public arrangements are deduced from
personal capacities defined as adapted to public arrangements.

More than logical error is at issue here. What the structure of
Rawls's argument indicates is a more fundamental feature of his
thought. This is an amphibious world, which contains just enough

---

10. *PL*, p. 19.
11. *PL*, p. 18.
12. *PL*, p. 225.
13. *PL*, p. 339.
14. *PL*, p. 308.

land of real social reference to avoid the tricky deeps of first philosophy (the gesture is roughly: let's start out from where we're at – in other words, Bush–Clinton country), while floating carefully enough on the waters of abstraction to avoid contact with the ground of actual political change (for example: what has happened in the US since the 1970s). The result is a kind of political *cabotage*, a critique of existing society that clings nervously to its shores. Readers of Rawls might well ask: where is the actual justice in the United States that corresponds to the ideal construct he offers us, if it is based on 'plain truths widely accepted by citizens'?[15] The question is never answered. *Political Liberalism* no longer speaks of any contemporary order as 'nearly just', but rather of a 'moderately well-governed democratic society'.[16] The social polarization of the last twenty years might never have occurred. In the entire book, the only place name from the geography of contemporary America is Malibu. The misery and despair, the greed and violence, of the daily urban scene are far away. The social infernos of *City of Quartz* could be on another planet.

Rawls's preoccupations lie elsewhere. He remarks in passing that the tendency of markets is for 'background justice to be eroded even when individuals act fairly',[17] without vouchsafing any explanation for this process, and approves of the principle of fiscal redistribution. But 'social and economic inequalities in the life prospects of citizens depending on their social origins' are nevertheless 'inevitable, or else necessary or highly advantageous in maintaining effective social cooperation'.[18] How far the difference principle might mitigate such inequalities is a matter too technical and sub-constitutional to detain the reader. By contrast, the state of the 'basic liberties' that have priority in the scheme of justice does merit sustained concern. Rawls devotes the two most engaged sections of the book to them. The issues he singles out for critical discussion are free speech and campaign finance. The case for the former, he argues, is not to be qualified in the name of protecting the constitution from revolutionary doctrines, on the grounds that they represent a 'clear and present danger' to the legal order – there could be restrictions on free political speech only if there were a general constitutional crisis such as a

---

15. *PL*, p. 225.
16. *PL*, pp. 347–348.
17. *PL*, p. 267.
18. *PL*, p. 270.

well-governed democracy precludes in the first place. Hence 'the free public use of our reason in questions of political and social justice would seem to be absolute'.[19] The sentiment is admirable, but the arguments used to support it are often surprisingly lax. So committed is Rawls to his conclusion that he maintains – in defiance of the obvious – that the First Amendment could not be constitutionally repealed, since whatever the Congress might do or the Court might say, it is 'validated by long historical practice'; even pronouncing the Sedition Act retroactively 'unconstitutional', whatever its validity at the time, because 'it has been tried by the court of history and found wanting'.[20] These are not exactly Kantian reasons, but they are consistent with a new inclination to find ad hoc warrants for the objects of Rawls's sympathy, wherever they are at variance with the logic of his theory. Protestant religion is manifestly a comprehensive doctrine of the kind *Political Liberalism* debars from a legitimate role in the discourse of public reason. Martin Luther King nevertheless slips past, since his biblical appeals 'fully support constitutional values' – likewise Abraham Lincoln, but on opposite grounds, that his pieties have 'no bearings on constitutional essentials'.[21] No doubt the same could be said of George Bush's call to prayer in 1991 as the bombers took off for Baghdad, but it unlikely Rawls would do so.

Free speech is not under serious threat in the United States today. Fair elections, on the other hand, are all but out of reach. Rawls's acknowledgement of the extent of their denial by the power of money is the one radical departure of *Political Liberalism*, where it moves beyond rather than behind *A Theory of Justice*. Equal political liberties, Rawls now stresses, are not enough – they must also be of equal practical worth, which they cannot be so long as elections are fought and won by force of superior wealth. Expressing dismay at Supreme Court rulings that have struck down (mostly nominal) limits on private expenditures in the campaign process, he envisages a measure of public funding of elections to assure 'fair value' to each citizen's political rights.[22] But there the matter rests. What institutional structures are required, for the first principle of justice to acquire reality, remains unfathomable – here once again, 'how best to proceed is a complex and difficult matter', in which 'the requisite historical

---

19. *PL*, p. 355.
20. *PL*, pp. 239, 343.
21. *PL*, pp. 250, 254.
22. *PL*, p. 328.

experience and theoretical understanding may be lacking'.[23] On closing *Political Liberalism*, the reader is no nearer a sight of electoral reform in the United States than when opening it. Rawls does not seem to have noticed that for political liberties to have equal worth, there would have to be the elementary change of proportional representation in the voting system, as well as equitable funding of the campaigning system. There is no hint in these pages that in 'the oldest democratic regime in the world',[24] half of the population never even votes. Instead we are invited – *inter alia* – to patriotic contemplation of 'the pride of a democratic people in distinguishing themselves from nondemocratic peoples'[25] (*sic*). The category of a non-democratic people is an unexpected political *trouvaille*.

Political Liberalism, as most of its reviewers have found, is a disappointing book. Its formal organization is poor, still bearing too many traces of the discrete lectures out of which it has been assembled, with a high rate of repetition and lack of independent direction. It belongs with that peculiar sub-set of books in which an author sets out to correct or defend a celebrated earlier work, and succeeds only in producing an arid shadow of it – Michel Foucault's *Archaeology of Knowledge* or Alasdair MacIntyre's *Whose Justice? Which Rationality?* are companion cases that come to mind. The experience of reading it is one of regret. The imperfect dignity of *A Theory of Justice* remains. If Rawls has taken the wrong turning away from it, a path of reduction rather than enlargement, the reason lies in part in a parochial self-enclosure of his intellectual world, now populated all but exclusively by like-minded colleagues and pupils. But it is also a consequence of the impossible desire that haunts his programme, what – adapting a phrase from Kant – we might call his unconforming conformity: the dream of extracting a radical alternative to our existing social world from the lineaments of its own description of itself. The contradiction between the postulates of consensus, to which Rawls continually subscribes, and the realities of dissensus, to which his best impulses belong, is incurable. There is no starker expression of it than the innocent passage from one key sentence to the next in the agenda of *Political Liberalism*. 'The aim', Rawls writes, is 'to work out a conception of political and social justice which is congenial to the most deep-seated convictions and traditions

---

23. *PL*, p. 328.
24. *PL*, p. 239.
25. *PL*, p. 204.

of a modern democratic state. The point of doing this is to see whether we can resolve the impasse in our recent political history; namely, that there is no agreement on the way basic social institutions should be arranged if they are to conform to the freedom and equality of citizens and persons.'[26] If the modern state is as described, deep in its democratic convictions and traditions, how could there possibly be a deadlock over the realization of freedom and equality for its citizens? The two halves of the statement fall apart. If he had pursued the logic of the second, rather than the will o'the wisp of the first, becoming less congenial to the state and more attentive to the impasse, Rawls would have written a better book. The needed sequel to his major work had another title – A Theory of Injustice.

1994

---

26. *PL*, pp. 300, 368.

5

NORMING FACTS:

Jürgen Habermas

What is still the most widely read of Jürgen Habermas's works is nearly the first: *The Structural Transformation of the Public Sphere*, published in 1962, when he was in his early thirties. Its enduring international influence is due to the way it combined historical, sociological and philosophical arguments in a single powerful narrative that spoke to the political present. In its striking interdisciplinary form, it remained truer to the original intentions of critical theory, as Horkheimer had proposed them in the early thirties, than any work of the pre-war Frankfurt School itself. In theme, however, the book offered a sharply revised account of the Enlightenment on which Adorno and Horkheimer had delivered their pitiless verdict twenty years earlier. The story told by *Dialectic of Enlightenment* was one of the hardening of reason into myth from its very inception: domination of nature requiring domination of others and of the self, already figured at the dawn of civilization in Homer's image of Odysseus lashing himself to the mast, while his oarsmen row beneath him, their ears plugged against the call of the Sirens. Bacon, Kant and Sade mark so many further steps in the instrumentalization of reason, in a logic of regression that can only end in the modern barbarisms of anti-Semitism and the culture industry of advanced capitalism – not as negations of Kant's conception of Enlightenment as the self-disciplined maturity of humanity, but as the bitter fulfilment of it.

The Structural Transformation of the Public Sphere is antithetical in method and argument. It proceeds, not by dramatic – and dramatically arbitrary – discursive projection, but by careful historical reconstruction, based on controllable empirical materials. It restores the origins of the Enlightenment to a determinate period and region, the late seventeenth and eighteenth centuries in Western Europe, rather than swathing them in the archaic mists of the Aegean. Most decisively, it switches the focus of enquiry from instrumental to what Habermas would later call communicative reason: that is, not conquest of nature, but consensus among persons, arrived at by a rational-critical exchange of views within an emergent public sphere, independent of the power of absolutism. Habermas traces the rise of this sphere through its successive institutional circuits: the conjugal family, the world of letters, the coffee-house and salon, the weekly and the novel, the circulating library and the newspaper, culminating in the codification of civil law that ushered in the bourgeois-constitutional state. Habermas furnishes a warm and vivid phenomenology of this whole process, as an impressive triumph of reason in its time.

Once so constituted, however, the public sphere of the Enlightenment began to reveal internal strains. Hegel pointed to the particularistic antagonisms within civil society, that could only be resolved in the universality of the state. Marx showed that the state was by no means universal, since it reflected a class-divided society – only democracy could make it so. Mill and Tocqueville perceived that democracy might induce mass conformity, and public opinion itself become a tyranny. These nineteenth-century tensions and forebodings had, by the mid-twentieth century, acquired daunting material shape. For the public sphere created in the time of the Enlightenment was now utterly altered.

Where state and society had once been separate, they now interpenetrated, as the economy became increasingly regulated and organized pressure groups invaded the administration. Corporations blurred the distinction between private and public institutions. The family was losing its role in socialization. Culture was ceasing to be a domain of critical reasoning, and becoming one of mere ideological consumption, as the massification of the means of communication – publishing, press, radio – tended to destroy genuinely independent publics. Political decisions had migrated away from parliaments, no longer reflecting the upshot of disinterested argument in a rational consensus, but rather compromises between special interests of different bargaining strength. Deputies in political assemblies were becoming passive implements of party machines, and elections increasingly reduced to the extraction of acclamations. At the end of this road would lie an all but complete decline – economic, social, familial, cultural and political – of the whole Enlightenment complex of the public sphere into mere 'publicity' or 'public relations', in their debased contemporary meanings.

Such developments might seem to trace the path of a destruction of communicative reason whose end-point would, paradoxically, not be so far from the bleakest outcome of Horkheimer and Adorno's dialectic of instrumental reason: the perdition of Enlightenment by another route. But Habermas did not think all was lost. The public sphere could be saved if the liberal-constutional state of the nineteenth century evolved into a social-welfare state, in which the effective participation of all citizens was secured by a consistent publicization of parties, of the media, and of administration, bringing these under democratic controls and so rationalizing the necessary exercise of social and political authority. But was the idea of a rational consensus around such goals not utopian, when unequal power relations profiting from the decline of the public sphere still obtained? Habermas admitted that the advent of the liberal-constitutional state itself had not come about by sheer force of the better argument, winning all hearers to the persuasion of a common reason. A divisive will had also been needed: 'the authority to legislate had so obviously been won in a tough struggle with the old powers that it could not be absolved from having the character of a "coercive power" itself'.[1]

But the prospect of a democratized social-welfare state could only be contemplated under the sign of union, not division. How could the necessary consensus for one be reached, in so unequal a society? The possibility of a harmonious agreement, Habermas ended by suggesting, lay in two developments. On the one hand, the onset of general abundance made it 'not unrealistic to assume that the continuing and increasing plurality of interests may lose the antagonistic edge of competing needs to the extent that the possibility of mutual satisfaction comes within reach'. On the other, the dangers of nuclear annihilation were 'so total that in relation to them divergent interests can be relativized without difficulty'.[2] The end of scarcity and the risks of self-destruction offered the chance of a united humanity, without need for the divisive struggles of the past.

Two decades later, Habermas had ceased to believe in the possibility of a self-governing society of the kind he envisaged in *Structural Transformation of the Public Sphere*. But he had come to the conclusion that this was no loss. Parsons was a better guide to modernity than Marx: the impersonal systems of the market and of bureaucratic administration were functional imperatives of a rational society,

---

1. *Strukturwandlung der Offentlichkeit*, Neuwied, 1968 edition, p. 94: *The Structural Transformation of the Public Sphere*, Cambridge, Mass., 1991, p. 82: 'coercive power' is *Gewalt* in the original, or violence.
2. *Strukturwandlung*, pp. 254–255; *Structural Transformation*, pp. 234–235.

inherently resistant to popular control. But that did not mean any diminution of the prospects for freedom or reason; rather it opened the way to a sounder basis for them. *The Theory of Communicative Action* (1981/85), in which Habermas engaged directly with Horkheimer and Adorno's *Dialectic of Enlightenment*, argued that the instrumental reason that necessarily governed the realms of money and power, the proper domain of systems theory, could and should be held in check by a communicative reason welling up from the life-world beyond them, in which action – in families, schools, voluntary associations, cultural ventures and the like – was oriented not to material success but to mutual understanding.

As capitalist modernization proceeded ever further in contemporary conditions, there was a danger of the systems colonizing the life-world: economic or technocratic pressures invading the natural forms of intimacy or sociability, and twisting them out of shape. But resistance to this overstepping tended to arise spontaneously within the life-world itself, as social movements and citizen initiatives – pacifist, feminist, environmentalist or other – contested such incursions. The arena in which these battles were fought out was the public sphere, intermediate between the two constitutive zones of modern society. The life-world could not hope to submit the systems to its own logic: historically, any such attempt – the idea of a producers' or any other kind of direct democracy – would lead to a fatal regression. But its impulses were capable of influencing the world of capital and government indirectly, in the form of a public opinion that at the limit could lay siege to the fortresses of money and power, even if it could never capture them.

Ten years later, looking back at *The Structural Transformation of the Public Sphere*, Habermas explained that if it had been too optimistic about the possibilities of a mass democracy, it had also been too pessimistic about the media, whose role was far more complex than he had allowed, and could often be distinctly positive. He was both more sanguine about the contemporary vitality of the public sphere, and less defiant than he had been.[3] What he meant by this comes most clearly into view in the work that appeared a few months later, and remains the major expression of his political philosophy to date. *Between Facts and Norms* is a homage to the role of law as the medium in which communicative power is converted into administrative power, freeing

---

3. 'Further Reflections on the Public Sphere', in Craig Calhoun (ed.), *Habermas and the Public Sphere*, Cambridge, Mass., 1992, pp. 438, 456–457.

actors in the life-world from the burdens of social integration by transferring these into a self-steering system. For legal norms, Habermas explains, possess at once facticity and validity. Based on both coercion and freedom, they form a set of constraints that must be obeyed to avoid sanctions, yet whose authority is grounded in more than fear of retribution. For the sources of the law lie in the social solidarities of the life-world, whose unforced communication confers a legitimacy on its rules beyond mere legality. So enabled, law can then not only reconstruct such institutions of the life-world itself as the family or the school, but also – more importantly – create the decisive new systems of modernity: markets, businesses, bureaucracies.

What guarantees that such conversion of springs of the life-world into dictates of the systems are indeed legitimate? Habermas's answer is that this becomes comprehensible once we understand democracy correctly, as the necessary flow of an unimpeded discourse towards consensus. So conceived, there is an internal relationship between the rule of law and democracy: private rights and public autonomies – let us say, freedom of expression and the vote – are co-original, rather than rank-ordered or sequenced, as in other standard accounts. The validity, as distinct from the facticity, of law derives from the procedures born of this connection. No collective subject is possible, authorizing legislation, as Rousseau or Jefferson had once envisaged. Rather, the democratic process that underlies modern law is a flux of 'subjectless communication' in an inescapably decentred society. But as such, it is modelled on the claims to truth embedded in the conditions of speech itself, that must seek unconstrained agreement. Citizens who communicate freely will reach a consensus capable of generating laws that are universally binding.

Habermas is aware how far such a vision is from the long and distinguished tradition, starting from Hobbes and continuing through to Weber, Schmitt and beyond, that sees law in realist fashion as a codification of power rather than of fellowship, finding its origin not in reason but in will, to use the terms of *Structural Transformation*. But he no more lingers on their negation of his assumptions than on the positivist theory of law that produced such great jurists as Kelsen or Hart; still less on the scepticism of contemporary critical legal studies. For such alternatives fail to grasp that legitimacy is inseparable from true legality, which cannot therefore be reduced to the contingencies of a sovereign command or an unappealable *Grundnorm*, or partisan judicial rulings. In this like the later Rawls, the Habermas of *Between Facts and Norms* inhabits a mental world in which virtually the only significant interlocutors are colleagues or pupils close enough not to derange any of the basic premises of the work.

The position is not quite the same with democracy. Here Habermas is more concerned to contrast his theory with the two rival contenders for a modern interpretation of its structure: liberalism, which views the negative freedoms of the individual as the foundation of any democratic order, and republicanism, which sees the active participation in public life of the citizen as the criterion of any real democracy. *Between Facts and Norms* situates itself between the two. A discourse theory of democracy, Habermas explains, is stronger than a liberal model of it, since it insists that positive freedoms – the right to vote and its concomitants – are not secondary to negative freedoms, but stand on an equiprimordial footing with them. But it is weaker than a republican model of democracy, since it requires no classical *virtù* from its citizens, and has abandoned the idea that their deliberate will could shape the life of the city.

For popular sovereignty can no longer be conceived as collective self-determination: its content is exhausted by competition between parties in a parliamentary system, and the autonomy of public spheres. Where does this leave the latter, whose decline Habermas once lamented? In keeping with the affirmative character of his new vision of Western democracy, at least formally in better fettle. The image of citizens arrayed in the public sphere laying siege to a – salutarily – untakable fortress of administration in *Theory of Communicative Action*, Habermas now explains, was too defeatist. Modern democracy should rather be envisaged as a core complex of parliamentary, judicial and bureaucratic institutions, and a periphery of social solidarities in the life-world, whose impulses flow towards the centre through the 'sluices' of the public sphere at its entrance, irrigating them with innovative norms or proposals, capable of reforming – to a certain extent, perhaps even democratizing – administration itself. It is therefore wrong, Habermas concludes, to think that because popular sovereignty must be conceived as 'subjectless communication' rather than self-governing agency, it thereby loses all radical potential. But if the triumph of the West in the Cold War has put paid to the dangerous delusions of a collective subject, the victors have so far been timorous in extending the scope of the 'higher level inter-subjectivity' in which the legal system of democracies is anchored. *Between Facts and Norms* shows why they could have greater courage.

How is this extended theoretical construction to be judged? The first, and most obvious, feature that separates Habermas's later treatment of law from his original study of the public sphere is its completely unhistorical method. Where *Structural Transformation* carefully traces the emergence of the different constituent elements of its object through time, and to some extent also across space – touching on its distinctive trajectories in England, France and Germany – *Between Facts and Norms* not only makes scant reference to the actual genesis, let alone variation, of modern legal systems: it is built on a postulate that is contradicted by the slightest glance at the history of constitutional law. In no country were private liberties and public rights ever co-original. Habermas is aware of this, at one point briefly noting Marshall's account of the successive emergence of civil, political and social rights, and rightly criticizing it as too linear – even observing that a constitutional state could grant the first and third without the second.[4] But the recognition is purely parenthetical, without incidence on the structure of his theory, which proceeds imperturbably to insist on the philosophical indissolubility of what history has unfailingly sequenced and sundered. Savigny or Dicey, Guizot or Bismarck, might as well never have existed. 'In normative terms', we are blandly assured, 'there is no such thing as a constitutional state without democracy.'[5] So much for the facts of the matter. The notion of 'co-originality' belongs neither to political science nor jurisprudence, but to an anthropological family: the myth of origins.

If history is banished from the architecture of *Between Facts and Norms*, this not is quite true, at least in the same way, of sociology. For Habermas warns us that 'the idealistic content of normative theories' of democracy and law 'has been evaporating under the sun of social science'.[6] This, however, is not simply 'a result of sobering evidence', but rather of 'empiricist folkore' and 'misguided conceptual strategies'. The aim of his intervention is above all directed against 'a false realism that underestimates the empirical impact of the normative presuppositions of existing legal practices'.[7] Thus, while

---

4. For the best exploration of variations in the sequence, see Michael Mann, 'Ruling Class Strategies and Citizenship', in *States, War and Capitalism*, Oxford 1988, pp. 188–209.

5. 'Normativ gesehen, gibt es keinen Rechtsstaat ohne Demokratie'. This pronouncement comes from *Die Einbeziehung des Anderen*, Frankfurt 1996, p. 251; *The Inclusion of the Other*, Cambridge Mass. 1998, p. 215. Henceforward *EA* and *IO*.

6. *Faktizität und Geltung*, Frankfurt 1992, p. 399; *Between Facts and Norms*, Cambridge, Mass., 1996. p. 329. Henceforward *FG* and *BFN*. Habermas revised and adapted the English translation himself.

7. *FG*, pp. 400, 11; *BFN*, pp. 330, xl. The dismissive gesture of 'in the light of empiricist folklore' does not appear in the German.

determined to repel what he calls the 'sociological undermining' of the normative authority of law, he also wishes to show that the sociology of actually existing democracies, properly understood, illustrates rather than contradicts his claims for it.

To do so, he must be able to show that in their fashion legal codes transmit the undistorted flow of communication between equals in the life-world into regulations of the modern state: in other words, that they do not rather reflect the distribution of unequal interests in society at large. To deliver this outcome, Habermas would need an account of contemporary democracies beyond even his powers of idealization. His solution is to sublimate the problem. Not social division between classes, but the technical division of labour in the production and diffusion of knowlege, and the (necessary) selectivity of the communications media, inevitably create 'asymmetries in the availability of information, that is, unequal chances to have access to the generation, validation, shaping and presentation of messages'. But these are *unavoidable* moments of inertia', since 'even under favourable conditions, no complex society could ever correspond to the model of purely communicative relations'.[8]

How does the legislation that prescribes the rules enforced by the courts then actually emerge? After once again expounding the vision of unconstrained communication flows, driven only by the current of the better argument, passing through the sluices of the public sphere to inform the wisdom of legislators, Habermas casually adds: 'to be sure, the normal business of politics, at least as it is routinely conducted in Western democracies, cannot satisfy such strong conditions'.[9] In practice, 'compromises make up the bulk of political decision-making processes', and are the outcome of bargaining between competing interests, not of intersubjective discourse.[10] Habermas notes that such bargaining 'may rely on power and mutual threats' – i.e.: the antithesis of everything his theory of democracy rests upon – but is undeterred. In situations 'where social power relations cannot be neutralized in the way rational discourse presupposes', the discourse principle can still 'regulate bargaining from the standpoint of fairness', by ensuring that there is an 'equal distribution of bargaining power between the parties'.[11] In other words, no matter how unequal the actual balance

---

8. *FG*, p. 396; *BFN*, pp. 325–326. Italics in the original.
9. *FG*, p. 432; *BFN*, p. 356.
10. *FG*, p. 344; *BFN*, p. 282.
11. *FG*, pp. 204–205; *BFN*, p. 166.

of power between – let us say, to use terms almost never to be found in *Between Facts and Norms* – capital and labour, the legal outcome of a bargaining process between them will be 'fair', provided they are given an equal opportunity to talk to each other. With this wave of the wand, inequality becomes something like equality again after all.

But even with such prestidigitation, what guarantees that laws issuing from particularistic negotiations have any general normative claim? Habermas offers two answers, each as self-contradictory as the other. On the one hand, they are the product of majority rule, which 'retains an internal relation to truth', for majorities may change, and their decisions are revocable by further rational argument, or other coalitions of interest.[12] Yet this proves no barrier to their erosion of the principles of any representative consensus. 'Formally correct majority decisions', Habermas remarks elsewhere, 'that merely reflect the status anxieties and self-assertive reflexes of a middle class threatened with the prospects of social decline, undermine the legitimacy of the procedures and instititutions of the democratic state.'[13] In the opening adverb and adjective, the emptiness of a purely procedural theory of law, as Habermas terms his own, is unwittingly laid bare. Indeed he is compelled to admit at one point in *Between Facts and Norms*, without dwelling on it, that 'often enough, law provides illegitimate power with the mere semblance of legitimacy'.[14] Then what distinguishes legitimate from illegitimate law? Here the answer changes register completely. 'A legal order can be legitimate', he writes, 'only if it does not contradict basic moral principles.'[15] What are such principles? Habermas's reply is radical. 'With moral questions, humanity or a presupposed world republic of citizens constitutes the reference system for justifying regulations that lie in the equal interest of all'.[16] But the moral criterion for the legitimacy of law proves on inspection to be as vacant as the procedural. For what legislation today lies 'in the equal interest' of all the inhabitants of an unimaginably unequal planet? If this were to be the yardstick by which to judge the law books of the Western world, nothing would be left of them.

The internal relationship that *Between Facts and Norms* seeks to establish between the rule of law and democracy logically extends the frailties of its theory of the first to its model of the second. Modern

---

12. *FG*, pp. 200–221; *BFN*, pp. 179–180.
13. *EA*, p. 149; *IO*, p. 123.
14. *FG*, p. 59; *BFN*, p. 40.
15. *FG*, p. 137; *BFN*, p. 106.
16. *FG*, p. 139; *BFN*, p. 108.

societies, Habermas insists, are composed of self-steering systems of money and power, and the social solidarity of the life-world. How should the relationship between these three be conceived? In his 'Further Reflections on the Public Sphere', Habermas had warned again of the dangers of a colonization of the life-world by the systems, and spoke of the need for a new balance between them, in which 'the power of solidarity can prevail over the powers of the other two control resources, ie. money and administrative power, and therewith successfully assert the practical demands of the life-world'.[17] Four years later, this had become simply 'an acceptable balance between money, power and solidarity'; and soon afterwards, the most that could be envisaged was that 'social solidarity may gain sufficient strength to hold its own against against the other two social forces – money and administrative power'.[18] Vague as all of these formulations are, the declension from 'prevail' to 'acceptable balance' to 'hold its own' traces a curve.

Between Facts and Norms has ceased to speak of the colonization of the life-world, whose resources are now said to replenish themselves spontaneously.[19] Nor does it use metaphors of a balance to represent the relations between communicative and instrumental power. The impersonal orders of money and power remain self-steering systems, the domain of discourse at a distance from them. But now the relations between them are depicted in other figures, at once spatial and temporal. The systems constitute the central complex of modernity, of which the life-world becomes the periphery. Between the two lie the locks and canals of the public sphere. The hierarchy of significance implied in this topography scarcely needs to be spelt out. Within the public sphere itself, the role of an active citizenry has dropped precipitously since its birth in the opening chapters of Habermas's portrait of the Enlightenment. Today, he remarks, the spontaneous associations and movements that make up civil society 'do not represent the most conspicuous element of a public sphere dominated by mass media and large agencies, observed by market and opinon research, and inundated by the public relations work, propaganda, and advertising of political parties and groups'.[20]

---

17. 'Further Reflections on the Public Sphere', p. 444.

18. *Die Normalität einer Berliner Republik,* Frankfurt 1995, p. 97; *A Berlin Republic: Writings on Germany,* Lincoln 1997, p. 92; henceforward *NBR* and *BR*; *EA*, p. 289 ('behaupten können'); *IO*, p. 249.

19. *EA*, p. 292; *IO*, p. 252.

20. *FG*, p. 444; *BFN*, p. 367.

What impact can such a reduced zone of undistorted communication have on the operations of government, let alone the market? Habermas defines it in temporal terms. At the centre, the normal business of politics (he does not discuss that of business proper) proceeds largely unaffected by eddies in the periphery. But *under certain circumstances* civil society can acquire influence in the public sphere, have an effect on the parliamentary complex (and the courts) through its own public opinions, and compel the political system to switch over to the official circulation of power'[21] – i.e. what is supposed to be a democratic representation of the will of the citizenry. The italics indicate just how unusual and precarious such episodes are. What triggers them are exceptional emergencies. 'In a perceived crisis situation, the *actors in civil society* thus far neglected in our scenario *can* assume a surprisingly active and momentous role.'[22]

Setting aside the degree of empirical success that movements around such issues have had in actually changing the order of things, the structural point is clear: outbreaks of solidarity in the life-world are the exception, not the rule. They are 'an extraordinary mode of problem solving', which like the fitful seizures of conscience or fear on which they depend can only be sporadic, and must give way if they collide too frontally with the ordinary system of decision-making. 'When conflicts become this intense, the political law-giver has the last word.' For, Habermas confesses, 'discourses do not govern'.[23] In practice, then, the role of the communicative reason that is held to underlie and inform the whole legal-political order of contemporary democracies is peripheral and exceptional within them. Involuntarily, Habermas himself offers the appropriate image of how the system really operates. Earlier, he had spoken of the 'sensors' needed to protect the life-world from the incursions of money and administration, in the language of electronic surveillance and private security firms. *Between Facts and Norms*, explaining how the joint efforts of citizens can on occasion affect the calculations of those who rule them, draws on another metaphor. 'The players in the arena owe their influence to the approval of those in the gallery.'[24] Just so: we are seated at the politics of the spectacle.

---

21. *FG*, p. 451; *BFN*, p. 37. Italics in original.

22. *FG*, p. 460; *BFN*, p. 380. Italics in original. Habermas cites the nuclear arms race, genetic engineering, ecological threats, Third World poverty, feminism and multiculturalism as issues creating a 'crisis consciousness' that has enabled civil society to make its voice heard.

23. *FG*, p. 433; *BFN*, p. 357; 'Further Reflections on the Public Sphere', p. 452.

24. *FG*, pp. 461–462; *BFN*, p. 382.

What of Habermas's own appreciation of the performance? The purpose of his earlier siege model of the role of communicative reason, he has explained, was to oppose the classical idea of revolution – that the state could be conquered, rather than surrounded. Only a gradual and reformist path to change is practicable and moral.[25] But change is indeed needed: the intention of his proceduralist theory of law is to 'tame the capitalist system'.[26] There is no doubting the sincerity of Habermas's conviction of the need to bridle capitalism, as a citizen. But his philosophy allows virtually no way to give it any content. The result is incoherence. The upshot of discourse theory is not merely formal, he insists. Yet at the same time he declares 'this paradigm of law, unlike the liberal and social-welfare models, no longer favours a particular ideal of society, a particular vision of the good life, or even a particular political option'.[27] So no specific proposals follow.[28] But if they do not, that is in part because *Between Facts and Norms* intimates that the necessary changes are already in train. What Habermas's theory offers is to 'provide a certain coherence to the reform efforts that are either under discussion or already under way' – for in practice 'the controversial *realization* of universalist constitutional principles has become a permanent process that is already under way in ordinary legislation'.[29]

But this affirmative vision, to all intents and purposes appearing to underwrite established arrangements *en bloc* as inherently self-improving, is never quite stabilized by the discourse theory of democracy. It is always shadowed and unsettled by more critical observations, without the two ever confronting each other. For Habermas can also write, still invoking the same principles but in antithetical register, that 'growing inequalities in economic power, assets, and living conditions have increasingly destroyed the factual preconditions for an equal opportunity to make effective use of equally distributed legal powers'.[30] Here it is not reform but reaction that sets the pace, voiding the very rights on which the procedural theory of law is based. The incompatibility between the two poles of

---

25. *NBR*, p. 139; *BR*, p. 135, where Habermas also explains why he now rejects a 'siege' for a 'sluice' model of communicative power; *FG*, p. 79; *BFN*, p. 57.

26. *FG*, p. 494; *BFN*, p. 410.

27. *FG*, p. 536 ; *BFN*, p. 445.

28. 'The putting into operation of lofty principles requires institutional imagination. I am not concerned with that': *NBR*, p. 81; *BR* 76.

29. *FG*, pp. 535, 629; *BFN*, pp. 444, 489. Italics in original.

30. *EA*, p. 302 ; *IO*, p. 261.

Habermas's rhetoric is accentuated by a pointed divergence in such prospects for reform as he does cautiously touch on. For the self-steering systems are not equally so in face of the life-world. Habermas can envisage a certain rationalization of administration that would render it more democratic. But this is excluded for the market. 'Power can be democratized; money cannot.'[31]

The dictum says much about its referents. One of the most striking anomalies in the architecture of Habermas's social theory, as set out in *Theory of Communicative Action*, and transferred without modification into *Between Facts and Norms* is the tacit elimination of the institutions of political representation from it. In the trinity – power: money: solidarity – the first denotes administration, that is the bureaucratic machinery of the state, alone. It has to do so, for to describe the elective machinery of the state as a self-steering system would destroy the credentials of the very democracy Habermas seeks to defend and illustrate. Popular sovereignty, in so far as it exists, is lodged first and foremost in these mechanisms of representation. But a paradoxical effect of Habermas's abstractions is to strip them of power, a term he reserves for the impersonal authority of public administration, alien to any exercise of popular will. Occasional concessions to the effect that bureaucratic agencies might be open to a certain 'internal' democratization could be read as a sign of unease with the logic of his schema – a substitute for what it omits. The representative institutions of modern government are a much more obvious object for political reform. But since they do not fit the dichotomy between systems and life-world, they are not allowed even this modicum of alteration.

More telling still, of course, is the immunity to any popular will Habermas's system grants the market. Money cannot be democratized. For better or worse – mainly better – a self-steering capitalist economy is one of the fundamental conditions of modernity, and cannot be reclaimed by the forces of social solidarity even to the extent that public adminstration may be. Economic democracy is, in effect, ruled out as a contradiction in terms. But if capital is structurally untouchable, what remedy is there for the growing economic inequalities that sap, in Habermas's more lucid moments, even the exercise of legal rights? The aim of his theory of law was to tame capitalism. But soon

---

31. *Die postnationale Konstellation*, Frankfurt 1998, p. 119; *The Postnational Constellation*, Cambridge, Mass., 2001, p. 78: the translation omits a limiting 'beispielsweise' from the first clause.

afterwards, he would himself write that 'the hackneyed, cure-all formula calling for the social and ecological "taming' of capitalism" is accepted on all sides'.[32] If so, was it worth devoting five hundred pages to a platitude incapable of checking its reversion to the wilds?

Habermas considers his theory of contemporary democracy more empirical and critical than that of Rawls. 'A sceptical evaluation of current world conditions is the background for my reflections. That is why my way can be distinguished from purely normative conceptions such as John Rawls's theory of justice, admirable as it is in itself.'[33] In his eyes, *Political Liberalism* does not truly repair this limitation, since it suffers from the opposite. The idea of an overlapping consensus is too weak and contingent a basis to ground the normative structure of constitutional democracy, which rests instead on the universal logic of communicative reason embedded in language. Likewise, Rawls's excessive concern with the political stabilization of a constitutional order forgets that 'radical-democratic embers' can be periodically reignited to take it further as a project, rather than simply receiving it as a heritage.[34] The result is to downplay public at the expense of private autonomy within the complex of liberties, in accord with the priority given the second over the first in Rawls's schedule of the principles of justice. To that extent, Habermas concludes that in their respective conceptions of democracy Rawls is a liberal, while he is a republican, albeit a Kantian one.

Rawls, vice versa, makes it clear he regards Habermas's theory as less sharp-edged than his own. Jefferson was wrong to think every generation should be equally constituent; a just constitution had no need of reinvention, but simply execution. Positive and negative liberties are indeed interdependent and of equal standing, but it is an illusion to think that therefore there can be no conflict between them. Habermas's procedural theory of law is less purely so than he presented it. But in taking legitimacy as its normative principle, it is sustantially weaker than a theory of justice as an instrument of political criticism, since legitimacy can be of all kinds – dynastic as much as democratic. In either case, it says nothing about how well the sovereign rules, as justice can. Rawls recalls such 'urgent matters' in the United States as the 'grave imbalance in fair political liberties' caused by private

---

32. *The Past as Future*, Lincoln 1994, p. 158, whose Afterword postdates *Vergangenheit als Zukunft*, Zurich 1990.

33. *NBR*, p. 136; *BR*, p. 132.

34. *EA*, p. 90; *IO*, pp. 69–70.

campaign financing, the 'wide disparities of income and wealth' that undermine equal opportunities in education and employment, the lack of universal health care – issues his theory of democracy could, and did, address in a way that Habermas's does not.[35]

The mutual reproaches are mild, remaining within the bounds of a family quarrel, as Habermas puts it. The kinship between the late work of the two thinkers derives from a common equivocation, more marked and insistent in *Between Facts and Norms* than *Political Liberalism*. What is the status of Habermas's discourse theory? It offers, he says at the outset, a reconstruction of law and democracy that can 'provide a critical standard against which actual practices – the opaque and perplexing reality of the constitutional state could be evaluated'.[36] How does it do so? By taking as its premise 'the idea that the counterfactual self-understanding of constitutional democracy finds expression in unavoidable, yet factually efficacious idealizations that are presupposed by the relevant practices'.[37] It follows there is no '*opposition* between the ideal and the real, for the normative content I initially set forth for reconstructive purposes is partially inscribed in the social facticity of observable political processes. A reconstructive sociology of democracy must therefore choose its basic concepts in such a way that it can identify particles and fragments of an "existing reason" already incorporated in political practices, however distorted these may be.'[38]

In such declarations lies the core strategy of *Between Facts and Norms*. What they trace is the continual movement of a theoretical shuttlecock, from the optative to the indicative and back again, that never comes to ground at either end. If Habermas's account of law and democracy is taxed with a fundamental abstraction from the empirical realities of a political order in which the formation of a popular will is at best fitful or vestigial, it can refer to its counterfactual vocation. If it is taxed with a complete lack of any specification of a desirable alternative, it can refer to the value of what already exists, in a bedrock of communication that only needs to be fulfilled. The result is a theory that answers to the responsibility neither of an accurate description of the real world, nor of critical proposals for a better one. It operates instead in a no man's land between the two, in

---

35. 'Reply to Habermas', in the paperback edition of *Political Liberalism*, New York 1996, pp. 408, 403, 419, 427–428, 407.

36. *FG*, p. 20; *BFN*, p. 5.

37. Postcript (1994) to *BFN*, p. 462.

38. *FG*, p. 349; *BFN*, p. 287.

unwitting mimicry of the title of the book – not law as a mediation, but philosophy as a *passe-passe* between facts and norms. What actual criticisms of the social order issue from the 'critical standard' it offers? Where precisely are we to find the 'efficacity' of the idealizations it discerns in existing practices, and why are these 'unavoidable'? Just how 'partial' is the inscription of norms in observable conducts, and how 'distorted'? What proportion of reality do the 'particles and fragments' of reason add up to? Such questions are beyond the remit of the theory, which is designed to elude them. Its effect is apologetic. Our societies are better than we know.

2004

6

PLOTTING VALUES:
Norberto Bobbio

Norberto Bobbio's intervention on the Right and Left marks a significant moment in the author's long and distinguished career as a political thinker. Published during the Italian electoral campaign of 1994, *Destra e sinistra* is one of his most topical and personal writings, whose popular success in Italy is not hard to understand.[1] Acclaim for its clarity, elegance and feeling is justified. The text, however, is more complex and less conclusive than it may appear. What are its theses?

Bobbio's starting point is the increasing frequency with which the notions of 'Right' and 'Left' are rejected in political discussion today – despite, he points out, their continued and even accentuated use in electoral competition. Why, he asks, is the traditional opposition between Left and Right now so often repudiated? There are currently three ways of contesting the dichotomy, he suggests. The first is to relativize the dyad by insisting on an 'Included Third': namely a moderate Centre situated between Left and Right, occupying most of the actual space of democratic political systems. The second way of rejecting the distinction is to dwell on the prospects of an 'Inclusive Third', integrating and superseding the legacies of Left and Right in some synthesis beyond them. The last is to point to the rise of a 'Transverse Third', penetrating across the camps of Left and Right, and displacing them from relevance – the role, he notes, often accorded Green politics. Bobbio's response to each of these claims is

---

1. Norberto Bobbio, *Destra e sinistra. Ragioni e significati di una distinzione politica*, Rome 1994; a revised and enlarged edition appeared in 1995, to which all page numbers below refer. Translated into English as *Left and Right*, Cambridge 1996. Henceforward *DS* and *LR*.

a firm *fin de non recevoir*. The existence of a Centre, however dominant, does not alter the contrast between polarities of Left and Right on each side of it. Notions of a synthesis beyond Left and Right typically conceal ambitions by one pole to absorb or neutralize the other. Finally, movements of opinion extending across Left and Right tend to redivide, like the Greens, into new versions of them. Nor – Bobbio further observes – do similarities between authoritarian movements of Right and Left, or shifts of individuals from one to the other, affect the political distinction itself. They relate to another opposition, which sets Extremists and Moderates apart in their attitudes to democracy – a fundamental contrast, but one orthogonal to the polarity of Left and Right, which does not cancel it: indeed in situations of crisis tends to yield before it, as in Italy in the early 1920s or 1940s.

If none of these reasons for doubting the validity of the dichotomy between Left and Right is valid, what then explains its intellectual rejection today? The real basis of the current opinion, Bobbio suggests, lies elsewhere. The distinction between Left and Right loses its meaning if one of the two ceases to exist. Without saying so directly, Bobbio implies that historically this has never occurred. But there have been situations in which one side has suffered such a deep defeat that its survivors have tended to argue that the distinction itself has lost all meaning, in a strategy of consolation designed to conceal their own weakness. Such was the stance of the Italian Right in the immediate post-war years, after the debacle of Fascism made the Left seem all-victorious. Today the boot is on the other foot. In the wake of the collapse of Communism, it is above all on the Left – or former thinkers of the Left – that the temptation to deny the distinction can be observed. The real reason for the new scepticism is once again a move of self-protection, compensating for an experience of defeat with a rhetoric of supersession.

Once Bobbio has dismissed the reasons subjectively adduced for discarding the dichotomy of Left and Right, and located the objective reason for the tendency to deny its validity, he has still to found the opposition as a rational political framework that has lost none of its force today. After considering a number of unsatisfactory attempts to do so – coding Right and Left as tradition versus emancipation, sacred versus profane, etc. – Bobbio offers his own definition. The division between Left and Right, he argues, is one of attitude towards equality. Given that human beings are manifestly at once – that is, in different respects – equal and unequal, 'on the one side are those who think men more equal than unequal, while on the other are those who think them more unequal than equal'.[2] This is the permanent, underlying contrast between Left and Right. It is accompanied by another. The Left believes that most inequalities are social and eliminable; the Right that most are natural and unalterable. For the first, equality is an ideal; for the second it is not.

Liberty is not a dividing-line between Left and Right, Bobbio goes on, in the same way. Anyway incommensurable with equality, as the status of a person rather than a relation between persons, it is the value that sets moderates apart from extremists within each camp. But in the opposition between Right and Left, it occupies the position of means rather than ends. Characteristically, Bobbio indulges no pious harmonics. Liberty cannot be equated with equality, and there is no reason to think the two always compatible. If some kinds of equality do not affect liberty, others – necessary constraints, like universal public education – do. It is over issues like these that Left and Right essentially join battle. Bobbio concludes his book with a personal avowal. Equality has always been the 'pole star' of his political life. The inequalities of this world – from the impoverished and excluded within rich Western societies, to the huge mass of misery in the poorer countries – remain staggering. It is enough, he writes, to look out at the 'social question on an international scale, to realize that the Left, far from coming to the end of its road, has only just started out on it'. The task is enormous. But the aspiration for an ever greater human equality, of which the rise of women's liberation is one of the most certain signs today, is – as Tocqueville understood already a century ago – 'irresistible'. Bobbio ends his book by urging us to look beyond the immediate skirmishes of the day, to the long sweep of the 'grandiose historical movement' bearing it forward.[3]

This is a powerful conclusion, that can leave few unmoved. We owe it the kind of intellectual respect Bobbio has always practised – a dispassionate critical scrutiny. Two sets of reflections are prompted by *Destra e sinistra*. One concerns the inner logic of Bobbio's argument, the other its exterior context. Let us look at the first. Bobbio's central claim is that the distinction between Left and Right remains alive and well, since it is based on two fundamentally different views of equality, which set Right and Left permanently apart. In the exposition of this difference, however, he tends to run together a number of propositions that are logically independent of each other. We can

---

2. *DS*, p. 105; *LR*, p. 66.
3. *DS*, pp. 128–132; *LR*, pp. 82–86.

distinguish four of these, which concern what we may stylize as the issues of (1) the factuality; (2) the alterability; (3) the functionality; and (4) the directionality of human inequality. In Bobbio's characterization, the Left holds the view that the natural inequality of human beings is less than their equality, that most forms of inequality are socially alterable, that few if any are positively functional, and that more and more will prove historically ephemeral. The Right, on the other hand, is committed to the view that the natural inequality of human beings is greater than their equality, that few forms of inequality are alterable, that most are socially functional, and that there is no directionality in their evolution.

The two packages thus presented are, however, dissociable. The first element in each poses an initial problem. Since the ways in human beings are at once similar and dissimilar differ so radically – Bobbio's illustration is the common fact of mortality, and the variable forms of death – how could they be aggregated in a single calculus, to yield a final balance? Bobbio's solution is in effect to introduce a specification: only those aspects of their nature that help people to live together – *per attuare una buona convivenza* – will be reckoned into the sum.[4] A conservative might reply that this is to build a *petitio principi* into the calculation from the start. Here we may overlook this difficulty, to note a greater one. There is no necessary connection between the first and second parts of each package. It is quite possible to believe that human beings are naturally more equal than unequal, and yet that most forms of inequality are ineliminable – and it is no less possible to believe that human beings are naturally more unequal than equal, and yet that many social inequalities can and should be eliminated.

These are not mere formal paradoxes. There is, after all, now a considerable literature bearing on the problems they might represent. To take only the second alternative, a growing body of thought has been concerned with the possibility that socially egalitarian programmes could ultimately have a counter-finality: by eliminating artificial forms of inequality, founded on power and culture, they could eventually highlight and crystallize natural forms of inequality far more dramatically than ever before, in a new hierarchical order founded on the genetic code. This was already the vision conjured up in Michael Young's *Rise of the Meritocracy*, the work of a moderate social-democrat in the fifties.[5] More recently, similar projections have come

4. *DS*, p. 105; *LR*, p. 66.
5. Michael Young, *The Rise of the Meritocracy 1870–2033. An Essay on Education and Equality*, London 1958.

from liberal or neo-conservative writers in the United States – Mickey Kaus or Charles Murray. Common to all these authors – who span the spectrum from Left to Right – is the foreboding that class divisions once cancelled, occupations would be determined by biological endowments – essentially degrees of innate intelligence – leading to new and harder forms of stratification, as endogamous strategies of marriage selection, now possessed of accurate genetic knowledge and choosing for comparable DNA, perpetuated a hereditary mental elite.

The validity or otherwise of these visions need not concern us here. What they point to, however, is something that Bobbio's argument passes over. For he writes as if views of human nature – and so of equality or inequality – were a question of ultimate philosophical choice, beyond which is no appeal. But in fact they are subject to scientific evidence, whose volume has been steadily increasing in recent years. Still – he might reply – so far few conclusive findings that bear on his theme have been reached. The prospect of further advance, however, casts a shadow over his distinction. Already, within his scheme, there is no reason why differences of viewpoint about natural or social inequality should be very extensive. Theoretically we could imagine that the natural variation in human beings of the estimated edge either of inequality over equality, or vice versa, was too small to generate any systematic political differences, indeed that there could be crossover in the list of particulars of each (since there is no reason why each side should weight every element consistently by inversion with the assessments of the other). To base the distinction between Left and Right on ontological judgements of the balance between human equality and inequality, in other words, is to rest it on a frail foundation – which the further development of science could strike away, by imposing inescapable convergence on a common empirical standpoint.

What then of the third element in Bobbio's set? Though he gives less attention to this, could it provide a more stable dividing-line? In principle, all parties might agree on the factual balance between natural equality and inequality, and on the alterability or otherwise of social inequalities, yet differ fundamentally over the question of whether the latter should be regarded as functional or dysfunctional for a flourishing society. Here questions of normative evaluation, unamenable to scientific arbitration, would enter into their own. Bobbio might have been expected to dwell on them. In fact, he touches on this third element in his characterization of Right and Left only cursorily, noting that inequalities are often viewed not just as inevitable but also as positive on the Right, without referring much to the opposite standpoint on the Left, which he perhaps took as self-evident.

But here, at any rate, we would appear to be on the surest ground for differentiating Right from Left. Nevertheless, a difficulty arises. Is it the case that the Left, as it actually exists in Europe today, denies all functionality to social inequalities? It is enough to observe the universal tribute paid to the market, and its incentive structures, to realize that this is not so. In many countries, actual indices of economic inequality have, indeed, notoriously increased under administrations of the Left as much or more as under those of the Right. Such has been the practice of recent decades. The theory of productive inequality, of course, has been developed mainly on the Right, above all in the powerful work of Hayek. The Left has by and large adapted to it, with softening but not necessarily effectual caveats. It is perhaps significant that Bobbio has never directly engaged with Hayek. He has, by contrast, referred approvingly to Rawls – the thinker of the moderate Left who has theorized justice as 'fairness', allowing economic inequalities only to the extent that they improve the lot of the worst-off. The formalism of the Difference Principle, however, leaves that extent absolutely indeterminate – potentially justifying virtually every inequality of the existing capitalist order on the grounds of the historically unprecedented productivity, benefiting every poorest citizen, that it has unleashed. It is little surprise Hayek himself could declare his fundamental agreement with Rawls, when *A Theory of Justice* first appeared.

The third component of Bobbio's package is thus more precarious than it seems too. He is aware of the difficulty – that in practice, the economic policies of Left and Right in the West appear to exhibit ever diminishing differences. He tries to resolve it by dismissing the practical 'compromises' the Left may have to make as irrelevant to the 'ideals' it continues to stand for, with which alone his intervention is concerned. But the two cannot so easily be separated. Bobbio himself, after all, appeals to the empirical fact that party politics in Italy has never been so shrilly and insistently coded in terms of Left and Right as today to give weight to his claim that the ideal distinction still holds. But there was a still more striking feature of the Italian electoral campaign of 1994. Never had the programmatic differences between the principal parties been so narrow as they were then – consequent, of course, upon the conversion of the former Communist Party to more or less neoliberal economic doctrines, symbolized by the pilgrimage of its leader to secure the *placet* of the City of London during the campaign. In 1996, the programmatic convergence of the two blocs has gone even further, to the point where each side is now publicly accusing the other of copying its platform. These are facts which tell against Bobbio's ideal types, and from which he cannot consistently insulate them.

Bobbio might reply that if such convergence has occurred in the rich countries, it has not in the poor countries in the world, where the overwhelming task before the Left – he insists – lies. But there too – in Latin America, in Black Africa, in South Asia – privatization and deregulation, the triumph of the market, are the doctrines of the hour, implemented by politicians and parties once of the Left as frequently as by forces of the Right. What does this tell us about Bobbio's fourth proposition – the directional trend of global inequality? Here it is noticeable that there is an asymmetry in his account. When he touches on the last element in his contrast between Left and Right, he refers only to the Left – which is to be encouraged on its path by a longer sense of the movement towards greater equality in human history. What view the Right might take of this prospect Bobbio does not suggest. But we can deduce that it must be unpalatable. Broad directionality of any kind, perhaps, might be thought incompatible with the traditional outlook of the Right.

In fact, however, we have before us a very recent example of a doctrine of the moderate Right with strong directionality, which bears directly on Bobbio's thesis. Famously, Francis Fukuyama's claim is that world history has reached a categorical, though not chronological conclusion, since there is no longer any viable alternative to liberal capitalism, whose incentive structures demand approximately the levels of inequality that now obtain in the advanced countries, and whose dynamic is now visibly starting to draw the poorer countries along the same path, towards a common – necessarily competitive, necessarily inegalitarian – prosperity.[6] Fukuyama could calmly agree with Bobbio that the movement of history is towards greater equality, since this is just what his Hegelian theory of the struggle for recognition recounts. He would merely note that the movement must halt somewhere, and that we can already see its stopping place in the kind of societies we have, give or take a few minor reforms on which all can agree. It is not clear how Bobbio, lacking any comparable historical theory, would reply. His concluding pages form a powerful moral statement. But is it an accident that they equivocate at one crucial point? The long-term trend towards ever greater human equality, Bobbio repeats, is 'irresistible'. Yet he writes in the same breath that this civilizing movement is 'not necessary', but only 'possible'.[7] The contradiction between the two claims needs no emphasis.

---

6. Francis Fukuyama, *The End of History and the Last Man*, London 1993.
7. *DS*, p. 132; *LR*, pp. 85–86.

Bobbio's theoretical defence of the distinction between Left and Right, for all its eloquence, may thus be more vulnerable than it appears. If we ask why this should be so, the answer surely lies in the difficulty of constructing an axiology of political values without coherent reference to the empirical social world. Bobbio often writes as if he could separate his ideal taxonomy from contemporary history, but of course he cannot. In practice he admits the political scenery of the present into his account selectively, for the purposes of his argument. But it is in that present that the deeper reasons and limits of his intervention lie. Bobbio spent the 1950s to the 1980s arguing against the traditions of Italian Marxism, first in their official and then their heterodox forms. From the start he was an outstandingly courageous, consistent and civil opponent of Communism in his own country and abroad, from the standpoint of what he wished to be a liberal socialism. When Communism collapsed in the Soviet bloc, however, Bobbio did not exult. His reaction was the very opposite of triumphalist. While greeting the overthrow of the Warsaw Pact regimes as a great episode of human emancipation, the end of an inverted utopia, his immediate fear was that Western capitalism now lacked any external pressure to reform itself in a more humane direction, of the kind the Soviet threat had once represented, in a world in which the larger part of humanity, outside the zones of Western privilege, remained the damned of the earth.[8]

His presentiment soon took specific shape in Italy, as a swelling chorus of voices on the Left, or former Left, declared the distinction between Right and Left henceforward an anachronism. This was just the kind of reaction to the events of 1989–1991 that Bobbio had warned against. Better than anyone, he could see the psychological springs of it, as he unerringly depicts them in *Destra e sinistra*. Against this relaxation of moral and political tension, he intervened with signal force to reaffirm the enduring identity of the Left. But if this gave all its strength to his polemic, it also fixed its limit. We might say that Bobbio's gaze remained too eastward. From Liberation onwards, he confronted a Left dominated by the most powerful Communist movement in the West, which demanded the best of his intellectual energy. His critique of it always remained much stronger than his alternative to it, after the demise of the Partito d'Azione and

---

8. 'L'Utopia capovolta', *La Stampa*, 9 June 1989, translated as 'The Upturned Utopia', *New Left Review* I/177, September–October 1989; republished in Bobbio's book of the same title, *L'Utopia capovolta*, Turin 1990.

the hopes of a 'liberal socialism' it had embodied for him. He was attracted by what he saw of Labourism in Britain, from a brief acquaintance during the Attlee years. But in Italy there was no equivalent. By the 1970s Bobbio saw himself as more or less a Social Democrat, in a country without Social Democracy. But he never gave the same degree of attention to the dominant Western version of the European Left that he did to the Eastern. Social Democracy remained a benign background haze, rather than an institutional phenomenon sharply focused in its own right.

Perhaps, unconsciously, Bobbio even avoided looking over his shoulder too much at what was taking shape behind him in the Britain of Wilson or Callaghan, the France of Mitterrand, the Spain of González. At all events, it is the repression of this experience that marks the limits of his intervention in *Destra e sinistra*. For by 1994 those who argued against the continuing validity of the categories of Right and Left were, of course, prompted to do so not just by the collapse of Communism in the East but by the demoralized effacement of Social Democracy in the West. The abandonment of full employment, reduction of social security, and universality of neoliberal doctrines for economic growth, put in question the traditional contrast between Left and Right in a more painful and pointed way than Bobbio's formal conspectus admits. The terms Left and Right are themselves, of course, as he concedes, purely relative. A Left could survive in an all-capitalist system – purged of any residual resistance to the market – that was to the Right of anything now in the centre. That would even be true today, if we compared – say – the record of recent Labour rule in New Zealand with that of the Swedish moderates.

In practice, however, it is doubtful how long the vocabulary of Right and Left would persist in such conditions. Europe, which invented the distinction, is inclined to think it has become universal. But that is not the case. In the United States, where a close approximation to an all-capitalist system has long existed, the terms Right and Left retain a limited currency in academic literature, but have virtually no purchase in public or popular discourse. This is not a foible of American cultural tradition, but an accurate reflection of the minimal difference, and sporadic interchangeability, between the country's two parties. It is enough to note that the domestic policies of the Democratic administration headed by Clinton are far more conservative than those of the Republican administration led by Nixon. No clear-cut line of principle, of any sort, separates the two duopolists. A very similiar situation – potentially perhaps even more pronounced – now obtains in Japan, with the liquidation of the former Social-Democratic Party and the split of the LDP. There is no sense in which the current government and opposition in Tokyo, essentially formed from the same magma, can be intelligibly classified as respectively Right or Left. Since the United States and Japan together form the larger and more dynamic part of the advanced capitalist world, there is reason to wonder whether Europe might not move towards the same horizon too.

This is not to argue that the concepts of Left and Right should be abandoned. Bobbio's passionate call to retain them merits our fullest sympathy. But they will not be saved by shutting one's eyes to the evacuation of their content by the trend of established politics today. A purely axiological defence of the idea of the Left, bereft of any historical theory or institutional attack capable of shaking the status quo, will not pass muster. Bobbio once looked to liberal socialism for such a challenge. Today he re-describes social democracy as liberal socialism, in a notable lowering of expectations – yet at the same time describes liberal socialism as a typical figure of the Inclusive Third, whose deceptive attempts to escape the dichotomy of Left and Right he elsewhere criticizes. The lesson of his book, however, is that the opposition between Left and Right has no axiomatic guarantee. If the Left is to survive as a meaningful force, in a world overwhelmingly dominated by the Right, it will have to fight for a real alternative to it.

This does not mean, of course, that the concepts of Left and Right should be abandoned. Bobbio's passionate call to retain them commands every respect. But to shut one's eyes to the evacuation of their content by the trend of established politics since the mid-seventies is not to safeguard, but to attenuate them. A purely axiological defense of the idea of the Left, bereft of any historical account of the present or institutional attack on the status quo, will not resist the turn of the time. Bobbio once looked to liberal socialism for such a challenge. Today he re-describes social democracy as liberal socialism, in a notable lowering of expectations – yet at the same time describes liberal socialism as a typical figure of the Inclusive Third, whose deceptive attempts to escape the dichotomy of Left and Right he elsewhere criticizes. It is a lesson of his book, however, that the opposition between Left and Right has no axiomatic guarantee.

Philosophically, Bobbio's response to the contemporary political condition of the West is the opposite of that of Rawls and Habermas. Where they have sought to efface the difference between *Sein* and *Sollen*, in a continual slide between idealizations of the existing world and factualizations of velleities beyond it, he has held fast to the principles of the legal positivism and political realism that formed him: values and facts are categorically separate domains, that are not to be confused. This is certainly an intellectual advantage he enjoys over them. But it comes at a price: to cut all connexion between the historical and the desirable risks delivering the world to what is undesirable, in the name of the same realism.

1996–2005

7

ARMS AND RIGHTS:
The Adjustable Centre

In the final decade of the the century that has just ended, three of the most distinguished political philosophers of the age turned their attention to the international scene. In the early nineties, each had published what could be seen as a culminating statement of their reflections on the internal life of Western liberal democracies: Jürgen Habermas's *Faktizität und Geltung* (1991), John Rawls's *Political Liberalism* (1993), and Norberto Bobbio's *Destra e sinistra* (1994). There followed, focusing now on external relations between states, Habermas's 'Kant's Idea of Perpetual Peace: At Two Hundred Years' Historical Remove' (1995) and 'The Post-National Constellation and the Future of Democracy' (1998), and Rawls's *The Law of Peoples* (1999).[1] Bobbio, who had started thinking about international relations much earlier, and anticipated many of their concerns in 'Democracy and the International System' (1989), produced more punctual interventions in these years, each arousing major intellectual debates. The apparent alteration in attention of Rawls and Habermas, previously often reproached with lack of concern for global issues, was by contrast striking. In the background to a new set of preoccupations, on the part of all three thinkers, stretched the frieze of world history, as the end of the Cold War brought not pacification of relations between states, but military engagements of a frequency not seen since the

---

1. Bobbio's essay first appeared in the revised third edition of *Il problema della guerra e le vie della pace*, Bologna 1989, and in English in Daniele Archibugi and David Held (eds), *Cosmopolitan Democracy*, Cambridge 1995, pp. 17–41. Habermas's essays appeared in, respectively, *Die Einbeziehung des Anderen*, Frankfurt 1996, pp. 192–236, and *Die postnationale Konstellation*, Frankfurt 1998, pp. 91–169; and in English in *The Inclusion of the Other*, Cambridge 1998, pp. 165–202, and *The Postnational Constellation*, Cambridge 2001, pp. 58–112.

sixties, in the Gulf, the Balkans, the Hindu Kush and Mesopotamia. Each philosopher sought to offer proposals appropriate to the time.

Of the three, it was Rawls who offered the most systematic outline of a desirable international order. *The Law of Peoples* extends the modelling devices of *A Theory of Justice* from a national to a global plane. How is international justice to be realized? Rawls argues that we should imagine an 'original position' for the various peoples of the earth parallel to that for individuals within a nation-state. In it, these collective actors choose the ideal conditions of justice from behind a veil of ignorance concealing their own size, resources or strength within the society of nations. The result, he argues, would be a 'law of peoples' comparable to the contract between citizens in a modern constitutional state. But whereas the latter is specifically a design for liberal democracies, the scope of the former extends beyond them to societies that cannot be called liberal, yet are orderly and decent, if more hierarchical. The principles of global justice that should govern democratic and decent peoples alike correspond by and large to existing rules of international law, and the Charter of the United Nations, but with two critical corollaries.

On the one hand, the Law of Peoples – so deduced from an original position – authorizes military intervention to protect human rights in states that are neither decent nor liberal, but whose conduct brands them as outlaws within the society of nations. These may be attacked on the grounds of their domestic policies, even if they present no threat to the comity of democratic nations, regardless of clauses to the contrary in the UN Charter. On the other hand, the Law of Peoples involves no obligation to economic redistribution between states comparable to the requirements of a justice within democratic states. The Difference Principle, Rawls explains, does not apply between peoples, since the disparities in their wealth are due not to inequality of resources, but principally to contrasts in culture. Each society is essentially responsible for its own economic fate. Better-off peoples have a duty of assistance to those that are historically more burdened by their culture, but this does not extend beyond helping them achieve the sufficiencies needed for a decent hierarchical order. A legal empyreum that conformed to these rules would have every chance of extending the peace that has reigned for more than a century between the world's democracies to all corners of earth. The Law of Peoples, inspired by the long experience of this silence of arms among liberal societies, configures a 'realistic utopia'.

Rawls explains at the outset of *The Law of Peoples* that the basic intention of his work was to offer a contemporary version of Kant's

For a Perpetual Peace: A Philosophical Sketch of 1795. Habermas, proceeding from the same inspiration, sought more explicitly to update Kant, reviewing the posthumous fortunes of his scheme, and where necessary adjusting it to present conditions. War could be abolished, Kant had believed, by the gradual emergence of a federation of republics in Europe, whose peoples would have none of the deadly impulses that drove absolute monarchs continually into battle with each other at the expense of their subjects – the drive for glory or power. Rather, interwoven by trade and enlightened by the exercise of reason, they would naturally banish an activity so destructive of their own lives and happiness. For well over a century, Habermas observes, history rebuffed this prospect. Democratic peoples showed they could be just as bellicose as autocratic princes. Instead of peace-giving trade, there came industrial revolution and class struggle, splitting rather than uniting society. The public sphere became prey to distortion and manipulation with the arrival of modern media. Yet since the close of the Second World War, Kant's vision has come to life again, as his premises have been fulfilled in altered conditions. Statistical research confirms that democracies do not war with each other. Within the OECD nations have become economically interdependent. The welfare state has pacified class antagonisms. NGOs and global summits on population or environment show that an international public sphere is taking shape.

But if Kant's diagnostic has today been vindicated, his institutional scheme for a perpetual peace has proved wanting. For a mere *foedus pacificum* – conceived by Kant on the model of a treaty between states, from which the partners could voluntarily withdraw – was insufficiently binding . A truly cosmopolitan order required force of law, not mere diplomatic consent. The UN Charter, in banning aggressive wars, and authorizing measures of collective security to protect peace, and the UN Declaration of Rights, laid some of the legal bases for one. But in continuing – inconsistently – to proclaim national sovereignty inviolable, the Charter had not advanced decisively beyond Kant's original conception. The transformative step still to be taken was for cosmopolitan law to bypass the nation-state and confer justiciable rights on individuals, to which they could appeal against the nation-state. Such a legal order required force: an armed capacity to override, where necessary, the outdated prerogatives of national sovereignty. The Security Council was an imperfect instrument of this imperative, since its composition was open to question and its actions were not always even-handed. It would better if it were closer in model to the Council of Ministers in the European Union, but – in this, unlike the latter – with a military force under its command. Nevertheless, the Gulf War was evidence that the UN was moving in the right direction. The present age should be seen as one of transition between international law of a traditional kind, regulating relations between states, and a cosmopolitan law establishing individuals as the subjects of universally enforceable rights.

Bobbio's starting point, by contrast, lay in Hobbes. For theorists of natural law, the passage from a state of nature to a civil union required two distinct contracts: the first an agreement between warring individuals to form an association, the second to submit to the decisions of an authority in case of disputes among them – a pact of non-aggression, and a pact for pacific settlement of conflicts. For Hobbes, neither were possible in relations between states. For them, peace could never be more than a temporary suspension of war, the inescapable condition of competing sovereign powers. This was an accurate description, Bobbio agreed, of the classical system of international relations, down to the twentieth century. But with the advent of the League of Nations, and then of the United Nations, for the first time a *pactum societatis* started to take shape between sovereign states. Still lacking, however, was any *pactum subiectionis* for the resolution of conflicts and the enforcement of rights. Democratic ideals plainly informed the UN's Declaration of Human Rights, and the representative equality of its General Assembly. But national sovereignty continued to frustrate the first, and the character of the Security Council to thwart the second. Transactions between the Great Powers still essentially determined the fate of the earth.

Yet now these coexisted with another and better framework. If it was wrong to idealize the UN, scepticism about it was also misplaced. The new system of international relations it half embodied had not done away with a much older one; but nor had the older one succeeded in dispatching this newer one. The two rubbed against each other – one still effective but no longer legitimate, the other legitimate but not yet effective.[2] For what was still missing from the contemporary inter-state system was the juridical figure of the Third – Arbiter, Mediator or Judge – created by any pact of submission, of which Hobbes's Leviathan, governing those who had voluntarily made themselves its subjects, had offered a compelling, if autocratic, intrastate model. Today, the abstract outline of such a Third could acquire a democratic form as a cosmopolitan sovereignty based on the consent

2. 'Democracy and the International System', pp. 22–31.

of states, empowered to enforce universal peace and a catalogue of human rights. The first condition of such a desirable order had already been perceived by Kant. It was the principle of transparency, abolishing the *arcana imperii* that had always characterized the foreign policies of democracies and tyrannies alike, under the pretext that affairs of state were too complex and delicate to broadcast to the public, and too dangerous to reveal to the enemy. Such secrecy could not but erode democracy itself, as innumerable actions – at home as well abroad – of the national security services of contemporary states testified. Here a vicious circle was at work. States could only become fully democratic once the international system became transparent, but the system could only become fully transparent once every state was democratic. Yet there were grounds for hope: the number of democracies was increasing, and a certain democratization of diplomacy was visible. As Kant had once seen in general enthusiasm for the French Revolution a 'premonitory sign' of the moral progress of humanity, so today universal acceptance of human rights, formal as this still might be, could be read as a portent of a pacified future to come.[3]

The similarity of these constructions, arrived at independently, is all the more notable for the differing profiles of their authors. Biographically, the formative experience of each lay in the Second World War, but these years were lived in sharply contrasting ways. Rawls (1921–2002), who came from a wealthy family in Maryland and originally intended to become a Protestant minister, fought as an infantryman in the New Guinea and Filipino theatres of the Pacific War. The moral crises of the battlefield seem to have affected him deeply, changing a religious into a philosophical vocation. Returning home to pursue an academic career, he became the most widely read political thinker of his time with the publication, in the early seventies, of *A Theory of Justice*. Although framed entirely abstractly, Rawls's work was at the same time consistently prescriptive, however ambiguous its practical implications might be. Intellectually, his horizon of reference could be described as quite narrow: principally, Anglo-American moral philosophy from the time of Victoria to the Cold War, and an animating inspiration from Kant. Politically, Rawls described himself as a Left liberal, and no doubt voted Democrat. But one of the most striking features of a thinker often admiringly described by colleagues as unworldly, was a complete abstention,

---

3. *Il Terzo Assente*, Milan 1989, pp. 115ff; henceforward *TA*.

throughout his life, from any commentary on contemporary public affairs.

Eight years younger, Habermas grew up in a small Rhenish town under Hitler. His father joined the Nazi Party in 1933, and Habermas himself briefly took part in defensive work with the Hitler Jugend at the end of the war. After discovering the realities of the Third Reich and breaking with Heidegger, his first major influence, Habermas became the major philosophical descendant of the Frankfurt School, absorbing its distinctive transformations of Marx, and then in turn criticizing these in the light of American pragmatism and systems theory. Intellectually heir to the totalizing ambitions of German Idealism, scarcely any major philosophical tradition has fallen outside the range of his interests, in which sociology – classical and contemporary – has also occupied a central place. As a political thinker, the pattern of Habermas's writing reverses that of Rawls, whom he has criticized for his inappropriately substantive intentions. His own political theory is purely procedural, abstaining from any programmatic proposals. On the other hand, Habermas has never hesitated to intervene politically on topical issues, adopting public positions on leading disputes of the day in Germany, as a citizen of the Left. His *Kleine politische Schriften* now run to nine volumes, rivalling the number of Sartre's *Situations*. At the same time, he has never been involved in any political organization, keeping his distance from SPD and Greens alike.

A generation older, Bobbio (1907–2004) was born into a well-connected family in Turin that, like most of the Italian bourgeoisie, welcomed the March on Rome and Mussolini's dictatorship. After early work on Husserl, he turned to the philosophy of law. In his late twenties, friendship with intellectuals in the anti-Fascist resistance led to brief arrest and release in 1935, after which he resumed a university career with a letter of submission to Mussolini, and intervention by an uncle acquainted with a leading hierarch of the regime. By the outbreak of the war he was a member of a clandestine liberal social-ist circle, and in 1942 became one of the founders of the *Partito d'Azione*, the leading force of the independent Left in the Italian Resistance. Active in the *Partito d'Azione* until 1948, when it faded from the scene, Bobbio became the most eloquent critical interlocutor of Italian Communism during the high Cold War. In 1966, when the long-divided Italian Socialists united again, he joined the reunified party, playing a major role both in its internal discussions and in public debates at large – after 1978, in sharp opposition to Craxi's leadership of the PSI. In 1984, on his retirement from the University of Turin, he was made a Senator for life, and in 1992 his name was canvassed as a candidate for President of the Republic.

If Bobbio's career was thus a much more intensely political one than that of Habermas, let alone Rawls, as a theorist he was less systematic or original – limitations he was the first to emphasize. Steeped in the philosophy of law, which he taught for most of his life, taking his primary inspiration from Kelsen's positivism, from the early seventies he occupied a chair of political science. In both fields he displayed a notably richer historical sense of his disciplines than either the American or German thinker. The most influential of his voluminous writings were concerned with the origins, fate and future of democracy, and its relations with socialism, in which he drew equally on Constant and Mill, on Weber and Pareto, to confront the legacy of Marx. These are texts that vividly reflect the energy and variety of Italian political culture in the post-war period, thrown into sharp relief against the monochrome landscape of the United States or the Federal Republic. To that extent, Bobbio's thought was the product of a national experience without equivalent elsewhere in the West. But in one critical respect he was also at an angle to his country. From the early sixties onwards, Bobbio was preoccupied with global problems of war and peace that had little, if any, resonance in Italy – a subordinate state within the American security system, with no post-war colonies, and hardly a foreign policy worth speaking of, whose political class and electorate, famously polarized by domestic conflicts, took correspondingly little interest in affairs beyond their borders. Acutely concerned by the dangers of thermonuclear war between East and West, Bobbio devoted a series of his finest essays to inter-state relations in the atomic age, first collected as *Il problema della guerra e le vie della pace* in 1979, long before either Rawls or Habermas had got around to considering the plane of international politics.

Service in America's war to regain the Pacific; a boyhood in Nazi Germany; underground resistance against Italian Fascism. It would be surprising if three such distinct experiences were without trace in the work of those who went through them. Rawls and Habermas offer the most clear-cut contrast. From the beginning, there were critics – nearly all also admirers – of *A Theory of Justice* who were puzzled by its tacit assumption, never argued through as such, that the only relevant unit for its imaginary 'original position', from which a just social contract could be derived, was the nation-state. How could a Kantian constructivism, deducing its outcome from universal principles, issue into the design merely of a particular community? The categorical imperative had known no territorial boundaries. At the time, the restriction could appear anodyne, since Rawls's two principles of justice, and their lexical order – first, equal rights to political liberty; second, only those socio-economic inequalities of benefit to all – presupposed conditions common to the wealthy capitalist countries of the West, with whom his commentators were also essentially concerned.

With the publication of *Political Liberalism*, however, the extent to which Rawls's preoccupations centred on just one – highly atypical – nation-state, his own, became clear. The whole problematic of this sequel, still couched in general terms, but now referring with diminishing compunction to strictly American questions or obsessions, revolved around the permissible role of religion in political life, an issue of small relevance in any major advanced society other than the United States. In the background, standard patriotic landmarks – the Declaration of Independence, the Bill of Rights, the Supreme Court, Lincoln's Inaugurals, the New Deal – demarcate the space of reflection. Moving into less familiar terrain, *The Law of Peoples* unfolds the logic of such introversion. Given that in *A Theory of Justice* it is the rational choice of individuals that is modelled in the original position, why does the same procedure not obtain for the law of peoples? Rawls's most impressive pupil, Thomas Pogge, deploring the conservative drift of his later work, has sought to extend its radical starting point in just the way Rawls refuses, offering a vision of 'global justice' based on the application of the difference principle to all human beings, rather than simply the citizens of certain states.[4] The reason why Rawls declined this amplification goes to the unspoken core of his theory. For individuals in the original position to reach unanimous agreement on the two principles of justice, Rawls had to endow them with a range of information and a set of attitudes derived from the very liberal democracies the original position was supposed to generate – its veil of ignorance screening the fortunes of each individual in the social order to be chosen, but not collective awareness of its typical institutions.

In *The Law of Peoples*, this circular knowledge resurfaces as the 'political culture' of a liberal society. But just because such a culture inevitably varies from nation to nation, the route to any simple universalization of the principles of justice is barred. States, not individuals, have to be contracting parties at a global level, since there is

---

4. See *Realizing Rawls*, Ithaca 1989, pp. 9–12; 'Priorities of Global Justice', in Thomas Pogge (ed.), *Global Justice*, Oxford 2001, pp. 6–23.

no commonality between the political cultures that inspire the citizens of each. More than this: it is precisely the differences between political cultures which explains the socio-economic inequality that divides them. 'The causes of the wealth of a people and the forms it takes lie in their political and the philosophical, moral and religious traditions that support the basic structure of the political institutions.'[5] Prosperous nations owe their success to the diligence fostered by such traditions; lacking the same, laggards have only themselves to blame if they are less prosperous. Thus Rawls, while insisting that there is a right to emigration from 'burdened' societies, rejects any comparable right to immigration into liberal societies, since that would only reward the feckless, who cannot look after their own property. Such peoples 'cannot make up for their irresponsibility in caring for their land and its natural resources' he argues, 'by migrating into other people's territory without their consent'.[6]

Decorating the cover of the work that contains these reflections is a blurred representation, swathed in a pale nimbus of gold, of a statue of Abraham Lincoln. The nationalist icon is appropriate. That the United States owes its own existence to the violent dispossession of native peoples on just the grounds alleged by Rawls for refusal of any redistribution of opportunity or wealth beyond its borders today – their inability to make 'responsible' use of its land or resources – never seems to have occurred to him. The Founders who presided over these clearances, and those who followed, are accorded a customary reverence in his late writings. Lincoln, however, held a special position in his pantheon, as *The Law of Peoples* – where he is hailed as an exemplar of the 'wisdom, strength and courage' of statesmen who, unlike Bismarck, 'guide their people in turbulent and dangerous times' – makes clear, and colleagues have since testified.[7] The abolition of slavery clearly loomed large in Rawls's admiration for him. Maryland was one of the slave states that rallied to the North at the outbreak of the Civil War, and it would still have been highly segegrated in Rawls's youth. But Lincoln, of course, did not fight the Civil War to free slaves, whose emancipation was an instrumental by-blow of the struggle. He waged it to preserve the Union, a standard nationalist objective. The cost in lives of securing the territorial integrity of the nation – 600,000

---

5. *The Law of Peoples*, Cambridge, Mass., 1999, p. 108. Henceforward *LP*.
6. *LP*, p. 39.
7. *LP*, p. 97. For Rawls's cult of Lincoln, see *inter alia* Thomas Nagel, 'Justice, Justice Thou Shalt Pursue', *New Republic*, 13 January 2000.

dead – was far higher than all Bismarck's wars combined; a generation later, emancipation was achieved in Brazil with scarcely any bloodshed. Official histories, rather than philosophers, exist to furnish mystiques of those who forged the nation. Rawls's style of patriotism sets him apart from Kant, and below him. *The Law of Peoples*, as he explained, is not a cosmopolitan view.[8]

Habermas offers the antipodal case. In post-war Germany, reaction against the cult of the nation was stronger in his generation, with personal memories of the Third Reich, than anywhere else in the West. Division of the country during the Cold War compounded it. Here there was little chance of taking the nation-state simply as an unspoken given of political reflection. For Habermas, the question was the opposite: what place could there be for the nation as a contingent community, whose frontiers were delimited by arms and accidents, within the necessary structure of liberal democracy? Since the *Rechtsstaat* embodies universal principles, how can it abide a particularistic core? Habermas offers two reasons, one theoretical and the other empirical. So far as the first is concerned, he observes that 'there is a conceptual gap in the legal construction of the constitutional state, that it is tempting to fill with a naturalistic conception of the people' – for 'one cannot explain in purely normative terms how the universe of those who come together to regulate their common life by means of positive law should be composed'.[9] As for the second, in historical practice the ideals of popular sovereignty and human rights were too abstract to arouse the energies needed to bring modern democracy into being. Ties of blood and language supplied the extra momentum for the mobilization required, in which the nation became an emotional driving force akin to religion, as 'a remnant of transcendence in the constitutional state'.[10] Nationalism then bred imperialism far into the twentieth century, sublimating class conflicts into wars of overseas conquest and external expansion.

Today, however, two broad forces are weakening the political grip of the nation-state. On the one hand, globalization of financial and commodity markets is undermining the capacity of the state to steer socio-economic life: neither tariff walls nor welfare arrangements are

---

8. *LP*, pp. 119–120.

9. *Die Einbeziehung des Anderen*, pp. 139–140; *The Inclusion of the Other*, p. 115; henceforward *EA* and *IO*.

10. *Die Normalität einer Berliner Republik*, Frankfurt 1995, pp. 177–179; *A Berlin Republic: Writings on Germany*, Lincoln 1997, pp. 170–172; henceforward *NBR* and *BR*.

of much avail against its pressure. On the other, increasing immigration and the rise of multi-culturalism are dissolving the ethnic
homogeneity of the nation. For Habermas, there are grave risks in
this two-sided process, as traditional life-worlds, with their own
ethical codes and social protections, face disintegration. To avert
these dangers, he argued, a contemporary equivalent of the social
response to classical laissez-faire that Polanyi had traced in *The Great
Transformation* was needed – a second remedial 'closure' of what had
become a new, 'liberally expanded', modernity.[11] The European
Union offered the model of what such a post-national constellation
might look like, in which the powers and protections of different
nation-states were transmitted upwards to a supra-national sovereignty that no longer required any common ethnic or linguistic
substratum, but derived its legitimacy solely from universalist political norms and the supply of social services. It is the combination of
these that defines a set of European values, learnt from painful historical experience, which can offer a moral compass to the Union.[12]

Such a European federation, marking as it would a historic advance
beyond the narrow framework of the nation-state, should in turn
assume its place within a world-wide community of shared risk. For
'the great, historically momentous dynamic of abstraction from the
local to dynastic, to national to democratic consciousness' can take
one more step forward.[13] World government remains impossible, but
a world domestic policy does not. Since political participation and the
expression of popular will, as Habermas puts it, are today no longer
the predominant bases of democratic legitimacy, there is no reason to
demand a planetary suffrage or representative assembly. The 'general
accessibility of a deliberative process whose structure grounds an
expectation of rational results' is now more significant, and in such
forms as a role for NGOs in international negotiations may largely
suffice for the necessary progress. For a cosmopolitan democracy
cannot reproduce the civic solidarity or welfare-state policies of the
European Union on a global scale. Its 'entire normative framework'
should consist simply of the protection of human rights – that is,
'legal norms with an exclusively moral content'.[14]

---

11. *Die postnationale Konstellation*, pp. 122–135; *The Postnational Constellation*,
pp. 80–88; henceforward *PK* and *PC*.
12. *PK*, pp. 155–156; *PC*, p. 103.
13. *PK*, p. 89; *PC*, p. 56.
14. *PK*, pp. 162–166; *PC*, pp. 108–111.

Beyond the obvious contrast in their valuations of the nation, a wider difference of outlook is noticeable in Rawls and Habermas here. Habermas's vision of the requirements of the time is more sociologically informed, offering an general account of objective changes in the contemporary world. Rawls, lacking such sociological imagination, appears – as Pogge notes – to have been blind to the implications of globalized capital markets for his account of the moral qualities that distinguish peoples in the tending of their natural assets. This is not a mistake Habermas could have made. On the other hand, unlike Rawls, he eschews any specific proposal for economic relations between rich and poor zones of the earth, even of the limitative sort advanced in *The Law of Peoples*. All that the community of shared risk involves is international enforcement of human rights. Here the two thinkers return to each other. For both, human rights are the global trampoline for vaulting over the barriers of national sovereignty, in the name of a better future.

How are these prerogatives derived in the two philosophies? In *A Theory of Justice*, they are an unproblematic deduction from the device of the original position, as rights that hypothetical individuals would rationally select, *inter alia*, behind the veil of ignorance. This was an elegant solution, that avoided determination of the status of rights claimed in the real world. By the time of *Political Liberalism*, concerned to construct an overlapping consensus from a variety of existing ideological standpoints – so inevitably requiring more empirical reference – this was no longer sufficient. To show that such a consensus would comprise his principles of justice, Rawls was now obliged to argue that all major religions contained moral codes compatible with them. In *The Law of Peoples*, the two lines of argument merge. Universal human rights are deducible from the choice that variant peoples, endowed as they are with differing faiths, would make if assembled together in an original position. Since they form a narrower set than the full range of liberal rights, decent as well as democratic societies will select them; symptomatically, Rawls's examples of the former are consistently Muslim.

Lacking a counter-factual artifice from which to derive them, Habermas is compelled to express a clearer view of human rights as they are actually invoked in the political world. Noting 'a certain philosophical embarrassment' surrounding them, he concedes that they cannot be taken as moral rights inherent in each human being, since they are 'juridical by the very nature' – that is, can exist only as determinations of positive law. Yet they are also 'supra-positive', for their justification, unlike that of other legal norms, can be exclusively moral, requiring no further arguments in support of them.[15] What is then the morality that legitimates them? Here Habermas directly rejoins Rawls. 'Does the claim to universality that we connect with human rights merely conceal a particularly subtle and deceitful instrument of Western domination?', he asks, 'or do the universal world religions *converge* on them in a core repertoire of moral intuitions?'. There are no prizes for guessing the answer. 'I am convinced Rawls is right, that the basic content of the moral principles embodied in international law is in harmony with the normative substance of the great world-historical prophetic doctrines and metaphysical world-views.'[16]

Habermas's more sociological side, however, which remembers Weber, cannot let the matter rest there. After all, surely the doctrine of human rights is specifically Western in origin, rather than of pan-confessional inspiration? Adjusting his sights, Habermas meets this objection by explaining that 'human rights stem less from the particular cultural background of Western civilization than from the attempt to answer specific challenges posed by a social modernity that has in the meantime covered the globe'.[17] How, in that case, is it that the social challenges of modernity happen to coincide with the moral intuitions of antiquity – the Atomic and Axial ages unexpectedly melting together in the eloquence of UN prose? Habermas has a proviso ready to square this circle. The faiths that so harmoniously agree with each other, and with lay wisdom, are not 'fundamentalist', but aware that their own 'religious truths must be brought into conformity with publicly recognized secular knowledge', and so 'like Christianity since the Reformation' are 'transformed into "reasonable comprehensive doctrines" under the reflexive pressure generated by modern life circumstances'.[18]

With this gloss, the vacancy of the claim that human rights are validated by all world religions is laid bare. The slightest acquaintance with the Pentateuch, Revelations, the Koran or the *Bhagavadgita* – replete with every kind of injunction to persecution and massacre – is enough to show how absurd such an anachronistic notion must be. All that is really postulated by Rawls and Habermas is that once religious

---

15. *EA*, pp. 221–224; *IO*, pp. 189–191.

16. *Vergangenheit als Zukunft*, Zurich 1991, p. 30; *The Past as Future*, Lincoln 1994, pp. 20–21; henceforward *VZ* and *PF*.

17. *PK*, p. 181; *PC*, p. 121.

18. *PK*, p. 191; *PC*, p. 128. Here too the reference – of 'reasonably comprehensive doctrines' – is explicitly to Rawls.

beliefs are rendered indistinguishable from 'public reason' or 'secular knowledge', they can be enlisted like any other platitude as sponsors of whatever conventional wisdom requires. The fact that in the real world, transcendent faiths continue to represent contradictory ethical imperatives, waging ideological or literal war with each other, becomes an irrelevant residue: the domain of a 'fundamentalism' that is no longer even quite religion, properly understood.

In Habermas's construction, something similar occurs to democracy. Once this is redefined as principally a matter of 'communication' and 'consciousness', political participation and popular will become residuals that can be bypassed in the design of a cosmopolitan legal order. Here too, the presiding concept assures the desirable outcome – Habermas's discourse theory functioning, like Rawls's public reason, to neutralize democracy as once religion. For rather than a critique of the involution of classic democratic ideals in the dispersed and depoliticized political systems of the West today, Habermas furnishes a metaphysical justification of it, in the name of the salutarily impersonal and decentred flux of communicative reason. The result is a political theory tailor-made for the further dissolution of popular sovereignty at a European level, and its vaporization altogther at a putative global level. To his credit, when writing on the actual European Union under his eyes , Habermas has sought to resist the logic of his own weakening of any idea of collective self-determination – calling, indeed, for more powers to the European Parliament and the formation of European parties. But when, untempered by any comparable experience, he envisages a cosmopolitan order to come, the logic of his projection ends in a political wraith: democracy without democracy, shorn even of elections or voters.

The intellectual framework of Bobbio's prospectus stands apart from these two. The reason for that is its quite distinct historical starting point. Rawls and Habermas were moved to reflections on the inter-state system only with the end of the Cold War. Their theories are plainly responses to the new world order announced in the wake of the Gulf War. By contrast Bobbio's concerns, predating theirs by three decades, were a product of the Cold War itself. The dangers of a nuclear exchange are completely absent from the analytics of either the American or the German. But it was these which determined the Italian's approach to the international scene. The lesson of Carlo Cattaneo in the time of the Risorgimento, and of his teacher Aldo Capitini in the Resistance, had been that the elimination of violence as a means of resolving conflicts, represented by the procedures of democracy within states, required a structural complement between states. Liberty and peace, whatever the empirical gaps or torsions between them, logically belonged together.

In the late eighteenth and mid-nineteenth centuries, a considerable range of thinkers had believed that history was in the process of delivering their union. Kant or Mazzini were confident that the spread of republican governments would do away with war. Saint-Simon, Comte and Spencer thought that industrial society made military conflict an anachronism. Cobden expected the growth of trade to ensure amity between nations. Bebel and Jaurès were sure socialism would bring lasting peace between peoples. All of these hopes, plausible as they seemed at the time, were dashed in the twentieth century. The barriers to which they had looked against mutual slaughter proved to be made of clay. Merchants did not replace warriors; peoples proved as truculent as princes; Communist states attacked each other.[19] Yet now that nuclear annihilation threatened humanity, peace was a universal imperative as it had never been before. Bobbio had no time for Cold War orthodoxy. Deterrence theory was self-contradictory, purporting to prevent the risk of atomic war by the very weapons that created it, and the balance of terror inherently unstable, preordained to escalation rather than equilibrium.[20] Disarmament treaties were welcome if secured, but did not constitute either a radical or reliable alternative.

Moral solutions to the problem of war, however noble, were not more satisfactory than such instrumental ones, since they required an improbable transformation of humanity. The most credible path for putting an end to the nuclear arms race was institutional. If the roots of war lay in the system of states, logically two remedies were possible. If conflicts were generated by the structure of international relations, a juridical solution was indicated; if their causes lay in the internal character of the states making up the system, the solution would have to be social. In the first case, peace could be secured only by the creation of a super-state, endowed with a global monopoly of force, capable of enforcing a uniform legal order across the world. In the second, it could come only by a transition to socialism, leading to a universal withering away of the state itself. A single Hobbesian sovereignty, or a Marxist *Sprung in der Freiheit*: such was the choice.[21]

---

19. *Il Problema della guerra e le vie della pace*, Bologna 1984, pp. 113–114, 143–146, henceforward *PGVP; TA*, pp. 34–38.
20. *PGVP*, pp. 50–55; *TA*, pp. 60–68.
21. *PGVP*, pp. 83–86.

Without claiming that it meant the elimination of coercion, since by definition the state was always a concentration of violence, Bobbio held the sole realistic prospect for global peace to be Hobbesian. The menace of a nuclear conflagration could be laid to rest only by a universal state. Structurally, that could become a super-despotism, such as Kant had feared.[22] But, unlike Rawls or Habermas, Bobbio was prepared to contemplate this risk, because it was less than the danger of planetary destruction they ignored.

Once the Cold War was over, Bobbio became more concerned to furnish his Hobbesian framework with a Lockean foundation, by stressing the need for a democratic, rather than authoritarian, incarnation of the Absent Third – one always preferable, but now that the Soviet bloc had collapsed, increasingly possible. Nevertheless, the world government he advocated remained a much more centralized structure than Rawls's law of the peoples or Habermas's cosmopolitan consciousness, and involved less idealization of its conditions. Even adjusted to post-Cold War circumstances, the link of any such authority to democracy was logically weaker, since its primary legitimation was pacification of inter-state relations rather than a mimesis of intra-state norms – not devices like the original position or discourse theory replicated at international level, but a supervening logic at that level itself, in keeping with Bobbio's dictum, unthinkable for the other two, that 'it cannot escape anyone who views history without illusions that relations between rulers and ruled are dominated by the primacy of foreign over domestic policies'.[23]

So too human rights, though they eventually played a role in Bobbio's prescriptions for a peaceful international order very similar to their position in the agendas of Rawls and Habermas, were always seen in a quite different light. At no point does Bobbio suggest that they magically harmonize the moral intuitions of the world's great religions, or can be regarded as principles of natural law, or are general requirements of modernity. They are not less precious to him for that. But a realistic view of them is incompatible with their standard descriptions. There are no 'fundamental' natural rights, since what seems basic is always determined by a given epoch or civilization. Since they were first proclaimed, the list of human rights has typically been ill-defined, variable and often contradictory. Such rights continually conflict with each other: private property with civic

22. *PGVP*, p. 116; *TA*, pp. 49–50.
23. *TA*, p. 94.

equality, freedom of choice with universal education, and more. Since ultimate values are antinomic, rights appealing to them are inevitably inconsistent. No historical synthesis between liberal and socialist conceptions has yet been realized. Human rights lack any philosophical foundation. Their only warrant is factual: today, all governments pay formal homage to the UN Declaration of Human Rights. This empirical consensus gives them a contingent universality that is their real basis.[24]

Bobbio's account of human rights is thus a far cry from the deontological versions of Rawls or Habermas. It is radically historical. For Hobbes, the only right was to life itself – the individual could refuse to lay it down for the state. Since his time, the list of rights claimed by citizens has been progressively extended: at first comprising liberties from the state, then liberties in the state, and eventually liberties through the state. The right to national self-determination, vehemently rejected by Habermas, belonged to these conquests. There was no end in sight to the dynamic of an 'Age of Rights' – today, rights to truthful information and to participation in economic power were on the agenda. But theoretical declamation was one thing; practical observance another. The new global ethos of human rights was resplendent only in solemn official declarations and learned commentaries. The reality was 'their systematic violation in virtually all countries of the world (perhaps we could say *all* countries, without fear of error), in relations between the powerful and the weak, the rich and the poor, the knowing and the uninstructed'.[25]

Law, in turn, could not be viewed in the starry-eyed fashion of Habermas or Rawls. Wars and revolution – the exercise of external and internal violence – were often the source of legal codes. Legitimacy was typically conferred by victory, not the other way around. Once in place, laws could be compared to a damming or canalization of the powers of existing social groups. When the dikes break, an extraordinary law-making power tumbles forth, creating a new legitimacy: ex *facto oritur jus*. 'Law cannot dispense with the use of force and is always founded in the last instance on the right of those who are strongest, which only sometimes, and contingently, coincides with the right of those who are most just.'[26] We are a long way from the premises of a Habermasian jurisprudence. Bobbio, though his

---

24. *PGVP* (first edition), Bologna 1970, pp. 119–157.
25. *Autobiografia*, Bari 1999, p. 261.
26. *PGVP*, p. 111; *TA*, p. 135.

accents could alter, never wavered from a basic fidelity to Hobbes's maxim: *auctoritatas sed non veritas facit legem*. The UN should be vested with powers to enforce the human rights it proclaimed. But the gap between its promises and performance remained wide. It had not secured the peace or friendship between nations that its charter had proclaimed. Its main achievement to date was never envisaged by its founders – the impetus given by the General Assembly in December 1960 to decolonization, the greatest single progress of political emancipation in the second half of the twentieth century.[27] Like Habermas, Bobbio proposed no determinate programme for reduction of social inequalities on a global scale. But the strength of his feeling about them set him apart too. The real problem of the time, which the nuclear arms race prevented any of the rich nations from addressing, was death by famine in the poor countries of the South.[28]

If such were the principal differences of theoretical prospectus, what of the political responses of the three thinkers to the new landscape of violence after the Cold War? Rawls, coherent with the silence of a life-time, made no comment on the *guerres en châine* of the nineties. But the logic of a sanction for them is written on every other page of *The Law of Peoples*. There the philosopher of justice not only offers a blank cheque for military interventions to protect human rights, without even specifying what authority, other than 'democratic peoples' at large, is empowered to decide them. He even exceeds State Department jargon with his talk of 'outlaw' states – a term inviting law-abiding nations to dispatch them still more swiftly than merely 'rogue' ones. The political assumptions at work in such language can be found in such historical illustrations as the book offers. Although Rawls mentions no contemporary political events, he touches on enough past ones to reveal, in this area, a disconcertingly uncritical mind. The slaughter of the First World War was inevitable, because 'no self-respecting liberal people' could have accepted German demands on France in 1914.[29] The fire-bombing of Hamburg was justified in the Second World War, if not that of Dresden. Though the destruction of Japanese cities, culminating in Hiroshima and Nagasaki, was a great wrong, it represented simply a 'failure of statesmanship' on the part of Truman, who otherwise – Loyalty Oaths, Greek intervention, the suborning of the UN presumably to

27. *TA*, pp. 108–109.
28. *TA*, p. 181.
29. *LP*, p. 48.

witness – was 'in many ways a good, at times a very good president'.[30] An excellent guide to just wars is provided by a work explaining why Israel's pre-emptive strike of 1967 was one.[31] Outlaw societies at one time included Habsburg Spain and Bourbon or Napoleonic France – but not Hanoverian or Victorian England, let alone Gilded Age America. Such miscreants are 'unsatisfied' powers. Nuclear weapons are essential to keep their modern counterparts in check.[32] Even Rawls's coinage of the notion of 'decent', as distinct from democratic, peoples simply shadows the geography of the US security system. The imaginary Muslim society of 'Kazanistan' that Rawls conjures up to illustrate the notion can be read as an idealized version of Kuwait or Saudi Arabia – reliable clients whose traditional, if less than liberal, political systems are to be respected, while outlaws in their neighbourhood are removed. Equipped with such credentials, Operation Desert Storm might well be described as the Law of the Peoples in real time.

Habermas was more explicit. The allied campaign to punish Iraq's brazen violation of international law in seizing Kuwait was an important step forward in the creation of a global public sphere. Although it was not fought under UN command, and was unaccountable to the Security Council, it invoked the UN and this was better than nothing: 'for the first time the United States and its allies were offered the objective possibility of temporarily assuming the (presumably neutral) role of police force to the United Nations'. Admittedly, the result was a hybrid action, since power-political calculations were not absent from its execution, but it was now plain that 'the enforcement of international law has to be carried out by an organized cooperation of the international community, not by some utopian (in the worst sense of the word) world government'. Moreover, and perhaps most importantly, the Gulf War was justified not merely by Iraq's annexation of Kuwait, but its menace to Israel, which posed 'the nightmare scenario of an Israel encircled by the entire Arab world and threatened with the most horrific kinds of weapons'.[33]

Since violations of international law had never hitherto troubled Habermas overmuch – when Turkey invaded Cyprus, Indonesia

---

30. *LP*, pp. 99–102; *Collected Papers*, Cambridge, Mass., 1999, p. 572.

31. 'I follow here Michael Walzer's *Just and Unjust Wars*. This is an impressive work, and what I say does not, I think, depart from it in any significant respect': *LP*, p. 95.

32. *LP*, pp. 48–49.

33. *VZ*, pp. 19, 18, 23; *PF*, pp. 12, 11, 15.

annexed East Timor, let alone when Israel seized East Jerusalem and occupied the West Bank, there is no record of his being moved to comment on them – it seems clear that political feelings rather than legal arguments were the principal pressure behind Habermas's endorsement of Desert Storm. On the one hand, there was his self-declared, long-standing posture of loyalty to the West. For forty years he had held that Germany could only be purged of its malign past, and put all suspect notions of a *Sonderweg* behind it, by an 'uncondi-tional orientation' to the West. This had been Adenauer's great achievement, which as a young man he had failed to understand, and which must remain the pole-star of the Federal Republic. After 1945, it was this orientation that had given Germans 'an upright posture'.[34] But there was also, after the Final Solution, and crucially, the special responsibility of Germany to Israel, a vulnerable democracy 'still obliged to act as an outpost of the Western world' in the Middle East. Since the founding of the Federal Republic, Habermas notes approv-ingly, 'solidarity with Israel has been an unwritten law of German foreign policy'; only anti-Semites could question it.[35] In the mixture of motivations for Habermas's support of the Gulf War, this was probably the most powerful.

Not a few admirers of Habermas, in Germany and outside it, were taken aback by this philosophical theorization of a war fought, on the admission of the US administration itself, essentially over the control of oil wells. Signs of an uneasy conscience could be detected in Habermas himself, who was quick to express reservations about the military tactics employed to win the war, and even to concede that the claim to UN legitimacy for it 'served largely as a pretext'.[36] But such qualifications, calculated to disarm critics, only underline the crudity of his subsequent conclusion, sweeping principles away in the name of deeds. Dismissing the objection that negotiations for a peaceful reso-lution of the conflict had scarcely been exhausted, Habermas declared in the spirit of a saloon-bar *Realpolitik*: 'It is a little academic to subject an event of such brutality to a pedantically normative assess-ment after the fact.'[37]

The rhetorical movement of Bobbio's response to the Gulf War was uncannily similar. Operation Desert Storm, Bobbio explained as it rolled into action, was a just war of legitimate defence against

---

34. *VZ*, p. 64; *PF*, p. 48; *NBR*, pp. 93–94, 108; *BR*, pp. 88–89, 102.
35. *VZ*, p. 28; *PF*, p. 18; 'Letter to America', *The Nation*, 16 December 2002.
36. *VZ*, p. 20; *PF*, p. 12.
37. *VZ*, p. 22; *PF*, p. 14.

aggression. Saddam Hussein, bidding to become a future emperor of Islam, was a great international danger. A sanguinary dictator at home, and an expansionist warlord abroad, he would multiply aggressions to the end of his days, if he were not checked now. Like Hitler, he was bent on extending the theatre of conflict ever further, as his raining of rockets on Israel showed.[38] Bobbio's position caused more of an uproar than Habermas's, in part because there was still a much stronger Left in Italy than in Germany, but also because he himself had been such an eloquent voice against the bellicism of the Cold War. Criticism from friends and pupils, shocked by his apparent volte-face, came thick and fast. In the face of this, Bobbio too, having approved the principle of the war, took his distance from the practice of it. 'I readily acknowledge that in the course of the fighting the relationship between the international organism and the conduct of the war has become ever more evanescent, with the result that that present conflict more and more resembles a traditional war, except for the disproportion in strength between the two combatants. Has a great historical opportunity been lost?', he asked after five weeks of uninterrupted American bombing. Looking around him, he confessed 'our conscience is disturbed'. The war was just, but – a separate question – was it obligatory? If so, did it have to be fought in this way? Bobbio's reply was taxative. Just as with Habermas, it served no purpose to scruple after the fact. 'Any answer to such questions comes too late to change the course of events. Not only would it be irrelevant – "what is done, is done" – but it could appear downright naive, for no one is in a position to say what would have happened if another path had been chosen to reach the same goal.'[39] The war might not have been necessary, or so bloody. But it was now an accomplished fact. What point was there in quarrelling with it?

Eight years later, Habermas greeted Operation Allied Force with more emphatic applause. NATO's attack on Yugoslavia was necessary to stop the crimes against humanity of the Milošević regime – '300,000 persons subjected to murder, terror and expulsion', before their rescue by American air-strikes began. There was no basis for casting suspicion on the motives of this intervention, from which the United States stood to gain little. It was a humanitarian war which, even if it lacked a UN mandate, had the 'tacit authorization of the international community'. The participation of the Bundeswehr in

---

38. *Una guerra giusta?*, Venice 1991, pp. 39, 22, 48, 60; henceforward *GG*.
39. *GG*, pp. 23, 90.

the attack was the decision of a Red–Green coalition, the first German government ever to be committed to a cosmopolitan legal order in the spirit of Kant and Kelsen. It expressed a public mood in the Federal Republic that was ressuringly similar to that in the rest of Western Europe. There might be some disagreements between the continental Europeans and the Anglo-Saxons on the importance of consulting the UN Secretary-General or squaring Russia. But 'after the failure of negotiations at Rambouillet', the US and member states of the EU proceeded from a common position.[40]

It was true, of course, that since human rights were only weakly institutionalized at the international level, 'the boundary between law and morality may blur, as in the present case'. Once authorization from the Security Council was denied, NATO could 'only appeal to the moral validity of international law'. But that did not mean Carl Schmitt's critique of the moralization of inter-state relations, as fatally radicalizing conflicts between them, applied. Rather, humanitarian interventions like the bombing of Yugoslavia were forced to anticipate the future cosmopolitan order they sought to create. Here there was a distinction between Washington and most European capitals. For the US, global enforcement of human rights supplied a moral compass for national goals. To that fruitful union of idealism and pragmatism, going back to Wilson and Roosevelt, Germans owed their own liberation, and it continued to be as vital as ever. 'The US has assumed the tasks of keeping order that are incumbent on a superpower in a world of states that is only weakly regulated by the UN.' But the moral imperatives it acted on needed to be institutionalized, as legal norms with binding international force. Happily, the UN was on the road to closing the gap between them, even if the transition between power politics and an emergent cosmopolitan order still involved a common learning process.[41]

In the Balkans as in the Gulf, Habermas was careful to season his plea for war with provisos of conscience. On the one hand, collateral damage to the civilian population of Yugoslavia created a sense of disquiet: were the brutal military means used to rescue the Kosovars always proportionate to the compassionate end? There was reason to

---

40. 'Bestialität und Humanität: Ein Krieg an der Grenze zwischen Recht und Moral', *Die Zeit*, 29 April 1999; in English as 'Bestiality and Humanity: A War on the Border between Law and Morality', in William Buckley (ed.), *Kosovo. Contending Voices on the Balkan Intervention*, Grand Rapids 2000, pp. 307–308, 312.

41. 'Bestiality and Humanity', pp. 313–316.

doubt it. On the other hand, what would happen if Operation Allied Force henceforth provided the model for humanitarian interventions at large? The West had been obliged to bypass the UN in this case: but that should remain an exception. 'NATO's self-authorization cannot be permitted to become a matter of routine.'[42] With this, ironically – in an essay whose title is taken from Schmitt's lapidary dictum 'humanity, bestiality', and is devoted to refuting it – Habermas ended by innocently illustrating the very theory of law he wished to refute. 'Sovereign is he who decides the exception' runs the most famous line of *Political Theology*. Not norms, but decisions, argued Schmitt, were the basis of any legal order. 'The rule proves nothing, the exception proves everything. It confirms not only the rule but also its existence, which derives only from the exception.'[43] Kant or Kelsen, invoked by Habermas at the outset, offered no affidavits for America's war in the Balkans; to justify it, he unwittingly found himself driven to reproduce Schmitt. For sovereign, in effect, was the superpower that delivered the ultimatum of Rambouillet designed to furnish the occasion for war, and disseminated the myth of a hundred thousand dead to motivate it; and sovereign the philosopher who now explained that the exception anticipated the rule of the future.

Unlike Habermas, Bobbio had admired and corresponded with Schmitt. But in justifying the Balkan War, he had a greater authority in mind. Milošević was a tyrant like Saddam, who needed to be wiped off the face of the earth: NATO's attack on him should be regarded as a police action rather than an international war, and its means be proportional to its ends. It made no sense to speak any longer of just or unjust wars: all that could be asked was whether a war was legal or not, and effective or not. But today another kind of warrant existed. For as a superpower the United States had acquired a kind of 'absolute right that puts it completely outside the constituted international order'. In practice, America had no need of legal justification for its wars, for its record in defending democracy in the three decisive battles of the twentieth century – the First World War, the Second World War and the Cold War – gave its *de facto* pre-eminence an ethical legitimacy. Europeans owed their freedom to the United States, and with it an unconditional gratitude. Wilson, Roosevelt and Reagan had fought the good cause, defeating the Central Powers, Fascism and Communism, and so making possible the normal democratic world we now live in.

---

42. 'Bestiality and Humanity', pp. 309, 316.
43. Carl Schmitt, *Politische Theologie*, Munich and Leipzig 1919, p. 15.

Hegel's *Philosophy of Right* had understood such a role. In every period of history, one nation is dominant, and possesses an 'absolute right as bearer of the present stage of the world spirit's development', leaving other nations without rights in face of it.[44]

This far-reaching accolade was, once again, not without troubled after-thoughts that were, once again, quieted with a further reassuring reflection. After seven weeks of bombing, Bobbio felt that Operation Allied Force had been incompetently executed, and produced a mess. Now expressing doubts that ethnic cleansing in Kosovo had started before the war, rather than being occasioned by it, he feared that a campaign to protect human rights was in the process of violating it. Yet this did not alter its general character, as an exercise of licit against illicit force. Habermas was right to maintain that international law was becoming – however imperfectly – institutionalized as a set of enforceable rules, in one of the most extraordinary and innovative developments of its history. Humanity was moving across the frontier from the moral to the juridical, as his German colleague had seen.[45]

By the time of the next Western military expedition, Bobbio had withdrawn from comment on public affairs. But in the Afghan war Habermas found vindication for his judgement of the trend of the time. Although the new Republican administration was deplorably unilateralist – European governments had some responsibility for failing to sustain sager counsels in Washington – the coalition against terrorism put together by it was a clever one, and had acted with good reason to remove the Taliban regime. True, the staggering asymmetry in weaponry between the the American armada in the skies and bearded tribesmen on the ground, in a country long victim of rival colonial ambitions, was a 'morally obscene sight'. But now it was over, and there was no point in repining . For 'in any case, the Taliban regime already belongs to history'. The UN was still too weak to fulfil its duties, so the US had taken the initiative, as in the Balkans. But with the UN-sponsored conference in Bonn to establish a new government in liberated Kabul, the outcome had been a happy step forward in the transition, which had begun with the establishment of no-fly zones over Iraq, from international to cosmopolitan law.[46]

---

44. 'Perché questa guerra ricorda una crociata', *L'Unità*, 25 April 1999.
45. 'La guerra dei diritti umani sta fallendo', *L'Unità*, 16 May 1999.
46. 'Fundamentalism and Terror', in Giovanna Borradori, *Philosophy in a Time of Terror. Dialogues with Jürgen Habermas and Jacques Derrida*, Chicago 2003, pp. 27–28.

A year later, Habermas was less serene. The new National Security Strategy of the Republican administration was provocatively unilateralist. The United States should not invade Iraq without the authorization of the United Nations – although the German government was also wrong in refusing such an invasion in advance, rather than declaring its unreserved respect for whatever the Security Council might decide. There might even have arisen something whose possibility Habermas had never imagined, 'a systematically distorted communication between the United States and Europe', setting the liberal nationalism of the one against the cosmopolitanism of the other.[47] Once launched, Operation Iraqi Freedom confirmed these forebodings. On the one hand, the liberation of a brutalized population from a barbaric regime was 'the greatest of all political goods'. On the other, in acting without a mandate from the United Nations, the US had violated international law, leaving its moral authority in ruins and setting a calamitous precedent for the future. For half a century, the United States had been the pacemaker of progress towards a cosmopolitan order vested with legal powers, overriding national sovereignty to prevent aggression and protect human rights. Now, however, neo-conservative ideologues in Washington had broken with the reformism of UN human rights policies, in favour of a revolutionary programme for enforcing these rights across the world. Such hegemonic unilateralism risked not only stretching American resources and alienating allies, but also generating side-effects that 'endangered the mission of improving the world according to the liberal vision'. Fortunately, the UN had suffered no really significant damage from this episode. Its reputation would only be injured 'were it to try, through compromises, to "redeem" the irredeemable'.[48]

Such thoughts did not last long. Six months later, when the UN Security Council unanimously passed a resolution endorsing the American occupation of Iraq and the client regime it had set up in Baghdad, Habermas offered no word of criticism. Though saddened by the change of political scene in America – 'I would never have imagined that such an exemplary liberal country as the United States could be so indoctrinated by its government' – he now had no doubt that Coalition Provisional Authority must be supported. 'We have no

---

47. 'Letter to America', *The Nation*, 16 December 2002.

48. 'Verschliessen wir nicht die Augen vor der Revolution der Weltordnung: Die normative Autorität Amerikas liegt in Trümmern', *Frankfurter Allgemeine Zeitung*, 17 April 2003; in English as 'Interpreting the Fall of a Monument', *Constellations*, Vol. 10, No. 3, 2003, pp. 364–370.

other option but to hope that the United States is successful in Iraq.'[49]

The response by the two philosophers to successive wars waged by the West after the collapse of the Soviet bloc thus exhibits a consistent pattern. First, military action by Washington and its allies is justified on normative grounds, invoking either international law (the Gulf), or human rights (Kosovo, Afghanistan), or liberation from tyranny (Iraq). Then, qualms are expressed over the actual way that violence is unleashed by the righteous party (Gulf, Kosovo, Afghanistan, Iraq), in a gesture of humanitarian punctilio. Finally, these in turn are casually minimized or forgotten in the name of the accomplished fact. The tell-tale formula '*in any case*', peremptorily ratifying the deed once done, says everything. The political complexion of such positions is clear enough. What is most striking about them, however, is their intellectual incoherence. No one could suspect Bobbio or Habermas of an inadequate background in logic, or inability to reason with rigour. Yet here philosophy gives way to such a lame jumble of mutually inconsistent claims and excuses that it would seem only bad conscience, or bad faith, could explain them.

Behind the dance-steps of this occasionalism – swaying back and forth between impartial principle, tender scruple and brute fact – can be detected a simpler drive shaping the theoretical constructions of all these thinkers. Rawls describes his Law of the Peoples as a 'realistic utopia': that is, an ideal design that withal arises out of and reflects the way of the world. Habermas's cosmopolitan democracy, a global projection of his procedural theory of law, has the same structure. Even Bobbio, in the past resistant to any such confusion between facts and values, eventually succumbed to his own, with sightings of a new *signum rememorativum* of historical development as humanity's improvement. In each case, the underlying wish is a philosophical version of a banal everyday inclination: to have one's cake and eat it. Against criticisms pointing to the disgraced reality of inter-state relations, the ideal can be upheld as a normative standard untainted by such empirical shortcomings. Against charges that it is an empty utopia, the course of the world can be represented as an increasingly hopeful pilgrimage towards it. In this *va-et-vient* between ostensible justifications by universal morality and surreptitious appeals to a providential history, the upshot is never in doubt: a licence for the American empire as placeholder for human progress.

---

49. 'Ojalá Estados Unidos tenga éxito en Iraq', *La Vanguardia*, 4 November 2003.

That this was not the original impulse of any of these thinkers is also clear, and there is something tragic in the descent that brought them to this pass. How is it to be explained? Part of the answer must lie in a *déphasage* of thinkers whose outlook was shaped by the Second World War, and its sequels, in the new landscape of power after the end of the Cold War. Old age mitigates judgement of the final conceptions of Rawls or Bobbio. When he published *The Law of the Peoples*, Rawls was already victim of a stroke, and writing against time. When he pronounced on the Balkan War, Bobbio was over ninety; and no contemporary has written so movingly of the infirmities of such advanced years, in *De Senectute*, one of the finest of all his texts.

But certainly, there was also long-standing blindness towards the global hegemon. In Rawls's case, superstitious veneration of totems like Washington and Lincoln ruled out any clear-eyed view of his country's role, either in North America itself or in the world at large. Regretting the US role in overthrowing Allende, Arbenz and Mossadegh – 'and, some would add, the Sandanistas [*sic*] in Nicaragua': here, presumably, he was unable to form his own opinion – the best explanation Rawls could muster for it was that while 'democratic peoples are not expansionist', they will 'defend their security interest', and in doing so can be misled by governments.[50] So much for the Mexican or Spanish-American Wars, innumerable interventions in the Caribbean, repeated conflicts in the Far East, and contemporary military bases in over a hundred countries round the world. 'A number of European nations engaged in empire-building in the eighteenth and nineteenth centuries', but – so it would seem – happily America never joined them.[51]

Habermas's vision of the United States is scarcely less roseate. Although undoubtedly culpable of lapses in such lands as Vietnam or Panama, Washington's overall record as a champion of liberty and law has been matchless – for half a century blazing the trail towards a disinterested cosmopolitan order. No exhortation recurs with such insistence in Habermas's political writing as his call to his compatriots to show unconditional loyalty to the West. The fact that Germany itself has usually been thought to belong to the West indicates the more specialized, tacit identification in Habermas's mind: intended are the Anglophone Allies who were the architects of the Federal Republic. If the United States looms so much larger than the United

---

50. *LP*, p. 53.
51. *LP*, pp. 53–54.

Kingdom in the ledger of gratitude and allegiance, this is not simply a reflection of the disproportion in power between the two. For Habermas, America is also a land of intellectual awakening in a way that Britain never became. To the political debt owed General Clay and Commissioner McCloy was added the philosophical education received from Peirce and Dewey, and the sociological light of Mead and Parsons. This was the West that had allowed Germans of Habermas's generation to stand erect again.

Against such a background, endorsement of American military interventions in the Gulf, the Balkans and Afghanistan came naturally. At the invasion of Iraq, however, Habermas baulked. The reason he gave for doing so is revealing: in marching to Baghdad, the United States acted without the authorization of the Security Council. But, of course, exactly the same was true of its attack on Belgrade. Since violation of human rights was, by common consent, far worse in Iraq than in Yugoslavia, why was a punitive expedition against the latter fully justified, but not the former? The difference, Habermas explains, is that the Balkan War was legitimated 'after the fact', not only by the need to stop ethnic cleansing and supply emergency aid, but above all by 'the undisputed democratic and rule-of-law-character of all the members of the acting military coalition' – even if the US and UK had approached the necessary task in a less pure spirit than Germany, France, Italy or other European members of NATO. Over Iraq, however, a once united 'international community' had split. The phrase, standard euphemism of every mendacious official broadcast and communiqué from Atlantic chancelleries, speaks for itself. The political confines of the community that stands in for the world are never in doubt: 'today, normative dissent has divided the West itself'.[52]

Yet since, in Habermas's own words, there can be no greater good than liberating a people from a brutal tyranny, why should prevention of ethnic cleansing or provision of aid – plainly lesser objectives – supply General Clark with philosophical credentials denied to General Franks? It is plain that the crucial *distinguo* lies elsewhere: in European responses to American initiatives. So long as both sides of the Atlantic concur, the international community remains whole, and the UN can be ignored. But if Europe demurs, the UN is sacrosanct. So naively self-serving an assumption invites, in one sense, only a smile. What it points to, however, is the disintegration of a larger one. The West upheld in Habermas's credo was always an ideological figure, an unexamined

---

52. 'Interpreting the Fall of a Monument', p. 366.

topos of the Cold War, whose assumption was that America and Europe could for all practical purposes be treated as a single democratic ecumene, under benevolent US leadership. The unwillingness of Berlin and Paris to rally behind Washington in the attack on Iraq undid that long-held construction, rendering an unconditional orientation to the West meaningless. In this emergency, Habermas fell back on European values, now distinct from – somewhat less commendable – American ones, as a substitute lode-star in international affairs. But, setting aside the work of lustration required to yield an uplifting common ethos out of Europe's bloody past, or even its self-satisfied present, the new construct is as incoherent as the old. Not only does Europe, as currently understood by Habermas, have to exclude Britain, for undue similarity of outlook to the United States, but it cannot even encompass the continental states of the EU itself, a majority of whose members supported rather than opposed the liberties taken by the US with the UN Charter. So in a further geopolitical contraction, Habermas has been driven to advocate a Franco-German 'core' as the final refuge out of which a future and better EU, more conscious of its social and international responsibilities, may one day emerge, harbinger of a wider cosmopolitan order.[53]

But this is a *reculer pour mieux sauter* without self-criticism. Habermas still appears to believe that NATO's attack on Yugoslavia – for him, a last precious moment of Euro-American unity – was warranted by Belgrade's refusal to treat, and determination to exterminate, heedless of well-advertised findings to the contrary. That the Rambouillet ultimatum was as deliberately framed to be unacceptable, furnishing a pretext for war, as the Austrian note to Serbia in 1914; that Operation Horseshoe, the plan for mass ethnic cleansing of Kosovo invoked by his Foreign Minister to justify the war, has been exposed as a forgery of the Bulgarian secret services; and that the number of Albanians in the region killed by Serb forces was closer to five than to the hundreds of thousands claimed by Western spokesmen – details like these can be swept under the ethical carpet as casually as before, for Yugoslavia too 'already belongs to history'. Even in Iraq, Habermas – in this like most of his fellow citizens in Germany or France – objects only to the American invasion, not occupation of the country. The

---

53. 'Unsere Erneuerung – Nach dem Krieg: Die Wiedergeburt Europas' (with Jacques Derrida), *Frankfurter Allgemeine Zeitung*, 31 May 2003; in English as 'February 15, or What Binds Europeans Together: A Plea for a Common Foreign Policy, Beginning in the Core of Europe', *Constellations*, September 2003, pp. 291–297.

deed once consummated, it becomes another accomplished fact, which he wishes well, even if he hopes it will not be repeated.

Bobbio's embrace of American hegemony was quite distinct in origin. Unlike Habermas, he never showed any special attachment to the United States after 1945, or even much interest in it. Did he so much as ever visit it? No reference of any intellectual significance for him seems to have been American. His post-war sympathies went to Britain, where he viewed the Labour experiment in person, and wrote warmly, if not uncritically about it. During the high Cold War, he sought energetically to resist polarization between East and West, and when he became active in the peace movements of the seventies and eighties, he never put the United States on a higher moral or political plane than the USSR as a nuclear power, holding them equally responsible for the dangers of an arms race threatening all humanity. America, however, was 'the more powerful of the two masters of our life and of our death', and it was therefore all the more discouraging to hear maxims from Reagan that could only be compared to the motto Louis XIV had inscribed on his cannon: *Extrema ratio regis*.[54]

But when the unexpected happened, and Gorbachev lowered the Soviet flag, ending the Cold War with a complete American victory, there was in Bobbio's outlook one tenacious idea that allowed him to make a radical adjustment to the new world order. He had always maintained that the most viable solution to the problem of endemic violence between states was the creation of a super-state with a monopoly of coercion over all others, as guarantor of universal peace. During the Cold War he envisaged this hitherto Absent Third ultimately materializing in the shape of a world government, representing a *de jure* union based on a multiplicity of states. But when instead, one existing state achieved a *de facto* paramountcy over all others of a kind never seen before, Bobbio could – without inconsistency – adapt to it as the unpredictable way history had realized his vision. America had become the planetary Leviathan for which he had called. So be it. The Hobbesian realism that had always distinguished him from Rawls or Habermas made him, who had been a far more critical voice of the international order as long as the Cold War persisted, ironically capable of a much more coherent apology for the US empire once the Cold War was over. Hobbes could explain, as they could not, why the *pax Americana* now so often required resort to arms, if a

---

54. *TA*, p. 208; written on 28 August 1983.

juridical order protected by a global monopoly of force was finally to be created. 'The law without a sword is but paper.'

Bobbio's realism, what can be seen as the conservative strand in his thinking, had always coexisted, however, with liberal and socialist strands for which he is better known, and that held his primary moral allegiance. The balance between them was never quite stable, synthesis lying beyond reach. But in extreme old age, he could no longer control their tensions. So it was that, instead of simply registering, or welcoming, the Hobbesian facts of American imperial power, he also tried to embellish them as the realization of democratic values, in a way that – perhaps for the first time in his career – rang false and was inconsistent with everything he had written before. The triptych of liberation invoked as world-historical justification for the Balkan War is so strained as virtually to refute itself. The victory of one set of imperialist powers over another in 1918, the American contribution to mutual massacre tipping the balance: a glorious chapter in the history of liberty? The D-Day landings of 1944, engaging less than a sixth of Hitler's armies, already shattered in the East: 'totally responsible for the salvation of Europe'?[55] An apotheosis of Reagan for his triumph in the Cold War: who would have imagined it from the descriptions of *Il Terzo Assente*? There was something desperate in this last-minute refrain, as if Bobbio was trying to silence his own intelligence.

It would be a mistake to deduce the late conclusions of all three thinkers in any simple way from the major body of their writing. That this is so can be seen from the chagrin of pupils and followers, steadfast in admiration for each man, but also to what they felt was the original inspiration of a great *œuvre*. Pogge's disappointment with *The Law of Peoples*, Matuštik's discomfort with *Between Facts and Norms*, and dismay at plaudits for the Balkan War, the reproaches of Bobbio's students to the claims of *Una guerra giusta?*, form a family of similar reactions among a cohort less disoriented in the new international conjuncture.[56] Nor would it be right to think that involution was ever complete in these philosophical minds themselves. To the end, flashes of a more radical temper can be found in them, like

---

55. 'Perché questa guerra ricorda una crociata', *L'Unità*, 25 April 1999.

56. See Thomas Pogge, *Global Justice*, pp. 15–17; Martin Beck Matuštik, *Jürgen Habermas. A Philosophical–Political Profile*, Lanham, MD 2001, pp. 247–251, 269–274; Eleonora Missana, Massimo Novarino, Enrico Passini, Stefano Roggero, Daniela Steila, Maria Grazia Terzi, Stefania Terzi, 'Guerra giusta, guerra ingiusta. Un gruppo di studenti torinesi risponde a Norberto Bobbio', *Il Manifesto*, 29 January 1991.

recollections of a past self. For all his apparent acceptance of capital as an unappealable condition of modernity, ratified by the irresponsible experiment of communism, Habermas could yet write, less reassuringly for its rulers, of a system breeding unemployment, homelessness and inequality: 'still written in the stars is the date that – one day – may mark the shipwreck of another regime, exercised anonymously through the world market'.[57] Bobbio, despite his approval of the Gulf and Balkan Wars, could in the interval between them denounce the 'odious bombardments of Baghdad' ordered by Clinton, and the 'vile and servile' connivance of other Western governments with them, as 'morally iniquitous'. Few intellectuals then spoke so strongly.[58] Rawls offers perhaps the most striking, and strangest case of all. In the last year of his life, when he could no longer work on them, he published lectures he had given over a decade earlier, under the title *Justice as Fairness*. Beneath the familiar, uninspiring pleonasm lay a series of propositions at arresting variance with the tenor of *Political Liberalism*, let alone *The Law of Peoples*.

It had been an error of *A Theory of Justice*, he explained, to suggest that a capitalist welfare state could be a just social order. The Difference Principle was compatible with only two general models of society: a property-owning democracy or liberal socialism. Neither of them included a right to private ownership of the means of production (as distinct from personal property). Both had to be conceived as 'an alternative to capitalism'. Of the two, a property-owning democracy – Rawls hinted that this would be the more congenial form in America, and liberal socialism in Europe – was open to Marx's criticism that it would re-create unacceptable inequalities over time, and do little for democracy in the workplace. Whether his objections could be met, or liberal socialism yield better results, only experience could tell. On the resolution of these questions, nothing less than 'the long-run prospects of a just constitutional regime may depend'.[59] Such thoughts are foreign to *Political Liberalism*. They outline, of course, only the range of ideal shapes that a just society might assume. What of actually existing ones? Rawls's answer is startling. After observing that favourable material circumstances are not enough to assure the existence of a constitutional regime, which requires a political will to maintain one, he suddenly – in utter contrast to anything he had ever

---

57. *NBR*, p. 17; *BR*, pp. 12–13.
58. 'Questa volta dico no', *La Stampa*, 1 July 1993.
59. *Justice as Fairness*, Cambridge, Mass., 2001, pp. 178–179; henceforward *JF*.

written before – remarks: 'Germany between 1870 and 1945 is an example of a country where reasonably favourable conditions existed – economic, technological and no lack of resources, an educated citizenry and more – but where the political will for a democratic regime was altogether lacking. One might say the same of the United States today, if one decides our constitutional regime is largely democratic in form only.'[60] The strained conditional – as if the nature of the American political system was a matter for decision, rather than of truth – barely hides the bitterness of the judgement. This is the society Rawls once intimated was nearly just, and whose institutions he could describe as the 'pride of a democratic people'. In one terse footnote, the entire bland universe of an overlapping consensus capsizes.

It is unlikely such flashes of candour were mere passing moments of disaffection. What they suggest is rather an acute tension buried under the serene surface of Rawls's theory of justice. Perhaps the most telling evidence for this is to be found in the unexpected entry of Hegel into his last published writings. In *Lectures on the History of Moral Philosophy* Rawls presents a respectful, indeed admiring portrait of Hegel as a liberal philosopher of freedom. What drew Rawls, against apparent temperamental probability, to the philosopher of Absolute Spirit? His reconstruction of *The Philosophy of Right* pays tribute to Hegel's institutional insight that 'the basic structure of society', rather than the singular individual, is 'the *first* subject of justice', and sets out his theory of civil society and the state with historical sympathy.[61] Here too a sharp aside says more than all the glozing pages of *Political Liberalism*. Hegel's constitutional scheme, Rawls remarks, may well strike us, with its three estates and lack of universal suffrage, as a quaint anachronism. 'But does a modern constitutional society do any better? Certainly not the United States, where the purchase of legislation by "special interests" is an everyday thing.'[62] Clinton's America as no improvement on a Frederick William's Prussia: a more damning verdict is difficult to imagine.

The principal interest of Hegel, however, lay elsewhere. For Rawls his most important contribution to political thinking, flagged at the outset of the relevant *Lectures*, and reiterated in *Justice as Fairness*,

---

60. *JF*, p. 101.
61. *Lectures on the History of Moral Philosophy*, Cambridge, Mass., 2000, p. 366; henceforward *LHMP*.
62. *LHMP*, p. 357.

was his claim that the task of philosophy was to reconcile us to our social world. Rawls emphasizes that reconciliation is not resignation. Rather, Hegel saw *Versöhnung* as the way in which we come to accept our political and social institutions positively, as a rational outcome of their development over time.[63] The idea of justice as fairness belongs to this conception of political philosophy as reconciliation, he explained. For 'situated as we may be in a corrupt society', in the light of its public reason we may still reflect that 'the world is not in itself inhospitable to political justice and good. Our social world might have been different and there is hope for those in another time and place.'[64]

In these touchingly incoherent sentences, Rawls's philosophy breaks down. Our society may be corrupt, but the world itself is not. What world? Not ours, which we can only wish would have been different, but another that is still invisible, generations and perhaps continents away. The wistful note is a far cry from Hegel. What the theme of reconciliation in Rawls expresses is something else: not the revelation that the real is rational, but the need for a bridge across the yawning gulf between the two, the ideal of a just society and the reality of a – not marginally, but radically – unjust one. That Rawls himself could not always bear the distance between them can be sensed from a single sentence. In accomplishing its task of reconciliation, 'political philosophy may try to calm our frustration and rage against our society and its history'.[65] Rage: who would have guessed Rawls capable of it – against his society or its history? But why should it be calmed?

Rawls resorted to Hegel in his internal reflections on a constitutional state. On the plane of inter-state relations, Kant remained his philosopher of reference, as the theorist of conditions for a perpetual peace. So too for Habermas. But since Kant failed to envisage the necessary legal framework for a cosmopolitan order, as it started to take shape through the permanent institutions of the United Nations, Habermas, when he came to review the progress made since 1945, also looked towards the philosopher of objective idealism. Measured against the sombre background of the disasters of the first half of the twentieth century, he decided, 'the World Spirit, as Hegel would have put it, has lurched forward'.[66] As we have seen, Bobbio was responsible

---

63. *LHMP*, pp. 331–332.
64. *JF*, pp. 37–38.
65. *JF*, p. 3.
66. *EA*, p. 207; *IO*, p. 178.

for the most pointed appeal to Hegel of all. In one sense, he was more entitled to do so. Welcoming Hegel's idea of reconciliation as akin to his own enterprise of public reason, Rawls drew the line at his vision of the international realm as a domain of violence and anarchy, in which contention between sovereign states was bound to be regulated by war. Habermas's gesture enlisted Hegel, on the contrary, as a patron of cosmopolitan peace. The first could not square his law of peoples with the lawlessness of Hegel's states, the second could only enroll Hegel for pacific progress by turning him philosophically inside out. Bobbio, by contrast, could take the measure of Hegel's conception of world history, as a ruthless march of great powers in which successive might founds overarching right, and invoke it in all logic to justify his approval of American imperial violence. Law was born of force, and the maxim of the conqueror – *prior in tempore, potior in jure* – still held. 'However difficult it is for me to share the Hegelian principle that "what is real is rational", it cannot be denied that sometimes history has vindicated Hegel.'[67] At the end of the twentieth century, reason had once again proved to be the rose in the cross of the present.

Yet three less Hegelian thinkers than these could hardly be imagined. The guiding light of all their hopes of international affairs remained Kant. In reaching out at the end for his antithesis, each in their different way engaged in a paradox destructive of their own conceptions of what a just order might be. Bobbio, who had most claim on Hegel, was aware of this, and tried to correct himself – he had intended not to justify, but only to interpret the course of the world in the register of the *Rechtsphilosophie*. There are coherent Hegelian constructions of the time, but they come from minds with whom these thinkers have little in common. Perhaps they would better have avoided wishful thinking by looking again at Kant himself, more realistic than his posterity in imagining a universal history for a race of devils.

2004

---

67. Perché questa guerra ricorda una crociata', *L'Unità*, 25 April 1999.

III. HISTORY

8

IN MEMORIAM:
Edward Thompson

Coming home one evening in the last weeks of 1962, I found a bottle of wine in the vacated room, with a note underneath. Edward Thompson had been completing *The Making of the English Working Class*. He lived in Halifax, and needed a final couple of weeks in the British Museum. In those days I lived in Talbot Road, newly wed to Juliet Mitchell. She was teaching in Leeds, while I was working for *New Left Review* in London. After hours Edward and I would exchange notes on our day, and fence aimiably about history and sociology. 'Do you *really* think Weber is more important than Bloch?' he would ask me with an air of mischievous puzzlement. If we were more circumspect about politics, this was partly a question of tact – he didn't want to lean on me too heavily, as a cub editor of the journal of which he was a founder, anxious for independence. But there was also a trick of perception to which I was subject.

Edward seemed not just one, but virtually two generations older, since between us lay those – the cohort of Stuart Hall or Raphael Samuel – who had co-founded the New Left, from beginnings in the fifties rather than the forties. His looks assisted the illusion, the handsome features at once melodramatically mobile and geologically deep-set, a landscape of wild scarp and gulley. It was the moment, of course, that clinched it – never did differences of age, however slight, loom so large as in those particular years. Larkin got the date roughly right, even if he skipped over the Stones. But at the time the librarian from Hull was probably no wiser than the historian from Halifax, who viewed talk of generational divisions impatiently, as a way of avoiding difficult arguments. The result was the same, even if it felt more like an inhibition than evasion to me. We had few political discussions. I was on the train down from Leeds as he came up from London, work complete, leaving behind what seemed like a still life of baffled good-will. It was not until the seventies that I realized, to my astonishment, that he was then thirty-seven.

In the following year, the connections between the founders of *NLR* and its new editors unravelled. The journal had been stranded by the ebb of CND, and was struggling without much success for a new direction. There had been disagreements about the best way to put it on a sound footing for some time, with the first impassioned resignations, apparent *sine qua non* of the life of the little magazine, I was to witness. Practical disputes and intellectual differences left Edward increasingly out of sympathy with the crew in Carlisle Street. He felt, justifiably, that the journal was drifting amorphously away from its past without having settled any account with it, and had no political confidence in its future. There were occasional explosions. But his attitude to the youngsters was fundamentally generous, and when the time came he ensured a clear hand-over of the old board to them, without rancour. Whatever his forebodings, he was not possessive.

When the journal found its feet, in the shape it more or less still has today, Edward's position altered. By the end of 1964, *NLR* had developed the kind of political perspective he had taxed us with lacking, and a set of historical theses about the relationship of the national past to the present British crisis, as we saw it. Edward liked neither part. But now, at last, a real confrontation was possible. Would the review, he wrote to me, be ready to publish a full-length critique by him – 'presumably written in my notoriously ill-natured polemical manner'? We would welcome one, I nervously replied, but didn't want a slanging-match. Sensibly, Edward let fly in *The Socialist Register* instead. The result was one of his most celebrated essays, 'The Peculiarities of the English'.[1] Stung by its ferocity, I replied in kind. The exchange had a sort of backhanded symmetry. Edward attacked us for inaccurate reading of historical evidence – I attacked him for inaccurate handling of textual evidence.[2] What had astonished me were the corners he cut in representing the arguments he wanted to refute, which I couldn't match with anything he stood for as a historian. This was a generic mistake on my part. I didn't understand the rules of polemic. This is a literary form whose history

---

1. Subsequently included, unexpurgated, in *The Poverty of Theory*, London 1978, pp. 35–91.
2. 'Socialism and Pseudo-Empiricism', *New Left Review* I/35, January–February 1966, pp. 2–42.

has yet to be written. One day critics will notice this, and read Jerome and his successors with new eyes. Polemic is a discourse of conflict, whose effect depends on a delicate balance between the requirements of truth and the enticements of anger, the duty to argue and the zest to inflame. Its rhetoric allows, even enforces, a certain figurative licence. Like epitaphs in Johnson's adage, it is not under oath.

I was not alone in failing to see this. A few years earlier, Edward had published a review of Raymond Williams's *Long Revolution* in *NLR*, which was more temperate in tone than his treatment of Tom Nairn and myself, but – here he miscalculated – more wounding in effect. One of his charges was that Raymond had become half absorbed, in manner and preoccupation, by the ruling-class academy. 'Oh, the sunlit quadrangle, the clinking of glasses of port, the quiet converse of enlightened men!'[3] It is not surprising a signalman's son took this amiss. But, perhaps without noticing it himself, Edward had admirably explained his address. Speaking of 'genuine communication', Raymond had said: 'you can feel the pause and effort: the necessary openness and honesty of a man listening to another, in good faith, and then replying'. Invoking the ancestry of *Culture and Society* against him, Edward replied: 'Burke abused, Cobbett inveighed, Arnold was capable of malicious insinuation, Carlyle, Ruskin and Lawrence, in their middle years, listened to no one. This may be regrettable: but I cannot see that the communication of anger, indignation, or even malice, is any less *genuine*.'[4] Here, *en toutes lettres*, is the polemicist's warrant. Edward's own indignations of this period were literary carmagnoles, without personal animus. A few months after my counter-attack on him, I ran into him into a pub off Tottenham Court Road. How I came to be there – I detest pubs – I cannot remember: perhaps simply to use their only civic function. It was my last night in England, before leaving the next morning for six months in Brazil. Edward, whom I hadn't seen for three years, was good nature itself.

It was another decade before I saw him again. In the winter of 1979, in a freezing church in Oxford, he rose like some wrathful divine to warn the congregation once more of the dangers of Gallican dogma. By now, his onslaught on Althusser in *The Poverty of Theory*, published the previous year, had roused much controversy. Disputation followed, before a rapt, shivering audience. One of the contestants

---

3. 'The Long Revolution', *New Left Review*, I/9, May–June 1961, p. 27.
4. Ibid., p. 25.

was Stuart Hall. I watched from the pews. My own reaction to *The Poverty of Theory* had been somewhat different. It seemed more important to take the measure of Thompson than Althusser. An attempt to do so came out a few months later.[5]

Just at this moment, the focus of Edward's energies suddenly altered. The second bout of intense Cold War had broken out, and he threw himself without reserve into a campaign to arouse resistance to it. I'd ended my writing about him by saying it would be good to leave old quarrels behind, and explore new issues together. He responded by publishing the manifesto of his fears in *New Left Review*, 'Notes on the Exterminism, the Last Stage of Civilization?', in the spring of 1980 – in effect, the founding text of the peace movement of the period.[6] The journal organized an international debate, with contributions from the US and USSR, Japan and Germany, France and Italy, as well as its own editors, around it. A book appeared, with Edward's conclusion.[7] The rift was over.

In 1986 we met in New York. Christopher Hill, Eric Hobsbawm, he and I had been brigaded to discuss agendas for radical history at the New School. By now, he was famous on another scale – a 'public person', as he sometimes complained, for much of the world. Explaining the toll on historical work his new role took, he mentioned the books awaiting completion, and the need for every radical to distrust 'assimilation by the host society'.[8] In the overflowing auditorium, hanging on his words, he was the image of a romantic orator: his bursts of passionate speech punctuated by that typical gesture, a sudden movement of the flat of his hand to his head – smiting his great brow or stroking his shock of grey hair? – whose effect always hovered between the histrionic and the playful. Afterwards, as we went off to an official supper, a somewhat incongruous quartet, something of the same trick of perception as when I first knew him recurred. The youngest of the three *doyens*, he seemed mysteriously senior – I wondered if it was simply because he was larger. Now, at all events, his aspect changed. I noticed for the first time a touch of the dandy, the slender waistcoat and raffish cheroot, hinting at a more classical silhouette. Our conversation turned to the Augustans. He

---

5. *Arguments within English Marxism*, London 1980.
6. *New Left Review* I/121, May–June 1980, pp. 3–31.
7. *Exterminism and Cold War*, edited by *New Left Review*, London 1982.
8. 'Agendas', *Radical History Review*, No. 36, September 1986, p. 42. Republished as the concluding text of the collection *Persons and Polemics*, London 1994, which he finished editing just before he died.

chaffed me for impudence about Swift, saying he was writing a novel conceived as a modern analogue of *Gulliver's Travels*, supreme critique of 'the reasons of power'.

It will take time to get a more settled sense of Thompson's distinction as a historian and a writer. His work spans too many forms for easy judgement, and its aura can be a temptation to short cuts. But a tension between what might be called his nineteenth and his eighteenth century sensibility was certainly at the creative centre of it. If the opening of *The Making of the English Working Class* bridges the two epochs, no one has ever doubted where the weight of its account lies. Where did Thompson's achievement point towards? There was an obvious answer – forward, to what became of the English working class, once made, in the Victorian epoch. Instead, he went in the opposite direction: back a full century to the 1720s. What motivated this alteration of field, an unusual jump – he spoke of a parachute – for any historian? In the nineteenth century Chartism was the terrain of his partner, Dorothy, he would remark. Beyond it, one might also suspect, the unrebellious world of mid-Victorian unionism, not to speak of subsequent Labourism, did not attract him: a come-down after Morris. But if there was a political element in his choice, some reluctance to pursue what might resemble the epilogue to *War and Peace*, personal ones must have been of greater significance.

Coinciding with the shift of period was a notable change of setting. In Yorkshire he lived in a draughty parsonage, perched high above the desolate black-red streets of Halifax, among the grimmest scoria of the industrial revolution. In Worcestershire his home was a Georgian mansion in rolling countryside, once a bishop's seat. The move allowed Williams, who remembered Thompson's apostrophe, a sly jest about 'country-house Marxism'. In fact, this was to be the headquarters of the most arduous political labour of his life. But there was a modulation in his writing, nonetheless. *Whigs and Hunters* is a different kind of book from *The Making of the English Working Class*, not only in scope, but in style. In a gesture of mimesis, romantic abundance yields to a sparer elegance, whose expression of passion is more often ironic than philippic. Their distributions varied thereafter. But in differing arrangements, the cadences of the two periods counterpoint in his prose to the end. The combination of idiom was the secret of its range. He was the greatest rhetorician of the age. This is an art foreign to the time, and its resistance is visible in the strain of Thompson's own relationship to the form. His touch was least certain when his diction was most contemporary. Typically, the lapses in his writing come from attempts at a twentieth-century demotic that miscue. The result can be startling. The obituaries have scarcely mentioned Thompson's poetry or fiction. He, rightly, did not regard them as marginal. His two longish poems, *The Place Called Choice* (1950), and *Powers and Names* (1986), which bear comparison in form and theme (atomic war – despotism), are vivid cases of this unevenness: passages of the tersest beauty side by side with others of pop galumphery. His novel, *The Sykaos Papers*, is the most complete single statement of his thought, giving imaginative form to ideas that find comparable expression nowhere else in his work. Needless to say, given the state of the trade, it is his only major book out of print. In it, the alien gaze of an incorporeal reason falls – too late – on the world of property and authority and war, as it moves towards nuclear destruction. The metaphysical argument is embedded in the liveliest of terrestrial narratives, meeting every maxim to move, to instruct, to delight. But there is still a striking contrast between minor opening sections of the novel, heavy-handed burlesque of the popular press and urban scene of the 1980s, whose humour can make one wince, and the major plot development that follows, glowing with energy and wit. Its climax, before the earth is extinguished, is the idyll in which reason becomes sexually incarnate, as the heroine takes the star captive into her arms – in an arcadian park 'landscaped in the 1740s', and 'made over in the early nineteenth century'.

Thompson's book on Blake, *Witness to the Beast*, in some ways reads like a scholarly companion to his novel. The same themes appear here in critical dress. Its original inspiration lies to a considerable extent in his relationship to Christopher Hill. At the New School, he told his audience how he had discovered Marxist history reading Hill in the sixth form, and already when *The Making of the English Working Class* came out, he would say he hoped one day to locate the underground tunnel that would connect Blake's ideas back to the world of the Civil War, directly linking up the two revolutionary epochs he and Hill had made their own. *Witness to the Beast* finds the filiation in the sect founded by John Reeve and Ludowick Muggleton in 1652. Blake's mother, Thompson suggests, may have been a Muggletonian, and many of his notions must have been derived from their brand of antinomianism. The respect and affection he shows for this mild, diminutive band – some two hundred souls by the mid eighteenth century – is winning. No theological nicety is neglected, as he delves into their complicated doctrine; though readers who recall rolling thunder against the obscurity of Parisian Marxism may be allowed a smile as they wrestle with the mysteries of the divine influx and the two seeds, the dispersal versus the unity of the godhead, painstakingly expounded here.

The larger purpose of the book, however, does not depend on the exactitude of the Muggletonian resuscitation. Its role is to suggest a new interpretation of Blake. Thompson argues that the poet inherited a long 'anti-hegemonic' tradition, rooted among artisans, which rejected the polite rationalism of the century for a religion of egalitarian love, hostile both to the new materialist science and to the moral law of the established church and state. But Blake transformed this antinomian outlook into a far more radical and original constellation, under the impact of Jacobinism and Deism. From the Painite mileu he developed a political vision of the evils of property and poverty, clergy and army, monarchy and marriage; while from Volney he arrived at a new critique of alienated faith, and the worldly powers it served. In each case, however, he saw deeper than his Enlightenment contemporaries – neither reducing human misery merely to social oppression or exploitation, nor religious feeling to priestly mystification. Not the reason of science or self-interest, but only the call of love could cure the curse of Cain. An alternative human nature, in keeping with the Everlasting Gospel, lay waiting to be realized. 'The intensity of this vision', Thompson writes, 'made it impossible for Blake to fall into the courses of apostasy' when the revolutionary fires burned low after 1801 – whereas 'the busy perfectionists and benevolent rationalists' of the time 'nearly all ended up as disenchanted men'.[9]

Witness against the Beast is a luminous *envoi* to an exceptional life's work. How best to honour its antinomian impulse? Not, certainly, by any new species of piety. Reading Edward's obituaries – right, left and centre – I do not know how many times I counted the citation of his desire to rescue 'even the deluded follower of Joanna Southcott from the enormous condescension of posterity'. The phrase is, of course, one of his most poignant and programmatic. But by dint of repetition, it risks becoming a PC tag. Edward, who was the most politically incorrect person in the world, would have had none of this. He rejoiced in irreverence, and we would do better to take after him, where we can. A start might be to note that Blake himself was the first to express condescension towards Joanna Southcott, about whose maidenhood he wrote a disdainful little ditty: 'Whate'er is done to her she cannot know, / And if you ask her she will swear it so, / Whether 'tis good or evil, none's to blame; / No one can take the pride, no one the blame.'

---

9. *Witness against the Beast. William Blake and the Moral Law*, Cambridge 1993, pp. 228–229.

But there is a wider point here, which bears on the argument of his last book. One writer of the eighteenth century who never attracted much attention from Thompson was its greatest historian. In *Witness to the Beast*, however, Gibbon does make an appearance. Here he figures as a foil – the Deist whose depiction of Constantine might have appealed to an antinomian, but whose sceptical view of Christianity understandably aroused Blake's poetic ire ('Gibbon arose with his lash of steel, / and Voltaire with a racking wheel', etc.). Thompson views his reaction, which stands at the head of the third chapter of *Jerusalem*, with sympathy. But the poem is actually a cameo of Blake's weaknesses – and at just the two points *Witness to the Beast* presents as strengths. In it, a piteous monk is tortured by Gibbon and Voltaire for failing to toast war: as if this was the burden of their critique of faith. The charge is wild enough to suggest a mind unable to face what disturbs it. Gibbon's *History* was indeed disturbing, and not alone to Blake. But if we ask why its medicine was so strong, Thompson's dictum can be reversed. The intellectual emancipation wrought by *The Decline and Fall* lay in what might well be described as its 'enormous condescension' – what else is the inimitable tone of those six famous volumes? – to the Christian, even Classical past. Thompson praises Blake's indignant annotations on Bishop Watson's *Apology for the Bible*, addressed to Paine. But Blake did not speak out publicly. It was Paine who replied to Watson, as Gibbon had done before him.

The origin of Blake's poem lay in his trial at Chichester, for an obscure affray with a soldier in his garden, in which he was acquitted.[10] Scared by the episode, he imagined himself one of the Grey Monks in whose one-time chancel the trial was held (the Duke of Richmond, presiding over it, would have been surprised to learn he was rack-master to Voltaire), broken yet triumphal: 'the bitter groan of a martyr's woe is / an arrow from the Almighty's bow!' Two years after the trial, still brooding on 'the full history of my spiritual sufferings', he dedicated engravings to the Queen. In the manuscript version of *Jerusalem* the friar is 'seditious'; but he had second thoughts, and changed it on publication to 'lazy'. There are no grounds for reproach in any of this. Blake had his timorous side; was prey to fears of persecution; was very badly off. It was a dangerous time for any radical. However, it is a mistake to present Blake as polit-

---

10. See David Erdman, *Blake. Prophet Against Empire*, Princeton 1969, pp. 403–415.

ically more intransigent than less mystic opponents of the Tory war regime. He pursued Robert and Leigh Hunt venomously, for having attacked his paintings of Nelson and Pitt as icons of reaction (a mistake, if it was one – Blake himself never said so – shared by not a few art historians), representing them as incarnations of evil, responsible for a war they were more outspoken about than he. Prosecuted three times, the brothers were eventually imprisoned for insulting the Regent, to Blake's jeers. 'How a monk can be a hypocrite, I cannot conceive', he admonished the Deists. The Enlightenment may, after all, have still had something to teach him.

To make these points is not to diminish the force of Thompson's affirmative case for Blake, as an iconoclast approaching genius. But it is to situate him more critically in the tradition to which Thompson draws our attention. The Muggletonians were an appealing company, as he shows. But they were also secretive and withdrawn, refraining from public worship or proselytism; their faith become quietist. Blake's absence from any collective form of radical politics, in a time of ferment, is very striking. His only experience even with a crowd seems to have been a dip in the Gordon Riots, when he was a boy. His reluctance to take risks that others accepted must have been in part temperamental – an artist's nervousness. Yet did it not also reflect the lie-low mentality of the background from which he probably came? The notion of an Everlasting Gospel afforded a ready line of retreat from any temporal hurly-burly. But descent from the Third Commission, however transfigured, had its costs. These were not just the limits of a political experience, but of a literary art too. The gnomic failures of Blake's later works were the issue of a self-isolation. More significant than his distance from Jacobin circles is the lack of any Romantic response to him, for all Crabb Robinson's valiant efforts to interest Wordsworth, Hazlitt or others. It is a good antidote to later patriotic bellowing of 'England's green and pleasant land' to remember that, while he was alive, the only significant report of Blake's work appeared in German.

Thompson's last article was about patriotism in that time. In a friendly if critical review of Linda Colley's work *Britons: Forging the Nation*, he questioned the consistency of popular loyalism during the French Wars, while not denying its existence, and had no patience with any too respectful treatment of it, that overlooked the flood of 'chauvinist humbug' in Volunteer ballading and parading.[11] If he could be irritated into gestures of Englishry himself, his deepest commitments were unequivocally internationalist. European nuclear disarmament was the cause to which he devoted himself for a decade. His imaginative response as a writer extended to China, India, Latin America, the United States. The unity of these engagements lay in his desire to dissolve the Cold War.

In the event, he proved to be the prophet of its end. That is remarkable enough. How far the peace movement contributed to the ending is another issue, the principal debate he left behind. On this we differed. Between the ideals of END and the realities of Soviet breakdown is a large gap. It is not a belittlement of the advocates of the end of the Cold War to distinguish them from its agents. The First World War was not terminated by the Zimmerwald Left or the Stockholm Appeal, although they had historical effects, but by the victory of the Entente. We do not honour them the less for that. Was the conclusion of the Cold War very different? Edward held, passionately, that it was. Certainly no one had more right to do so. His interim judgement, 'Ends and Histories', completed in the spring of 1990, and published in Mary Kaldor's *Europe from Below*,[12] is in part a reply to Francis Fukuyama, about whom we had opposite opinions. It is one of his most attractive statements, at once autobiographical and visionary. People will return to it after more conventional verdicts are forgotten.

It was first drafted, he explains, just before the old order was swept away in Prague, and he nearly died in a New York hospital. His last years were dogged by repeated illness. Readers of the *LRB* may remember a piece about the NHS.[13] He died young, by contemporary standards. We have missed a lot. Christopher Hill, in the twelve years since he passed the same age, has published seven books. What might Edward have gone on to write? At the height of the peace movement he tended to set aside other politics, as divisive of a common cause. With the Cold War over, he might have helped to renew the Left once more. There are hints of that in 'Ends and Histories'. Whatever shape his ideas would have taken, the book on Blake makes one thing probable. They would have been uncovenanted. He was not in a mood to settle. *A Life of Dissent* is the affecting film Tariq Ali made of Edward and Dorothy Thompson earlier this year, recently re-shown. While it was being shot, there

---

11. 'The Making of a Ruling Class', *Dissent*, Summer 1993, pp. 377–382, now included in *Persons and Polemics*, under the title 'Which Britons?'.

12. Mary Kaldor (ed.), *Europe from Below*, London 1991, pp. 7–25.

13. 'Diary', *London Review of Books*, 7 May 1987.

was talk of mutual acquaintances. 'What's Perry up to these days?', he enquired. Tariq mentioned something I'd written on conservatism. 'Yes, I know,' Edward replied. 'Oakeshott was a scoundrel. Tell him to stiffen his tone.'

1993

9

PHILOLOGIST EXTRAORDINARY:

Sebastiano Timpanaro

Philology has a bad name – worse than that of the dismal science, which at least can claim a bearing on production – as a discipline encouraging sterile pedantry. In public association, the shadow of Eliot's Casaubon has lingered. Even its eminences have not escaped it: the aridity of Housman's labours over Manilius regularly contrasted (or invidiously connected) with the lushness of his poetry, the authority of Wilamowitz mocked by the posthumous triumph of Nietzsche. Today, few could cite a contemporary practitioner. But the discipline had at least one remarkable after-life, contradicting every preconception against it, in the strange career of Sebastiano Timpanaro, the Italian scholar and thinker who died in November 2000, one of the purest and most original minds of the second half of the century.

He was born in Parma in 1923, son of a Sicilian intellectual of the same name, who through most of his childhood taught science in a Florentine high school, before becoming director of the Domus Galileana in Pisa. His father, who joined the Italian Socialist Party after the war, collected drawings and championed a humanistic science in the tradition of Leonardo and Galileo. His mother edited Proclus and Pythagoras. When his father died after a long illness in 1949, the young Timpanaro brought together a posthumous collection of his essays on the history of science.[1] The physical resemblance between them must have been striking. In the darkened hall of the family flat in Florence in the eighties, there hung a gaunt, arresting portrait which at first glance looked – notwithstanding period features – as if it must be his: a mistake his wife, who works on eighteenth-century history, had

---

1. *Scritti di storia e critica della scienza*, Florence 1952.

more than one occasion to correct. Although their fields differed, filiation was clearly spiritual as much visual.

Sebastiano Timpanaro Jr, as he signed his first preface, studied
classical philology during the war at the University of Florence under
the acknowledged master of the discipline in Italy, Giorgio Pasquali.
Later, he was a favourite younger colleague of the famous German
exile Eduard Fraenkel, who often taught seminars in Italy as a relief
from duties in Oxford. By his mid-twenties, he was publishing recon-
structions of the early Latin poet Ennius, and Fraenkel looked to him
to produce a new critical edition of Virgil. But in this he was to be
disappointed. Timpanaro lacked the patience, as he freely said, for
this immense task. His outstanding gifts of textual criticism took the
form of *adversaria*, punctual annotations, that eventually yielded
well over a thousand pages of meticulous dissection of passages from
Lucretius, Martial, Virgil, Fronto, Ovid, Seneca, Lucan, Servius,
Sallust, the Historia Augusta – 'the minor writings of a philologist
with no major writings to his credit', as he put it.[2] He once described
this traditional practice as that of the micro-historian within his discipline. His first book, written when he had turned thirty, was a
rediscovery of the textual findings of Leopardi, whose fame as a poet
had long obscured the seriousness of his classical philology.[3] His
second was a study, immediately recognized as a fundamental
revision, of the emergence during the Restoration of the textual procedures associated with the German scholar Karl Lachmann, usually
regarded as the main originator of modern techniques of recension –
as opposed to emendation – of ancient texts, famously applied by
him to Lucretius, the *Nibelungenlied* and St Luke alike.[4] *The Genesis
of the Lachmann Method* assured Timpanaro an international reputation in his field, amplified by the steady stream of corrections and
conjectures that followed it. In due course he was elected to the
Accademia dei Lincei and the British Academy.

But there was always an anomaly. This distinguished expert in a
highly technical field, a province *par excellence* of academic scholarship, never held a position in a university, or indeed in any other
institution of learning. Nor did he have independent means. For a
living, Timpanaro worked as a proof-reader – a job never much
regarded, let alone well-paid, that often left him in financial difficulties

---

2. *Contributi di filologia e di storia della lingua latina*, Rome 1978, p. 7.
3. *La filologia di Giacomo Leopardi*, Florence 1955.
4. *La genesi del metodo del Lachmann*, Florence 1963.

– for a small publisher in Florence, *La Nuova Italia*, owned by the Codignola family. Report of this circumstance appears to have reached George Steiner, the central character of whose novella *Proofs* is often identified by Italians with Timpanaro. The association rests on a *qui pro quo* more revealing of its makers than its object. Steiner's proof-reader is a benighted Communist, struggling with the destruction of his illusions in melodramatic dialogues with a Catholic comrade-priest, equally hostile to capitalist consumerism, but more clear- sighted about Stalinism, at whose climax the unhappy protagonist exclaims 'we are the children of Hagar' – 'there can be no real Communist who is not, at bottom, a Jew'[5] – before relapsing into a pitiful surrender to a Party now thoroughly adjusted to capitalism, that no longer wants him. Whatever else may be said of this *Granta* showcase, its author can hardly be taxed with inaccuracy for a fable which speaks of preoccupations so peculiarly his own.

Timpanaro belonged to another world. Like his father, he joined the Italian Socialist Party in 1945, and was active on its Left for nearly twenty years. At the elections of 1948 – the turning point in the post-war history of the country – the PSI opted for a common Socialist-Communist list with the PCI, against the Christian Democratic Party backed by the Vatican and the CIA. Timpanaro was among the socialist youth who bitterly opposed this decision, regarding the PCI leadership as little better than a lay version of the Holy Office, and in despair wrote a savage parody of the PSI Congress that was pushed into it, mimicking the forms of a Greek tragedy.[6] But hostility to Stalinism never inclined him to indulgence towards Social Democracy, in any of its guises. So long as the PSI maintained its opposition to Christian Democracy, he remained within it, but when in an eventual volte-face the party formed a coalition with the DC in 1964 – the first Centre-Left government of the post-war period – its more radical wing, rightly predicting that the experience would transform the PSI rather than reform Italian society, abandoned the Party to create its own formation. Timpanaro remained a militant in this organization and its sequel until the middle seventies. His commitment to revolutionary socialism was not just a sentimental attachment. Later, rejecting descriptions of himself as an isolated intellectual, he wrote: 'I have spent more hours taking part in political discussions and

---

5. *Proofs and Three Parables*, London 1992, p. 35.
6. 'Il Congresso del partito. Scherzo filologico-politico', *Il Ponte*, January 1981, pp. 65–80; the text was written, as Timpanaro explains, in 1949.

demonstrations, in undertaking the tasks of a so-called "intermediate cadre" (rather closer to the base than the summit) than in studying: by this I mean a literal computation of time, without any populist exhibitionism, if anything with a certain retrospective self-irony'.[7] His politics were Marxist, and anti-Stalinist; critical too – this was much rarer on the far Left in Italy – of Maoism.

In certain temperaments, intellectual skills and political sympathies have little or no connection. Frege's anti-semitism or Wittgenstein's philo-stalinism lacked significant leads to their philosophy. Such cases are common enough. Timpanaro was not one of them. His political commitments were not a personal foible or random *point d'honneur* of the philologist. They informed and transformed his work. The highly technical starting point in Leopardi proved to be no accident. Formally speaking, what happened was that Timpanaro widened his field of operations from textual criticism to intellectual history. Substantively, what drove the amplification of focus was his political engagement. Leopardi was the bridge between the two: the classical philologist who was also the most implacable adversary of Restoration culture, the poet who was a visionary materialist. Each of the two central works of Timpanaro's mid-career were built round his heritage. *Classicismo e illuminismo nell'ottocento italiano* (1965) and *Sul Materialismo* (1970) offer intellectual landscapes of the nineteenth and twentieth centuries – the former on an Italian, the latter on a Western scale – seen through the prism of selected figures and movements, whose trajectories could be said to define the time.

The first book revolves around the peculiar position occupied by Leopardi, flanked at some distance by his friend Pietro Giordani, in Italian culture of the post-Napoleonic period, and ends with a consideration of the line from the liberal patriot Carlo Cattaneo – hero of the rising against Austrian rule in Milan in 1848 – to the comparative linguist Graziadio Ascoli after the Risorgimento. The second develops a systematic critique of Western Marxism for relinquishing the materialist legacy of Engels, and at the same time of structuralism for distorting the linguistic heritage of Saussure. Timpanaro could intervene on each terrain with particular authority. Few scholars had mastered the corpus of Leopardi or Ascoli so thoroughly as he; and in the vast literature on (or of) structuralism, none rivalled his grasp of the comparative history of Western linguistics. The briskness with which he could handle the edifying intentions of Manzoni,

---

7. *Antileopardiani e neomoderati*, Pisa 1982, p. 12.

or despatch the dicta of such venerated notables as Lévi-Strauss or Chomsky, came from professional knowledge.

Three themes governed Timpanaro's output in this period. The first was specifically cultural. If European Romanticism swept the board as ideology and aesthetic under the Restoration, he argued that its success was due to a distinctive combination of traits. On the one hand, as a post-revolutionary outlook, it benefited from the break-up of the aristocratic side of the Enlightenment – displacing its etiquette of surface gallantry with a new sense of seriousness and inward passion. It could draw on valid elements in the continental struggle against Napoleonic expansionism – the right of peoples to independence, longing for peace, rejection of the cult of military glory. Finally, of course, it could claim to have liberated art from the tyranny of classical imitation – conventional Aristotelian unities, too marmoreal diction. On the other hand, Romanticism fulfilled at the same time the need of new bourgeois classes to assert themselves as the emergent social force of the time, without running the risk of a plebeian radicalization of the battle against Absolutism, of the kind that had marked Jacobinism. To this end the most serviceable ideology was a flexible post-revolutionary Christianity, melding apposite doses of tradition and progress. Politically, the Romanticism of this period was by no means always conservative – for every Chateaubriand or Novalis there was to be a Hugo or Mazzini. Nonetheless two characteristic limits defined virtually all its varieties: a diffuse religiosity exhaled in any number of idiosyncratic forms, and a lachrymose populism of nativist more than democratic bent.

It was against this dominant pattern, Timpanaro maintained, that a counter-culture ranged itself – the classicist tradition whose greatest voice was Leopardi. Within this classicism there were purely or largely nostalgic currents, fixated on dead forms. But its most intransigent and coherent expression defied the sentimental verities of the age. Rejecting the Romantic cult of the Middle Ages, it looked back to the republican virtues of Athens and Rome, and scorning every brand of spiritualism, it reclaimed the most unflinchingly materialist thinkers of the Enlightenment: La Mettrie, Helvétius, Holbach. This was a classicism, isolated from popular feeling in a season of counter-revolutionary stagnation, whose aesthetic forms were often deliberately archaizing, vehicles of a polemical disdain for the pandering rhythms around them, as those of Lucretius had been before them. But its intellectual and political outlook – refusal of any compromise with the broken-backed world of the restored monarchies – was far in advance of typical Romantic postures, half at home in them.

In the work of Leopardi, this post-mortem classicism brought into exceptional focus a tension still for the most part latent in the Enlightenment itself. Here was Timpanaro's second fundamental theme. For once he had detached himself from his upbringing, Leopardi combined the progressive social and political impulses of the radical Enlightenment with an unyielding pessimism about the prospects for human happiness, even under the best society, that marked his work off sharply from the main line of the Age of Reason. Nature, to which so many eighteenth-century thinkers had appealed as the beneficent force by which the tyranny of prejudice and artifice of custom stood judged, gradually changed shape in his vision, becoming the malignant step-mother whose cruelties – illness, infirmity, senescence, death – ultimately condemned all human beings to helpless misery. A consistent materialism afforded no intellectual comforts. But the temper of Leopardi's pessimism was not stoic: it recommended no renunciation of the passions, remaining loyal to what pleasures could be found in the world. Nor did its conclusions have anything in common with Schopenhauer's later metaphysic of misanthropic resignation. Leopardi's response to the weakness and insignificance of human life in the cosmos was the opposite – a 'titanism' calling for universal solidarity in the battle against nature, that every life must lose.

Timpanaro, a leading authority on Leopardi – whose descendants denied him the right to edit the poet's early philosophical writings for political reasons, though they were technically in the public domain – was hardly unusual in admiring his genius. Nor was he the first to suggest his significance for a modern Left. Others had made this case, often with a degree of overstatement and anachronism. Standard appropriations of Leopardi dwelt on his hostility to clericalism or egalitarian republicanism – his proto-politics – or his materialism. Timpanaro, however, singled out his pessimism as Leopardi's most original and important contribution to a contemporary culture of the Left. This was a much more unsettling move. Gramsci, another hunchback, had famously recommended – the formula came from Romain Rolland – 'optimism of the will, pessimism of the intelligence'. But this was a pessimism of tactical calculation, the precaution of any lucid strategist not to underestimate the enemy. In prison, Gramsci did not see Leopardi as a kindred spirit, criticizing him for his conception of nature as fundamentally hostile to man. Indeed, in a revealing mistake, Gramsci took this to be an expression of 'turbid romanticism', blind to historical progress.[8] Reversing Gramsci's judgement,

---

8. *Quaderni del carcere*, II, Turin 1974, p. 1187.

Timpanaro argued that just this vision was not merely compatible with a revolutionary Marxism, but its necessary complement.

This was an untimely message in Italy, where the insurgencies of the late sixties lasted through to the mid-seventies. For Timpanaro warned the far Left to which he belonged that any one-sided exaltation of 'praxis' ignored at its cost the ineliminable element of passivity in human experience, all that is inevitably suffered rather than done. To acknowledge it, he insisted, was incumbent on any true materialism. In a time of jubilant activism, a more disconcerting and unpopular message could hardly be imagined. Timpanaro was at pains to point out that psychologistic dismissals of Leopardi's pessimism as the despair of a deformed invalid – a traditional stock-in-trade of his critics – were of no avail. The poet's scoliosis certainly forced his attention to the relation between human beings and nature, but 'the experience of deformity and disease is always registered in Leopardi's work at a level that transcends individual lament for a purely private and biographical fact; it is not even to be explained in terms of a purely poetic introspection, but becomes a formidable instrument of cognition'.[9] In fact, Timpanaro reminded his unwilling readers, Leopardi's larger cosmic pessimism, his absolute conviction of the impending annihilation of the world – 'a refutation of every myth of the immortality of human works' – was shared by the most sanguine of Marxists, Friedrich Engels, physically and temperamentally his opposite. It was the co-author of the *Communist Manifesto* who wrote: 'Millions of years may elapse, hundreds of thousands of generations be born and die, but inexorably the time will come when the declining warmth of the sun will no longer suffice to melt the ice thrusting itself forward from the poles; when the human race, crowding more and more about the equator, will finally no longer find even there enough heat for life; when gradually even the last trace of organic life will vanish; and the earth, an extinct frozen globe like the moon, will circle in deepest darkness and in an ever narrower orbit about the equally extinct sun, and at last fall into it'.[10] This was the ultimate fate – the end of the human race, from which successive militants from Blanqui to Lyotard were to dream of inter-planetary escape – that put all voluntarism into proportion.

Culturally, however, the moment of the late Engels was separated from the time of Leopardi by a significant mutation. By the last

---

9. *Classicismo e illuminismo nell'ottocento italiano*, Pisa 1965, p. 158.
10. *Dialectics of Nature*, New York 1942, p. 20.

quarter of the nineteenth century, Romanticism was a spent force and classicist reactions against it had vanished – Leopardi is the last major European writer to be a direct interlocutor of Antiquity. Now, in the wake of broadening scientific advances, the dominant outlook of the age was positivist. A century later, no ideology had a worse press on the Left. In decrying its baleful legacy, all varieties of Western Marxism were united. Here, once again, Timpanaro went clean against the consensus of his own party (in the sense that Marx would have used the term). Whatever its limits or eventual simplifications, he maintained, the positivist culture of the late nineteenth century represented a break with religious myth and folkloric superstition, at a time when scientific truth could still seem a condition of bourgeois progress, and high culture had not yet cut all connection with popular aspirations.[11] Philosophically it may have been mediocre, but its record in other fields – from the natural sciences to history, linguistics to fiction – was considerable. Clausius himself, who predicted the cooling of the sun, not to speak of Darwin, Bernard, Helmholz, Delbruck, Zola, were among the lights of this culture.

By the turn of the century, however – Timpanaro was, of course, not the first to notice this – there was a marked shift. From the age of imperialism onwards, another outlook took hold whose cast was in varying measure idealist, subjectivist, vitalist. Scientific and techno-logical advance continued unabated, indeed even accelerated. But it was now increasingly framed by anti-objectivist epistemologies and demarcations – conventionalism, empirio-criticism, contingentism: Poincaré, Mach, Boutroux – whose target was any consistently mate-rialist view of the world, which could now be dismissed as the illusions of a vulgar 'common sense' refuted by the development of the sciences themselves. In the arts, naturalist report yielded to sym-bolist experiment, depth-charges of wayward interiority, mystical longings or intimations of epiphany. The result was a culture of great brilliance, but much more cut off from popular life than its predeces-sor. Henceforward there would be a sharp divide between the high forms of an educated elite and second-rate fare destined for the masses – a populist semi-culture typically 'instilling petty-bourgeois ideals of moralism and maudlin sentimentalism'.[12] The tasks of cultural unification that positivism had once set for itself were

11. *Classicismo e illuminismo*, pp. 2–5ff.

12. *Sul materialismo*, Pisa 1970, pp. 113–118; *On Materialism*, London 1975, pp. 122–127.

abandoned. This split-level structure, Timpanaro argued, had persisted right through the new century and was still basically intact. The style of mass culture might have changed, but the disposition of the elite culture had not. At these altitudes, idealism in one variant or another – most of them subjectivist – remained the norm.

One famous episode of the traverse at the turn of the century held Timpanaro's particular attention. Freud had started out as a typical product of the positivist culture of the Victorian medical profession. His original premises were robustly materialist, but as his theory of psychoanalysis developed, it became more and more detached from the neurophysiological hypotheses that initially underpinned it, ending in a speculative system that had effectively cast off scientific controls. 'Doctrines which started as more or less imaginative "metaphysics" and later became serious sciences are common enough (it is enough to cite evolutionary theory in biology)', Timpanaro wrote. 'Psychoanalysis has pursued the opposite path: though its aspirations were seriously scientific at its birth, from the outset it contained an admixture of speculative tendencies and then increasingly regressed to a myth.' On the other hand, if it was true that 'psychoanalysis as a therapy records ever more failures, while psychoanalysis as a theory finds its most ardent advocates among literary critics and philosophers',[13] this did not mean that it was intellectually nugatory. There could be no doubt that Freud had greatly enriched our knowledge of ourselves. But he had done so in the sense of Musil or Joyce, rather than Darwin or Einstein.

To demonstrate the difference, Timpanaro took for his object a text that Freud himself declared to be not only an indispensable part of his theory as a whole, but which he asserted had found more general acceptance than any other, *The Psychopathology of Everyday Life*. The work Timpanaro devoted to this touchstone is a technical *tour de force* that is also the most entertaining of his writings. *The Freudian Slip* brings the skills of the philologist to bear on the claims of the psychoanalyst, using the procedures of textual criticism to query the machinery of Freud's explanation of parapraxes. Examining Freud's examples in *The Psychopathology* one by one, Timpanaro showed how often errors of memory or slips of the tongue that Freud had attributed to repressed sexual materials were to be explained more persuasively by a standard set of deviations from the lexical norm,

---

13. *Il lapsus freudiano*, Florence 1974, p. 201; *The Freudian Slip*, London 1976, pp. 223–224.

'corruptions' of which philologists had developed their own fine-grained classification. Freud's explanations, by contrast, were typically captious and arbitrary, resting on chains of association that could be altered or alembicated more or less at will – Timpanaro had fun generating his own variants, from the same materials and with the same logic, reaching even more far-fetched conclusions. True cases of 'Freudian' slips undoubtedly exist, he argued, but the great majority of those discussed by Freud – *a fortiori* in daily life – were closer to the mistakes of ancient or medieval copyists: dipthography, *lectio facilior*, haplography, *saut du même au même*, metathesis, *faute critique*, polar slip, and so on. Psychically repressed material could find its way to the surface through parapraxes, but Freud's insistence that the springs of these must be sexual in origin was a further weakness of his account of them, since it could equally well be social or existential, apprehension of the lower orders or fear of death that had escaped the censor.

The Freudian Slip is a firework display of erudition – alternating tracers of playful and polemical learning criss-crossing the analytic night. Here the combination of Timpanaro's recondite skills and anomalous occupation found their perfect object. He read the examples of *The Psychopathology* with the eye of a proof-reader, and the mind of a classical scholar. Freud's choice of the misremembrance by a 'young Austrian Jew' of Dido's dying appeal in the *Aeneid* for an avenger – *Exoriare aliquis nostris ex ossibus ultor* – for the most extended of all his exercises in the interpretation of a parapraxis, could hardly have been selected more piquantly for posthumous retribution. You do not have to have much first-hand Latin to enjoy Timpanaro's explanation of the strangeness of Virgil's construction, and the reasons why anyone might forget *aliquis*, regardless of erotic anxieties. 'Let someone arise from my bones as an Avenger': it could be the poet himself, appealing down the centuries against misuse to the philologist.

Behind the wit and energy of *The Freudian Slip*, there lay the secret of Timpanaro's occupation. He was a proof-reader not out of choice or circumstance, but under the pressure of intense neurotic distress. In conversation he once said: 'my rancour against Freud comes from the failure of psychoanalysis to cure me'. He was paralysed by two fears. The first was of speaking in public. It was that, he explained, which had made it impossible for him to take any academic post. The notion of teaching in a university filled him with terror at being struck dumb at the lectern. The only time in his life, he told me, when he lost all fear, and suddenly found he could address audiences quite fluently, was in the late sixties. 'In that atmosphere, my inhibitions vanished and to my surprise I had no difficulty in taking the floor at mass meetings.' He reported the exception that political turmoil had made without a hint of pentecostal complaisance, a touch ironically. At such moments his expressive features would sketch a grimace. In his youth, Timpanaro's looks must have been striking: a strong, delicate face, with a hint of acquilinity, firm, flat mouth and dark piercing eyes. By the time I knew him one could sense handicaps, which he did not conceal. Below average height, his voice was harsh and his walk faintly rigid and mechanical, with a slight splay of the feet. His eyes, of luminous beauty and intelligence, dominated every other feature.

The stiffness of his gait could have had something to do with his other fear. He suffered from severe agoraphobia, dreading any kind of travel. If my recollection of a rueful remark by his wife is right, only once in his life did he leave Italy, for a short trip into Yugoslavia. My impression is that over time, he became increasingly a prisoner of Florence itself, a city he spoke of without admiration, ruined by infestation of tourism. A glimpse of what it may have meant to move even within Florence can perhaps be had from a passage in a text set down some years after *The Freudian Slip*. 'Anyone with any knowledge of neurosis, which need not be that of a psychiatrist but may be that of a "victim" knows that agoraphobia can be "overcome" in a number of ways. One may succeed in crossing a public square, but only at the cost of palpitations, tremors, disorientation, terror of being unable to "hold out" to the far side', he wrote. Yet in such cases, 'the "victory" is in truth a defeat, for the price paid is too high and will discourage further attempts: the phobia might admittedly have led to worse things (a sense of vertigo causing its victim to collapse in mid-course, an irresistible impulse to turn back after the first faltering steps), but it has been exacerbated'.[14]

These words occur in a wonderful essay on 'Freud's Roman Phobia', written in 1984. Its subject was Freud's keen desire, yet for many years inner inability, to travel to Rome. What was the source of his fear of the Eternal City? Timpanaro surveyed the explanations offered by subsequent analysts or psycho-historians – Ernest Jones, Marthe Robert, Carl Schorske, Cesare Musatti – who had interpreted the phobia either as the expression of an ambivalence towards Christian Rome, as the destroyer of the Ancient Rome that he loved, or as the

---

14. 'Freud's "Roman Phobia"', *New Left Review*, No. I/147, September–October 1984, p. 25.

mask of an incestuous longing to possess his mother, and dispelled each of them. Paradoxically, he pointed out, all had dismissed Freud's own account of his aversion, which was much more compelling: namely, that he identified Rome with the Catholic Church whose bigotry and anti-Semitism he had experienced early in life, leading him to identify passionately with Hannibal as the Semitic hero of military triumphs over Rome, who in the end never finally reached it. If at first Freud's cult of Hannibal was, as Timpanaro put it, no more than 'a typical schoolboy affection for defeated heroes, such as has inclined all of us to prefer Hector to Achilles (I myself was led by a "Hannibalism" of this kind, which lasted right into my adolescence, to consume in indigestible quantities the most varied literature on the second Punic War)',[15] it became something much more pointed. In Freud's words: 'To my youthful mind Hannibal and Rome symbolized the tenacity of Jewry and the organization of the Catholic Church' – where the euphemism 'organization' itself continues to testify to the intimidating power and menace of the Vatican.

Timpanaro's vindication of Freud's political explanation of his phobia was characteristic of his turn of mind, in its fairness to a figure he had otherwise criticized so sharply, and in its sense of historical context. But there was also a contemporary purpose behind his essay. In it he expressed in the strongest terms his loathing of Catholic persecution of the Jews, and sympathy with the nature of Freud's identification with his people. 'All his life, Freud remained convinced that his discovery of a theory so anti-conformist and "revolutionary" as psychoanalysis had been made easier by his Jewishness, which involved him in battling against a conformist, deeply prejudiced "compact majority" hostile to anyone who chose to differ from it. When he joined the B'nai B'rith association in 1926, he declared quite openly that, being neither a practising Jew nor a "Jewish nationalist", he felt bound to the Jewish community, and proud to be a Jew, only because this left him free "from many prejudices which restricted others in the use of their intellect".'[16] Timpanaro's admiration for this free spirit of loyal detachment is unconcealed.

But he ended his essay with a reminder that things had changed. 'To accept psychoanalysis or to be a Jew is no longer to be marked out as a lonely and courageous non-conformist, struggling with the notorious

15. 'Freud's "Roman Phobia"', p. 8.
16. 'Freud's "Roman Phobia"', p. 9.

"compact majority". There are certainly still upsurges of Nazi and clerical anti-semitism, attacks "from the Right" on the "immorality" of psychoanalysis still occur, and we shall always need to be on our guard against these tendencies. Overall, however, psychoanalysis has been integrated within conformist bourgeois culture, where it has become a more sophisticated substitute for the old traditional religions. Today, the lonely non-conformists are often those who are prepared (without dismissing it out of hand) to submit it to critical discussion'. Nor was this all. 'Furthermore, there now exists a Jewish "compact majority", the State of Israel, which not only claims (with absolute justice) its own right to exist, but denies that right to another people whose claim is equally just, submitting it to a murderous abuse of power worthy of the European colonialism which helped to establish it. This State would not be able to pursue its evil policies without the backing of a much larger "compact majority" – the Western, so-called democratic world. Today the very term 'anti-Semitic' has lost all meaning, since the most immediate victims of Israeli arrogance are of Semitic descent, while the Israelis are sustained in their crimes, financed and supplied with arms by devout Christians'. Those in the Diaspora who kept alive the tolerant traditions of cosmopolitan Jewry, disowning what was done in their name by Tel Aviv, were still too few. Today it was not for Israelis, or Jewish apologists for Israel, to identify with Hannibal, the isolated Semitic hero, but 'Palestinians defending the claims of the Palestinian people'.[17]

Timpanaro's politics did not falter with age. They find their fullest expression in a singular book of the same period, *Il Socialismo di Edmondo de Amicis* (1983), a work of translucent advocacy that has a special place in his writing. Its focus is one of the oddest literary careers of nineteenth-century Europe. In the history of Italian literature, Edmondo de Amicis (1846–1908) is mainly remembered for the two disparate works that originally made his name. The first, *Vita Militare* (1868), was a work of patriotic edification based on de Amicis's experience as a Piedmontese officer in the last phase of the Risorgimento, when he had served against the Austrians at Custoza. The second, *Cuore* (1886), is a cloying children's story that became an enormous bestseller – over 200 editions by the time it was translated into English and other European languages a decade later – and is still a standard text in Italian elementary schools. Franco Moretti has skewered it in a brilliant essay on the functions of the tear-jerker

---

17. 'Freud's "Roman Phobia"', pp. 30–31.

(taking *Misunderstood* as its English-language counterpart). By this time de Amicis had become a byword for *bien-pensant* civics lessons and sententious moralism.

In the early seventies, however, Italo Calvino 'rediscovered' one of his late novels, *Amore e ginnastica*, praising its erotic mordancy. Then in 1980, the manuscript of a novel de Amicis had written nearly a hundred years earlier, but had left in a drawer, was published. Its title was *Primo Maggio*: a novel about socialism. It was well known that in his last years, de Amicis had preached what was generally held to be a sentimental doctrine of social commiseration and inter-class harmony. The all but unanimous reaction of critics – indeed of the editors of the text itself – to *Primo Maggio* was to dismiss it as a botched product of these emotional shallows, of scant political and no aesthetic interest. Timpanaro's book is a scathing polemic against this reception of the novel. In a close reading, he was able to show that far from being a lifeless tract of weak-minded reformism, trundling cardboard figures through predictable motions, *Primo Maggio* not only displayed considerable skill and nuance of characterization, but embodied a revolutionary critique of the bourgeois social order of the time, of such intransigence that de Amicis may well have left it unpublished for fear of prosecution if it saw the light of day. Passing in review the novel's major themes – de Amicis's treatment of army, school, religion, family; his picture of the relations between capital and labour; his imagery of women and case for sexual freedom; his conception of revolution, and what a socialist state should not look like; his sympathy for anarchism in its very opposition to socialism – Timpanaro's commentary has a crispness of intellectual attack that suggests a rapid and passionate composition. *Primo Maggio* was not a fictional pamphlet; in it de Amicis gave persuasive voice to critics of any idea of a working-class revolution, and graphic representation of the costs of any miscalculated demonstration against the established order. The novel undoubtedly had its weaknesses: more ambitious, it was also less achieved than *Amore e ginnastica*. No one would consider it a masterpiece, but so what? Timpanaro ended his book with these gaily taunting words: 'And now you want to tell me that Alberto Bianchini [the central character of *Primo Maggio*] is no Julien Sorel, nor Giulia [his wife] Madame de Renal or Anna Karenina? That even a socialist has more to learn from *A la recherche* or *The Conscience of Zeno*, or even *Germinal*, which is not dear to you, than from *Primo Maggio*? That a great reactionary writer is, against his own intentions, more revolutionary than a lesser socialist one? These things are so obvious that even I know them. But joys in life are few; and if instructing me in all this gives you even the smallest pleasure, why I should grudge you it?'[18]

If the transformed figure of de Amicis who emerges from Timpanaro's pages appears a sport of culture, a kind of cross between William Morris and Erich Kästner, such possibilities belonged to the epoch. *Primo Maggio* is a contemporary of *News from Nowhere*, to which it might best be compared. We are at the confident beginning of Donald Sassoon's hundred years of socialism. Timpanaro was writing at their end, and in retrospect *Il socialismo di Edmondo de Amicis* seems like a moving finale of a classical tradition, bringing back to life a world of revolutionary thought and movement in all its freshness for one last time, on the verge of its extinction. He was aware of what probably lay ahead. Locally, he had foreseen the complete destruction of the Italian socialism in which he grew up, at a time when some of his former companions were still pinning hopes on Craxi. A little later – 1982 – he remarked more generally that perhaps more 'Homo sapiens would turn out to be a zoological species capable of language, thought, art and so many other excellent things, but incapable of equality or collective self-government'.[19] By the mid-nineties he was writing that *On Materialism* now looked 'like a fossil, and will remain so for a long time or for ever'.[20] But the defeat of his political hopes did not mean any philosophical retreat. In his last years, he produced new translations of Holbach's *Bon sens* and Cicero's *De divinatione*, each with a long introductory essay, of pointed scholarship and intent. If the battle against religious superstition had not yet been won, there was more chance of swinging veteran battering-rams like these against it than of unseating the rule of capital.

Through all this, he never ceased to work as a highly technical philologist. One of his last books is devoted to the tradition of Virgilian scholarship in Antiquity. Its concern is to rescue a line of textual commentary in the Roman world often dismissed as beneath modern attention. The central figure of Timpanaro's account is a now obscure grammarian of the first century AD, Valerius Probus of Beirut – a philologist, he argued in detail, perfectly entitled to contemporary respect: his merits neither to be overstated, as they were by

---

18. *Il socialismo di Edmondo de Amicis. Lettura del 'Primo Maggio'*, Verona 1983, p. 192.

19. *Antileopardiani e neomoderati nella sinistra italiana*, p. 327.

20. *Nuovi studi sul nostro ottocento*, Pisa 1995, p. xi.

his disciples, nor minimized, as they had been by subsequent posterity.[21] Here lay a figure in the carpet, one of the deepest motifs in all Timpanaro's work. It can be seen as inextricable from his philological impulse itself – what made his vocation. The recovery of neglected talents or writers to their proper reputation belonged to the same enterprise as the restoring of ancient texts to their integrity. Timpanaro started his career with a revaluation of Leopardi's classical scholarship, cast into the shadows by his poetry. When he came to write his book on the genesis of the Lachmann method, quote marks became necessary round the phrase, since his central finding was that genealogical classification of manuscript versions did not actually originate with Lachmann, but less well-known scholars of the time – Madvig, Zumpt, Bernays – whose more polymathic work had not achieved the same canonization as that of Lachmann, 'a great simplifier, with the virtues and defects that implies'.[22] Writing on Italian classicism, he put Pietro Giordani into unaccustomed relief alongside Leopardi; on materialism, he defied received opinion on the Left by giving pride of place to Engels rather than Marx.

After writing his book on Freud, a friend told him of an essay published in 1923 by Rudolf Meringer, a German linguist, criticizing *The Psychopathology of Everyday Life* along lines that anticipated some of his own. He immediately translated and edited it, with a long postscript, to make sure that credit was paid to a pioneer where it was due, and insisted that any reprint of *The Freudian Slip* contain an acknowledgment of the precession.[23] Of all his acts of retrospective justice, the most sustained was his recuperation of *Primo Maggio*, doubly contemned, the suppressed work of an author decried for other reasons. But perhaps the most affecting is his portrait of the freethinker Carlo Bini of Livorno, a minor *carbonaro* who translated Byron and helped Mazzini, author of splendidly corrosive texts from prison in Elba, before relapsing into silence, illness and a premature bohemian death, to the scandal of right-thinking associates.[24] Timpanaro's long essay on Bini is one of his most personal. A modest man himself, who

---

21. *Per la storia della filologia virgiliana antica*, Rome 1986, pp. 18, 127.

22. *La genesi del metodo del Lachmann*, pp. 69–72.

23. Rudolf Meringer, 'Die täglichen Fehler im Sprechen, Lesen und Handeln', and Sebastiano Timpanaro, 'Postscriptum a Meringer', *Critica Storica*, No. 3, 1982, pp. 393–485.

24. 'Alcuni chiarimenti su Carlo Bini', *Antileopardiani e neomoderati*, pp. 199–285; see also 'Due cospiratori che negarono di aver cospirato', in *Nuovi studi sull nostro ottocento*, pp. 103–125.

stressed his own limitations, there may have been an element of fellow-feeling in his sympathy for the undeservedly obscure or defeated. But behind it was something it else – an unusually strong, instinctive egalitarianism. In conversation, he rarely used the formal *lei* with anyone. In matters of style, he deprecated any hint of exhibition or pretension, detesting above all what he called intellectual 'foppery' (*civetteria*). As for questions of character, his categories retained an eighteenth-century ring: his most frequent term of dispraise was *mascalzone* – 'scoundrel'.

What of his concerns? The philosophical-political contrast he drew between Romanticism and classicism in the epoch of the Restoration is posed as a continental phenomenon. But its demonstration remains national, tested out in Italy. There the evidence is striking, but Timpanaro did not probe its conditions of possibility very far. Historically, however, it is pretty clear that it was the very backwardness of Italy – its political and cultural stunting, under foreign rule and clerical censorship – that produced the paradox of a vanguard/rearguard classicism so late. Here the Enlightenment, largely over elsewhere, still had a powerful unspent momentum, capable of carrying it beyond even the most intrepid naturalistic outposts of the *philosophes*, while at the same confining it to an isolate. Remarking that the one great figure of Restoration Europe to owe allegiance to Romanticism yet remain faithful to the legacy of Helvétius and Destutt de Tracy was Stendhal, Timpanaro overlooked the opposite paradox, that it was in Italy Beyle found a life of the emotions and the senses he identified with all that was Romantic, in contrast to the arid conventions of his rationalist homeland. This sort of question did not preoccupy Timpanaro. Hostile to nationalism of any stripe – a caustic critic of contemporary uses of the Gramscian concept of the 'national-popular' – he was disinclined to compare countries. Nor was there anything historicist in his formation. More than most intellectuals on the Left, he was averse to the influence of Croce. But what he most reproached Croce for was helping to 'bar doors and windows' against non-Italian culture under Fascism, and so inflicting a double damage. As he put it in an essay on Giorgio Pasquali, who had resisted Croce's example, 'first we had provincial closure; now, by way of reaction, we have no less provincial – uncritical – enthusiasm for European, and especially French, culture'.[25]

---

25. 'Pasquali, la metrica, e la cultura di Roma arcaica', introduction to Giorgio Pasquali, *Preistoria della poesia romana* (re-edition), Florence 1971, pp. 48–49.

What was Timpanaro's position within his own culture? There is a sense in which his outlier existence was not so untypical. The Italian university system – in many respects archaic and bureaucratic to a degree – has long driven many of the country's best minds to exasperated refuge abroad. Arnaldo Momigliano, originally an exile in England, chose not to come back to Italy after the war, though in his case the reasons were to do with the memory of his forced emigration itself. Luca Cavalli-Sforza, Carlo Cipolla, Franco Modigliani and Giovanni Sartori took chairs in America. In the next levy, Carlo Ginzburg, Franco Moretti and Giovanni Arrighi all gave up posts at home, more or or less in despair, to make their way across the Atlantic. This has never been a real intellectual emigration, since figures like these have typically continued to participate actively in the cultural life of Italy, during spells at home or from abroad. But it has reduced the significance of native academic institutions for the circulation of ideas at large. If Timpanaro was isolated in his own country, it was not due to his occupation as a proof-reader, but to the unpalatibility of his themes to the surrounding culture. The extent of his solitude should not be exaggerated. He was a correspondent on an eighteenth-century scale, not only with fellow philologists. In Florence he was a regular contributor, for over thirty years, to the country's most distinguished and nonconformist 'journal of various humanities', *Belfagor* – founded by Luigi Russo, the post-war director of the Scuola Normale, who named it after Machiavelli's wanton devil against the express admonitions of Croce (*'un titolo troppo chiassoso'*) who told him not to mix literature with politics. It is difficult to imagine Timpanaro's productivity without its support. Abroad, the most serious responses to his work seem to have come from England, where Raymond Williams wrote an admiring critique of his conception of nature, proposing an alternative materialist sensibility, and Charles Rycroft, from within psychoanalysis, largely endorsed his account of parapraxes. *New Left Review*, which published texts by and about him, was a point of external reference, though a journal where he regularly suffered the worst typographical indignities for one of his temperament and training, a stream of misprints flowing through his very diagnosis of just such errors ('Australian Jew' on the first page of a dismantling of *The Psychopathology*, etc.). He minded about such carelessness.

While the angle at which Timpanaro stood to the academic world in Italy was never the same as that of his compatriots abroad – he was much less economically secure, and enjoyed no overseas collegiality to offset potential cold shoulders at home – there is a common element in the style of this detachment of thinkers that is the obverse of the atmosphere of murky intrigue and fustiness that still clings to many local universities. Just because higher education has never been truly modernized in Italy, much of it remaining in a kind of suspended delapidation, academic professionalization in the post-war sense has never entirely taken hold. The drawbacks of this have often been pointed out. It has also, however, meant a relative underdevelopment of baneful effects familiar elsewhere: peer-group fixation, index-of-citations mania, gratuitous apparatuses, pretentious jargons, guild conceit – everything that stands between mind and thought in our culture. Absent much of this, Italian conditions can produce a relationship to ideas, unmediated by any institutional protocols, of a *sui generis* purity and directness. This effect – it could be called an advantage of quasi-backwardness – is not confined to any particular standpoint or location. Right, Centre and Left are equally represented among the overseas scholars; while Norberto Bobbio, who has always worked within the Italian university, is just as much an illustration of it as Giovanni Arrighi, who abandoned the system. At the same time, the appalling quality of Italian mass culture – TV shows capable of deterring the most dedicated follower of folk-fashion – has been a safeguard against populist affectations that elsewhere have become a typical compensation for professorial involution.

Without the MLA or BBC, so to speak, the space for an older kind of imagination has survived. Two features mark it out. The first is an ability to engage with ideas of the past – proximate or remote – as if they were as immediate as those of the present, without any strain of reference or exhibition of learning. Rousseau or Mill in Sartori, Bodin or Vico in the pages of Bobbio, Augustine or Voltaire in Ginzburg, Hegel or Rilke in Moretti, Weber or Hicks in Arrighi, speak with vivid directness to us, as though by some magic of intellectual disintermediation. This is in part an effect of the second gift of this Italianate mode, its distinctive clarity and economy of expression. Sartre once remarked that the Italian language of the post-war period was *trop pompeuse pour être maniable*, like a decaying palace in which writers wandered around at a loss, no longer knowing quite how to take up residence. A too capacious syntax, permitting virtually any shape or shapelessness of sentence, has been part of the sumptuous *décombres*. Anyone who has ever heard a political speech, looked at an administrative document, or glanced at a daily newspaper in Italy will have a sense of this. The writing of what could be called – with some but not complete variation of meaning – the enlightened counter-culture of this period has been formed in reaction against the euphuistic slackness of so much public discourse in Italy. What its different practitioners have in common is a planed-down terseness and transparency. More obviously than any contemporary variant of French, it could be described as a classical prose.

Timpanaro belonged to this national set, though with traits that placed him somewhat apart within it. Suspicious of any deliberate literary effect, he wrote straightforwardly and forcefully, where necessary at the cost of formal finish. Lucan or Bopp appear with more contextual distance, in keeping with his training, but bluntly and powerfully enough to jolt conventional expectations. These were nuances. Where he really differed was in his complete indifference to intellectual fashion – his considered rejection of every consecrated school of thought in his time. Judging the overwhelming propensity of the Western intelligentsia to be anti-materialist, in one specious guise or another, he took his ground outside any consensus, conservative or progressive. The claim that high culture since at least the Belle Epoque has always been predominantly idealist in tendency is a sweeping one. Was he wrong? He came to this conclusion long before the high tide of post-structuralism in the arts and conventionalism in the sciences: neither Kuhn nor Derrida, let alone Geertz or Rorty, rate a mention in his verdict on the epistemological slide of the age. It could well be thought that, as he denounced it, all he described was yet to reach its paroxysm.

But the overall balance of intellectual forces is another matter. There were many signs, as the century approached its end, that the tables were being turned. Most conspicuously, the new genetics has started to have the same kind of cultural impact as the old in the age of Darwin. Evolutionary models borrowed from the latest biology are spreading everywhere: in economics, psychology, literature, sociology, international relations – the talk is all of adaptation, exaptation, mutation, replication. Popularizers like Gould or Dawkins rival the fame of Spencer or Huxley in their day, naturally at a higher level. Even in philosophy, traditional nursery of every refinement of idealism, neurophysiology now has belligerent champions. Lent confidence by the spectacular successes of the natural sciences over the past twenty-five years, stretching from astrophysics to the genome, positivism – not the name, still faintly ungrateful, but the thing – is back in force. How far its return in these forms would have been a source of satisfaction to Timpanaro is imponderable. Certainly it was not accompanied by any displacement to the Left in the political world; famously, the reverse. But then he had never equated intellectual with social progress.

Historically, even in the greatest minds of the Enlightenment, they could be at variance. Rousseau, the most advanced political thinker of his generation, was emotionally a pietist; Voltaire, politically at ease with a benevolent absolutism, scorned the consolations of Savoyard Christianity. For Timpanaro, Leopardi had represented the possibility of a synthesis beyond either: firm republicanism, unswerving atheism. A generation later, Georg Büchner – it seems strange Timpanaro never touched on him – would make a fiercer join of his own. Both died before the political logic of their pessimistic materialism could really be tested. In Leopardi's case, Timpanaro conceded that his republican convictions had receded as his cosmic despair – 'existence is a disfiguring birthmark on the face of nothingness' – deepened, prompting sporadic expressions of political indifferentism. Yet by the end, he argued, Leopardi had reached some kind of difficult equilibrium between them. But it was true that his understanding of society always remained limited – it was absurd to present him as a proto-socialist. Still more absurd was the attempt to make of him an ecologist *ante diem*. One of Timpanaro's last major polemics was with his friend Adriano Sofri, once leader of *Lotta Continua*, now in jail for the duration in Pisa on trumped-up – *pentito* – evidence. At the time Sofri was a theorist of Green politics, who had sought to annex Leopardi for what Timpanaro saw as an emollient environmentalism, rising above class conflicts in a rescue mission to save Mother Nature, in which all could impartially join.[26] Leopardi's vision of nature as malign stepmother, visiting ills 'infinite and immedicable' on human beings, was the antithesis of such a conception. His pessimism could not be put to any kind of Gaian service.

What of Timpanaro's own? He made no secret of its biographical sources. It was not an expression of political withdrawal or bookish influence, but the product of 'direct, personal reflection on all that vast part of human unhappiness that is not related to man's social but his biological being'.[27] From a number of scattered passages, it is clear that his father's long, painful illness and death were deeply traumatic for Timpanaro, bringing him close to breakdown. His own psychic disabilities, however related to this experience, must have reinforced the intellectual effects of it, and would have drawn him to Leopardi anyway. Suffering from another kind of deformity, he arrived at a parallel pessimism, equally impersonal, equally reasoned. It was not

---

26. 'Il "Leopardi verde"', *Belfagor*, November 1987, pp. 613–637.
27. *Antileopardiani e neomoderati*, p. 11.

the same, because Timpanaro had so much stronger a sense of social oppression and injustice, above and beyond our natural caducity. At times, in the scales of misery, society seemed of small account to Leopardi – emperor and beggar alike pitched into the grave. So conceived, philosophical pessimism always risked becoming political defeatism. Timpanaro was not subject to this temptation. He was intensely – even on occasion, he admitted, too vehemently – political. But he was also quite free from the monomania of any 'pan-politicism', as he once called it. The ideas of historical progress and natural catastrophe were not at odds in him. Yet perhaps time played a trick on him all the same. He had started out believing that an egalitarian revolution was possible, and amendment of our natural condition impossible. Ironically, today, it is the opposite opinion that holds sway: capitalism cannot be abolished, but infirmity might be. In the seventeenth century, Descartes was sure that science would soon let people live for ever. His confidence shows signs of returning. When Timpanaro died, he was termed by another philologist an enemy of the twentieth century. In such conditions, how could he remain actual in the new one? He would have had no truck with the question. '"Actuality"', he once wrote, 'is a reductive, anti-historical and philistine criterion of judgement.'[28]

2001

---

28. 'Pasquali, la metrica e la cultura di Roma antica', p. 76.

10

TROPICAL RECALL:
Gabriel García Márquez

As ways of writing about a past, memoirs and autobiographies, although in practice they may often overlap, are different undertakings. At the limit, a memoir can recreate a world lavishly peopled with others, while saying very little about the author himself. An autobiography, on the other hand, can take the form of a pure portrait of the self; the world and others featuring only as *mise-en-scène* for the inner adventure of the narrator. In recounting their lives, novelists have produced bravura performances in either genre. Among modern writers, Anthony Powell's *To Keep the Ball Rolling* – four leisurely, yet laconic volumes – offers a masterpiece of the first form. Sartre's brief *Words* is perhaps the greatest example of the second. Gabriel García Márquez's *Living to Tell the Tale* is billed by its publishers a memoir, and there is little doubt that on the whole it falls to that side of the divide.[1] Márquez is, of course, a legendary story-teller. But he also has an acutely self-reflective intelligence, as a glance at *The Fragrance of Guava*, his biographical conversations with Plinio Apuleyo Mendoza of twenty years ago, shows.[2]

In *Living to the Tell the Tale*, Márquez exercises this side of his gifts very sparingly. By artistic choice he has instead constructed a memoir as close in form to a novel as perhaps has ever been written. It opens with the arrival of his mother in Barranquilla, to take her son – then twenty-three – back with her to sell the family house in Aracataca, on the trip that made him the novelist he became; and ends with the ultimatum he wrote on a plane to Geneva, five years later, that made the

---

1. *Vivir para contarla*, Madrid 2002; *Living to Tell the Tale*, New York 2003. Henceforward *VC* and *LTT*.
2. *El olor de la guayaba*, Bogotá 1982; *The Fragrance of Guava*, London 1984.

elusive sweetheart of his adolescence his future wife. Between these two parallel *coups de théâtre*, the author recounts his life up the point when he left Colombia in 1955, in a narrative that obeys not the untidy patterns of experience or memory, with all their unevenness, but rules of a perfectly symmetrical composition. The book is divided into eight chapters of virtually identical length – an arrangement least of all corresponding to the way any life can actually be lived, as if to underline that we are in the presence of another supreme artifice.

From the start, Márquez has practised two relatively distinct styles of writing: the figurally charged prose already on brilliant display in his earliest fiction *Leaf Storm*, which was rejected for publication at the time, with the concession that it was 'poetic'; and the objective concision of such tales as *No-one Writes to the Colonel* or reportages like *News of a Kidnapping*. If technically the register of *Living to Tell Tale* lies somewhere between the two, the tone and effect of the whole – this follows from the conception of the memoirs – has the crisp, sumptuous grandeur of his major novels. We are in the world of *A Hundred Years* or *The General in his Labyrinth*, with its metaphoric density and trade-mark dialogue: lofty one-liners that function like near-epigrams, of inimitable pungency and good-humoured irony.

Formally, what we are told is the tale of Márquez's youth in Colombia. Vivid portraits of his grandparents and parents establish the strangest of family settings. We then are given his childhood, up to the age of eight, with his grandfather in the banana zone of the Caribbean coast; early schooldays in poverty in Barranquilla, and holidays in a more Edenic hinterland; passage up the Magdalena river to an Andean *liceo;* entry into university at Bogotá; an eyewitness description of the apocalyptic riots in the capital after the assassination of the country's leading populist politician, Eliécer Gaitán; flight from the conflagration back to the coast; early journalism in Cartagena; literary enthusiasm and bohemian dissipation in Barranquilla again; finally a regular reporter's job in Bogotá, and dispatch abroad to cover the Geneva Conference of 1955. All this with a wealth of striking incident, intriguing detail and flamboyant chance that few works of fiction could equal.

Yet its sum is not a *Bildungsroman* of the author, whose personality is rarely front-lit, but the recreation of an astonishing universe, the Caribbean coastlands of Colombia in the first half of the last century. Anyone who might think that a factual counterpart of Márquez's fictions could be at best only a pallid duplicate can be reassured. Scene after remarkable scene, character after arresting character, cascades of gestures beyond logic and coincidences beyond reason, make of *Living to Tell the Tale* a cousin of the great novels. This first volume of Márquez's final enterprise is a major, meditated edifice of literary imagination. It is tempting therefore to read it simply as a work of art, independently of its status as a biographical document.

That would diminish its interest, however. One way of seeing why this is so is to consider its relationship to the memoirs of the Latin American writer most often associated with Márquez, and second only in fame to himself. Mario Vargas Llosa's *A Fish in Water*, published over a decade ago, has a less conventional structure.[3] Written in the aftermath of the defeat of his candidacy to the presidency of Peru in 1991, it consisted of chapters alternating between the writer's childhood and youth in his native country, and his campaign to become its ruler when he was in fifties – a switching device he has used more than once in his fiction, from *Aunt Julia and the Scriptwriter* to the recent *Way to Paradise*. Within this form, the three years of his presidential campaign take up more space than the twenty-two years of his passage to adulthood. That alone makes it a very different kind of memoir from Márquez's. All the more striking, then, are the resemblances between their early experiences, in many respects uncannily close.

Both writers spent their crucial first years as small boys under the roof of an adoring grandfather, the patriarch of the family – a civil war veteran in Colombia, a planter and prefect in Bolivia/Peru. Their fathers, who had similar jobs (a telegraph operator, a radio operator), and made similar marriages (against in-law resistance, above their station) were absent: blank positions in the emotional structures of childhood, in which even mothers played a secondary role. Sexual initiation came early, in brothels of which each writes with a wry affection. Later, each married a home-town girl. As adolescents, both were sent against their will to boarding schools by their fathers. Each was happily formed in the provinces, and experienced arrival in the capital as a misfortune.

At university, both plunged into a side-life of journalism and nocturnal carousal. Each turned a hand to radio soap operas, even inspired by the same tear-jerker – 'Felix B. Caignet's *El Derecho de nacer*' (no anachronistic pro-life connotations). In both cases, the great literary discovery of their youth was Faulkner, whose novels they report marking them more deeply than any other. Each ends his memoir of those years at the same fateful point, as the writer – having

---

3. *El pez en el agua*, Barcelona 1994; *A Fish in Water*, New York 1994. Henceforward *PA* and *FW*.

just learnt something of the unknown interior of the land (El Chocó; Amazonas) – leaves his native country for Europe, never to fix his residence there again.

A set of parallels like these is an invitation to some future Plutarch of Latin American letters. Yet what they serve to throw into relief are finally the contrasts between the two novelists, and their memoirs. For all the similarities in their family constellations, Vargas Llosa came – on his mother's side – from a more privileged social background, a clan of the Arequipa elite that produced Peru's first post-war President, Bustamante y Rivero. Class and colour situated him higher up the social scale, in what was also a more rigidly racist society, than a mestizo boy would be in Colombia. Formal education, too, separated them. Márquez explains how thoroughly disaffected he was from his studies at university, where his father had insisted he take law, and he eventually dropped out. Vargas Llosa, on the other hand, had a brilliant student *cursus*, becoming an assistant to a leading local historian in Lima before even graduating. The university was a central experience for him, where it meant nothing to Márquez. That difference explains why he got to Europe much earlier in his career, with a scholarship to Madrid. So too, once in Europe, he has never really left it, living essentially in Paris, London, Madrid, with trips back to Lima; while as a journalist Márquez soon returned to Latin America, and would ultimately settle in Mexico.

These divergent trajectories have their atmospheric correlates in the work of each. In their lifetimes, the history of their two countries – measured in terms of slaughter, repression, frustration, corruption – could hardly have been grimmer, and these of course find expression in their novels. But Márquez's depictions of his homeland, even at its worst, are infused with a lyrical warmth, an immutable love, that have no counterpart in Vargas Llosa's world, where the writer's relationship to the land of his origins is always tense and ambiguous.

Part of the reason for this difference can be found in their individual situations. For if the configuration of the two families from which they came was strikingly similar, their emotional voltage was quite opposite. Márquez's mother, of whom he paints a loving portrait, was clearly a woman of great strength of character, capable of managing her spirited, if wayward, husband and eleven children, in penury or precarious prosperity alike. Vargas Llosa's father, abandoning his spouse without a word when she was five months' pregnant, and appearing out of the blue ten years later to repossess her and shanghai him, was by contrast a traumatic nightmare: feared by his wife and hated by his son. Showing no attachment to his native land, he eventually emigrated to the US, dying a janitor in Pasadena.

Even the melodramas of the early sexual experience of the two writers, set pieces of Latin honour and outrage, reflect this contrast. When Vargas Llosa married his aunt – in this semi-deracinate family, not coincidentally a Bolivian – his father, after brandishing a revolver, denounced him to the police in Lima, and threatened to kill him with five bullets, like a rabid dog. García Márquez, caught *in flagrante* with the black wife of a policeman in the backlands, was faced with a pistol too, and the words: 'cheating in bed is settled with lead'. [4] But the affronted sergeant let the terrified boy off with an humiliation, as thanks for a medical service from his father, and when last seen is drinking with him. The two scenes, each set pieces of a theatrical machismo, speak in their way of differing societies. The poetry and humanity of the Colombian episode capture the general spirit of *Living to Tell the Tale*, and the ties of its author with the community in which he grew up, whereas the title of *A Fish in Water* inverts the story it actually tells. This is more accurately conveyed by its first draft, released as 'A Fish Out of Water' – a reversal that is not the least oddity of Vargas Llosa's memoir as a whole.[5] Composed at a moment of acute political disappointment, and inevitably somewhat discoloured by it, the book is nevertheless shot through with detestation of much – social and cultural, as well as political – in Peruvian life that clearly expresses sentiments of long standing.

The literary consequences of this difference are not what might be expected. The – now shop-worn – label of 'magical realism' is customarily applied to Márquez's novels. It has never fitted Vargas Llosa, who disavows the adjective. 'I have an invincible weakness for so-called realism', he remarks in *A Fish in Water*.[6] One of the most significant contrasts between their fiction follows from – or perhaps dictates – these distinct options. The bulk of Vargas Llosa's work is set in the Peruvian present, contemporary with his own experience. The principal exceptions are displacements, not just of time but of space – the Brazil of *War of the End of the World*, or the France and

---

4. *PA*, pp. 333–334; *FW*, p. 329; *VC*, p. 255; *LTT*, p. 217.
5. See 'A Fish out of Water', *Granta* No. 36, June 1991, pp. 15–75, an issue that also contains an account of his presidential campaign by the British consultant Mark Malloch Brown, previously an adviser in the same capacity to Gonzalo Sánchez Losada – a Bolivian President later obliged to flee from the population to Miami – and today right-hand man of Kofi Annan in the United Nations Secretariat.
6. *PA*, p. 469; *FW*, p. 462.

South Seas of *Way of Paradise*. Within his own country, he has been unwaveringly *à la page*. None of García Márquez's major novels, on the other hand, represents the epoch in which he himself became a writer. Macondo vanishes in the Great Depression. The patriarch belongs to the rustic world of Juan Vicente Gomez (*fl.* 1908–35). The time of cholera is Victorian. The General expires as the Restoration ends. Modernity is allergic to magic. Márquez's powers have always needed a recession into the past to be exercised with full freedom.

In the public mind, of course, what probably distinguishes the two writers most are conventional images of their politics – García Márquez as the friend of Fidel, Vargas Llosa as a devotee of Thatcher, figures respectively of an ecumenical Left and a liberal Right. That polarity exists, of course. But if one looks at the writing, rather than the affiliations, it is another contrast that is more striking. Vargas Llosa was from the beginning, and has remained, a political animal. As a student in Lima under the Odría dictatorship, he was an active Communist militant, inducted into the Party by Héctor Béjar, who would lead the first Peruvian guerrilla in the sixties; and after arriving in Europe, steeped himself in Marxist theory as an enthusiast for the Cuban Revolution. When he broke with the Left over Cuba in the early seventies, he did not simply retreat into literature , as did others, but became a passionate admirer of Hayek and Friedman, and a leading advocate of free-market capitalism in Latin America. His run for the presidency of Peru, with the support of the traditional Right, was not a sudden caprice, but the outcome of a decade of consistent public activity. Logically, his fiction – from his earliest depiction of the military academy in *The Time of the Hero*, through the revolutionary conspiracies of *Conversation in the Cathedral* or *Alejandro Majtà* to *Feast of the Goat* – takes contemporary political conflicts directly as an organizing theme.

This has never been the case with García Márquez, and *Living to Tell the Tale* helps to explain why, though patches of mystery remain. He depicts a youngster, coming from the coast in the highlands in his teens, so absorbed in literary matters – at first poetry, above all – as to have virtually no interest in public affairs. Colombia was already in a high state of political tension in his last school years, and just as he arrived at university, the country descended into civil war. *Living to Tell the Tale* contains – its most powerful single chapter – a Goyaesque panorama of the social earthquake that engulfed Bogotá when Gaitán, its most popular politician, was murdered in 1948. From his *pension* three blocks away, García Márquez rushed to the scene, arriving to witness the lynching of the assassin and the outbreak of the tidal wave of rioting and looting that swept the city. But his reaction, as he records it, was simply to go back to the boarding-house to finish his lunch. Meeting him on the street, an older relative – who became one of the leaders of the revolutionary junta that tried to steer the turmoil into an uprising against the Conservative government – urged him to participate in the student protests against the murder. In vain. Terrified by the wholesale destructions and killings of the next days, when the army moved into the city to restore order, his one desire was to escape.

The *Violencia* that ravaged Colombia for the next decade, pitting Liberals against the ruling Conservatives, took 200,000 lives – a catastrophe worse than any endured in Peru. This was the historical background to Márquez's early career as a journalist and writer. But he seems to have remained eerily untouched by it. Although a regular columnist for a Cartagena daily, he writes that 'in my political obfuscation at the time, I did not even know that martial law had been reimposed in the country'.[7] In Barranquilla, a little later, 'the truth of my soul was that the drama of Colombia reached me like a remote echo and moved me only when it spilled over into rivers of blood'.[8] The confession is disarming, but the distinction untenable: Colombia's drama *was* the spilling of rivers of blood. The reality seems to have been that the young littérateur, entirely wrapped up in discoveries and experiments of the imagination, in these years effectively ignored the fate of his country.

This was easier to do in the coastal cities, since the Caribbean littoral, although not immune to sectarian killing, was spared the worst of the *Violencia* raging along the coffee frontiers of the highlands. Márquez's identification with his region – 'the only place where I really feel at home' – has given his writing its luminous intensity, but also seems to have shielded, or blinded, him from larger national patterns and forces. 'Colombia', he writes, 'had always been a country with a Caribbean identity that opened to the world by means of the umbilical cord of Panama. Its forced amputation condemned us to be what we are today: a nation with an Andean mentality whose circumstances favor the canal between the two oceans belonging not to us but to the United States.'[9]

---

7. *VC*, p. 405; *LTT*, p. 343.
8. *VC*, p. 431; *LTT*, pp. 364–365.
9. *VC*, p. 532; *LTT*, pp. 449–450.

The regret is palpable, and consequential. It would be not much of an exaggeration to say that the Andean uplands that form the core of Colombian society have remained something of a closed book to Márquez. Hence in part, no doubt, the blankness of *Living to Tell the Tale* about the civil war within which much of it unfolds. The novelist's one venture into contemporary history, *News of a Kidnapping*, humane and gripping though it is as the account of a closing episode in Pablo Escobar's career, confirms a certain intellectual mountain-sickness. For it lacks either much sense of the social context of Colombia's drug wars or critical vision of the oligarchy presiding over them. Reading it, one might be tempted to think that at bottom Márquez has remained as unpolitical as when he started out.

That would be a mistake, as the sequel to *Living to Tell the Tale* will certainly show. But both this memoir and his fiction suggest a mind with a marvellous intuitive sensibility for the temper, the colour and the details of the world in which he grew up, without much thought for definition of its relationships or structures. From this account, it would be difficult to locate Márquez's family with any accuracy in a social scale. His grandfather, though represented as a patriarch of some substance, appears to have been originally little more than an artisan, albeit a goldsmith: the economic basis of the legendary household in Aracataca – his father is described as seeking the hand of a 'daughter of a wealthy family' – remains obscure. The ups and downs in his father's fortunes, from extreme poverty to modest comfort – seemingly unrelated to the proliferation of eleven offspring – are only a little less elusive. In due course, clan connections reveal themselves: an uncle in the Cartagena police, capable of dispensing jobs, a professor in Bogotá, owner of a major bookstore. How all this fitted the young Gabito into a complicated hierarchy of class and colour we are left to work out for ourselves.

What, finally, of the self-portrait that emerges from this memoir? It is curiously glancing. Márquez provides us with a thorough account of the development of his literary vocation, from schooldays to his mid-twenties, and many a captivating incident or enthralling encounter in his journey to maturity. But what he was like as a boy or a young man is not so clear. The self-confidence his grandfather gave him as a child seems never to have left him, save for the briefest of adolescent turbulences. But there is little sign of deliberate ambition. He dwells on his shyness, but he was obviously lively company, since he was never short of friends. But how far he sought them, or they saw him as other than a mad-cap bohemian, is not revealed. In transactions with the opposite sex, seductions came mostly from women rather than himself. Though he says that when he returned to Barranquilla 'I had the timidity of a quail, which I tried to counteract with insufferable arrogance and brutal frankness',[10] he seems to have been on generally good terms with his elders and peers, in one setting after another. Apart from conflict with his father over choice of career, no major quarrel marks this progress. Only occasionally does he allude to other, more volcanic sides to his personality – 'fits of rage for any reason at all', 'puerile tantrums'[11] – but these hints are not enlarged upon.

Rather than any sustained self-analysis, Márquez extends a generous mirror to his contemporaries. *Living to Tell the Tale* contains a teeming gallery of relatives, paramours, class-mates, mentors and confederates, captured in a paragraph or page or two. This is enough to make Anglo-Saxon readers impatient, but it is an attractive loyalty, which also sets these memoirs apart from Vargas Llosa's. *A Fish in Water*, aimed at an international public from the start, is thinner in this respect. Márquez's memoirs are designed for Colombian readers first of all.

They announce their principle of construction at the outset, in the manifesto set like an epigraph at the head of the book: 'Life is not what one lived, but what one remembers and how one remembers it in order to recount it.' Taken literally, this is an invitation to selective recall, with all the facilities of a convenient amnesia. There is no reason to suppose Márquez has abused his maxim. Yet it always remains legitimate to ask how far memories correspond to facts. However much licence we are willing to grant an artist in reconstructing the past, we would not value the result in the same way, if all proved imaginary.

In this case, the narrative allows for some question-marks in the margin. Sex, politics, literature: each leaves a penumbra of uncertainty around the edges. Commenting on his father's 'furtive hunter's ways', Márquez mentions there was a period when he was tempted to imitate him, but soon discovered this was 'the most arid form of solitude'.[12] Nothing in his account relates to this brief avowal. In *The Fragrance of Guava* he says he belonged to a cell of the Colombian Communist Party when he was at university.[13] There is no trace of this

---

10. *VC*, p. 430; *LTT*, p. 363.
11. *VC*, pp. 404, 459; *LTT*, pp. 342, 388. The same word, *berrinche*, is used each time.
12. *VC*, p. 60; *LTT*, pp. 51–52.
13. *El olor de la guayaba*, p. 102.

in *Living to Tell the Tale*. Of authors who shaped him, he emphasises Faulkner. But his rule that 'each sentence ought to be responsible for the entire structure',[14] and the celestial use of the adjective (he reports his aversion to adverbs) that is the signature of his prose, derive from Borges, whom he barely mentions. His abandonment of the Barranquilla group that produced the literary journal *Crónica*, the crucible of his first flourishing as a writer, is presented as an amicable parting, without trouble or resentment. Yet it slips out of the sleeve that he had resigned as editor in a fury some time before, for reasons unspecified. The break might have been more painful than he suggests. Do such discrepancies matter? The epigraph absolves them. But a life and a tale are never the same thing, and the interstices – wider or narrower – between them are inescapably part of the interest of each. In the resplendent light of these memories, there is a faint shimmer in the distance, proper to the latitude.

2005

---

14. *VC*, pp. 436, 310; *LTT*, pp. 369, 264.

11

ATLAS OF THE FAMILY:
Göran Therborn

Few topics of fundamental importance have, at first glance, generated so much numbing literature as the family. The appearance is unjust, but not incomprehensible. For the discrepancy between the vivid existential drama into which virtually every human being is plunged at birth, and the generalized statistical pall of demographic surveys and household studies often looks irremediable: as if subjective experience and objective calibration have no meeting-point. Anthropological studies of kinship remain the most technical area of the discipline. Images of crushing dullness have been alleviated, but not greatly altered, by popularizations of the past: works like *The World We Have Lost* by the doyen of Cambridge family reconstruction, Peter Laslett, fond albums of a time when 'the whole of life went forward in the family, in a circle of loved, familiar faces', within a 'one-class society'.[1] The one outstanding contemporary synthesis, William Goode's *World Revolution and Family Patterns*, which argued in the early sixties that the model of the Western conjugal family was likely to become universal, since it best fulfilled the needs of industrialization, has never acquired the standing its generosity of scope and spirit deserved.[2] Family studies are certainly no desert. They are densely populated, but much of the terrain forms a featureless plain of functions and numbers, stretching away to the horizon, broken only by clumps of sentiment.

---

1. *The World We Have Lost*, London 1965, pp. 22–23ff. A work subject to one of Edward Thompson's most devastating reviews: 'The Book of Numbers', *Times Literary Supplement*, 9 December 1965.

2. Out of the unpromising functionalism of modernization theory, Goode produced a balanced and intelligent survey of family systems across the world, that treated the USSR – in 1963 – as part of a Western pattern, and omitted only Latin America and the Caribbean.

Over this landscape, Göran Therborn's *Between Sex and Power* rises up like some majestic volcano. Throwing up a billowing column of ideas and arguments, while a lava of evidence flows down its slopes, this is a great work of historical intellect and imagination, the effect of a rare combination of gifts. Trained as a sociologist, Therborn is a highly conceptual thinker, allying the formal rigour of his discipline at its best, with command of a vast range of empirical data.[3] The result is a powerful theoretical structure, supported by a fascinating body of evidence. But it is also a set of macro-narratives that compose perhaps the first true example of a work of global history we possess. Most writing that lays claim to this term, whatever other merits it may display, ventures beyond certain core zones of attention only selectively and patchily. In the case of general histories of the world, of which there are now more than a few, problems of sheer scale alone have dictated strict limits to even the finest enterprises.

Therborn, by contrast, by focusing on just one dimension of existence, develops a map of human changes over time that is faithful to the complexity and diversity of the world in a quite new way, omitting no corner of the planet. Not just every continent is included in this history, but differences within each between nations or regions – from China and Japan to Uruguay and Colombia, North to South India, Gabon to Burkina Faso, Turkey to Persia, Norway to Portugal – are scanned with a precise eye. Such ecumenical curiosity, the antithesis of Barrington Moore's conviction that only big countries matter for comparative history, is the attractive product of a small one. Therborn's sensibility belongs to his nationality. In modern times Sweden, situated in the northern margins of Europe, with a population about the size of New Jersey, has for the most part been an inconspicuous spectator of world politics. But in the affairs of the family, it has more than once been a pace-setter. That the comparative *tour de force* on them should be Swedish is peculiarly appropriate.

Surveying the world, Therborn distinguishes five major family systems: European (including New World and Pacific settlements), East Asian, sub-Saharan African, West Asian/North African, and Subcontinental, with a further two more 'interstitial' ones, South-East

---

Asian and Creole American. Although each of the major systems is the heartland of a distinctive religious or ethical code – Christian, Confucian, Animist, Muslim, Hindu – and the interstitial ones are zones of overlapping codes, the systems themselves form so many 'geocultures' in which sediments of a common history can override contrasts of belief within them. This cultural backdrop lends its colour and texture to *Between Sex and Power*. The tone of the book recalls aspects of Eric Hobsbawm, in its crisp judgements and dry wit. While Therborn is necessarily far more statistical in style, something of the same literary and anecdotal liveliness is present too. Amid an abundance of gripping arithmetic, novels and plays, memoirs and marriage ads have their place in the narrative. Most striking of all, in a field so dominated by social or merely technical registers, is the political construction Therborn gives to the history of the family in the twentieth century.

What are the central propositions of the book? All traditional family systems, Therborn argues, have comprised three regimes: of patriarchy, marriage, and fertility. Crudely summarized – who calls the shots in the family, how people hitch up, what kids result. *Between Sex and Power* sets out to trace the modern history of each. For Therborn patriarchy is male family power, typically invested in fathers and husbands, not the subordination or discrimination of women in general – gender inequality being a broader phenomenon. At the beginning of his story, around 1900, patriarchy in this classical sense was a universal pattern, if with uneven gradations. In Europe, the French Revolution had failed to challenge it, issuing into the ferocious family clauses of the Code Napoleon, while subsequent industrial capitalism – in North America as in Europe – relied no less on patriarchal norms as a sheet-anchor of moral stability. Confucian and Muslim codes were far more draconian, though the 'minute regulations' of the former set some limits to the potential 'blank cheque' for male power in the latter.[4] Arrangements were looser in much of sub-Saharan Africa, Creole America and South-East Asia. Harshest of all was the Hindu system of North India, in a league by itself for repression. As Therborn notes, this is one of the very few parts of the world where men live longer than women, even today.

By 2000, however, patriarchy had become 'the big loser of the twentieth century', as Therborn puts it, yielding far more ground than

4. *Between Sex and Power: Family in the World, 1900–2000*, London 2004, p. 63. Henceforward *BSP*.

religion or tyranny. 'Probably no other social institution has been forced to retreat as much.'[5] This roll-back was not just an outcome of gradual processes of modernization, in the neutral scheme of structural-functional sociology. It was principally the product of three political hammer-blows. The first of these, Therborn shows, came in the throes of the First World War, when full legal parity between husband and wife was first enacted in Sweden, and then, in a more radical series of measures, the October Revolution dismantled the whole juridical apparatus of patriarchy in Russia, with a much more overt emphasis on sexual equality as such. Conduct, of course, was never the same as codification. 'The legal revolution of the Bolsheviks was very much ahead of Russian societal time, and Soviet family practices did not immediately dance to political music, however loud and powerful.'[6] But the shock wave in the world at large of the Russian example was, Therborn rightly emphasizes, enormous.

The Second World War delivered the next great blow on the other side of the world, again in contrasted neighbouring forms. In occupied Japan, MacArthur's staff imposed a Constitution proclaiming 'the essential equality of the sexes' – a notion, of course, that has still to find a place in the American Constitution – and a Civil Code based on conjugal symmetry. In liberated China, the victory of Communism 'meant a full-scale assault on the most ancient and elaborate patriarchy of the world', obliterating all legal traces of the Confucian order.[7] Finally, a third wave of emancipation was unleashed by the youth rebellions of the late sixties – when the revolt of May 1968 erupted in France, the country's High Court was still upholding the French husband's right to forbid his wife to move out, even if he was publicly maintaining a mistress – that segued into modern feminism. Here the inauguration by the UN of an International Decade for Women in 1975 (also the ultimate outcome of a Communist initiative, in the person of the Finnish daughter of one of Khruschev's Politburo veterans) is taken by Therborn as the turning point in a global discrediting of patriarchy, whose last legal redoubt in the US – in Louisiana – was struck down by the Supreme Court as late as 1981.

The rule of the father has not disappeared. In the world at large, West Asia, Africa and South Asia remain the principal hold-outs.

---

5. *BSP*, p. 73.
6. *BSP*, p. 85.
7. *BSP*, p. 93.

Islam itself, Therborn suggests, may be less to blame for the resistance of Arab patriarchy than the corruption of the secular forces
once opposed to it, abetted by America and Israel. In India, on the
other hand, there is no mistaking the degree of misogyny in caste and
religion, even if the mediation of patriarchal authority by market
mechanisms has its postmodern ambiguities. Surveying the 'blatant
instrumentalism' of the matrimonial pages of a middle-class Indian
press, in which 'more than 99 per cent of ads vaunt socio-economic
offers and desires' he wonders: 'To what extent are parents the
"agents" of young people, in the same sense as any money-seeking
athlete, musician or writer has an agent?'[8] At the opposite extreme is
Euro-American post-patriarchy, in which men and women possess
equal rights, but still far from equal resources – women enjoying not
much more than half (55–60 per cent) the income and wealth of men.

In between these poles come the homelands of the Communist revolutions, which did so much to transform the landscape of patriarchy
in the last century. The collapse of the Soviet bloc has not seen any
restoration here, whatever other regressions it may involve ('the power
of fathers and husbands does not seem to have increased', though
'that of pimps certainly has').[9] Therborn ventures the guess that in
both Russia and Eastern Europe, the original revolutionary in this
respect here may prove Comunism's most lasting legacy. In China, on
the other hand, there is much further to go, amid more signs of recidi-
vist urges in civil society. Still, he points out, not only is gender
inequality in wages and salaries far lower in the PRC than in Taiwan
– by a factor of three – but patriarchy proper, as indicated by conjugal
residence and division of labour, continues to be weaker.

The first part of Therborn's story is thus eminently political, As he
remarks, this is logical enough, since patriarchy is about power. His
second part moves to sex. In questions of marriage, Europe diverged
from the rest of the world far earlier than in matters of patriarchy –
or more precisely, Western Europe and those of its marchlands
affected by German colonization in the Middle Ages. In this zone a
unique marital regime developed already in pre-industrial times, combining late monogamy, significant numbers of unmarried, and
Christian norms of conjugal duty, contradictorily surrounded by a
certain penumbra of informal sex. The key result was 'neo-locality',
or the exit of wedded couples from parental households. Everywhere

---

8. *BSP*, p. 109.
9. *BSP*, p. 127.

else in the world, Therborn maintains that the rule was universal marriage, typically at earlier ages, as the necessary entry into adulthood. (He does not make it clear whether he thinks this applies to all pre-class societies, where such a rule might be doubted.)

Paradoxically, however, although patterns of marriage might be thought to have varied more widely around the world than forms of patriarchy, Therborn is much briefer about them. Polyandry is never mentioned, the map of monogamy is unexplored, nor is any taxonomy of polygamy offered, beyond a tacit distinction between elite and mass variants (the latter peculiar to sub-Sahara). The baseline of his tale of marriage is set by a contrast between two deviant areas and all other arrangements. The first of these is the West European anomaly, with its subsequent overseas projections into North America and the Pacific. The second is the Creole, born in plantation and mining zones of the Caribbean and Latin America with a substantial black, mulatto or mestizo population, where a uniquely deregulated sexual regime developed.

Some startling figures emerge from Therborn's comparison of these. If sexual mores in Europe first became widely relaxed in aristocratic circles of the eighteenth century, flouting of conventional norms reached epidemic proportions among the lower classes of many cities in the nineteenth, if only by reason of the costs of marriage. At various points in the latter part of the century, a third of all births in Paris, a half in Vienna, and over two-thirds in Klagenfurt, were out of wedlock. By 1900 such figures had fallen, and national averages of illegitimacy become quite modest (Austrians still outpacing Afro-Americans, however). Matters were much wilder in the Creole system, readers of García Márquez will not be surprised to learn. 'Iberian colonial America and the West Indies were the stage of the largest-scale assault on marriage in history.'[10] In the mid-nineteenth century between a third and a half of the population of Bahia never tied a knot; in the Rio de la Plata region, extra-marital births were four to five times the levels in Spain or Italy; around 1900 as many as fourth-fifths of sexual unions in Mexico City may have been without benefit of clergy.

These were the colourful exceptions. Throughout Asia, Africa, Russia and most of Eastern Europe, marriage in one form or another was inescapable. A century later, Therborn's account suggests, much less has changed than in the order of patriarchy. Creole America has become more marital, at least in periods of relative prosperity, but

---

10. *BSP*, p. 157.

remains the most casual about the institution. In Asia, now mostly monogamous, and sub-Saharan Africa, still largely polygamous, marriage continues to be a universal norm – with pockets of slippage only in the big cities of Japan, South-East Asia and South Africa; but the age at which it is contracted has risen. If divorce of one kind or another has become nearly universal as a legal possibility, its practice is much more restricted – in the Hindu cow-belt, virtually zero. At the top end of the scale, in born-again America and post-Communist Russia, any wedding guest is entitled to be quizzical: half of all marriages break up. But with successive tries at conjugal bliss, the crude marriage rate has not fallen in the US. Globally, it would seem, the predominant note is stability.

In one zone, however, Therborn tracks a major change. After marrying as never before in the middle decades of the century, West Europeans started to secede from altar and registry in increasing numbers. Sweden was once again the vanguard country, and still remains well ahead even of its Scandinavian neighbours, not to speak of lands further south. The innovation it pioneered, from the late sixties onwards, was mass informal cohabitation. Thirty years later, the great majority of Swedish women giving birth to their first child – nearly 70 per cent – were either cohabiting or single mothers. Marriage might or might not follow cohabitation. What now became a minority option, in one country after another – the UK, France, Germany – was marriage before it. In Catholic France and Protestant England alike, extra-marital births jumped from 6–8 to 40–42 per cent in the space of four decades.

Manifestly, the sexual revolution of the sixties and seventies lay behind this spectacular transformation. Therborn notes the arrival of pill and IUD, as facilitating conditions, but is more interested in consequences. What did it add up to? In effect a double liberation: more partners and – especially for women – more pleasure. In Finland, women had bedded an average of three men in the early seventies, six in the early nineties; by then the gap in erotic satisfaction between the sexes had closed. In Sweden, the median of lovers more than trebled, a much greater increase than for men. 'More than anything else', Therborn concludes, 'this is what the sexual revolution has brought about: a long period for pre-marital sex, and a plurality of sexual partners over a lifetime becoming a "normal" phenomenon in a statistical as well as in a moral sense.'[11]

---

11. *BSP*, p. 210.

How far does the US conform to the emergent European pattern? Only in part, as its different religious and political complexion would lead one to think. Europeans will be astonished to learn that in 2000 about a fifth of American eighteen- to twenty-four-year-olds claimed to be virgins on marriage. Only 6 per cent of American couples cohabited. Over 70 per cent of mothers at first birth are married. On the other hand, the US has nearly twice as many teenage births per cohort as the highest country in the EU, and an extra-marital birth rate higher than the Netherlands. Without going much into race or region, Therborn describes the American system as 'dualist'. But from the evidence he provides, it might be thought electoral divisions are reflected in sexual contrasts, blue and red in the boudoir too.

In the last part of his book, Therborn moves to fertility. Here the conundrum is the 'demographic transition' – the standard term for the shift from a regime of low growth, combining lots of children and much early death, to one of high growth, combining many children but fewer deaths, and then back to another one of low growth, this time with both many fewer deaths and fewer children. There is no mystery about the way medical advances and better diets led to falling rates of mortality in nineteenth-century Europe, and eventually reached most of the world, to similar effect, in the second half of the twentieth century. The big question is why birth rates fell, first in Europe and North America between the 1880s and 1930s, and then for the majority of human race from the mid-1970s onwards, in two uncannily similar waves. In each case, 'a process rapidly cutting through and across state boundaries, levels of industrialization, urbanization, and levels of income, across religions, ideologies and family systems'[12] slashed fertility rates by 30–40 per cent in three decades. Today, the average family has no more than two to three children throughout most of the former Third World.

What explains these gigantic changes? The first nations to experience a significant fall in fertility were France and the United States, by 1830 – generations in advance of all others. What they had in common, Therborn suggests, was their popular revolutions, which had given ordinary people a sense of self-mastery. Once the benefits of smaller families became clear in these societies, neo-locality allowed couples to make their own decisions to improve their lives before any modern means of contraception were available. Fifty years later, perhaps triggered initially by the onset of a world recession,

---

12. *BSP*, p. 236.

mass birth control began to roll through Europe, eventually sweeping all the way from Portugal to Russia. This time, Therborn's hypothesis runs, it was a combination of radical socialist and secular movements popularizing the idea of family planning, together with the spread of literacy, that brought lower fertility as part of an increasingly self-conscious culture of modernity. This was birth control from below.

In the Third World, by contrast, contraception – now an easy technology – was typically propagated or imposed from above, by political fiat of the state. China's one-child policy has been the most dramatic, if extreme example. Once lower birth rates became a general goal of governments committed to modernization, it was family systems that then determined the order in which societies entered the new regime: East Asia in the lead, North India and Black Africa far in the rearguard. Here too it was a sense of mastery, of human ability to command nature – not always bureaucratic in origin, since the better-off societies of Latin America moved more spontaneously in the same direction – that powered the change. Its consequences, of which we can still see only the beginnings, are enormous. Without it, the earth would now have some two billion more inhabitants.

In Europe and Japan, meanwhile, fertility has moved no less dramatically in the opposite direction, falling below net reproduction rates. This collapse in the birth rate, from which the US is saved essentially by immigration, promises rapid ageing of these nations in the short run, and, if unchecked, virtual extinction of them in the long run. There is now a growing literature of public alarm about this prospect, what the French historian Pierre Chaunu denounces as a 'White Death' threatening the Old World. Therborn eschews it. Negative rates of reproduction in these rich, socially advanced societies do not correspond to any birth-strike by women, he suggests, but rather to their desire to have both two to three children and careers that are the equal of men's, which the existing social order does not yet allow them to do. In denying themselves the offspring they want, European parents are 'moving against themselves',[13] not with the grain of any deeper cultural change.

Between Sex and Power ends its narratives with four principal conclusions. The different family systems of the world reveal little internal dynamic of change. They have been recast from the outside,

---

13. *BSP*, pp. 284ff.

and the history of their transformations has been neither unilinear nor evolutionary, but rather determined by a series of unevenly timed international conjunctures, of markedly political character. The result has not been one of convergence, other than in a general decline of patriarchy, due more to wars and revolutions than to any 'feminist world spirit'. In the South, the differential pace of changes in fertility continues to shift the distribution of global population further towards the Subcontinent and Africa, and away from Europe, Japan and Russia. In the North, European marriage has altered its forms, but is proving itself supple and creative in adapting to a new range of desires: conventional jeremiads notwithstanding, it is in good shape. Predictions? Serenely declined. 'The best bet for the future is in the inexhaustible innovative capacity of humankind, which eventually surpasses all social science'.[14]

In due course, an army of specialists will gather round *Between Sex and Power*, like so many expert sports fans, to pore over its multitudinous argument. What can a layman say, beyond the magnitude of its achievement? Tentatively, perhaps only this. In the architectonic of the book, there is something of a gap between the notion of a family system and the triad of patriarchy, marriage and fertility that follows it. In effect, the way these three interconnect to form the *structure* of any family system goes unstated in the separate treatment accorded each. But if we consider the trio as an abstract combinatory, it would seem that logically – as the order in which Therborn proceeds to them itself suggests – patriarchy must command the other two, as the 'dominant', since it will typically lay down the rules of marriage and set the norms of reproduction. There is, in other words, a hierarchy of determinations built into any family system.

This has a bearing on Therborn's conclusions. His final emphasis falls, unhesitatingly, on the divergence between major family systems today. After stressing continuing worldwide dissimilarities between fertility and marital regimes, he concedes that 'the patriarchal outcome is somewhat different'.[15] His own evidence suggests this is an understatement. For what it shows is a powerful process of convergence, far from complete in extent, but unequivocal in direction. But if the variegated forms of patriarchy are what historically determined the main parameters of marriage and reproduction, would not any ongoing decline of them across family systems towards a common

---

14. *BSP*, p. 315.
15. *BSP*, p. 306.

juridical zero-point imply that birth rates and marriage customs are eventually likely to converge, in significant measure, at their own pace too? That seems, at any rate, a possible deduction side-stepped by Therborn, but which his story of fertility appears to bear out. For what is clear from his account is that the astonishing fall in birth rates in most of the underdeveloped world has been the product of precisely a collapse in patriarchal authority, as its powers of life and death have been transferred to the state, which now determines how many are born and how many survive.

What then of marriage? Here certainly contrasts remain greatest. In speaking of 'the core of romantic freedom and commitment in the modern European (and New World) family system', Therborn implies this remains specific to the West. But while the caste system or the shariah plainly preclude extempore love, does it show no signs of spreading, as ideal or realization, in the big cities of East Asia or Latin America? The imagination of urban Japan, he shows, is already half seized with it. Not, of course, that the aeration of marriage in Western Europe, with the advent of mass cohabitation, has so far been replicated anywhere else. But here a different sort of question might be asked. Is it really the case that the negative rates of repro-duction that have accompanied this pattern are as unwished for as Therborn suggests? He relies on the discrepancy between surveys in which women explain how many children they expect, and those they actually have. But this could just mean that in practice their desire for children proved weaker than for a well-paid job, a satisfying career, or more than one lover at time. Voters in the West regularly say they want better schools and health care, and in principle expect to pay for them, and commentators on the Left often pin high hopes on such declarations. But once such citizens get to the polling booth they tend to stick to lower taxes. The same kind of self-deception could apply to children. If so, it would be difficult to say European marriage was in such good shape, since there would be no stopping place in sight for its plunge of society into an actuarial abyss.

Therborn resists such thoughts. Although *Between Sex and Power* pays handsome homage to the role of Communism in the dismantling of patriarchy in the twentieth century, it displays no especially Marxist stance towards the family. Engels would have not shared the author's satisfaction that marriage was flourishing, however ductile the forms it has adopted. In expressing his attachment to them never-theless, Therborn speaks with the humane voice of a level-headed Swedish reformism that he understandably admires, without himself having ever altogether coincided with it. In looking on the bright side of the EU marital regime, he is consistent with the case he has made in the past for its welfare states too, surviving in much better condition than its critics or mourners believe.[16] It is in the same spirit, one might say, that he insists on the persistent divergence of family systems across the world. Uniformity is the one condition every part of the political spectrum deplores. The most unflinching neo-liberals invariably explain that universal free markets are the best of all guardians of diversity. Social Democrats reassure their followers that the capitalism to which they must adjust is becoming steadily more various. Traditional conservatives expatiate on the irreducible multiplicity of faiths and civilizations. Homogeneity has no friends, at least since Alexandre Kojève. But when any claim becomes too choral, a flicker of doubt is indicated. It scarcely affects the magnificence of this book. In it, you can find the largest changes in human relations of modern times.

2005

16. 'The Prospects of Labour and the Transformation of Advanced Capitalism', *New Left Review* I/145, May–June 1984, pp. 5–38, still a basic text; for a striking political vision of the world two decades later, see 'Into the Twenty-First Century', *New Left Review* 10, July–August 2001, pp. 87–110.

12

CIVIL WAR, GLOBAL DISTEMPER:

Robert Brenner

I

The English Civil War occupies a strange niche in contemporary memory. To all official appearances, no episode of the country's modern past is so parenthetical. Leaving no reputable trace in common traditions or public institutions, it looks in established retrospect like a blackout in the growth of the collective psyche. Our only republic remains under ban, a historical freak. Rosebery could raise a statue to Cromwell outside Parliament: eighty years later, Benn could not even get him onto a postage stamp, at a time when Rosa Luxemburg adorned ordinary West German mail.

Such treatment, it might be argued, is not without all justice. For in a comparative perspective, did not the English Civil War – however traumatic at the time – prove in the end to be the least significant of the political upheavals that accompanied the birth of the leading nation-states of the capitalist world? Set beside the Dutch Revolt, America's War for Independence, the French Revolution, Italy's Risorgimento, the unification of Germany, let alone the Meiji Restoration in Japan, the overthrow of the English monarchy seems of a different order: not a modern starting point of institutional development, more an exotic intermission. If this is so, however, there remains a paradox. For what would be the most barren convulsion has produced the most fertile literature. The volume of modern writing on the French Revolution – the only possible rival – is larger than on the English. But intellectually it is thinner. The difference here has much to do with the respective situations of the revisionism that has dominated each side of the Channel in recent years. Where the French variant, personified by François Furet, has been fashioned as a polemic against what it has identified as a single historiographic tradition, the Jacobin–Leninist continuum running from Mathiez through Lefebvre to Soboul, the English school has developed as an argument with two conflicting traditions – the Whig view descending from Notestein through Hexter, and the Social Interpretation passing from Tawney through Hill. Ideologically, the consequences can appear marked. English revisionism often looks more unequivocally like a historiographic Right, locked in struggle with a liberal Centre and a socialist Left – where French revisionism tends to occupy both Right and Centre positions in its polemic against the local Left, shifting from liberal-conservative to conservative-liberal accents as the occasion demands. That might seem a politically more commodious posture. Intellectually, however, the topographical contrast between the two countries has benefited the English historians. Seeking to displace not just one but two pre-existent explanatory paradigms, they have had to display greater ingenuity. The outcome has been more tough-minded and original.

It has been also more various, as can readily be seen from the cluster of *summa* just published by three leading historians, whose work has set the agenda for debate on the English Revolution since the seventies. Kevin Sharpe's *Personal Rule of Charles I*, Conrad Russell's *Fall of the British Monarchies*, and John Morrill's *Nature of the English Revolution* all represent distinct standpoints – of which the last, and hitherto least noticed, is the most interesting.[1] But for all the divergences between them, certain common features continue to stand out. Rejecting both constitutional explanations of the Caroline crisis, and class interpretations of the Civil War, these histories focus on the politics of royal finance and court faction, clerical administration and diplomatic manoeuvre, at the apex of the state, and of parochial lobby or credal grievance in the localities below. If the new costs of war placed unfamiliar strains on the traditional compact between the monarchy and gentry in the mid-seventeenth century, the breakdown of a fundamentally consensual polity was fortuitous – the result of a sequence of mishaps, springing from management of the Stuart patrimonies in Scotland and Ireland, rather than any incurable division within England itself. The targets of criticism remain Whig or Marxist conceptions of the Civil War as a struggle grounded in long-term oppositions of either juridical principle or social interest.

Taxing such accounts with anachronism, the revisionists insist on the primacy of palace imbroglios and theological feuds, and the

---

1. Respectively: London 1992; Oxford 1991; London 1991.

fumbling collisions attending them, as the stuff of politics in the age of Buckingham and Pym. Not that the new orthodoxy is at all abstemious itself in mixing past and present, for its own purposes. The revisionists, indeed, relish gestures of a swashbuckling topicality. Sharpe depicts Henrietta Maria as a bubbly twin of Princess Diana, and even transvests Charles I into a baroque Margaret Thatcher, closing 700 pages on the King with the words: 'He believed some principles worth adhering to whatever the repercussions – and, well, he may even have been right.'[2] Russell will compare Ship Money to the Poll Tax, and describe the arrival of James I in London as a foretaste of the Single European Act. Such are the playful flourishes of a scholarly ascendancy. Blair Worden has even ventured the view that Russell's 'hegemony' over civil war studies has 'banished controversy to the margins'.[3] There, pockets of Whig resistance no doubt remain – readers of Lawrence Stone's correspondence with Russell in the *TLS* might be surprised to learn the field had become so pacific. Yet even Stone has conceded the second part of the victory the revisionists claim. For he too has opined that the Marxist interpretation of the Civil War is dead.[4]

Merchants and Revolution, dedicated to Stone, comprehensively overturns that judgement. Its author, Robert Brenner, belongs to that rare group of historians who have given their name to a whole literature – the 'Brenner Debate' on the origins of agrarian capitalism in Europe recalling the 'Pirenne Thesis' of old. His new book, in which the name of Marx is never mentioned but his spirit is omnipresent, transforms the landscape of the English Revolution. *Merchants and Revolution* is distinguished by three achievements, any one of which would be impressive enough. Together, their combination is an extraordinary feat. The first of them is simply the magnitude of the research the book embodies. Brenner's archival investigation into the activities of the leading merchant networks of Stuart England – a quest that often reads like a vast, intricate detective story – has no counterpart in recent literature. Moving below the level of the landed elite, Brenner has made more discoveries of importance about the period than any of his contemporaries. To read *Merchants and Revolution* is to realize how far revisionist histories – for the all the acuity of their negative insights – have tended to tinker at the edges of existing stocks

---

2. *The Personal Rule of Charles I*, p. 934.
3. 'Conrad Russell's Civil War', *London Review of Books*, 29 August 1991.
4. 'The Century of Revolution', *New York Review of Books*, 26 February 1987.

of positive knowledge, delving further into official papers or truffling in county holdings. Brenner's book opens another world.

No less striking is a second feature of the work. *Merchants and Revolution* restores narrative to the seventeenth-century crisis, on a grand scale. Here too the contrast with the revisionist corpus is marked, and again has its wry side. For in principle the revisionists are committed to a variant of the English one-damn-thing-after-another view of the past, stressing acceptance of the contingency of historical events as a condition of understanding them, which ought to have generated a narrative school. In fact, the reverse has been closer to the case. Russell's *Fall of the British Monarchies*, as Worden has pointed out, is a selective patchwork of themes, that makes no attempt to recount the actual process of breakdown to which its title alludes. Ironically, Russell in turn has lodged the same objection against Sharpe, complaining that his study of *The Personal Rule*, for all its bulk, lacks any coherent narrative.[5] For its part, Morrill's *Nature of the English Revolution* is a splendid collection of essays, from which we learn that the author has for the moment desisted from a projected history of *England's Wars of Religion*. An earlier work, Anthony Fletcher's *Outbreak of the Civil War*, offers a genuine chronology, but one so clotted and short-winded as often to defeat its purpose – impenetrable trees and sparse wood. For truer narratives, we have to move forward in time to historians – Underdown, Woolrych, Worden, Gentles – more sympathetic to the revolutionary experience itself, who have written the modern accounts of Pride's Purge, the Putney Debates, the Rump, or the New Model Army. But, with the exception of the last, these still cover relatively brief episodes. Brenner's work is of an altogether different range. Its subtitle indicates a span of a century, but although there is a necessary preamble starting in Elizabethan times, what the book actually offers is a sustained account of its subject from the accession of James I to the arrival of Cromwell as Protector – with a crucial flash-forward to the overthrow of James II. This timescale sets the English Revolution within a longer dynamic than any other study of comparable detail has afforded.

The narrative here is an analytic one. Rather than plotting the movements of individual actors, or the evolution of political factions, Brenner's account reconstructs the trajectory of the social forces that led to the Civil War and its aftermath. It does so through the prism of one particular, hitherto largely unnoticed, but crucial player in the

---

5. 'Draining the Whig Bathwater', *London Review of Books*, 10 June 1993.

drama – that sector of the London merchant community which made
its fortunes in the Americas, rather than in trade with Europe or Asia,
under the early Stuarts. By focusing on this pivotal group, and its
development within the wider constellation of power and property in
the first half of the century, Brenner rearranges the whole look of the
time. The upshot is the most powerful social explanation of the
breakdown of the Caroline monarchy we now possess. *Merchants and
Revolution* connects structure and event in a continuous tale of
pointed historical meaning.

What is the gist of this account? Brenner shows that, contrary to
received opinion, the expansion of English trade after the acute commercial crisis of the mid-sixteenth century was not powered by the
search for new markets to sustain staple cloth exports, but was essentially import-driven. The Merchant Adventurers who monopolized
the cloth trade with northern Europe continued to dominate the City
establishment in Jacobean times, but were now increasingly chal-
lenged by the Levant and East India companies, controlled by a quite
distinct group of merchants, engaged in the import of Mediterranean
or Oriental delicacies and luxury goods – wines, currants, silks,
spices. By the end of the 1630s, the leaders of this combine were typically wealthier than the cloth traders, and had displaced them from
hegemony in London's municipal power system. The two groupings,
however, still shared a common interest in tight political regulation of
their respective trades – legal exclusion of outsiders from them, and
monopolistic price-setting within them. By contrast, in the Americas
there emerged a very different kind of merchant, accumulating capital
in a zone of free competition open to new entrants. Here the valuable
commodities were tobacco, sugar or furs. The growth of these
westward trades spawned a third commercial interest, whose rise is
Brenner's particular concern. Forming an intricate network, tied by
criss-crossing bonds of kinship and partnership, the merchants of the
New World were a breed apart as chancers and innovators. Brenner
picks out as the central figure among them one Maurice Thomson.
His career makes an amazing story.

Born in the Home Counties about 1600, the eldest of five brothers,
Thomson emigrated to Virginia in his teens, where he soon became a
ship's captain, acquired land, and entered the tobacco trade.
Returning to London in his mid-twenties, he pioneered slave planta-
tions in the Caribbean, and within a decade had become the major
tobacco merchant in the Atlantic, with sidelines in New England
provisioning and fisheries. Supply contracts for colonial ventures off
Honduras, prospecting for silver in Panama, and raids on Venezuela

followed. By the 1640s, Thomson and his associates were planting Barbados with sugar, and stocking it with slaves from West Africa. In doing so, they embarked on another huge arc of operations, breaking into the *chasses gardées* of the Old World, with voyages to the Guinea coast and then schemes for bases in Madagascar and the Celebes. On the eve of the Civil War, these interlopers were second only in scale of wealth to the Levant–East Indies combine itself.[6]

Where did these rival complexes of merchant capital stand on the political chequerboard of the time? Between the chartered companies and the monarchy there was in normal conditions a natural symbiosis: the Merchant Adventurers and the eastward traders needed royal power to enforce their monopolies, and the King needed taxes on overseas commerce and loans from merchant syndicates to cover state expenditures. The logic of the bargain – a kind of exchange of letters of marque – was so strong that even when Charles I's war-time exactions of 1627–29 did drive the City elite into indignant alliance with the Parliamentary opposition, triggering a shipping strike against the government, the conflict was rapidly absorbed. The years of Personal Rule, bypassing Parliament altogether, soon restored working relationships rooted in mutual dependence. By contrast, Brenner argues, there was no comparable nexus between the English gentry and the Stuart monarchy. For landowners now typically derived their incomes from a capitalist agriculture that did not require extra-economic forms of coercion, and so gave no reason for consenting to arbitrary impositions, which threatened the principle of unconditional rights in property even when directed at trade rather than land. Hence the paradox that customs levies generally accepted by the merchants on whom they fell were fiercely resisted by MPs who were not directly affected by them.[7]

Overlaying this basic economic discord between the monarchy and the gentry was a further ideological divergence. The Tudor state, Brenner argues, had performed invaluable service to the English landowning class by quelling unruly magnates and subduing peasant discontent, rife in late feudalism. Once these conditions of internal order had been achieved, however, the focus of the gentry's interest in the state came increasingly to bear on its external role. Formally, the Elizabethan church had settled the religious issue. But the national brand of Reformation it represented at home still left the diplomatic

---

6. *Merchants and Revolution*, Princeton 1993, pp. 118–184: henceforward *MR*.
7. *MR*, pp. 670–673.

position of England relatively indeterminate. Here a potential field of conflict opened up. For dynastic sense of dignity pulled one way, impulses of doctrinal solidarity another. The only Western monarchies of suitable rank for matrimonial alliance were Catholic, the one republic of strategic power was Protestant. Warfare was increasingly expensive, and England lacked a standing army. For reasons both of prestige and of prudence, the Throne was wary of letting religious sentiment get the upper hand in its diplomatic manoeuvres – where Parliament, less troubled by either issues of precedence or calculations of risk, tended to view foreign policy through a more theological lens. So disputes were all but inevitable. Brenner does not share Russell's low opinion of the Parliamentary opposition to the monarchy's European stance, as ill-informed and irresponsible. He stresses rather the coherence of a forward policy against Spain, to be waged by cheap naval campaigns in the Caribbean, that became the hobby-horse of militant Puritans in the House.[8]

This was not a general conviction of the landed class. It was the fixed objective of one particular coterie within it, the 'colonizing aristocrats' around the Earl of Warwick and their clients, Pym prominent among them, who financed and organized a range of Puritan settlements in the New World. In the course of such ventures, this group had quietly started to draw upon the resources of the network of interloper merchants. Here, at the opposite end of the trading spectrum, they found allies whose objective position – unlike that of regulated commerce – gave them no economic reason for loyalty to the monarchy, still less any political bond with it, of the kind that parliamentary representation accorded even the most disgruntled landowners. What, on the other hand, the new merchants did possess were strong ties with popular strata in London – domestic traders, sea captains, small shopkeepers, from whose ranks they had often sprung, and with whom they shared exclusion from municipal power. The informal collaboration between colonizing nobles and interloping traders thus had a wider potential undertow. Beneath the carapace of personal rule, a fateful mixture was brewing.

When the king's peace was broken by Scottish rebellion, Brenner shows, it was this alliance that seized the initiative in challenging Charles's regime, and then forced the pace in the slide to civil war. In September 1640, Warwick's group fired off the first elite demand for a recall of Parliament – synchronized with a mass petition from

---

8. *MR*, pp. 244, 318, 676.

London, brought up to the King at York by Thomson. In November, three of the four MPs elected to the Long Parliament from London had links to the interloper connection. By December, the radicals in the City were already launching a campaign to do away with bishops. With the Scots still in occupation of the border, and the Long Parliament facing a recalcitrant King, the new merchants occupied an increasingly strategic position. By regulating the flow of loans from the City to Parliament, for onward payment to the Scots, and orchestrating the tide of popular demonstrations against the Court, they brought critical pressure to bear on the course of gentry politics in the Commons. Two results were decisive. In the spring of 1641 Strafford's attainder was pushed through, over the hesitation of Pym and the resistance of the Lords, and Charles was deprived of the power to dissolve Parliament without its consent, a measure nicely motivated as a surety for its creditors.

By the summer of 1641 the apparatus of personal rule had been dismantled, to the all but unanimous satisfaction of the landed class. Why then did Civil War break out a year later? The revisionist answer singles out religion as the principal reason. English landowners – the argument runs – were broadly united in constitutional outlook. But they were separated by their conceptions of the church. While the great majority wished to return to what they imagined had been a happy Elizabethan mean, a vehement minority now pressed for a more radical reformation, with an intransigence which split the ranks of the gentry. For Russell, it was Scottish leverage which forced Puritan zeal up the agenda of an English Parliament dependent on Covenanter military insurance against Charles, but itself containing few committed Presbyterians.[9] For Morrill, the dynamic of a new Calvinist bigotry in England itself was quite sufficient for the task. In either case, it was the religious issue – as it first crystallized around the dispute over bishops, and then precipitated rebellion in Ireland, under threat from a still more punitive Protestantism – which pushed the landed class over the brink, into a fratricidal conflict that eventually brought down the monarchy itself.[10]

Brenner's analysis challenges this orthodox account. What it suggests is that the polarizing force which divided the gentry was not disputation over the church, but unrest in the capital. Parliamentary opposition to the King, he argues, was from the outset structurally

9. *The Causes of the English Civil War*, Oxford 1990, pp. 15–16; *The Fall of the British Monarchies 1637–1642*, pp. 203–205, 523–524.

10. *The Nature of the English Revolution*, pp. 42–44 *et seq.*

intertwined with municipal insurgency in the City. It was coordination between Pym's leadership in the Commons and the new merchant
radicals in London, controlling money supply and mobilizing street
intimidation, which corralled the monarchy in the first session of the
Long Parliament. That victory, however, remained insecure so long as
the Commons was unarmed and Charles bent on revenge. The only
effective counter-weight to the coercive reserves of the monarchy lay
in the citizenry of the capital – mob or militia. But for many MPs, the
escalation of popular activism in London was becoming steadily more
alarming. In Brenner's account, it was the inescapable choice between
two political evils which came to divide the country's rulers. Which
was to be feared more – a vindictive king or a turbulent people: the
threat to a traditional order from above, or below?

The new salience of religion in the autumn of 1641, Brenner
contends, was an effect of this dilemma. For as spiritual ferment in
London blended with popular insubordination, in a climate of
increasing hostility to the established church, the episcopacy that
had earlier been widely perceived among the gentry as a nursery of
overbearing clericalism came to seem to many landowners as, after
all, a necessary fixture of the social hierarchy. In that change of mind
lay the route to subsequent royalism. If Pym and his band moved in
the opposite direction, towards root-and-branch Puritanism, the
reason was not only that they were more exposed to vengeance in the
event of a royal comeback. It was also, and above all, that they had
greater confidence in their ability to handle a mass movement in
London, because of their long-standing ties to the new merchants
behind it.

When Catholic rebellion in Ireland brought the political situation
in England to flashpoint in the winter of 1641, as Pym's caucus
demanded control of the King's ministers and the army, and the King
tried to recover power in the capital by securing the Tower, it was the
radical movement in London that settled the outcome. Mass peti-
tions against royal moves poured in, apprentices threatened a
counter-coup, shops shut down, the City gave shelter to the ringlead-
ers of the Commons, and the streets bristled with arms. At the helm
of resistance there emerged a Committee of Safety, conspicuously
dominated by the American merchant interest. Faced down by this
show of force, Charles evacuated the capital. Municipal revolution
followed. The Levant–East Indies combine, which had remained
loyal to the monarchy throughout the crisis, fell from power as the
oligarchic constitution of the City was opened up, and the mayor
replaced. London had saved Parliament, and the Parliament that

remained – half its members left to join the King – accepted the remodelling of London.

The interloper merchants lost no time in demonstrating their new position of strength, with two spectacular enterprises undertaken before the start of the Civil War in August 1642 – a major land-and-sea expedition to plunder Ireland, under the direction of Maurice Thomson and associates of such later fame as Thomas Rainsborough and Hugh Peter; and a naval rampage round the Spanish possessions in the Caribbean, from Maracaibo to Jamaica to Guatemala, in collusion with Warwick. Once the fighting in England broke out, the same syndicate moved into control of the financial and naval machinery of Parliament's war effort, capturing the customs in the process. As Royalist forces gained initial advantage, the new merchants and their radical allies in the City pressed for more resolute pursuit of the war and the formation of a volunteer army. By the summer of 1643, with Parliamentary fortunes at their nadir, the Commons was cornered into accepting a mass petition demanding the creation of a Committee for a General Rising – or a new popular army under militant command, designed to shunt the Earl of Essex's mainline forces aside. Brenner describes this move, calculated to wrest overall military power from Pym's leadership itself, as the climax of the radical drive in London. But in making it, the political front around the American combine overreached itself. The General Rising failed to materialize, Parliament assembled the New Model Army, and as its victories turned the tide against the King, moderates regained ascendancy in the City.

In a careful analysis, Brenner shows that power in London now passed away from the major overseas merchants to smaller domestic trades, with some representation from the older cloth exporters. The result was to invert the relationship between the Parliamentary leadership and the City. For if the municipal oligarchs of the mid-1640s shared with leading MPs the political priority of winning the war, their religious aim – a Presbyterian settlement along Scottish lines – was more conservative than the centre of gravity in Parliament. Brenner explains this option as a symptom of social insecurity. Landowners, enjoying traditional authority in their localities, required no clerical busybodies to police their parishes – *parvenu* retailers in the big city, on the other hand, watching the religious ferment around them with dismay, sought the discipline of elders to check the risks of popular anarchy. In this frame of mind, the City Presbyterians naturally came to view the New Model Army, with its unprecedented freedom of religious expression, with even greater apprehension than did moderate civilian MPs, once victory on the battlefield was secure. The result was the repeated efforts of a bloc between the Commons majority and the City fathers to settle a peace with the King at the expense of the Army in 1646–48 – in which there was a faster slide towards outright royalism in London than at Westminster.

With the outbreak of the Second Civil War, the spotlight of Brenner's narrative swings back to the new merchants. The radicalization of the New Model Army now gave them their opportunity. In the emergency of 1647, with royalist forces at the gates of London, Maurice Thomson was securing the Thames and fetching vessels from Holland, his brother George – now Army colonel and MP for Southwark – manning the perimeter of the South Bank; one of his partners was ensconced as private secretary to Cromwell; a year later, another was to figure in joint planning with the Levellers for the coup to put an end to an unregenerate Parliament. Pride's Purge accomplished, the interlopers were immediately restored to power in the City, and after the execution of the King became central pillars of the new republican regime.

For the Commonwealth, Brenner argues, proved to be a virtually perfect framework for the realization of new merchant goals. Thomson and his friends were put in charge of the navy and customs, excise and assessments, City and suburban militias. North American and Caribbean colonies were rapidly wrested back from Royalist settlers; the East India Company was prised open; Levant trade was accorded government escort. Most fatefully, war was unleashed against the Dutch, when they refused to abandon commercial competition for political union with England. The very narrowness of the social base of the Commonwealth favoured the interlopers. The gentry were by now disaffected; the soldiers away on campaigns in Ireland or Scotland; the Levellers dispersed. So power at the centre fell into the hands of the small group of committed republicans in what remained of the Commons, whose imperialist aims made them ideal interlocutors for the new merchants. So intimate became the cohabitation of the two that when the officers returned to the capital and, discontented with the lack of electoral reform, dissolved the Rump, the American connection immediately expressed its solidarity with it – although, a point Brenner does not make, it had no particular stake in the Rump's domestic conservatism as against the Army's more radical attitude on constitutional issues. Its collective protest to Cromwell, however, ensured its exclusion from the counsels of the Protectorate. Cromwell's personal rule was ultimately to see a move back to a regime somewhat more accommodating to the gentry, in which merchant lobbies had less direct leverage. But this was not on the cards in 1653. Brenner is content to rest his case with the fall of the Commonwealth.

What became of his chief actors in later years we are not told – save for a tantalizing glimpse of Maurice Thomson and one of his brothers under the Restoration, perhaps now secret agents for the Dutch. But if the ending of Brenner's story is frustratingly abrupt, an arresting coda follows. For his narrative inevitably poses the question: was the nexus between 'merchants and revolution' ultimately sterile – in the long run a dead end in the nation's development, largely hidden from modern attention because of little further moment? Brenner's answer is quite precise. The sequels to the alliance of 1640–42 are to be found in the Exclusion Crisis of 1679–81 and the Glorious Revolution of 1688–89. The project of an English absolutism did not disappear with Charles I, and when his sons renewed it they ran into the same oppositional front as their father. On each occasion, aristocratic landowners in Parliament once again came together with unregulated traders in the City. The Whig campaign under Charles II failed, because the gentry remembered the lessons of the Civil War – Green had been the Leveller colour too. But James II could be safely banished, once a Dutch army had – in Brenner's words – performed 'the veritable miracle' of checking the monarchy for the gentry, without their having this time to appeal to the people.[11] The regime of grandees and merchants which oversaw the financial revolution and the war against France in the 1690s was a descendant of the compact of colonists in the 1630s. Brenner's book concludes with the words: 'The Revolution of 1688 and its sequels not only realized the project of 1640–1641 of the parliamentary capitalist aristocracy; in so doing, it also realized, in a politically subordinated form, the project of 1649–1653 of its leading allies outside the landed classes, the American colonial and East Indian-interloping leadership.'[12]

Formidable both in its volume of evidence and concentration of argument, *Merchants and Revolution* will shift the parameters of all future discussion of the Civil War. To gain a sense of how radically new is the scene it offers, it is enough to note that the central figure of Brenner's narrative, recurring on page after page, is mentioned just once in Russell's *Fall of the British Monarchies*, as in Worden's *Rump Parliament*, and figures not at all in Morrill's *Nature of the English Revolution*. No image, indeed, of any of the Thomson brothers

---

11. *MR*, p. 713.
12. *MR*, p. 716.

seems to have survived, though the hooded gaze of their partner Thomas Andrewes, first Mayor of London under the Commonwealth, whose handsome portrait adorns the cover of Brenner's book, projects the appropriate sense of collective power. It will take time to assimilate the implications of Brenner's account for the aspects of the Civil War it does not discuss. A number of obvious questions, however, are posed by it.

The English Revolution, unlike the French, was a conflict ultimately fought out in the countryside. It was decided, not by insurrectionary *journées* in urban squares, but in pitched battles in open fields. Yet the capital city was of much greater structural weight in England than in France. In 1640 London had perhaps 450,000 inhabitants out of a population of 4.5 million, and was over ten times larger than any other town – whereas in 1789 Paris had no more than 650,000 out of a population of 25 million, a qualitatively lesser magnitude. The economic disparity between the two centres was even greater, because of London's role as a major port as well as manufacturing centre. Although the importance of the City in the Civil War has been familiar enough in outline to historians, since the pioneering work of Valerie Pearl, the effect of Brenner's work is to make it clear that the full extent of its contribution to the English Revolution has not been registered. Certainly, merchant operations have escaped the revisionist problematic, with its nobiliary bias, almost entirely.

At the same time, the blazing light in which they emerge from Brenner's treatment only deepens the darkness in which other levels of London life remain. In particular, the trajectory of popular politics in the capital becomes yet more of an enigma. If, as Brenner maintains, the American-based merchants possessed a special advantage in their downward links to shopkeepers and small traders, allowing them to mobilize mass pressure for radical causes in 1640–42, why were their Presbyterian opponents able to reverse the situation so easily after late 1643, and dominate the streets for the rest of the Civil War – indeed even through the rise of Leveller agitation in 1647? Ian Gentles has suggested that Presbyterian strength was based on a combination of the wealthier tradesmen and the poorest layers of porters, watermen and sailors, in which apprentices from the more substantial guilds acted as a shock-force, against an Independent – later Leveller – constituency of artisans and smaller traders.[13]

---

13. 'The Struggle for London in the Second Civil War', *Historical Journal* 26: 2, June 1983, pp. 282–283.

If such was the correlation of forces, what was its social logic and how long did it hold? Sharp swings of mood, and abrupt ideological volte-faces, punctuate the history of London crowds in the seventeenth century. The two later Stuart crises Brenner enlists for his overall argument exemplify the point. The mass fervour aroused by Shaftesbury for Exclusion exceeded any mobilization witnessed by Pym, leading to a virtually insurrectionary atmosphere in London by 1681. But when James fled in 1688, leaving a vacuum of power behind in the capital, the populace scarcely moved. By the 1690s, indeed, the geography of London politics in the 1640s had undergone an all but complete reversal. During the Civil War, a relatively moderate inner City was surrounded by more radical suburbs. By the time of the Financial Revolution, the centre of London had become a Whig stronghold, while the outlying districts were hotbeds of Toryism.[14] The pattern of such volatility among the *menu peuple* calls for the kind of close focus, by sector and by conjuncture, Brenner has provided for the municipal elites, although the evidence is unlikely to be as clear-cut.

A second area of query must be religion. Brenner presents the monarchy and aristocracy as potentially at loggerheads over the church from the Elizabethan settlement onwards – the bulk of the landed class attracted to a more rigid Calvinism of conscience, while royal rulers preferred hieratic forms of worship with the greater stress on ceremony. The tension between doctrine and discipline was, indeed, an original fault-line in the Anglican church. But it was long containable. Why did it widen so dramatically from the 1620s onwards? The proximate answer is the Arminian turn of the monarchy, which caused an uproar in Parliament from the start. In Brenner's framework, with its emphasis on the long-range structural logic of social conflicts, it is tempting to conclude that this religious option – suspect of crypto-Catholicism for many gentlemen – was the appropriate clerical trapping for the more absolutist ambitions of Charles I, just as a radicalized Calvinism, gravitating towards a second Reformation, could be predicted among the most determined Parliamentary opponents of the King's will, in sympathy with urban Puritanism.

Such theological associations, however, lacked any compelling necessity. Absolutism could consort perfectly well with Calvinism, as the Great Elector in Prussia – far more autocratic than Charles I –

---

14. Gary De Krey, *A Fractured Society. The Politics of London in the First Age of Party*, Oxford 1985, pp. 171–176.

showed. Arminianism, on the other hand, was in its country of inven-
tion the creed of a mercantile Dutch patriciate in conflict with an
Orange dynasty sponsoring Calvinist orthodoxy – the exact opposite
of the English configuration. Such vagaries present no difficulty for
the nominalism of the revisionists, committed on principle to just-so
stories. But they do pose a problem for Brenner, as a critic of these.
In an European perspective, the religious policies of Charles I look
under-determined. It is more plausible to view the Laudian church less
as a token of some elective affinity between royal and clerical
ceremony, than as the sign of a disorder in the reason of state – a
monarchy that was losing its functional bearings in landed society,
slipping into contingency. Political authoritarianism did not require
theological provocation.

Once the dynamic of religious passions was unleashed, how should
their contribution to the Civil War be weighed? Brenner's contention
that, once personal rule had been scrapped, it was the popular
eruption into politics rather than the Puritan campaign against the
bishops which divided the landed class, leaves a number of issues
unresolved. The strongest version of the claim would require significant numbers of Parliamentarians to have put aside partiality for
bishops in the interests of rallying the people, and of Royalists to have
stifled aversion towards them out of greater fear of the people. But if
a few of the latter can be found, were there any of the former? Tacitly,
Brenner's case must appeal to the operation of a 'coincidence'
between political militancy and religious zeal in Pym's wing of the
Commons, which its terms do not explain. On his own showing,
moreover, confidence in an ability to control mass agitation in the
capital can only have been shared by the relatively narrow circle of
peers and MPs with ties to the new merchant leaders: scarcely by half
of the landowning class, the overwhelming majority of whom had not
the slightest purchase on London politics.

The process that converted a small majority in the Commons into a
moiety of Parliamentary counties must have involved other determi-
nants. Morrill has cogently argued for the asymmetrical effect of
religion in the genesis of the Civil War, on the grounds that
Puritanism mustered an intensity of zeal that Anglicanism did not.
For most Parliamentary landowners, trust in God is likely to have been
more important than trust in the people, even where a common faith
might allow one to envisage a measure of the other. In a larger sense,
moreover, there is not the slightest doubt that religion was the decisive
trigger of the Civil War, since it was the Scottish rebellion against the
Caroline Prayer Book which put the King at the mercy of Parliament,

and a Catholic revolt in Ireland which unsheathed swords between the two in England. The British matrix of the Civil War is not broached by Brenner: it is an intriguing question how far his line of analysis could be extended to encompass it.

Within his English framework, however, the division of the country poses a further problem. What determined the territorial configuration of the two camps, as fighting started? Why did most of the countryside in the North and West rally to the King, in the South and East to Parliament? Can either religious conviction or political confidence be regarded as plausible markers for the distribution? Even if they were, we would still be left with the question why they had taken this geographical pattern. No answer is to be found in either the revisionist literature or Brenner's reply to it. Two alternative explanations have traditionally been available. The first suggests that the diagonal split in the country in the summer of 1642 was essentially a function of Parliament's original control of London, and of the King's physical presence in York, each becoming a fortuitous magnet for the surrounding zones, subsequently consolidated along strategic – not social or ideological – lines. How plausible is such a view?

There can be no doubt that most Civil Wars do involve a certain random distribution of the cards, in which military control may correspond less to political strength than to chances of terrain or logistics. The map of Republican and Nationalist regions in the Spanish Civil War can be superimposed on the electoral geography of today's Socialist and Popular Parties with a high degree of fit – save for Andalucia and Extremadura, now bastions of the Left, but whose proximity to Morocco handed them to the Right in 1936, once the Moorish Legion was airlifted across the Straits. In China, Yenan was far from being a natural home of the CCP, whose principal areas of strength had been in the South-East, until it was driven there as a refuge more inaccessible to the KMT. Even in the American Civil War, where regional and political frontiers in principle coincided most completely, Maryland and Kentucky found themselves on the wrong side of the Mason–Dixon line. Nevertheless, the accidents of war have seldom, if ever, radically erased the ecology of class or belief when a country is gripped by civil strife. Even the most aleatory readings of the division of England in 1642 concede the logic of a Parliamentary London.

The second kind of explanation looks for systematic differences behind the territorial separation. In the richest analysis, David Underdown has argued that two antagonistic rural cultures – quite close to popular images of Cavalier and Roundhead – existed in sheep–corn lowlands and wood–pasture uplands, based on distinct village and manorial patterns, and that it was these which shaped the geography of political choice in the Civil War. But his concern is with popular rather than elite allegiances, and his evidence, drawn from three Western counties, is intra- rather than inter-regional.[15] At the national level, the broad contrast between Wales and East Anglia inverts rather confirms Underdown's dichotomy. The older hypothesis advanced by Christopher Hill was less fine-grained. It simply pointed to the fact the capitalist agriculture had developed further in the South and East of England than in the more backward North and West, and suggested that this was the setting for the dominant options of the gentry in each zone. Hill's argument was integral to a social interpretation of the Civil War that saw the Stuart monarchy as a nascent absolutism capable of calling upon reserves of feudal custom in the outer regions of the country.

What is Brenner's position? In keeping with his famous account in *The Brenner Debate* of precocious economic development in England, based on competitive leases and insecure tenures, *Merchants and Revolution* insists that by the time of the Civil War the landowning class as a whole was capitalist – not 'divided into advanced and backward sectors', but 'extraordinarily homogeneous' in its forms of exploitation.[16] The polarization between Royalists and Parliamentarians, therefore, was without any socio-economic basis. 'In so homogeneous a landed class as that of England in the 1640s, whence could such social differences have arisen?'[17] This seems categorical enough. Yet looked at a little closer, Brenner's formulations sometimes fluctuate. The landed class, it emerges, was only 'by and large' – 'for the most part' – 'not of course uniformly' – capitalist, and 'further consolidation' would be necessary later in the century.[18] Does the note of hesitation here suggest the underlying issue remains less than completely resolved? Certainly, the agrarian world of manorial courts and copyholds, wardships and entry fines, advowsons and impropriations, was still a good way from that of Charles Townshend.

Brenner's central argument for the capitalist character of English agriculture under the early Stuarts is that agrarian property was no longer 'politically constituted' – that is, landowners no longer

---

15. *Revel, Riot and Rebellion: Popular Politics and Culture in England 1603–1660*, Oxford 1985. The counties Underdown studied were Dorset, Somerset and Wiltshire.

16. *MR*, p. 642.

17. *MR*, p. 643.

18. *MR*, pp. 641–642, 711.

depended on extra-economic powers of coercion to extract a surplus from the cultivators, along medieval lines.[19] What this contrast, focussing essentially on the 'direct exercise of force', as Brenner puts it, perhaps understates is the extent to which landed property was still 'ideologically constituted' – that is, remained encased in pre-capitalist relations of justification. The power of such 'extra-economic legitimation', as we might call it, was subject to erosion from the rationale of the market. But if we are looking at the regional pattern of the divide within the landed class in the 1640s, it is here we might find part of the answer. It is clear that Royalists and Roundheads cannot simply be decanted in two different categories of estate management, since there were plenty of the most up-to-date landlords on the King's side. But for there to be a social logic to the division, such a symmetry is not necessary.

Just as religion worked asymmetrically within a broadly common Protestant outlook to polarize the Parliamentary side, so – we might surmise – tradition worked asymmetrically within a broadly improving agrarian class to polarize the Royalist side. In other words, the attachment of many 'progressive' landlords to the King does not mean that equal numbers of 'conservative' landlords rallied to Parliament. The magnetic pull of London ensured that market forces permeated the South-East more thoroughly than the North or West; and the less modern the setting, the more effective were bonds of loyalty and dependence tying property and authority together, in a traditional hierarchy. We can glimpse this contrast even within the most Roundhead of zones, the Eastern Association – Norfolk, Cambridge and Huntingdon lagging noticeably behind Essex, Suffolk and Herts in ardour for the Parliamentary cause.[20]

Royal ability to secure feudal exactions during personal rule is one kind of testimony to the continuing strength of the forms of ideologically constituted property. The pledges of allegiance received by the King once war seemed inescapable were another, and more decisive one: feudal conceptions of order and honour were not dead in the hinterland of the kingdom, or yet closer to the centre. Eventually, in the second round of the Civil War, even Kent or Surrey saw Royalist revolts. In Denbigh or Cumberland, on the other hand, no Parliamentary spark ever flared. The spectacle of popular disorder in London, divisive

---

19. *MR*, pp. 650–652.
20. See Clive Holmes, *The Eastern Association in the English Civil War*, Cambridge 1974, pp. 25–68.

though it certainly was, does not suffice to explain the split of 1642 – indeed, it might have been thought the gentry of the localities closest to the epicentre would be most alarmed, those further away less moved by it. Over much of the country, it seems likely that fear of the urban mob was less of a recruiter for royalism than codes of rural fealty to the King.

The ideological role of the monarchy as the keystone of an aristo-cratic order, holding the arch of ranks upright, has been emphasized by other Marxist historians of the period, notably Brian Manning.[21] Brenner tends to neglect it. His description of English monarchy as 'patrimonial' is a Weberian islet within his categories, whose consis-tency with them goes unexplained.[22] Patrimonialism was one of Weber's vaguest and most polymorphous notions, and its use has often been indiscriminate since. In the context of Brenner's analysis, however, the thrust of the term 'patrimonial' is clear enough: it is designed to suggest the distance between the Stuart monarchy, con-ceived as a self-contained household, and the landed class outside it – in other words, its lack of roots in the social soil at large. The unspoken antonym is feudal. This picture of the state is no quirk: it is a logical requirement of the claim that the aristocracy was homoge-neously capitalist. For where could that leave the monarchy, other than in structural isolation?

The depiction of the English landowning class in *Merchants and Revolution* is coherent with the account of its evolution in *The Brenner Debate*, which sets the late medieval stage for the early modern trans-formation of the gentry, now presented as all but complete. Nevertheless, there is a deep paradox in Brenner's sequel as a whole. For the great iconoclastic theme of his original theory of European economic development was the relative unimportance of towns or trade for the transition from feudalism to capitalism. Everything, in that vision, turned on agriculture, and only in England, it claimed, did agriculture turn. Historically, it was the unique self-transformation of the English landowners in the countryside which ushered in the world of capital – and it alone.

If one side of Brenner's polemic was aimed at neo-Malthusian orthodoxies, stressing the primacy of demography in early modern economic history, the other was targeted at neo-Smithian accounts that gave priority to cities and commerce – unwisely adopted, in Brenner's view, by too many Marxists. In subsequent work, he then

---

21. *The English People and the English Revolution*, London 1991, pp. 319–325.
22. *MR*, pp. 653–657.

went on to draw the conclusion that the idea of a 'bourgeois revolution', lodged in the Marxist tradition, was misplaced – no bourgeoisie
was needed to overthrow a feudal aristocracy, since the latter had
changed itself and got to capitalism first anyway. The break with feudalism came not from any accumulation in trade or assault on
absolute monarchy, but through an agrarian catharsis. Beside the self-
conversion of the English landlords, every other strand in the
emergence of capitalism was marginal.

For all the power of this case, there were always difficulties with its
overall context. The idea of capitalism in one country, taken literally,
is only a bit more plausible than that of socialism. For Marx the different moments of the modern biography of capital were distributed
in a cumulative sequence, from the Italian cities to the towns of
Flanders and Holland, to the empires of Portugal or Spain and the
ports of France, before being 'systematically combined in England at
the end of the seventeenth century'.[23] Historically, it makes better
sense to view the emergence of capitalism like this: as a value-added
process gaining in complexity as it moved along a chain of inter-
related sites. In this story, the role of cities was always central.
English landowners could never have started their conversion to commercial agriculture without the market for wool in Flemish towns –
just as Dutch farming was by Stuart times in advance of English, not
least because it was conjoined to a richer urban society. It might still
be argued that, even if the 'bourgeois' contribution to the economic
genesis of capitalism is conceded, this does not mean that any political 'revolution' was necessary to smooth its path. That would have
been one possible reading of Brenner's case, with its emphasis on the
immanent dynamism of competitive production for the market.
Where does his new work leave the issue?

Merchants and Revolution does not argue that the Civil War was
inevitable, but that a political collision between the monarchy and the
landowning class was inherently likely. What converted a parliamentary revolt into an armed revolution was, on Brenner's showing, the
catalytic role of the new merchants in London. Here, if ever, were
indeed revolutionary bourgeois. The species declared a fiction in
France was *bel et bien* a reality in England, a hundred and fifty years
before the Convention. There is a nice irony that it should be massive
historical evidence, running against – not with – a theoretical conviction, which has brought a Marxist scholar to this conclusion. The

---

23. Marx, *Capital*, Vol. I, London 1976, p. 915.

detractor of the significance of merchant capital in principle has been the first to establish, in spellbinding detail, its role as demiurge in practice. When the revisionists draw their lessons from the Civil War for Ukania today, Lord Russell – recalling the need for prudent management of Scots affairs and tamping down of ideal passions – dwells on the dangers of a disunited realm. Brenner's account of the hour of the Committee of Safety reminds us of that other question, the conditions of a durable republic.

The historical intelligence that has generated both the comparative logic of *The Brenner Debate* and the narrative depth of *Merchants and Revolution* is without close counterpart. This is a body of writing centred on the medieval and early modern worlds. It is an awesome thought that its author is now at work on the central puzzle of our own time, which has so far defeated every analyst. Why has the world economy been sunk in the intractable slow-down of the past twenty years, whose social consequences lie strewn without number around us? The answer will be worth waiting for.

II

Brenner's move into contemporary history is now before us, with the publication of two works on the world economy, *The Economics of Global Turbulence* and *The Boom and Bubble* that together amount to a body of writing close in size to *Merchants and Revolution*.[24] Their appearance offers an occasion to consider the relationship been the three great blocs of Brenner's oeuvre – his account of the feudal economies of medieval Europe, of the roots of revolution in early modern England, and of the dynamics of global capitalism in modern to postmodern times. The empirical wealth of each of these sets of writing, and the relative discontinuity between them – roughly speaking, they focus on the thirteenth to fifteenth centuries, the mid seventeenth and the late twentieth centuries – encourages, properly enough, specialist discussion of them by period or topic, for which there is no substitute. But to get a sense of Brenner's enterprise as a whole, some reflection on the general structure of his historical thought is also required. His recent writing provides a topical starting point.

Since at least the seventies it has been clear that, causally, the power

---

24. Respectively, London and New York 2005 and 2002. The first was originally published as a special issue of *New Left Review*, I/229, May–June 1998, but has now been updated, with a new introduction.

of the world economy to determine the fate of earth's population has been far greater than any other force. Yet, analytically, it has remained intractable. For years economics as an academic discipline has been moving steadily away from explanation of the real world towards formalized axioms and mathematical models with only a precarious bearing on actuality. Kenneth Arrow, architect of general equilibrium theory, has famously remarked that the profession has 'tended to shy away from the grandest themes. The fundamental questions of economic change, the theme of Schumpeter's work, are not discussed'.[25] Weekly commentators fill the gap as best they can, but in the absence of any real underlying scholarship, journalism – even at its most intuitively acute – is vulnerable to the myopias of immediacy or fashion. The deeper enigmas of post-war development have remained in either case largely untouched.

This is the background against which Brenner's current work acquires relief. In it, Arrow's 'grand theme' – the foundations of economic change in the post-war epoch – is directly taken up, and the result is on the appropriate grand scale. *The Economics of Global Turbulence* and *The Boom and the Bubble* present a detailed narrative of the trajectory of the three central capitalist economies – the United States, Japan and Germany – over the past half century, that has no counterpart in the literature. Brenner writes as a historian in the tradition of Marx, and no other recent work offers such a compelling use of its legacy to tackle large problems that have baffled other approaches. But this is an original Marxism that has little in common with what has often passed for orthodox deductions from *Capital*. No axioms of crisis based on a rising organic composition of capital, and therewith falling return on investment, are to be found in it. Brenner rejects such aprioristic equations on the Left as logical fallacies, just as he criticizes many conventional notions of the Centre and Right as lacking support in evidence. What distinguishes his own account of the long-term path of the world economy is an unmatched ability to hold the two sides of any satisfactory explanation together: a clearcut analytical model of how capitalist development can generate crises, and a detailed historical narrative of their empirical occurrence, testing and controlling the theoretical starting point. The minds of the economist and historian typically work in such antithetical ways that a true combination of their strengths – articulated

---

25. 'Economists', he intimated, display 'strong risk aversion in their own choice of research topics': K. Arrow and S. Honkapohja (eds), *Frontiers of Economics*, Oxford 1985, p. 19.

formal rigour and meticulous factual care – is very unusual. Here they are exceptionally united.

Brenner opens *The Economics of Global Turbulence* by posing the central question of why the world capitalist economy, after a long upturn of extraordinary dynamism after 1945, lapsed into an equally protracted downturn in the early 1970s, as decade by decade, the combined macro-economic performance of the advanced economies has fallen. For thirty years, this problem has frustrated a legion of analysts and commentators. For long, the most popular explanation – developed in various forms by Left and Right alike – was that the mechanisms of capitalist growth were undermined by the very success of post-war full employment, which eventually allowed trade unions to take advantage of tight labour markets to force up wages and hold back innovations. The result, so this interpretation went, was a cumulative squeeze on profits that broke the springs of investment, sending the world into prolonged recession. Brenner argues with great force that this cannot have been the case. Theoretically, he contends, no system-wide pressure of labour on capital is conceivable that would be capable of achieving a universal long-term lowering of rates of profit across the globe. International factor mobility is simply too asymmetric for this, since capital can always outflank labour by shifting elsewhere.[26] Empirically, moreover, the statistical evidence confirms what first principles would indicate: that wage pressures could not have determined by the onset of the downturn.

What, then, does explain the huge sea-change that overcame the advanced economies in the 1970s? Brenner's answer is testimony to his open-mindedness as a historian. Against all then received opinions, his work on the transition from feudalism to capitalism located its key mechanisms in the balance of forces between peasant producers and seigneurial proprietors on the land. There it was the variable outcome of the conflict between classes that essentially determined the path of agrarian development. However, in today's world of a fully consolidated industrial capitalism, Brenner reaches the opposite conclusion. Here it is not the vertical relationship between capital and labour that in the last resort decides the fate of modern economies, but the horizontal relationship between capital and capital. It is the logic of competition, not class struggle, that governs the deeper rhythms of growth or recession.

---

26. *The Economics of Global Turbulence*, pp. 20–26. Henceforward *EGT*.

For its champions, of course, competition has always been the central virtue of capitalism – the discipline that makes it inherently innovative, and gave it easy victory over the command economies in the Cold War. Brenner takes the system at its word, and shows how its strongest mechanism to raise productivity also fatally brings on loss of momentum and recurrent crisis. Typically, he argues, successful competition in manufacturing requires the sinking of large amounts of investment in complexes of fixed capital. These, however, will tend to become outdated by technologically newer complexes, initially erected in spaces beyond immediate reprisal by the original enterprises. The competitive pressure of the later arrivals then inevitably depresses the rate of return on the older enterprises. But these cannot immediately liquidate the capital sunk in fixed plant, with a normal life-span still to run, to exit smoothly into other lines of production. Instead, their rational response will be to lower their margins to meet the challenge from more efficient newcomers.[27] The result is a pattern of over-competition forcing down the rate of profit throughout the branch concerned. Once such competition becomes generalized, opportunities for profit contract, investment declines, and at some stage a sharp downturn becomes inevitable – which will last until sufficient obsolete capital has been flushed out of the system to restart the mechanisms of accumulation again.

If such was the general logic of the long downturn that set in around 1973, it was precipitated – this is Brenner's second theme – by a specific pattern of uneven development between competing blocs of capital. Historically, a condition of the post-war boom was the still relatively segmented national economies of the period, which allowed Germany and Japan to construct technological complexes that would in time become equal or superior to those of the world leader, the United States itself. In an economic space still largely protected by national frontiers, the conditions of a challenge to first-comers in any

---

27. *EGT*, pp. 29–41. The perverse logic of this process was first pointed out by Alexandre Lamfalussy, later head of the Bank of International Settlements in Basle, in his analysis of 'defensive investment' by Belgian industrial firms in the fifties: *Investment and Growth in Mature Economies: The Case of Belgium*, London 1961, pp. 79–94. In his pioneering work *The Limits of Capital* (Oxford 1982), David Harvey treated it as a 'switching crisis', in which the inertia of sunk capital obstructs exit from decreasingly profitable lines: pp. 428–429. Harvey's reconstruction of a Marxist theory of crises, preceding Brenner's work, can be regarded as the principal alternative to it, one that is conceptually much more systematic, but cast as a categorical structure, without historical instantiation.

given branch of production could be assembled, without danger of
being stifled at birth. Japanese and German capitalism, moreover,
enjoyed not just the technical advantages of an unencumbered modernization of fixed capital, but key institutional advantages in their
competition with American capitalism. These included not just the
availability of cheaper labour, but also a superior ability to sustain
high levels of investment and to control costs, based on tighter coordination of banks, firms and unions, and more effective state
intervention.

Brenner argues that it was when German and Japanese products
started to penetrate the American market on a major scale, with the
rapid growth of international trade during the 1960s, that the conditions for the long downturn were prepared. Once rival complexes of
fixed capital were locked in national confrontation with each other,
with no easy escape into alternative lines of production, profits fell
dramatically and in tandem across the whole advanced capitalist
world, at the turn of the seventies. Three decades later they have still
not recovered. Brenner traces the successive policy attempts by the
governments of the three major states to revive growth: first, expansion of debt to sustain demand in (open or disguised) Keynesian style;
then, efforts to prime supply by deregulation and deflation along
monetarist lines; eventually, improvised operations to fine-tune credit
or alter exchange rates. None, he documents, have been able to
restore system-wide profitability to anything near the levels of the
post-war boom. But, as the end of the century approached, uneven
development once again moved centre-stage.

This time it was the US that turned the tables on Japan and
Germany, by exploiting two advantages denied its rivals. American
competitive recovery, Brenner shows, was in good measure based on a
successful wage repression that held the growth of labour costs in
manufacturing far below German or Japanese levels. This complete
reversal of the pattern of the 1950s was possible for the very reason
that the US had never embedded the wage contract in the kind of
social arrangements that were once of such assistance to Germany or
Japan, but have since become fetters. Class struggle, in other words,
while of limited effect on the plane of the international system as a
whole, where the logic of inter-capitalist competition requires radical
devalorization to ignite a major upturn, can significantly affect the
fate of national economies within the overall system – that is, on the
plane of uneven development. Even here, however, Brenner suggests
that between the Plaza Accord of 1985 and its reversal in 1995, the
more important weapon of American competition was horizontal

rather than vertical, as the Treasury engineered successive devaluations of its currency. For a decade, a combination of lower wage growth and a lower dollar allowed the US to regain ground with a reinvigorated export drive and a sharp rise in manufacturing profitability.

By 1995, however, the heights to which the yen had been pushed under this regime were threatening Japan with an economic contraction that risked rebounding on the United States itself, should Japanese investors be forced to liquidate their holdings of American financial assets. Alarmed by the recent Mexican crisis and the prospect of system-wide financial instability, the Clinton administration reversed course, driving the dollar up in exchange for a huge increase in Japanese and other foreign purchases of US government securities. *The Boom and the Bubble* traces the story of what followed. With the inversion of the Plaza regime, a falling yen undermined exports from rival centres in the region around Japan whose currencies were pegged to the dollar, setting off the East Asian financial crisis in the summer of 1997. In the US, manufacturing profits flattened out as the dollar appreciated, while the stock market soared on a wave of incoming money from abroad and diving real interest rates – until, in the autumn of 1998, the Russian default brought one of the largest hedge funds on Wall Street to the verge of ruin overnight. At this point, faced with the danger of a worldwide financial crash, the Federal Reserve stepped in with a bail-out and successive interest-rate reductions, injecting huge amounts of credit into the US economy to sustain equity prices.[28]

Given a second life, the Clinton bubble that had started in 1996 took stock values – not least by firms buying up their own equity – to multiples of corporate earnings beyond all previous records. For a further brief spell, manufacturing firms, now awash with liquidity derived from record borrowings and overvalued stock issues, shadowed this speculative euphoria with an investment boom, much of it – notably in telecommunications – disastrously misallocated. But by mid-2000, the bubble had become unsustainable, and within another six months the stock market plunged, and manufacturing profitability along with it, taking the US economy into recession as Clinton departed. Since then, a precarious revival has rested on two further injections of liquidity into the system: the engineering of low mortgage rates by the Federal Reserve, that has enabled widespread cashing-out from a housing boom to take over the role of stock appreciation in fuelling consump-

---

28. *The Boom and the Bubble*, pp. 134–176.

tion, and the tax cuts of the Bush administration.[29] Profitability in the American economy has in these conditions come back fairly well, albeit to nowhere the levels of the long boom, mainly at the expense of wages. High productivity growth, too, has been achieved, but by intensified pressures – speed-up and stretch-out – rather than further investment. The result has been a largely jobless recovery, with high levels of concealed unemployment as labour-force participation has declined. The structural weakness of American labour, which has allowed business to manage repeated shake-outs, scrapping obsolete plant and redistributing the workforce, in each of the periodic sharp recessions within the long downturn, continues. Brenner does not underestimate the accomplishments these represent. The possibility that sufficient devalorization of fixed capital will eventually have occurred for the American economy to pull out of the downturn, and lift the global economy with it, cannot be ruled out. But for the moment, the signs point in the opposite direction. Notwithstanding the partial depreciation of the dollar, US exports continue to fall further behind the demand of American consumers for imports. The steadily widening US trade deficit is covered only by a huge influx of capital from Asian central banks, while Europe and Japan remain mired in stagnation. For Brenner, the underlying cause of this triangular impasse is the persistence of over-capacity in the leading branches of industrial production across the developed countries. The system has yet to be purged of its excess of sunk capital, that still discourages investment and employment, and now finds its counterpart in a mountain of debt and huge financial bubbles. The spectre of over-competition has not been banished.

Whatever particular judgements may be made of the different parts of this argument, it is plain that here, as in no other body of work today, Marx's enterprise has found a successor. To have developed as coherent, detailed and deep-going an attempt to understand the history of the world market – where Marx left off in *Capital* – since the Second World War must be regarded, by any standards, as an extraordinary accomplishment. It is one that at the same time leaves open a number of problems, theoretical or empirical. The first of these is the role of labour in the narrative. It is fundamental to

---

29. For the astonishing part in sustaining growth that devolved on housing debt, see 'New Boom or New Bubble', *New Left Review* 25, January–February 2004, pp. 78–82.

Brenner's case that 'labour cannot, as a rule, bring about a tempo-
rally-extended, systemic downturn', since 'what might be called the
potential sphere of investment for capital in any line of production
generally extends beyond the labour market that is affected by unions
and/or political parties or is regulated by norms, values and institutions supported by the state'.[30] In principle this argument, made well
before the current global wave of out-sourcing, seems irrefutable.
However, two questions are left unresolved by it. Empirically,
Brenner's own account indicates that if wage pressures cannot have
determined the onset, let alone persistence, of the long downturn,
wage repression was critical to the competitive recovery of American
capitalism between 1980 and 1995.

Is there a contradiction here? Not if all that was involved was
another twist in the pattern of uneven development in the world
market, where the position of competitors is subject to perpetual
change – Germany and Japan having benefited from lower wage
costs than the US during the long boom, the ROK or Taiwan from
still lower ones from the long downturn. At times, however, Brenner
suggests that a full recovery of profitability in the US could unleash
a virtuous circle of investment and growth outside it, given the centrality of the American economy within the overall system.[31] But if
local wage repression could help trigger a global upturn, it would
appear to follow that wage pressures could prolong or deepen a
down-turn, making labour a more independent variable than at first
sight. Brenner seems readier to introduce wages as a significant
variable when they are low rather than when they are high, much as
militants are typically reluctant to admit that workers' demands
could contribute to an economic crisis, but are quite prepared to
accept that workers' defeats have boosted capitalist profits. Perhaps
too much weight should not be put on Brenner's occasional conjectures of a US-led escape, based in large part on wage repression,
from the system-wide trough of the past thirty years. They pose the
question, however, of whether a general theory of wage determination is implied by his narrative. What is the relative weight to be
accorded to industrial struggles between workers and employers, as
opposed to the tightness of labour markets, or inherited expectations?
If 'labour forces in regions with long histories of economic development tend to receive wages which are substantially higher than can be

30. *EGT*, p. 25.
31. *EGT*, pp. 291–292.

explained simply by reference to their relative level of productive-
ness',[32] what explains such uneven development of wage costs?

A less empirical query attaches to the logic of competition between
capitals. If the potential sphere of investment, as Brenner argues,
always exceeds the area in which trade-union, party or state action
can affect wages, how far does this potential usually become actual?
For if firms with sunk capital in a given line of production find it difficult, when confronted with new lower-cost competitors, to exit
cleanly into other lines, would not the same constraints inhibit them
from easily shifting the location of their enterprises, since this would
mean scrapping existing fixed assets and building new plant with new
equipment, in much the same way? At a superficial glance, the difference between changing product lines and production sites does not
look decisive, in terms of impact on fixed capital.

Here, however, a more general issue posed by *The Economics of
Global Turbulence* arises. Brenner's narrative repeatedly points to the
contrasting fate of the non-manufacturing sectors of the American,
Japanese and German economies, where prices could be raised
without fear of foreign competition, and so profits more easily sustained, as proof of the constraints of over-competition in the
manufacturing sector, where this was not possible. These demonstrations are in themselves convincing. But they raise the question of why,
if prices can be increased with greater impunity in non-tradeables,
and the weight of this sector is constantly increasing in the developed
world, there has not been more inflationary pressure since the
eighties. More formalistically, given that the share of manufactures in
the GDP of all the advanced countries has been steadily declining
through the long downturn – in the US, it is now not much above
12 per cent – why should the future not lie in the emergence of increasingly pure service economies in these societies, generating sufficient
external surpluses from their financial sectors to pay for needed manufactures from the less developed economies? That might be thought
an appropriate *reductio ad absurdum* of theories of post-industrial
society. But what it points to is a heuristic gap in Brenner's exposition,
which assumes rather than explains the reasons why material production must remain the core of any major economy, and the vicissitudes
of manufacturing underlie tectonic shifts in the system as whole.

One consequence of this gap is an unspoken hiatus between the
structural account of over-accumulation in *The Economics of Global*

---

32. *EGT*, p. 22.

Turbulence and the conjunctural path of the downturn in which it resulted. The first sets out a powerful model of the destructive consequences of competition between firms with fixed capital of different vintages within common sectors of industry, and of the ways in which their spread-effects can become worldwide. Everything here happens within the world of material production. When the analysis moves to the history of the long downturn, however, both the agents and the instruments of competition change: states intervene to defend the interests of firms, and alterations of exchange rates are capable – at any rate temporarily – of halting or reversing outcomes on the company battlefield. Turning points in the story become such moments as the Plaza and Reverse Plaza Accords. Left ambiguous is how far, across the period as a whole, currency adjustments were essentially an automatic process built into the uneven development of the system, regardless of the particular distribution of its parts, and how far they reflected a contingent asymmetry between the 'continental' weight of the US economy as against its 'national' counterparts in Japan and Germany – the primacy of the dollar as an international reserve currency giving the American state a special freedom of manoeuvre in the monetary field, from the time of Nixon's break with gold onwards.

What is clear, however, from Brenner's account is that from the turn of the eighties through to the mid-nineties, the appreciation of the yen and D-mark against the dollar, permitting large competitive gains for American industry, was the principal factor in the recovery of manufacturing profitability in the US. In other words, the monetary economy – the market for currencies, not commodities – operated as a 'corrector' of outcomes in the material economy, in the uneven development of the system. But while this result is registered empirically, there is no theoretical explanation of how and why exchange rates can so decisively affect mechanisms of competition postulated independently of them. A more formal model of how the material and the monetary planes interact seems required by the narrative itself. Brenner is not, of course, alone here. Money was essentially ignored not only in Marx's system, but equally in neo-classical theory, whose formally perfected versions – from Walras's *tâtonnement* to Arrow and Debreu's general equilibrium – render it redundant. In Austrian economics too, it remained, as Hayek confessed, a 'loose joint'. Keynes is the exception, and it is no accident that there are echoes of him in Brenner's explanation of the reasons why the long downturn has not led to any classic crash, involving a cathartic devalorization of older capitals, that would allow accumulation to pick up pace again at higher levels of profit in a global upturn. What has stabilized the system so far has been massive injections of credit, not just by government spending when so required, but by the multiplication of bank money and the growth of consumer and corporate debt, culminating in the stock and housing frenzies of *The Boom and the Bubble*.

That these offer no solution for the dilemmas of over-competition, but only palliatives or postponements of them, is integral to Brenner's case. But they raise a more general issue for the framework of his theory. Within it, demand is essentially treated as a function of the growth of investment, and therewith of employment and wages, governed in turn by the rate of profit. Once over-competition sets in, and profitability declines, this model must presuppose that the market is limited in advance. For otherwise, it might be asked why older-established firms could not compensate for the lower prices imposed on them by cost-cutting competitors, with enhanced returns to scale from a larger volume of sales, in an expanding market that afforded leeway for both new and old producers. So indeed, throughout *The Economics of Global Turbulence*, certain demand parameters – 'continuing barriers to manufacturing dynamism anywhere in the advanced capitalist world'[33] – appear as a relatively stationary background to the narrative.

But as the specification of the final phrase suggests, there is a spatial dimension to any structure of demand. Brenner's initial account of the mechanisms of over-competition rests on the premise of a segmented territorial system, organized in national units, behind whose protection challenges can be mounted by newcomer against old-timer firms. A vast and illuminating historical narrative flows from this. But the abstract postulate of territorial division is never cashed out into a commensurately concrete description of the overall space of the system. Rather, Brenner explains, *The Economics of Global Turbulence* focuses for practical reasons on the US, German and Japanese cases, which after all, he points out, accounted for as much as two-thirds of OECD output in the mid-nineties.[34] One effect of this decision is that the European Union becomes close to a null factor in the story: it is as if Germany stands as a proxy for the Europe as a whole, while its own path of development is related essentially to movements of the American economy.

---

33. *EGT*, p. 233.
34. *EGT*, p. 12.

Yet Europe has always been a much more important market for German exports than the US; while the sheer size of the EU, with a GDP larger than that of the US itself, make it difficult to treat as just a penumbra of the German economy. On the other side of the world, Japan is given a more regional context than Germany in *The Economics of Global Turbulence*, as the smaller East Asian economies stage a dramatic entry into the story, invading American markets and reorienting Japanese trade and investment in the 1990s. It is with the crisis of 1997–98 in this region that *The Boom and the Bubble* opens, and no reader of Brenner could by then be uncertain of its importance for his history of the present. But his selection of the USA, Germany and Japan as a stylized *abrégé* of the world economy as a whole remains substantially unaltered. The theoretical implications of a major expansion of the space of industrial capitalism *since* the long downturn are not explicitly confronted. Simply, the new entrants into the ring – South Korea, Taiwan, Hong Kong, Singapore – figure as doughty additional combatants in the battle for export markets, intensifying global over-competition yet further. The question of how they could have achieved this status, without either the substantial domestic markets or the long international boom that powered German and Japanese expansion after the war, is left to one side.

Today, the emergence in the twenty-first century of China as one of world's largest industrial powers, the principal trading partner not only of the United States but also of Japan, poses a challenge to Brenner's conceptualization of the space of over-competition of an altogether different magnitude. Brenner crisply rejects the traditional Marxist theorem of the tendency of the rate of profit to fall as the organic composition of capital rises.[35] But he has never directly addressed what was one development from it, Luxemburg's notion that the opening-up of hitherto non-capitalist territories could be a solution, partial or provisional, for crises of over-accumulation. Imperialism, in her eyes, was best understood as a drive to offset failing demand at home, by prising exogenous demand loose from regions hitherto inaccessible for socio-political reasons, and so to give accumulation a fresh lease of life. Along these lines, the decommunization of the Soviet bloc could be regarded as offering something like such an outlet for particular branches of Western industry. But what of the far larger gravitational mass of post-Maoist China?

---

35. *EGT*, pp. 15–16.

Dreams of a boundless market for European and American goods in China were already commonplace among Western merchants and projectors in the nineteenth century. The contemporary pursuit of Chinese consumers by Microsoft or News Corp has a considerable ancestry. But macro-economically, the boot has so far been on the other foot, as China racks up enormous trade surpluses, importing primarily raw materials and capital goods, against manufacturing exports not only in labour-intensive, but also increasingly in medium or high-tech lines. Despite the size of the Chinese market, and the sigificance of foreign investment in it, the net impact of this emergent colossus on the world economy would thus, on Brenner's showing, seem to have been less to mitigate over-competition in the most advanced economies by opening up new avenues of demand, than to aggravate it by piling yet further supply pressure on higher-cost producers. At any rate, that appears to be one possible deduction from the way China figures in his narrative to date.

But if this is so, it raises two questions. The basic premise of Brenner's theory of the long downturn is that inter-capitalist struggle between US, Japanese and German firms leads to over-competition because they are typically fighting for market shares in the same lines of production. But why, in the case of a newcomer like China, should there not be more complementarity than competition in its trade relations with the US or Japan, or for that matter Europe – China exporting simpler goods and importing more sophisticated ones, in a virtuous circle of growth all round? Why, indeed, are thoroughgoing national specializations along classic Ricardian lines – English cloth for Portuguese wine – so limited a phenomenon in the contemporary world, cases like the former Japanese semi-monopoly of consumer electronics, or the US semi-monopoly of wide-bodied jets, transient exceptions rather than the rule? Implied in the notion of over-competition is an antithesis whose formal conditions and historical exemplifications are little explored. Complementarity features in the argument as what has failed to materialize, not as an object in its own right. In the case of China, this theoretical neglect is the more pertinent because of an empirical feature of East Asian growth, that Brenner notes in the case of post-war Japan, but does not linger on – the very high rate of household savings that has always underlain domestic investment in the region. In the PRC, this has assumed extraordinary dimensions – savings running at 40 per cent of GDP, powering rates of investment of nearly 50 per cent. Much of this huge spending spree on fixed capital, a great deal going into infrastructure rather than plant, is not yielding a rate of profit that would be remotely acceptable in the OECD. It answers to another logic of accumulation. But does that mean it has no implications for a deadlock in world demand?

Such questions return us to the space of the system. There, at least, one thing is clear: the time has passed when the United States, Japan and Germany could still function as a shorthand for the world economy. How is this change likely to affect the shape of Brenner's argument? To get a sense of its possible directions, it may be useful to look at the ways in which his work as a historian has been received to date, and the pattern of his response to them. Few scholars working on the past have made such a spectacular mark so early on. His first major essay, 'Agrarian Class Structure and Economic Development in Pre-Industrial Europe', published in *Past and Present* in 1976, was the subject of an international debate in 1978–79, involving leading economic historians from four countries, among them such eminences as Postan, Le Roy Ladurie, Cooper and Hilton. Three years later came Brenner's comprehensive rejoinder, taking up the range of objections put to him, and expanding his original case, both empirically and conceptually. The whole exchange then appeared as *The Brenner Debate* in the mid-1980s. Thereafter, for a decade all discussion of his theses virtually ceased. It was not until the mid-1990s that a group of young Belgian and Dutch historians returned full-tilt to them, in a second collective engagement that in due course produced a volume as substantial as the first, *Farmers into Peasants?*, which appeared in 2001.[36]

The most consequential gap in Brenner's taxonomy of agrarian relations and the origins of capitalism had always been the Low Countries. There, in the most densely urbanized region in Europe, commercial farming in the early modern period achieved higher levels of productivity than in England, on an owner-operator basis without significant aristocratic landlords. How did such apparent self-emancipation of a peasantry fit his schema? With characteristic thoroughness, Brenner set out his answer in the long concluding essay of

---

36. Peter Hoppenbrouwers and Jan Luiten van Zanden (eds), *Peasants into Farmers? The Transformation of Rural Economy and Society in the Low Countries during the Later Mediaeval and Early Modern Periods in the Light of the Brenner Debate*, Turnhout 2001, which contains nine detailed studies by local historians, more supportive of Brenner than his respondents in *Past and Present*, and with much more documentation, together with an essay by Jan de Vries from Berkeley, doyen of early modern Dutch economic history and coiner of the notion of an 'industrious revolution' predating the industrial revolution.

Farmers into Peasants?. In it, he showed that the mere presence of towns and absence of major seigneurial exploitation was insufficient to unleash a transition to capitalist agriculture in the most developed area of the medieval Low Countries, inland Flanders. There, peasants could still assure part of their subsistence on their own small plots, but were forced by demographic pressures to supplement cultivation for the household with intensive husbandry – fodder crops, legumes, flax – for the market, and eventually widespread domestic industry. The result, however, was not development, since there was no true dependence on the market, and so exposure to its cost-cutting imperatives, as long as households could still cling to rudiments of subsistence. Rather, in a vicious circle, labour productivity fell as peasants redoubled their efforts on ever more subdivided plots, and rural misery became widespread.

By contrast, in the maritime north of the Low Countries, also a region of weak lordship but far poorer and less urbanized than the south, soil decline – the penetration of water into peat on reclaimed lands – made arable cultivation increasingly unviable in the later Middle Ages. The consequence was to force peasants, still in possession of their land but now altogether unable to use it for subsistence purposes, to specialize in dairy farming on larger holdings, often using wage labour.[37] Out of this ecological contingency emerged a true capitalist agriculture, albeit with a quite different pattern of property and production from England, that laid the basis for the spectacular urban growth and commercial dynamism of the Dutch Republic in the early modern period. Yet this model of development, Brenner argues, had an Achilles heel that ensured its English rival, at first far slower to take off, would ultimately surpass it. The Dutch lead depended on exports. Its dairy products, textiles and porcelain were sold in Europe-wide markets, where its shipping dominated the carrying trade. Once the pre-industrial European economy was struck by widespread Malthusian crisis in the seventeenth century, the Netherlands lacked a sufficient domestic market to offset the general contraction abroad. For all its own wealth and modernity, it formed too small a territory and population to avoid the fatality of symbiosis with its pre-modern environment, condemning the Republic to stagnation and eventually regression, while the English economy – no

---

37. To the contrast between an inland South and maritime North of the Low Countries, Brenner adds a diagonal pendant: social relations in the coastal belt of Flanders inclining to a commercial landlordism, in the inland regions of the North to feudal agriculture.

less capitalist, but with a much larger home market, proof against setbacks in Europe – gathered speed and in due course overtook it.

If the Netherlands had presented the principal challenge to Brenner's original account of the 'agrarian roots of European capitalism', what of economies outside Europe? Here, plainly, the largest case was China, universally acknowledged to have been far more prosperous and developed than medieval Europe in Song times. In recent years, moreover, claims have been increasingly made that the economy of the wealthiest Chinese region, the Yangzi delta, was fully as advanced as that of any part of Europe, if not more so, down to the end of the eighteenth century – a view shared by a contemporary like Montesquieu, who compared the irrigated fertility of Jiangnan and Zhejiang, indeed, to that of Holland.[38] In *The Great Divergence*, the most the ambitious work along these lines, Kenneth Pomeranz has argued that in both early modern England and the Yangzi delta rapid development was driven by an increase in demand set off by the combination of demographic growth and free markets, leading – in classic Smithian fashion – to an intensification of the division of labour, specialization of productive activities and corresponding expansion of supply. If China fell behind England – and Europe more generally – in the nineteenth century, this was essentially because it lacked two critical facilities that allowed the industrial revolution to occur in the West: coal and colonies.[39] It was these that gave first England and then much of the continent access to windfalls of inorganic energy and overseas land supply, without which they would have encountered the same Malthusian barriers to further growth that brought the Qing economy to a halt by the time of the Opium War.

In this case, Brenner has been a critic in a wider debate, rather than the object of one, since the view that eighteenth century China was on an economic par with England is rejected by the leading authority on the country's agrarian history, Philip Huang, author of commanding works on the northern plains and the Yangzi delta alike. Yet here again, Brenner's intervention, co-authored with Christopher

---

38. 'The ancient emperors of China were not conquerors. The first thing they did to aggrandize themselves was what gave highest proof of their wisdom. They raised from beneath the waters two of the finest provinces of the empire; these owe their existence to the labour of man. And it is the inexpressible fertility of these two provinces which has given Europe such ideas of the felicity of that vast country': *The Spirit of the Laws*, New York 1949, p. 274.

39. *The Great Divergence. Europe, China and the Making of the Modern World Economy*, Princeton 2000, pp. 66–67, 264–80 et seq.

Isett, has been as courteous and decisive as was once his reply to Le Roy Ladurie on France. What the two show is how vast was in fact the distance between English and Jiangnan paths of development, from as early as the sixteenth century onwards. This was a divergence culminating by the end of the eighteenth century in sizes of agricultural holdings in Engand over a hundred times those in the Yangzi delta, and characterized by a prolonged secular rise in labour productivity as against a sharp fall, much higher levels of urbanization and popular living standards, and longer life expectancy.[40] Such contrasts were rooted, as in Europe itself, in the ability of the Chinese peasant families to maintain subsistence on micro-plots, investing ever greater inputs of labour for decreasing returns while resorting to commercial activities for supplementary income, in a pattern reminiscent of Flemish rather than Dutch development. In the Jiangnan, even remarkable progress in rice yields and flourishing urban consumption – not to speak of abundant seams of unutilized coal, and a vast empire in Central Asia – were ultimately of little avail against agrarian involution, once labour intensification could go no further and a land frontier was reached. As forests were stripped and marginal lands became barren, the inevitable upshot was overpopulation, falling life expectancy, and economic stagnation. The Smithian notion that market mechanisms and an industrious people can of themselves deliver self-sustaining growth stands revealed, in meticulous detail, as a mirage.[41]

This lesson can, in effect, can be regarded as the core proposition of everything that Brenner has written on the origins of capitalism. Its consistent theme is that only a grasp of comparative property relations in the tradition of Marx, rather than an appeal to timeless axioms of Smith or Malthus, can account for the variant outcomes of pre-modern economies in Europe as in Asia. Given the dominance of neo-classical assumptions, taken as self-evident truths, by the economic profession and allied historians, it is no surprise that this should be an unpalatable conclusion to many, among whom the political cult of the market that has been a signature of recent decades has merely reinforced a

---

40. 'England's Divergence from China's Yangzi Delta: Property Relations, Microeconomics, and Patterns of Development', *Journal of Asian Studies*, 61: 2, May 2002, pp. 609–662.

41. Not touched on are the cultural contrasts – in science, philosophy, social and political thought – between the two societies by mid-Qing times, alone enough to make attempts to minimize the economic differences between them something of a quixotic enterprise.

long-standing intellectual faith that predates it. Resistance to any alternative vision of development, no matter how well argued or documented, is virtually automatic among such believers. But if this has been a common submerged motif in reactions among economic historians to Brenner's work on the logic of property relations for patterns of development, the reception by Stuart specialists of *Merchants and Revolution* has been quite distinct. When it first appeared, responses were generally laudatory. Brenner's identification of the salience of North American-based merchants in the Civil War was – in Robert Ashton's judgement, echoed by others – a 'signal and indisputable contribution to the historiography of both commercial reorientation and political revolution'.[42] There were qualifications. Levant and East Indies merchants may have been less favourable to the monarchy, and domestic traders more significant in the opposition to it, than Brenner had allowed. But his general map of different interests in the City was not contested.

Criticism focused instead on what was taken to be the implication that economic positions, rather than religious convictions, determined the political agenda of the interloper connection.[43] In fact, Brenner had dismissed the idea that commercial considerations could of themselves explain the role of the colonial merchants in the Civil War, and himself stressed the importance of a religious outlook in this network, one not exclusive to it, that would in time become Independency. *Merchants and Revolution* – correctly described by Ashton as a 'monumental exercise in *l'histoire intégrale*' – never counterposed what such critics separated. The most striking feature of the book's reception, however, lay elsewhere. Although virtually every historian who reviewed the work noted that Brenner had

---

42. *English Historical Review*, February 1994, p 116. Conrad Russell: 'The pivotal finding of the book is that support for parliament in the City in 1640–1642 came overwhelmingly from those involved in the colonial trades, and especially in tobacco. This finding appears to be substantially correct and is clearly of major significance': *International History Review*, February 1994, p. 128.

43. 'To *assume* that their economic activity drove them to radical religion, and radical religion to radical politics, is both illogical and improbable. It is much more probable that most of his radicals began in other forms of economic activity, and were drawn into radical religion and through that into investment/and or participation in colonial trade': John Morrill, 'Conflict Probable or Inevitable?', *New Left Review* I/207, September–October 1994, p. 118 – an objection shared by Ian Gentles, for whom Brenner lacks 'understanding of the inwardness of puritan belief': 'A New Social Interpretation', ibid., p. 110. These are the two most detailed and substantial considerations of *Merchants and Revolution*.

proposed a new social interpretation of the Civil War, none engaged with it. Russell's claim that he did not even 'know for certain what "feudalism" or "capitalism" are' , let alone 'whether there was ever a "transition" between them', can be taken as more or less representative.[44] Such professions of blankness, intended as condescension, were in part, of course, simply codewords for an aversion to Marxism *de rigueur* in this period, as opposed to the time of *The Brenner Debate*. No doubt, too, they in some degree reflected a more general difficulty historians can experience in coping with theoretical structures for which their intellectual equipment has not prepared them. Yet behind the inability to confront Brenner's larger argument was perhaps also something more specific to this periodic field, a growing indifference to economic history of any kind.

Whatever the mixture of such reasons, the deepening silence that has covered Brenner's work in the decade since the publication of *Merchants and Revolution* suggests the extent to which the run of Stuart historians have been not only out of sorts, but out of depth with it. If the high tide of revisionism has ebbed, and along with it much of the polemical zest and curiosity it brought to thinking about the period, work on Stuart history has continued to come thick and fast. But the temperature of the time can be taken from three examples of recent scholarship that abut directly onto the terrain explored by Brenner: the Civil War, the relation of the mid-century Republic to the Revolution of 1688–89, and rival historiographic interpretations of the period at large. All three suppress any reference

---

44. 'Like an Englishman unwillingly abroad, forced to shape his mouth around menacing foreign syllables', a younger historian would later caustically note, Russell 'pleads a delicate inability to discuss the conclusion of Brenner's book, because he does not know for certain what "feudalism" or "capitalism" are" – a perennial strategem, as R.H. Tawney pointed out in 1926: "After more than half a century of work by scholars of half a dozen different nationalities and of every variety of political opinion, to deny that the phenomenon exists; or to suggest that if it does exist, it is unique among human institutions in having, like Melchizedek, existed from eternity, or to imply, if it has a history, propriety forbids that history to be disinterred, is to run wilfully in blinkers"': James Holstun, 'Brian Manning and the Dialectics of Revolt', paper at a conference on *Making Social Movements*, 2002. The one exception to the pattern came from Manning, who criticized Brenner's social interpretation of the Civil War for overstating the contribution of the gentry to the development of an agrarian capitalism at the expense of the role of yeomen, and more generally of paying insufficient attention to small producers, also in industry, in the genesis of the conflict: 'The English Revolution and the Transition from Feudalism to Capitalism', *International Socialism*, Summer 1994, pp. 75–86.

to his work. The principal synthesis on the Civil Wars and Inter-regnum, Austyn Woolrych's *Britain in Revolution 1625–1660*, eight hundred pages of detailed narrative, full of minor as well as major characters, wipes the record bare of any trace of the North American syndicate, managing the feat of not even mentioning *Merchants and Revolution* in its five-part bibliography of relevant scholarship. Here return to an older style of imagination yields a panegyric of Cromwell at which Victorians might have blushed.[45] The most ambitious attempt to reconnect the successive crises of the seventeenth century within a single framework, Jonathan Scott's *England's Troubles*, is programmatically innocent of any reference to economic changes in the country. Its leading premise is that an understanding of the time must not depart from the beliefs of (selected) contemporaries about them : essentially, fear of popery – to be taken not simply at face value, but internalized by the historian to the point of describing Charles I's Arminianism, in the language of his enemies, as a stealthy version of it.[46] Here, immune to intrusion from structural develop-ments in society as a whole, military and fiscal issues of state-building, and ideological discourses, principally of religion, can be choreographed into a rigidly stylized, virtually balletic suite at the fancy of the director.

More pointed still is Ronald Hutton's recent survey of *Debates in Stuart History*, where it might be thought the topic itself would render notice of *Merchants and Revolution* inescapable. But in an attractive book, generally fair as well as lively in its judgements of authors and arguments, Brenner's work is again conspicuous by its

---

45. For withering comments on partisan anachronisms in the narrative as a whole, see Mark Kishlansky, 'The Price of Treason', *Times Literary Supplement*, 8 November 2002. If revisionism was sometimes, unjustly, associated with the political climate of Thatcherism, such post-revisionism has on occasion had something of the tone of the subsequent regime. Had he ever leafed through *Britain in Revolution*, the late director of communications at Downing Street might have admired the presentation of its hero, and other commendable *dramatis personae* – certainly not Levellers – at delicate junc-tures in their careers.

46. 'It is not difficult to get modern students to see why these policies provoked contemporary fears of popery. What is more difficult, within the existing English story, is to get them to take seriously the possibility that it was popery, that when contemporaries believed they were witnessing the eradication of English protestantism they were correct': *England's Troubles*, Cambridge 2000, p. 126. The oxymoron of 'counter-reformation protestantism', freely used as an alternative formulation to the same ends, could hardly be a more strident example of what the book deplores, a category inconceivable to contemporaries.

absence. In this case, the lapsus is the more striking in that Hutton sets himself the goal of a self-reflexive account of his subject, not without success – offering, among other things, far the best account of the origins and lights of revisionism, setting these in generational, professional and social contexts that historians have rarely vouchsafed of their own practice.[47] But amid much collegial and autobiographical candour, and no lack of self-critical irony, Hutton appears to have no inkling of the limitations that could have led to his oversight: not simply the automatic belief that Marxism must now be as dead as the Soviet Union, an assumption as lazy as its fashionable opposite would have been thirty years ago, but a more general tendency to write as if economic history – apparently banished from 'debates in Stuart history' – no longer existed. It is the combination of the two as a professional disposition that has assigned Brenner to a peculiar limbo of the imagination in these years. But over time, as with the Brenner Debate itself, a *rebondissement* can be expected. When the forthcoming work of the American historian Steven Pincus on the revolution of 1688–89 appears,[48] offering an integrated account of the depth charges in English society that blew up the final attempt to build a Stuart Absolutism, the absurdity of continuing to write the political history of the country in abstraction from its economy will become obvious. The *longue durée* of *Merchants and Revolution* is likely to be vindicated in more than one sense.

If Brenner's work on late medieval history has aroused repeated, if widely spaced debates, whereas on the seventeenth century it has been, after initial acknowledgement, all but censored within the profession, the fate of *Global Turbulence* has differed again. Here, there has been a bifurcation of response. A bombardment of rejoinders in small journals of the Left met its first appearance, most of them concerned with points of doctrine, none attempting to deal with its history of

---

47. *Debates in Stuart History*, pp. 6–31. For another, detailed overview of Stuart historiography since 1992, see the preface to the third edition of Barry Coward, *The Stuart Age*, London 2003, pp. xiv–xxxviii, no less unable to remember *Merchants and Revolution*.

48. Thought to be nearing completion. In his first book, Pincus differed from Brenner over the origins of the first Anglo-Dutch War – more religious and political than commercial, in his view – but went out of his way to endorse Brenner's critique of the dominant historiography of the early seventeenth century: *Protestantism and Patriotism*, Cambridge 1996, p. 13. Pincus was himself subsequently berated by Scott for an unwarrantably secular view of Restoration opinion about foreign affairs: *England's Troubles*, pp. 351–354.

post-war economic development as a whole.[49] In mainstream venues, it was ignored. Nor was this duality greatly altered with the publication of *The Boom and the Bubble*, favourably noticed in the press but unexamined by the profession. Five years after Brenner's vision of the world economy entered circulation, however, it has elicited a fuller and deeper critical response than to any other part of his work to date. Giovanni Arrighi's long essay, 'The Social and Political Economy of Global Turbulence' seeks to reframe the story Brenner tells in a more extended historical perspective, reworking his arguments into an alternative theoretical and narrative structure, comparable in argument and scale, but with other turning points and conclusions.[50]

Concurring with Brenner that the long downturn since 1973 has been an effect of over-competition, similar in this to the protracted depression of 1873–96, Arrighi argues that that there are both critical differences between the two long cycles of crisis, that need to be grasped if the novelty of the present period is to be understood, and a common underlying solution that capital has adopted in each epoch to escape from over-accumulation. What were the differences? In the late nineteenth century, labour in the major industrial countries of the North succeeded in resisting a fall in nominal wages after the onset of the depression, while the South was everywhere falling prey to imperial penetration and conquest; a hundred years later, labour in the North was far stronger, its wage pressures precipitating the downturn itself, while national liberation movements had liberated most of the South and were on the verge of victory over America in Vietnam. In both periods, however, the typical response of manufacturing firms to falling profitability was the same. It was not to defend existing fixed capital, as Brenner maintained, but to switch their assets out of production into finance, where high levels of profit could for an era still be realized.

The hallmark of each cycle has thus, in Arrighi's view, been growing liquidity and a general process of 'financialization', typified equally by the unhealthy flush of Asquith's England and of Reagan's America. But the outcomes have necessarily diverged, since the deflation that marked the nineteenth century downturn was no longer a politically

---

49. The principal barrage, numbering some seventeen articles and over four hundred pages, can be found in two successive numbers of *Historical Materialism*, 4: 1 and 5: 1, 1999.

50. 'The Social and Political Economy of Global Turbulence', *New Left Review* 20, March–April 2003, pp. 5–71. The analysis builds on Arrighi's famous *Long Twentieth Century*, London 1994, and with Beverly Silver, *Chaos and Governance in the Modern World System*, Minneapolis 1999.

viable option for capital – labour being so much stronger – in the late twentieth century, inducing it to choose instead inflation as a way to erode wage gains. But once the costs of the Vietnam War had broken the Bretton Woods system apart, the US paid the price of this solution: a falling dollar that repelled rather attracting the mass of mobile capital set loose by worldwide financialization. It was only with the turn to a strict monetarism at the bend of the eighties that this flow was reversed. With a strong dollar and sky-high interest rates, the US could now draw in huge volumes of footloose finance that allowed it to fund Western victory in the Cold War and check anti-systemic movements in both North and South. But by the new century the dependence of the United States on capital inflows to cover an ever-widening trade deficit, combined with imperial over-reach in Iraq, made its position in many ways weaker than that of Edwardian England, a power that was still exporting capital and maintaining an Indian army at no cost to itself. For Arrighi the crisis of profitability on which Brenner has concentrated is thus an aspect of a crisis of hegemony that runs deeper, and will bring down the US as the world's premier power in a foreseeable future.[51]

It remains to be seen how Brenner will respond to this challenge. Formally speaking, the two bodies of work are in many ways complementary opposites. Arrighi has the advantage of a continuous timescale, stretching back in his writing to the Renaissance, and a more global geopolitical scope. His primary focus has long been on trade and finance – at times all but identified with capitalism itself, after the manner of Braudel – rather than production, and his style more broadly analytic than tightly statistical. Brenner has the advantage of greater empirical command and a deeper research strategy, the care of a historian rather than the sweep of a sociologist. His focus is on manufacturing, and his framework closer to Marx. When he comes to take up the issues that are posed by Arrighi's account of the downturn – the significance of inflation in its first phase; developments in the periphery of the system; financialization as an escape route from declining profits; the idea of inter-state competition for mobile capital; the functions of hegemony – it will no doubt be with these qualities and predispositions.

Something of what is likely to result can be surmised from the overall structure and sequence of his work as a historian. For there is

---

51. For this conclusion, see Arrighi's sequel: ''Hegemony Unravelling' , New Left Review 32 and 33, March–April and May–June 2005, pp. 23–80 and 83–116, which emphasizes the rise of China as an economic power.

a marked pattern to it. Not totalizing but tunnelling, in his account both of the original breakthrough to capitalism, which made him famous, and of the protracted malaise of the system in recent decades, Brenner's intellectual strategy has been the same. In each case, he has picked one sector as the key to economic development at large, and tracked it largely through one determining society within a comparative set. In defiance of conventional opinion, his explanation of the origins of capitalism pivots on agriculture alone, giving towns and trade little more than walk-on parts in the break-out from feudalism. In the same way, in his explanation of the long downturn, everything revolves around the fate of manufacturing, relegating services – typically comprising a much larger sector of the economy – to compensations or after-effects. In the transition to capitalism, England commands the stage; in the deceleration of capitalism, America. In a deliberate sacrifice of width for depth, the focus is unwavering: on a single dominant, in a single arena.

But this narrowing of the beam of research is the opposite of any provincial limitation. In both historical fields, Brenner constructs his argument comparatively. In *The Brenner Debate*, the demonstration of England's unique path to an agrarian capitalism proceeds by way of a double contrast: with France on the one hand, and Eastern Europe on the other. Whereas beyond the Elbe the balance of class forces was so overwhelmingly in favour of lords that the outcome of the general crisis of late feudalism, in newly colonized zones where village communities were typically weak, was imposition of a 'second serfdom', in France peasant communities remained so strong that lords could not dislodge the customary rights of tenants to possession of their plots. In either case the result was to block the development of cost-cutting production for the market. In England alone were landowners able to prevent peasant security of tenure with entry fines and variable leases, opening the way to competitive rents, consolidation of holdings, and commercial farming based on wage labour, at progressively higher levels of productivity. In *The Economics of Global Turbulence*, it is Japan and Germany that function as the equivalent contrasts with the United States, here in the opposite direction from Eastern Europe and France, as economies enjoying the technological and institutional advantages of late-comers over the leader of the post-war boom, and so able to challenge it for market shares.

In each case, the comparative framework is selective: no attempt is made to furnish a full typology of agrarian relations in late medieval Europe, and no attention is paid to the OECD as a whole. Instead of proceeding to what is missed out in these comparisons, Brenner's next move was again strikingly similar in both time zones. After *The Brenner Debate* came *Merchants and Revolution* – a withdrawal from comparative to solo study, concentrating in far greater detail just on England; as after *Global Turbulence* came *The Boom and the Bubble*, focusing at much closer range on the United States. In each case, a formal narrowing of geographical ambit was accompanied by a major broadening of substantive analysis, making good what had been significant lacunae in the original comparative studies. In *Merchants and Revolution*, Brenner took up the roles of trade, towns and the state in the transition from feudalism to capitalism, set aside in *The Brenner Debate*, with a vengeance. In *The Boom and the Bubble*, as much space is devoted to speculation as to production, to stocks and mortgages as to manufactures.

With his essays on the pre-modern economies of the Low Countries and China, a third movement in this work is visible: a dialectical return to its original comparative starting points, to complete the parts of the puzzle they omitted. The logic of this widening of Brenner's comparative scope at the beginning of his long-run account of capitalism indicates a matching expansion at the end of it. That would mean, in the first place, a thorough explanation of the pattern of China's high-speed growth today, and monitoring of the displacement effect of its huge economy as it descends the slipway into the global waters. In between, there lies the whole period of the industrial revolution itself, and the ways in which it spread to a continental Europe that never experienced the kind of agrarian capitalism that was the platform for industrialization in England. This is so far untouched territory for Brenner, where many a historiographic lion – Wrigley, Pollard, Crafts, Landes – lies in wait. It would be surprising if he had no hypotheses in mind to make a reckoning with it. One would expect them to be as spare and rigorous a combination as those employed to unlock the the end of banal lordship or the onset of defensive investment. In its very austerity lies the secret of this work, whose ambition is nothing less than to track the abstract essentials – the property relations and competitive mechanisms – that have generated the forms of modern capitalist life through their economic consequences, with a density and tenacity of detail otherwise associated with the most *terre-à-terre* of empirical historians. Only a very stubborn and original mind could have conceived such a formidable project.

1993–2005

13

THE VANQUISHED LEFT:
Eric Hobsbawm

I

What apter practicioners of autobiography than historians? Trained to examine the past with an impartial eye, alert to oddities of context and artifices of narrative, they would appear to be the ideal candidates for the difficult task of the self-description of a life. Yet strangely it is not they, but philosophers who have excelled at the genre – indeed all but invented it. In principle, autobiography is the most intimately particular of all forms of writing, philosophy the most abstract and impersonal. They should be oil and water. But it was Augustine and Rousseau who gave us the sexual and personal confession and Descartes who offered the first 'history of my mind': in modern times Mill and Nietzsche, Collingwood and Russell, Sartre and Quine, all left records of themselves more memorable than anything else written about them. The number of historians who have produced autobiographies of any distinction, on the other hand, is remarkably small. In the nineteenth century, the self-serving memoirs of Guizot and Tocqueville, rarely consulted today, are of interest mainly as testimonials of political evasion. Closer to hand, Marc Bloch's post-mortem on 1940, with its mixture of personal report and general requisitory, is a poignant document, but too circumscribed for more than flashes of self-revelation. More recently, we have the eccentric cameos of Richard Cobb and *causeries* of A.J.P. Taylor, of which he said they were evidence that he had run out of historical subjects. In all, in the genre for which it seems so well designed, the craft of the historian has yielded perhaps only two classics – Gibbon's graceful mirror at the end of the eighteenth century, and Henry Adams's baroque *Wunderkammer* at the beginning of the twentieth.

In this generally disappointing field, Eric Hobsbawm has entered the lists with a work he invites us to read as the 'flip-side' of his great history of the twentieth century, *Age of Extremes*: 'not world history illustrated by the experiences of an individual, but world history shaping that experience' – and the life-choices it offered him. Published at the age of eighty-five, in its energy and trenchancy *Interesting Times* could have been written at forty.[1] Its qualities are such, in fact, that it is almost impossible to read without being drawn back to his work as a historian, so many insights does it offer, casually or deliberately, about what he has accomplished as a whole. We are dealing with a kind of fifth volume, in more personal register, of a continuous project. This one could be called simply The Age of EJH.

As such, it offers an autobiography composed of three quite distinct parts. The first of these, which covers the author's early years up to the threshold of university, has many claims to be the finest piece of writing this famously accomplished stylist has ever produced. With delicacy and reserve, yet also a tense candour, Hobsbawm takes us from his accidental birth in Alexandria to a precarious childhood in post-war Vienna; brief but exalted schooling in the last days of Weimar Berlin; removal from Nazism to England and final ascent towards Cambridge, on the eve of the Spanish Civil War. Touching portraits of his parents – hapless English father and fragile Austrian mother, both dead by the time he was fourteen – sketch one psychological background; Jewish descent in the most anti-Semitic city in Europe, another. He explains the kind of loyalty to family origins he learnt from his mother, and his corresponding 'lack of any emotional obligation to the small, militarist, culturally disappointing and politically aggressive nation-state which asks for my solidarity on racial grounds'.[2]

Shifted to Berlin, where a rackety uncle (on the English side) was working in the film business, Hobsbawm describes his discovery of Communism at the age of fifteen, in a traditional Prussian Gymnasium, with Hitler at the gates of power. There have been few such vivid evocations of the electric atmosphere of the revolutionary Left in Germany in those months. It is little wonder that memories of the final, guttering parade of a doomed KPD through the twilight of Berlin should have marked him more deeply than schooldays in the becalmed London of the National Government. Of his subsequent experience at St Marylebone Grammar School he writes with affectionate good humour ('I took to examinations like ice-cream').[3] In the

---

1. London, 2002, p. xiii; henceforward *IT*.
2. *IT*, p. 24.
3. *IT*, p. 93.

composition of these contrasting scenes, the historian's intelligence is always at work, setting the accidents of an individual life in the cross-currents of a graphically delineated space and time. The picture that emerges, with considerable artistry, is of a boy unlike conventional images of the man: solitary, initially drawn to nature rather than politics, somewhat abstracted and introspective, gradually more confident of his powers. The tone of the self-portrait with which he wound up his adolescence recalls something of Kepler's horoscope of himself: 'Eric John Ernest Hobsbawm, a tall, angular, dangly, ugly, fair-haired fellow of eighteen and a half, quick on the uptake, with a considerable if superficial stock of knowledge and a lot of original ideas, general and theoretical. An incorrigible striker of attitudes, which is all the more dangerous and at times effective, as he talks himself into believing them himself ... Has no sense of morality, thoroughly selfish. Some people find him extremely disagreeable, others likeable, yet others (the majority) just ridiculous ... He is vain and conceited. He is a coward. He loves nature deeply. And he forgets the German language'.[4]

So ends the first part of *Interesting Times*. From a literary point of view, it could well have stopped there. We would then have had something close to those *chefs d'œuvre* of calm truncation, moving and tantalizing in equal measure, that Constant or Sartre have left us – journeys to the age of reason, or passion, that leave us at their threshold. If this thought is not incongruous, it is because, rather than preparing the way for a portrait of the historian as a young man, the passage quoted above closes the door on further exploration of the self of this kind. A deeply felt, imaginative recreation of the youth he once was abruptly gives way to another kind of enterprise. We never glimpse the same interior landscape again. Without notice of any change of gear, the next chapter shifts us into the second part of *Interesting Times*, which covers Hobsbawm's membership of the Communist Party of Great Britain from the late thirties to its dissolution in the early nineties. Here he recounts his time at Cambridge, at the zenith of its student Communism; his beaching during the war as suspect to the authorities; his outlook as a Party member and his semi-marginalization as an academic, during the Cold War; his reactions to the crisis that engulfed the Communist movement with Khruschev's revelations and the Hungarian Revolt in 1956; the reasons why he stayed in the Party after most of his fellow-Marxist

4. *IT*, pp. 98–99.

historians had left, and believes his choice was more fruitful than theirs; how he eventually helped, in his own eyes, to save the Labour Party even as the CPGB itself went under.

These chapters mark a complete alteration of register. The difference sets in from the very first page, in which – before even attempting to describe his own experience of Cambridge – Hobsbawm feels obliged to explain how little was his acquaintance with Burgess and Maclean, Philby and Blunt, all of whom preceded his time at the university. Honourably enough, he adds that had he later been asked to carry out the same kind of mission, he would have done so. But a sensation of discomfort remains, as if another sort of reader is starting to hover in the background of the narrative. The depiction of Cambridge that follows offers deft sketches of the archaism of tutors and institutions, and of the motives and characters of student radicalism. Pointing out that the Left at its peak numbered perhaps a fifth of the undergraduate body, of which the Communist contingent in turn was no more than a tenth, Hobsbawm stresses the informal influence the Party nonetheless exercised in the university – a product of its energetic campaigning and commitment to academic success, and the buoyancy of its budding activists. The scene so presented is convincing, but essentially generic. Of Hobsbawm's personal path through it we are told very little: nothing at all of his intellectual development, virtually nothing of his emotional life, scarcely a hint even of his political ideas. The persistent pronoun is now the anonymous, generational 'we'. The first person singular is reserved for less charged moments, as when a more conventional *cursus* is touched upon: 'My last term, May–June 1939, was pretty good. I edited *Granta*, was elected to the Apostles and got a starred First in the Tripos, which also gave me a Studentship at King's.'[5]

Just how misleading this suppression of a subjectivity must be, can be seen from the curious displacement of decisive episodes of this phase of the author's life to much later chapters, separated by hundreds of pages from his account of these student years. Towards the end of his chapter on Cambridge, summer vacations spent in Paris, working with James Klugmann for a front organization of the Comintern, are casually mentioned, in connection with Margot Heinemann. Of the former, Hobsbawm delphically remarks: 'What did one know about him? He gave nothing away'; of the latter, he says simply: 'she probably had more influence on me than any other

---

5. *IT*, p. 124.

person I have known', after which terse tribute she never appears again.[6] It is not until one reaches a set of concluding reminiscences of different parts of the world Hobsbawm has visited, at the very end of the book, that – under the objective headings of France and Spain – a sense slips through of what private feelings might lie behind such clipped phrases.

For there is nothing in his account of Cambridge to touch the passion of his description of Bastille Day in the first year of the Popular Front, when he drove round a celebrating Paris on a newsreel team of the French Socialist Party – 'It was one of the rare days when my mind was on autopilot. I only felt and experienced' – then drank and danced till dawn: a different sort of trance from the funeral march in Berlin.[7] It would be strange if these sojourns in Paris, working as a translator in what was then the hub of all Comintern networks in Europe, surrounded by the ferment of the Popular Front, did not mean more to him than Party chores in the Socialist Club at Cambridge. Perhaps by some unconscious association, in this other setting he even – in a memoir otherwise rigorously tight-lipped in such matters – uncharacteristically confides sexual initiation, 'in a bed surrounded with mirrors', in a brothel near the Rue Sébastopol. Earlier, venturing an illegal entry to Spain soon after the outbreak of the Civil War, around the time John Cornford enrolled in Barcelona, did he consider taking up arms for the Republic? Again, the page in which he retrospectively questions himself about that possible cross-roads has an enigmatic depth and beauty that stands out against the drabber English story.[8] What is missing – deliberately averted – is an attempt to bring these scattered elements of a youthful revolutionary together in any interior synthesis. As the narrative proceeds, the cost of increasing externality is dispersion.

Chronologically, after Cambridge came the war – a relatively empty experience for Hobsbawm, as he complains with legitimate bitterness, the War Office confining him to a sapper regiment until it was sent to Singapore, and then to mock duties at home in the Education Corps, probably as much because he came from Austria as because he was a Communist. But from his time with the Engineers, he learnt to appreciate at first hand the traditional qualities of English workers, for whom he formed a 'permanent, if exasperated admiration', the

---

6. *IT*, pp. 122–123.
7. *IT*, pp. 73–74, 323.
8. *IT*, pp. 315, 340–341.

beginning of an imaginative sympathy that has marked everything he has since written about popular classes.[9] The acute economic insecurity, at times close to penury, of his own background in Vienna would anyway have brought him closer to the proletarian experience than most English intellectuals of his generation. It was also during the war that he got married for the first time, to a fellow-Communist civil servant, about whom he says scarcely anything. Once belatedly demobbed, he started to work as a historian, soon getting a job at Birkbeck. But then he found what should have been a brilliant career – after such a flying start at King's – deflected from its natural path by the Cold War, when all Communists were frozen out of advancement. He implies, in a dignified way, his hurt at the denial of the posts he might have expected in Cambridge.

But reading between the lines, his account of this bend in his career contains some mysteries. He reveals that not only did he take part in the reconstitution of the Apostles – a coterie of insiders, if there ever was one – after the war, but was actually in charge of it, as the society's organizer, and continued to recruit new undergraduates to it into the mid-fifties. Was there any connection between this role and the fellowship he was granted at King's in 1949, not before but at the height of the Cold War, or the dispatch with which he was accorded congenial lodgings, on which he comments himself, when his marriage broke up? An inkling that there may be more to this story than appears is suggested by a puzzling absence: the name of Noel Annan, Fellow and later Provost of King's, a close friend, does not figure in it.

If in principle such matters have their place in an autobiography, they are of slight moment otherwise. The main burden of Hobsbawm's treatment of these years is political. Three substantial chapters are devoted to explaining what it meant to be a Communist in this epoch, out of power or in power; what problems were posed for British Communists by the evolution of the Soviet system during the Cold War; and how de-Stalinization detonated a crisis in the CPGB that left him one of the few intellectuals remaining in the Party. Throughout, he returns again and again to the question: why did he stay to the bitter end? The effect of these extended reflections is mixed. Viewing the choice for Communism on a very general level, from the October Revolution to the end of the War, Hobsbawm offers an eloquent defence and illustration of what it meant for those who

---

9. *IT*, p. 159.

made it, alternating social observation and individual examples, heroic or humdrum. His emphasis falls on an ethos of selfless obedience and practicality – 'business efficiency', as he puts it – as the real hallmark of the Third International. 'Communist Parties were not for romantics. On the contrary, they were for organization and routine ... The secret of the Leninist Party lay neither in dreaming about standing on barricades or even Marxist theory. It can be summed up in two phrases: "decisions must be verified" and "Party discipline". The appeal of the Party was that it got things done when others did not.'[10]

Historically, it must be said, this picture is strangely lop-sided. A movement that counted revolutionaries like Serge or Trotsky, Roy or Mariategui, Sneevliet or Sorge, not for romantics? For that matter what of Mao, for better or worse a somewhat larger figure in the history of Communism than any of the loyal European functionaries or militants to whom we are introduced here? Elsewhere, indeed, Hobsbawm has precisely condemned him as a 'romantic'.[11] The reality is that a counterposition of barricades and theory to business efficiency and getting things done is *post facto* rhetoric that at best indicates something of the self-image of the Stalinized European Comintern, post-1926, in which Hobsbawm himself was formed, but does not adequately capture even its ambiguities. The cult of hard-headed routine and practicality, as expressed here, was often just another form of romanticism, and by no means always the most effective. Fortunately, Hobsbawm himself does not consistently live up to it, as his affecting portrait of the Austrian revolutionary Franz Marek, the moral centrepiece of his reflections on 'Being Communist', makes clear.

What then were his own convictions as an individual, in the time no longer of the Comintern, dissolved in 1943, but of the Cominform assembled by Zhdanov in 1948 for duty in the high Cold War? It is not easy to say. In part this is because *Interesting Times* skirts any too meticulous chronology in its discussion of his own Communism. His general meditation on the Communist experience, which extends more or less datelessly from Lenin all the way to Gorbachev, is placed immediately after his account of Cambridge, before even the war. When he resumes the topic in his personal history, it is to evoke the attitude of intellectuals in the British Party to the developments of the

10. *IT*, p. 133.
11. *Age of Extremes*, London 1994, p. 468.

Cominform period that troubled them – the excommunication of Tito, the show trials of Kostov, Rajk and Slansky. Here too the reference is insistently collective: 'what were we to think?' – 'none of us believed' – 'we clearly underestimated' – 'people like myself' – 'we too recognized'.[12]

Of Hobsbawm's personal views, we learn little, beyond the fact that he was sceptical that Basil Davidson, whom he knew personally, could have been a British agent as charged along with Rajk. There is no clue to his opinion of the Moscow Trials that destroyed the Old Bolsheviks and set the pattern for the sequels in Sofia, Budapest and Prague after the war. He never mentions any reading of the considerable literature surrounding these events. The gist of his account is that British Communists, or at any rate Party intellectuals, did not believe the official versions of any of them. This is not quite the same thing as knowing they were a pack of lies, since unofficial versions circulated too. When Khruschev finally laid bare the foundations of the whole grotesque edifice of confessions, in Stalin's torture-chambers, Hobsbawm stresses the shock that his revelations – containing, of course, little not already widely known outside it – caused the international Communist movement. 'The reason', he writes, 'is obvious. We were not told the truth about something that had to affect the very nature of a communist's belief.'[13] Even if, once again, the pronoun leaves a margin of ambiguity, the implication must be that Hobsbawm himself had in some way continued to believe in Stalin's honour. In what way? The construction of the narrative makes it impossible to guess. What is clear is that, not independent sources critically checked, but the word of authority was expected to deliver the truth. To all appearances, militant and historian had remained separate identities.

The crisis that Khrushchev's speech in April 1956 – followed within months by the Hungarian Revolt – set off in the CPGB is described with an image of agitated emotion by Hobsbawm. 'For more than a year, British communists lived on the edge of the political equivalent of a collective nervous breakdown.'[14] The Party Historians' Group, of which he was then chairman, became the centre of opposition to officialdom, and virtually all its members, with the exception of himself, had left the Party by the summer of 1957. Why did he stay? He offers

---

12. *IT*, pp. 192, 194, 195.
13. *IT*, p. 204.
14. *IT*, p. 206.

two answers, and a postilla. 'I did not come into communism as a young Briton in England, but as a central European in the collapsing Weimar Republic. And I came into it when being a communist meant not simply fighting fascism but the world revolution. I still belong to the tail-end of the first generation of communists, the ones for whom the October Revolution was the central point of reference in the political universe'. It was therefore, he writes, 'for someone who came from and when I did, quite simply more difficult to break with the Party than for those who came later and from elsewhere.'[15]

This is surely the plain biographical truth, well stated. But if both the emergency and the hope that brought him into the Communist movement were more intense than was typical of his English contemporaries, it is less clear that the second contrast would have been more significant than the first, as he suggests. Was the October Revolution so peripheral for Christopher Hill, who joined the Party in 1932, learnt Russian – as Hobsbawm explains he never did – and wrote a book on Lenin? At all events, in spelling out what he takes to be the larger difference, of time rather than space, Hobsbawm offers another illuminating remark about himself. 'Politically', he says, having joined the CP in 1936, he belongs to the era of the Popular Front, that pursued an alliance between capital and labour which has determined his strategic thinking to this day; 'emotionally', however, as a teenage convert in the Berlin of 1932, he remained tied to the original revolutionary agenda of Bolshevism.[16] This is a dichotomy with more than one bearing on his work as a whole.

Yet if such were the deeper biographical reasons why Hobsbawm remained a Communist after 1956, one would still have expected some more ordinary political assessments to have been at work as well. For after all, de-Stalinization did not stop in that year. With the defeat of Malenkov and Molotov in the summer of 1957, Khruschev pursued it more vigorously in the USSR than before. The camps were emptied, living standards improved, intellectual debate revived, solidarity extended to the latest chapter of world revolution in the Caribbean. Further steps to cleanse the record of the past were taken at the Twenty-Second Party Congress in 1962. Such developments persuaded many Communists shaken in 1956 that the legacy of the October Revolution was, if with zig-zags, being gradually redeemed rather than irretrievably abandoned. It would be surprising if

---

15. *IT*, pp. 217–218.
16. *IT*, p. 218.

Hobsbawm never thought along these, perfectly understandable, lines. But if he did, there is no trace of it here. As throughout his treatment of the Communist experience, there is no discussion of the actual political history of the period, *stricto sensu*, at all. Instead, he concludes his reasons for staying in the Party by appending a 'private emotion: pride', explaining that if he had left it, he would have improved his career prospects, but just for that reason stayed, to 'prove myself to myself by succeeding as a known communist – 'whatever "success" meant' – in spite of that handicap'.[17]

Hobsbawm calls this combination of loyalty and ambition a form of egoism, which he does not defend. Most people would see in it evidence of an exceptional integrity and strength of character: a courage to take unpopular positions all the more striking in one for whom success has plainly mattered so much. *Interesting Times* records the different forms – we can take that airy parenthesis as a propitiatory gesture – that success has assumed: a worldwide reader- ship in four score languages, simultaneous chairs in three countries, academies and honorary degrees *ad libitum*, interviews and audiences galore, homages from the Front Bench and the Viminale. Still others are omitted: English readers will think of the Company of Honour, to which he also belongs, alongside Lords Tebbit, Hurd and Hailsham. Early on in this account of his life, Hobsbawm explains that he has 'accepted at least some the signs of public recognition' that have made him a 'member of the official British cultural establish- ment' because nothing would have given such happiness to his mother in her last years – adding, with a disarming smile securing all exits, that in saying this he 'would be no more honest or dishonest than Sir Isaiah Berlin who used to excuse taking his knighthood by saying he had only done it give pleasure to *his* mother'.[18]

Great men have foibles for which they can be forgiven; including an occasional failure to see where their greatness lies, or what might diminish it. In Britain an inability to resist gewgaws is anyway as common among eminent scholars – historians of all stripes foremost among them – as once African agents of the slave trade. In Hobsbawm's case, its interest lies not in any dissociation, but in the connection between political loyalty and social accommodation. Just because he remained so steadfast in an execrated cause, entry into the acceptance world seems to have acquired all the more value. Inwardly,

---

17. *IT*, p. 218.
18. *IT*, p. 40.

each advance in the one could be chalked up as refracted lustre for the other. Psychologically, such intricate balance-wheels are normal enough. But they come at a cost. At the heart of *Interesting Times* is a sustained effort to explain the meaning of a Communist life. But explain to whom?

If there is something painful in the repeated, nervous adversion to that quest, it is because – not consistently, but too often for comfort: from the first swivel to the Cambridge spies, to the last swell of satisfaction that Heath and Heseltine should have adorned *Marxism Today* – the unspoken addressee is as if an established order to which an accounting of the self is due in exchange. This appears to be the logic of that absence of close political discussion, or any real intellectual engagement with the issues that haunted the trajectory of European Communism, which is so unexpected a feature of these pages. 'It must now be obvious', he writes of the Russian Revolution, that 'failure was built into the enterprise from the start.'[19] He offers no reason for a conclusion so entirely at variance with his insistence on the practicality of the Stalinist tradition. But since such failure is self-evident for the readership in mind, why bother with explaining it? To do that would require another style of orientation, and a different set of references, starting with some names and clairvoyant ideas – Kautsky, Luxemburg, Trotsky – this memoir chooses to avoid.

Nevertheless, after all qualifications or demurrers have been entered, Hobsbawm's elegy to the political tradition to which he dedicated his life has a dignity and passion that must command anyone's respect. His treatment of the traditions of others is much less impressive. Here a lack of generosity disfigures too many judgements, producing one grudging solecism after another. The problem starts at the very moment he seeks to explain why he did not leave the Party in 1956. Before reaching the valid biographical reasons for his own decision, he sets out, as if it were a necessary preliminary to justify himself, to disparage those who made the opposite choice. A profile of Raphael Samuel – 'this eager vagabond figure, the absolute negation of administrative and executive efficiency' – devotes itself principally to denouncing his 'hare-brained project' for a coffee-house in London, and bemoaning his own indulgence in this 'lunatic enterprise', with a disconcerting lack of any sense of proportion.[20] Reading it, no one would guess that Samuel, after six years in the CPGB,

---

19. *IT*, p. 127.
20. *IT*, pp. 212–214.

produced a political anthropology of the Party, 'The Lost World of British Communism', whose riches make Hobsbawm's recollections of it, after a membership eight times as long, look a touch skeletal.[21]

Of Edward Thompson, we are likewise given to understand that he 'lacked any inbuilt compass', and after writing *The Making of the English Working Class* – a work of genius, albeit aggressively brief and narrow in focus – essentially wasted his time, with a 'criminal' diversion of energies into theoretical dispute rather than empirical research, against which Hobsbawm warned him. Thompson would have been surprised to find himself described as 'insecure' in these pages.[22] No doubt this can be said in some measure of all human beings. But we can be fairly sure that in this case he would have thought the boot on the other foot. 'In practical terms', Hobsbawm continues, the various New Lefts that emerged from the crisis of 1956 were negligible. Still worse were the student radicals of North America or Europe of the sixties – to whom 'my generation would remain strangers' – responsible not even for 'a botched attempt at one kind of revolution, but an effective ratification of another: the one that abolished traditional politics, and in the end the politics of the traditonal left'. As for the 'contemporary ultra-left in and outside South America (all of whose Guevarist attempts at guerrilla insurrection were spectacular failures)', inspired by the Cuban Revolution, 'they neither understood nor wanted to understand what might move Latin American peasants to take up arms', unlike the FARC in Colombia or Sendero Luminoso in Peru.[23]

Scarcely an item in this sour retrospect withstands careful scrutiny. The New Left of the late fifties was integral to the Campaign for Nuclear Disarmament, which did not achieve its objectives, but was rather less negligible as a force for change than the unreconstructed CPGB. The student movements of Europe and America not only, as Hobsbawm himself in a forgetful moment remembers, helped to cripple the regimes of De Gaulle and Nixon, but – as he does not recall – were critical in bringing the war in Vietnam to an end in the US, and setting off the most powerful working-class mobilizations of the post-war period in France and Italy. In Latin America, the only

---

21. 'The Lost World of British Communism', *New Left Review* I/154, November–December 1985, pp. 3–53; I/156, March–April 1986, pp. 63–113; I/165, September–October 1987, pp. 52–91.

22. *IT*, p. 215.

23. *IT*, pp. 251–252, 375.

successful revolution, in Nicaragua, was not only directly inspired, but assisted by Cuba. As for Peru and Colombia, Hobsbawm tells us he could not but welcome the crushing of Sendero by Fujimori; why not now the FARC by Uribe?

Counterpointing such exercises in futility, Hobsbawm recounts another and – in his eyes – more fruitful enterprise under way by the early eighties. This was the campaign he waged in the pages of *Marxism Today* to rescue the Labour Party from the perils of Bennery. Here legitimate pride and fatal delusion are curiously interwoven. Before the fall of the Callaghan government, Hobsbawm rightly pointed out that the militant trade unionism of the seventies, for all its striking industrial successes, was not being carried by any underlying expansion of working-class strength or organization; and after Thatcher came to power, that capture of a weakened Labour machine by the Left would not suffice to defeat the new Conservatism.[24] But the conclusions he drew from these correct observations were extraordinarily simple-minded: essentially, that the overriding task was to ensure the restoration at any cost of a 'moderate' leadership capable of attracting middle-class voters back to the Party again – regardless of the obvious fact that it was just the exhaustion of this kind of traditional Labourism, demonstrated at dismal length through the late sixties and seventies, which had led to the rise of the Left in the first place.

Hobsbawm recounts with relish, but overestimates, his role in the media outcry that finished off Benn and put the pitiable figure of Kinnock in office. Since the whole of Fleet Street, from the *Sun* and *Mirror* through to the *Guardian* and the *Telegraph*, was baying for Benn's head, it is doubtful how much difference his personal bark made. Once Kinnock had conducted the necessary purges of the Party, he assures us, 'its future was safe'. Alas, even with Thatcher out of the way, the new leader proved a fiasco at the polls in 1992. 'I am not alone', Hobsbawm writes mournfully, 'in recalling that election night as the saddest and most desperate in my political experience'.[25] So much for March 1933. Such absurd inflation is a measure of the loss of contact with reality that his crusade to 'save the Labour Party' – Gaitskell's old slogan dusted off again – seems temporarily to have induced in the historian. For, of course, far from being saved, in

---

24. See his essays in Martin Jacques and Francis Mulhern (eds), *The Forward March of Labour Halted?*, London 1981; and *Politics for a Rational Left*, London 1989.

25. *IT*, p. 276.

the sense he wanted, it was turned inside out to produce what he himself now calls a 'Thatcher in trousers'.

Remarking that, since his rescue operation of the party, a Labour Left no longer exists, he seems unable to grasp that just this was one of the conditions of the rise of Blairism he now deplores. It is obvious enough that on a minor scale *Marxism Today* – journalistically lively, but with no intellectual or political stamina (it disappeared in 1991 with the party that kept it) – played the role of a sorcerer's apprentice, not least in preparing the cult of Thatcher as a model of radical government that was taken over with a vengeance by New Labour. Hobsbawm ends by grieving that the Blair regime 'drove us out of "real" politics', and sadly cites the admonition to him of an MT stalwart now ensconced in Downing Street, that critique is no longer enough, since New Labour 'must operate in a market economy and fit in with its requirements'. To which all he can reply is: 'True enough' – adding to such humble minimalism only a protest that still, the leadership does have excessive faith in neo-liberal ideology.[26] This episode is not the whole Hobsbawm, by any means. What it shows is only what had become of that side of his background that he says has always guided his strategic thinking. The Popular Front could once awaken masses to political life and mobilize genuine enthusiasm, but even at its height, in France and Spain in the thirties, it lacked any realistic calculus of power, and ended in disaster. The transference of its freight of sentimental illusions into post-war conditions, where there was never any comparable popular mobilization behind it, had more banal outcomes: the bewildered ejection of one Communist Party after another from continental governments in 1946–47, the futile quest for a Historic Compromise in Italy in the seventies, finally – cold cinders of the glowing hopes of 1936 – the forlorn attempt to put the cracked shell of Labourism together again in the eighties.

The last third of *Interesting Times* shifts register again, dropping any narrative sequence for surveys of Hobsbawm's profession and travels. Here the pace slackens and the book appears to become more conventional, though the same sharp intelligence flashes through even flatter stretches. He gives a good account of the rise of the analytic social history associated with the *Annales* and *Past and Present* at the expense of earlier high-political narratives, regretting its later retreat with the cultural turn of the eighties. The historians who pioneered it he describes as 'modernizers' – a term too vague and bureaucratic,

---

26. *IT*, pp. 276–277.

quite apart from its other connotations ('the main railway network along which the trains of historiography would roll had been built'), to be of much theoretical use.[27] Here he sells himself short. To see how original his own thinking about the study of the past has been – more than Braudel's, by whom he says he was somewhat overawed – one needs to turn to his collection *On History*. For what this part of *Interesting Times* brings home again is how little this autobiography offers any direct account of Hobsbawm's engagement with the world of ideas. From beginning to end, scarcely a work of thought is mentioned as having seriously impinged on him. Of his Marxism, virtually all we are told is that he read the *Communist Manifesto* at high school in Berlin. Noting that literature was the substitute for philosophy in English sixth forms, he associates himself with other British Marxist historians in coming to history through an initial passion for the arts. But beyond saying that St Marylebone Grammar School introduced him to 'the astonishing marvels of English poetry and prose',[28] we are no wiser as what to his reading actually was. When he comes to politics, lines from Brecht and Neruda are quoted, but conceptually there is a complete blank.

Perhaps this abstention is no more than an eye to a public uninterested in such questions. Travel is another matter. The book ends with Hobsbawm's experiences of France, Spain, Italy, Latin America and the United States. Of the first four he writes with consistent affection, without claiming any special insight into them. He confesses, in fact, that in different ways he has been disconcerted or disappointed at the development of each – finding the politics and culture of the Fifth Republic an uncongenial sequel to the France of late thirties and forties; caught by surprise at the speed with which capitalism has transformed Spain; flabbergasted by the success of Craxi and Berlusconi in Italy, and the shrivelling of the Communist movement to which he felt closest; resigned to the lack of any real political progress in Latin America, amidst sweeping social changes. But in other respects, these chapters are agreeable enough records of pleasures and friendships in societies of which he is fond.

The United States, where Hobsbawm has spent more time than in all the others combined, is another matter. Manhattan excepted, by his own account he learnt more about the country from a few months exploring the jazz scene in 1960, than from a dozen years of seasonal

27. *IT*, p. 293.
28. *IT*, p. 95.

teaching in the eighties and nineties. These seem, if anything, to have reinforced a sense of distance from it – an antipathy without his usual quotient of curiosity. However impressive its achievements, he writes, American social inequality and political paralysis, self-absorption and megalomania, are traits that make him glad to belong to another culture. The remark is a reminder that the country which has meant most to Hobsbawm does not figure in this survey. After describing boyhood impressions, *Interesting Times* – though it contains a brief intermezzo on holidays in Wales – never returns to England again. This is certainly not a sign of indifference. It is clear from contemporaries that already at Cambridge he felt more British than they expected, patriotic sentiments that later found expression in a strong defence of the integrity of the United Kingdom, and perhaps mixed feelings about the Falklands War. His relationship to his legally native, but culturally adopted, country is an area of complexity he leaves aside in this self-portrait.

Interesting Times comes to a close with a magnificent coda on September 11, and its political exploitation – above all 'the sheer effrontery of presenting the establishment of a US global empire as the defensive reaction of a civilization about to be overrun by nameless barbarian horrors unless it destroyed "international terrorism"'.[29] In a historical perspective, the new American imperium will be more dangerous than was the British Empire, because run by a much larger power. But it is unlikely to last longer. Indeed capitalism itself, Hobsbawm suggests, is once again earning the distrust of the young, as vaster forces of social change bowl the world beyond all known horizons. Defining himself as a historian who benefited from never wholly belonging to any one community, whose ideal is 'the migrant bird, at home in arctic and tropic, overflying half the globe', he calls on newer generations to shun the fetishes of identity, and make common cause with the poor and weak. 'Let us not disarm, even in unsatisfactory times. Social injustice still needs to be denounced and fought. The world will not get better on its own.'[30] On closing these pages, for all the differences of composition within them as a memoir, and of the reflections these suggest, the abiding impression is of the largeness of this mind, and the complex distinction of the life it reports. They are a fitting accompaniment to the achievement of the historian. A brusque vitality has defied the years.

---

29. *IT*, p. 412.
30. *IT*, p. 418.

II

Presented as a pendant to *Age of Extremes*, a personal portrait hung opposite the historical landscape, what light does *Interesting Times* throw on Hobsbawm's vision of the twentieth century, and overall narrative of modernity? In overarching conception, *The Age of Revolution*, *The Age of Capital*, *The Age of Empire* and *Age of Extremes* can be regarded as single enterprise – a tetralogy which has no equal as a systematic account of how the contemporary world was made. All display the same astonishing fusion of gifts: economy of synthesis; vividness of detail; global scope, yet acute sense of regional difference; polymathic fluency, at ease with crops and stock-markets, nations and classes, statesmen and peasants, sciences and arts; breadth of sympathies for disparate social agents; power of analytic narrative; and not least a style of remarkable clarity and energy, whose signature is the sudden bolt of metaphoric electricity across the even surface of cool, pungent argument. It is striking how often these flashes of figuration are drawn from the natural world to which he says he felt so close in his youth: 'religion, from being something the sky, from which no man can escape and which contains all that is above the earth, became something like a bank of clouds, a large but limited and changing feature of the human firmament' – 'the iron plough of industrialization multiplied its crops of hard-faced businessmen under the rainy clouds of the North' – 'fascism dissolved like a clump of earth thrown into a river'.[31]

Still, within the epic span of these four volumes, there is a definite break between the first three, conceived early on as a trilogy, and the last, which is more self-standing, with features that mark it off from its predecessors. Covering the epoch from the French Revolution to the First World War, the trilogy follows a consistent scheme, classically Marxist in its logic: each volume begins with an account of the economic foundations of the period, then a narrative of its political conflicts – in the first two volumes, headed 'developments'; followed by a panorama of social classes, and then a survey of the cultural and intellectual scene – headed 'results'. There is no clanking of theoretical armour; base and superstructure are never mentioned. Within the series, individual treatments repeatedly stand out: wonderful chapters on the Napoleonic Wars, on Romanticism, on the World Boom of the 1850s and its losers, on the origins of the First World War, and many

---

31. *The Age of Revolution*, London 1962, pp. 227, 267; *Age of Extremes*, p. 175.

others. A decade before the term became common currency, 'global-ization' is already a theme in *The Age of Empire*.

The political sympathies of the trilogy are forthright. It is rare to find a historian writing – this is *The Age of Capital* – 'the author of this book cannot conceal a certain distaste, perhaps a certain contempt for the age with which it deals, though one mitigated by admiration for its titanic material achievements and by the effort to understand even what he does not like'.[32] Hobsbawm's general verdicts are often searing: 'Altogether the introduction of liberalism on the land was like some sort of silent bombardment which shattered the social structure [the peasant] had always inhabited and left nothing in its place but the rich: a solitude called freedom.'[33] But the tang of particular judgements is always individual, and rarely pre-dictable. Who would have thought to see the Congress of Vienna praised as sensible and realistic, or expected Louis Napoleon to receive more favourable treatment than Proudhon or Bakunin?

If the three *Ages* enjoy a well-nigh universal admiration, they have attracted less critical discussion than they deserve. That is partly, of course, a matter of the scale of their performance, which virtually defies any all-round view of them. Lacking that, particular points of dissent or reflection are bound to remain somewhat arbitary or marginal. But if the test of any major work is also the questions it prompts, a few loose thoughts may be worth bouncing off these superbly polished surfaces. The axis around which the trilogy organ-izes the history of the 'long nineteenth century' – running as it were from 1776 or 1789 to 1914 – is, in Hobsbawm's words 'the triumph and transformation of capitalism in the historically specific forms of bourgeois society in its liberal version'.[34] Here we have, *in nuce*, the trio of objects of analysis – economic: social: political – that control the unfolding of each volume.

Describing the aim of his work as 'not detailed narrative, but inter-pretation or what the French call *haute vulgarisation*',[35] Hobsbawm leaves open the question of how far this commits him to explanation, a distinction that is not irrelevant to his achievement. At the outset of his enterprise, he remarks that *The Age of Revolution* will not try to explain the origins of capitalism, which lie in sixteenth- or seventeenth-

32. *The Age of Capital*, London 1975, p. 17.
33. *The Age of Revolution*, p. 194.
34. *The Age of Empire*, London 1987, pp. 8–9.
35. *The Age of Revolution*, p. 11.

century Europe, but the breakthrough of the industrial revolution in England from the 1780s onwards. He keeps his promise with a powerfully focused account of the imperial foundations of British industrialization. 'Launched, like a glider, by the colonial trade to which it was attached', the cotton industry – its raw materials furnished essentially by slaves, its markets secured by naval power – represented the triumph of exports over domestic consumption.[36] Subsequent historians have stressed the comparative advantage afforded by Britain's coal-based energy as a key condition of the industrial revolution, a notion others have sought to do away with all together. But none has seriously shaken Hobsbawm's argument.

On the other hand, when we come to the second major epoch of industrial expansion, the global take-off of the 1850s that is the starting point of *The Age of Capital*, a gradual lowering of explanatory pressure sets in. 'Why did economic expansion accelerate so spectacularly in our period?' Hobsbawm asks, only to reply that 'the question ought really to be reversed' – the problem being rather why it did not do so earlier.[37] This *fin de non recevoir* seems something of an obfuscation, but in any case is not pursued. Instead, we are offered a more scattered menu of factors – the railway, improved communications, new gold supplies – that never really matches the scale of the change invoked, tailing away rather inconclusively with the spread of economic liberalism ('how far the global movement to liberalise was cause, concomitant or consequence of economic expansion must be left an open question').[38]

At the next crucial juncture of the world economy, the slide into the Great Depression of 1873, even less is vouchsafed – indeed, while there is a graphic depiction of the uneven character of the slump, scarcely any causal analysis of it is ventured at all. Rather, when the tide turns again with the upswing of the 1890s, Hobsbawm simply notes that the whole period of *The Age of Empire* appears to have moved to a Kondratiev rhythm – some twenty years of recession, followed by twenty of expansion. But 'since we cannot explain them, the Kondratiev periodicities do not help us much'.[39] Little is said of the possible reasons for the upturn, beyond the increased purchasing power of the big cities, after the price deflation of the downswing.

---

36. *The Age of Revolution*, pp. 50–52.
37. *The Age of Capital*, p. 47.
38. *The Age of Capital*, p. 53.
39. *The Age of Empire*, p. 48.

Perhaps abstention from deeper probing is the price of the stream-
lined elegance of the trilogy, whose pace militates against the kind of
patient economic excavation Hobsbawm once practised, in essays like
'The Crisis of the Seventeenth Century'.[40]

If we move from the first to the second term of the trilogy's programme, a different set of issues is posed, conceptual more than
empirical. It might be said these begin with the famous idea of the
dual revolution itself – 'twin craters of a larger regional volcano'.[41]
The problem here can be put very simply. At the end of the eighteenth
century, the industrial revolution occurred in Britain, the political
revolution in France. But why were they dissociated? According to
traditional Marxist premises, a political revolution should occur
when the advance of new economic forces of production bursts
through the carapace of outmoded social relations. Yet in one country
the blast of modern industry shook neither monarchy nor oligarchy;
in the other, the eruption of the people brought no acceleration of
advanced technology, but rather – as Hobsbawm notes – a consolidation of traditional peasant property. For a Marxist historian, this
reciprocal asymmetry might seem to call for something more than
empirical registration. To tax any work of magnitude with what it
does not say, rather than learn from what it does, always risks being
captious. But in this instance, the grace with which Hobsbawm's
histoire raisonnée glides across analytic thin ice presages difficulties
later on. For what it finesses is the nature of the relationship between
'capitalism' and 'bourgeois society', of which the trinitarian formula
of the *Ages* says only that one is a historically specific form of the
other, without further particulars.

The neuralgic point here is the career of the European bourgeoisie
as a political class. In his first volume, after describing the
Restoration settlement of 1815, Hobsbawm writes of the revolutionary wave of 1830: 'In effect, it marked the definitive defeat of
aristocratic by bourgeois power in Western Europe. The ruling class
of the next fifty years was to be the "grande bourgeoisie" of bankers,
big industrialists and sometimes top civil servants, accepted by an
aristocracy which effaced itself or agreed to promote primarily bourgeois policies, unchallenged as yet by universal suffrage, though
harassed from the outside by the agitations of the lesser or unsatisfied

---

40. *Past and Present*, Nos 8 and 9, May and November 1954, pp. 33–53 and
45–65, republished in T. Aston (ed.), *Crisis in Europe 1560–1660*, London 1965.
41. *The Age of Revolution*, p. 14.

businessmen, the petty bourgeoisie and the early labour movements'.[42]
This seems a trifle premature. If the bourgeoisie were already the
rulers of Western Europe in the time of Lola Montez and King
Bomba, what need for the upheavals of 1848? Why indeed conclude,
at the end of an admirable survey of these, that it was now that 'the
bourgeoisie ceased to be a revolutionary force'?[43] For that matter, in
the half century after 1830, universal male suffrage had arrived in
both France and Germany, but were Bismarck and MacMahon mere
burghers?

The second volume suggests another periodization, but one that
compounds rather than resolves such uncertainties. The years from
1850 to 1875 represent, above all, 'the era of the triumphant bourgeois, when its ascendancy 'seemed beyond doubt or challenge'. Yet
at the same time, Hobsbawm concedes, 'in most countries the bourgeoisie, however defined, plainly did not control or exercise political
power. What it did exercise was hegemony, and what it increasingly
determined was policy. There was no alternative to capitalism as a
method of economic development.'[44] What this description implies,
but does not say, is that between economic and political realms, there
was not a match but a torsion. The rule of capital did not necessarily
mean bourgeois rulers. Here too is a central paradox, that appears to
call for explanation. But again the narrative eludes it. In this case, it
does so in part by dispersion. The great political upheavals of the
period form a set that concentrates all the elements of this epochal
twist: the Unifications of Germany and Italy, the American Civil War
and the Meiji Restoration in Japan. *The Age of Capital* covers all of
them, but distributing them under different chapter headings –
'Conflicts and Wars', 'Building Nations, 'Winners' – does not relate
them in a way that would force the underlying historical issue.

If, at the height of its powers, the European bourgeoisie was never
actually quite in power, enjoying mastery of the state, what was the
curve of its development after the 'brief and impermanent'[45] moment
of its triumph? *The Age of Empire* shifts emphasis to the third term
of the originating formula. 'This book surveys the moment in history
when it became clear that the society and civilization created by and
for the western liberal bourgeoisie represented not the permanent

---

42. *The Age of Revolution*, p. 140.
43. *The Age of Capital*, p. 33.
44. *The Age of Capital*, pp. 293, 291.
45. *The Age of Capital*, p. 17.

form of the modern industrial world, but only one phase of its early development.'[46] In other words, here for the first time Hobsbawm starts explicitly to disconnect economic form and social force. After a careful discussion of the fluid composition and boundaries of the class, he remarks that 'the problem of defining the bourgeoisie *as a group of men and women*, and the line between these and the "lower-middle-classes", has no direct bearing on the analysis of capitalist development at this stage' – for 'the economic structures which sustain the twentieth century world, even when they are capitalist, are no longer those of "private enterprise" in the sense businessmen would have accepted in 1870'.[47]

The Age of Empire does not dwell on the continuing grip of aristocratic and agrarian elites at the summit of state and society in the Belle Epoque, in the way that a historian like Arno Mayer has done. But it traces a 'dissolution of the firm contours of the nineteenth century bourgeoisie' in the emergence of the modern corporation, the emancipation of women, and above all in the crisis of liberalism – a moral and ideological self-destruction leading to 1914. 'As bourgeois Europe moved in growing material comfort towards its catastrophe, we observe the curious phenomenon of a bourgeoisie, or at least a significant part of its youth and its intellectuals, which plunged willingly, even enthusastically into the abyss.'[48] In effect, the upshot of the trilogy is a snapping of the links between the constituent elements that set it in motion. Capitalism no longer requires – this: or any? – bourgeoisie. The bourgeoisie is no longer committed to – this: or any? – liberalism. The demonstratives remain indeterminate, leaving the difference between the particular and the generic in suspense.

Chronologically, *Age of Extremes* resumes the narrative at the point where its predecessor ends, with the outbreak of the First World War – a continuity underlined by the anticipation of some of its key themes in the epilogue that concludes the trilogy, looking ahead to the history of the twentieth century. But conceptually, and architectonically, there is a break. Half as long again as the earlier volumes, the fourth is erected on a larger scale. Coming to it after them is rather as if, having clambered along what appeared to be the crest-line of a great mountain range, one were suddenly to find a peak of Andean proportions rearing up overhead beyond it. There is no doubt at all

---

46. *The Age of Empire*, p. 11.
47. *The Age of Empire*, pp. 173, 11.
48. *The Age of Empire*, pp. 188, 190.

that *Age of Extremes* is Hobsbawm's masterpiece. Its presentation and internal construction repay close attention. The title is already a signal: the definite articles of the trilogy have gone, as have their pointed substantives. The replacements belong to another semantic set: less categorical and political, more existential. The actors have changed too. The most striking single discontinuity of the fourth volume is the complete disappearance from sight of the bourgeoisie, which – unlike chess, drugs or football – does not even rate an entry in the index. Did it vanish historically in August 1914? No historian is obliged to return to earlier themes, and a wish to break new ground is always commendable. But such a sharp caesura is unlikely to be just a matter of changing the subject, without significance for the direction of what follows.

Age of Extremes delivers its fundamental argument in the form of a periodization. The 'short twentieth century' between 1914 and 1991 can be divided into three phases. The first, 'the Age of Catastrophe', extends from the slaughter of the First World War, through the Great Depression and the rise of Fascism, to the cataclysm of the Second World War and its immediate consequences, including the end of European empires. The second, 'The Golden Age', stretching approximately from 1950 to 1973, saw historically unprecedented rates of growth and a new popular prosperity in the advanced capitalist world, with a spread of mixed economies and social security systems; accompanied by rising living standards in the Soviet bloc, and the 'end of the Middle Ages' in the Third World, as the peasantry streamed off the land into modern cities in post-colonial states. The third phase, 'Landslide', starting with the oil crisis and onset of recession in 1973, and continuing into the present, has witnessed economic stagnation and political atrophy in the West, the collapse of the USSR in the East, socio-cultural anomie across the whole of the North, and the spread of vicious ethnic conflicts in the South. The signs of these times are: less growth, less order, less security. The barometer of human welfare is falling.

This is a powerful view of the century. The contrast it draws between the first and second phases is clear-cut enough, and gives its force to the title of the book. What of the dividing-lines between the second and third? Here there is an obvious sense in which Hobsbawm has remained faithful to his Marxist origins, since the primary demarcation between the two is economic. Each period, he observes, corresponds to a Kondratiev long wave – a quarter century of dynamic upswing, followed by a another of sluggish downswing. Once again he reiterates that Kondratiev cycles seem to exist, but have defied explanation. Since *Age of Extremes* opens by saying that 'my object has been to understand and explain *why* things turned out the way they did' – a stronger emphasis than the 'interpretation' promised by the trilogy – reliance on the same inscrutable mechanism could be held a more serious admission of limit, since the coherence of the whole narrative in a sense turns on this *deus absconditus*.[49]

As it happens, Hobsbawm does offer partial explanations of the Great Depression of the thirties, of the boom of the Golden Age, and even – if more obliquely – of the Long Downswing. The first he attributes essentially to insufficient demand (wage stagnation) in the United States of the Jazz Age, anyway perhaps too isolationist for a responsible role in the world economy at large. The second he puts down to effective management of demand in the mixed economies of a chastened post-war capitalism, assuring regular wage increases to absorb output, and far better international coordination of trade and investment. The third he implies was due to excessive demand, as wages outstripped productivity in the late sixties, unleashing generalized inflation, just as the gold-dollar system of the Bretton Woods epoch broke down. The symmetry of these suggestions is plain enough. Mostly Hobsbawm lets them fall without emphasis, with the sceptical air of a historian who distrusts the dogmas of economists of any sort, so too much weight should not be put on them. Yet they remain conventional, and surprisingly unaffected by contrary indications. Robert Brenner has shown, pretty conclusively, how little the onset of the Slump in America can be explained by wage repression, or the end of the post-war boom by wage explosion.[50] He has also proposed a genuine theoretical explanation, of the kind Kondratiev was unable to provide, of the Long Downswing, backed by very detailed empirical evidence. The box is not quite so black as Hobsbawm suggests.

Still, whatever the reasons, the fact that in the second half of the past century the economic history of advanced capitalism divides at the point and in the way that Hobsbawm describes is beyond dispute. Out of the sea-change of the early seventies, however, Hobsbawm develops a much more far-reaching contrast of epochs, tending to encompass every dimension of social life and every part of the globe.

---

49. *Age of Extremes*, pp. 87, 268, 3.

50. See Robert Brenner and Mark Glick, 'The Regulation Approach: Theory and History', *New Left Review*, I/188, July–August 1991, pp. 45–117, and *The Economics of Global Turbulence*, discussed above.

How sound is the superstructure built on this foundation? Virtually by definition, every Golden Age is suspect of legend. In this case, Hobsbawm has taken the phrase from a description of the post-war boom in the OECD zone by Anglo-American economists of the Left – Andrew Glyn, David Gordon and others – and totalized a phase of world history under it. The notion, as always and as he himself concedes, is a retrospective one: treasure discovered after the event. It is amidst the rubble of the landslide that what preceded it appear ingots. The validity of this contrast can be looked at in a number of ways. But if we confine ourselves to the principal issues addressed by Hobsbawm, three suggest themselves.

First, has the period since 1973 delivered sustantially less material improvement for the majority of the world's population than the period before it? Slower rates of growth, flatter wages, more unemployment and rising inequality in the rich Atlantic and Antipodean zones, do not by themselves mean that the answer is yes. For the period of the Long Downswing has also seen a dramatic shift in the relative wealth of the most densely inhabited regions of the earth. China alone, after all, has a population larger than North America, Europe and Russia combined. Its growth rates in the period of the Landslide dwarf those of the Golden Age. Notwithstanding the acute economic crisis of 1997–98, South-East Asia – with a population considerably larger than South America – has posted faster development since the seventies than in the fifties and sixties. Even India somewhat accelerated over the same span. In all this part of the world, where some three-fifths of humanity live, the sum of misery has been reduced more significantly than in the halcyon days of the Atlantic boom.

Thus, even allowing for the pit into which most of the former Soviet Union has fallen, the indescribable abyss of large regions of sub-Saharan Africa, and the universal increase of inequality, on any moderately Benthamite calculation the balance of well-being tips towards the later, not the earlier period. For confirmation, we can take Hobsbawm's own most striking image of human improvement. The peasantry did not become extinct in the Golden Age, and has far from disappeared after three decades of Landslide. It is still about 45 per cent of the world's population. But the greatest drop in its numbers, by a long way, has occurred in the past thirty years of break-neck Third World urbanization. The Middle Ages, in the sense intended, ended for most of humanity in the age of Reagan, not Eisenhower.

A second central theme of *Age of Extremes* is the political violence of the century – the 187 million deaths by war, massacre, execution or famine that Hobsbawm places at the outset of his history. How do the Golden Age and the Landslide compare on this scale? The shape of the former was inseparable from the Cold War, to which Hobsbawm devotes a crisp chapter, putting the onus for it essentially on the United States, rather than either Soviet Union, or both powers. The apocalyptic tone and crusading zeal of the conflict came, he argues, from Washington alone. Yet no imminent danger of world war existed, each side accepted the division of the globe after 1945, and nuclear arms, irrationally accumulated and strategically inconsequential, were never used. The effect of this account of the high Cold War is to soften the dangers of mutual destruction so widely feared at the time, which might be thought to compromise the image of a Golden Age. *Interesting Times*, more consistently and candidly, speaks of life 'under the black cloud of nuclear apocalypse'.[51]

Still, even setting this aside, the period was murderous enough. The years from 1950 to 1972 included the Korean War, the French wars in Indochina and Algeria, three Middle Eastern wars, the Portuguese wars in Africa, the Biafran conflict, the Indonesian massacres, the Great Leap Forward and Cultural Revolution, and the American war in Vietnam. Total dead: perhaps 45 million. By comparison, the global kill ratio dropped steeply during the Landslide. From 1973 to 1994, when *Age of Extremes* appeared, its worst episodes were the Iraq–Iran War, the Cambodian massacres, the genocide in Rwanda, counter-revolutionary terror in South and Central America, the fourth and fifth Middle Eastern wars, and ethnic cleansing in the Balkans. Approximate deaths: 5 million. The barbarities of the present age are far from over. But in that respect there is no cause to regret its predecessor.

Why should the analytic schema of *Age of Extremes* be to this extent out of kilter with the historical record, in the two leading measures it selects for appraising the century? One reason in common suggests itself. In both, it is the weight of East Asia, and above all of China, that makes the difference – with far the largest casualties in the Golden Age, and far the highest rates of growth in the Landslide. In his autobiography, Hobsbawm writes: 'To this day I find myself treating the memory and tradition of the USSR with an indulgence and tenderness which I do not feel towards Communist China, because I belong to the generation for whom the October Revolution represented the hope of the world, as China never did.'[52] There is a

51. *IT*, p. 228.
52. *IT*, p. 56.

touch of over-generalization in this: Brecht, from an earlier generation, or Althusser from his own, did not feel this way. But it can be
taken as a personal fact, relevant to the historian. Given the extraordinary internationalism of Hobsbawm's cast of mind, compound
of political experience, professional erudition and imaginative
sympathy, it would be absurd to reproach him for his European formation. But *Age of Extremes* retains the angle of vision of its origins
in Vienna, Berlin and London, as the autobiography describes them.
China lacks its proportionate place in the balance of the century.
Japan, too, figures less than it should, not least during the Golden
Age itself, or as its role in *The Age of Capital* would warrant. The
only member of the nation to earn a mention is Kurosawa. Here
cultural distance probably makes itself felt. Once asked what the
country was like, after a visit, the historian stared into the middle
distance and replied, simply: 'Mars'. Affinities are always selective:
the condition of engaging deeply with some foreign cultures, however
many, is inevitably less contact with others.

The third major theme running through Hobsbawm's account of the
last half century is 'the disintegration of the old patterns of human
social relationships, and with it, incidentally the snapping of links
between the generations, that is to say, between past and present'.[53]
The socio-cultural comparator is not so clear-cut as the material or
lethal, but the emphasis of the narrative falls on the 'crisis decades' of
the seventies and eighties as the time when moral ties that had given
immemorial cohesion to human life – of family, birthplace, work,
religion, class: solidarities of any ethical substance – crumbled most
decisively. The result has been the spread of 'an absolute a-social
individualism', whose psychological costs have incresingly found compensation in the twisted collective fixations of identity politics. Here,
certainly, it is more plausible to assume an overall uni-directional
development than in the case of economic growth or violent death.
Since, reasonably enough, Hobsbawm dates the inception in the West
of a cultural revolution against every known form of tradition to the
sixties, it follows that the wider impact of this transformation must
fall in the subsequent decades.

The timing of such changes is one thing; evaluation of them another.
Hobsbawm's depictions of the sixties and their aftermath, both in
Age of Extremes and *Interesting Times*, are generally dyspeptic. In
direction, they can be ranged together with the suggestions first

53. *Age of Extremes*, p. 15.

adumbrated on the Left by Régis Debray, and then developed by Mark Lilla on the Right, that the hedonistic libertarianism of the period sprang from the same moral soil as the unbridled neo-liberalism of its successor – in the casting-off of all restraints, first of sex and then of greed, in pursuit of naked individual desire.[54] Hobsbawm does not make this connection quite so expressly, giving more importance to the autonomization of youth as a historically unprecedented phenomenon, but his negative verdict on the 'cultural revolution' is clear.

There is, however, an obvious rejoinder to any jeremiad here. Has there been any single consequence of the great transvaluation as general and profound as the worldwide advance in the emancipation of women? This is a development whose brunt falls squarely into the Landslide. Modern feminism as a movement, and the mass entry of women into the labour-force of the industrialized world on less unequal terms with men, essentially dates from the seventies. Hobsbawm accords these all the sociological importance they merit, naturally without censure. But they do not figure much in his moral reckoning of the dissolution of traditional ties. With scarcely a word, the bourgeois family and its patriarchs, objects of withering analysis in *The Age of Empire*, have crept off the scene. Tacitly, their demise has ceased to be altogether a liberation.

With this we arrive back at the missing actors of the short twentieth century. The changing position of women is allocated to the 'social revolution', as distinct from the deleterious cultural one, covered in the next chapter. Here Hobsbawm lays out the major collective forces of the contemporary world, in a counterpart survey to his panoramas of class in the nineteenth century. What does it contain? In order: peasants (going or gone); students (multiplying); workers (declining); women (rising). Absent is any sequel or equivalent to the bourgeois who commanded the heights of the trilogy. Were they without descendants? The architecture of *Age of Extremes* masks the difficulty here, by not including any cross-section of Western societies between 1914 and 1950. In effect, we pole-jump from the milieu of the Belle Epoque, with which *Age of Empire* ends, over the inter-war period, into the latter part of the Golden Age or even the Landslide. This conceals, yet also deepens, the hiatus within the series as a whole. For clearly the Western bourgeoisies, however understood, did not pack

---

54. Régis Debray, *Modeste contribution aux discours et cérémonies du dixième anniversaire*, Paris 1978, pp. 35–63 ; Mark Lilla, 'A Tale of Two Reactions', *New York Review of Books*, 14 May 1998.

up at Versailles, but continued to loom large through the Age of Catastrophe – as Hobsbawm, arriving in Baldwin's England, has every reason to know. Why then does he factor them out?

One clue to an answer may lie in a spatial anomaly of *Age of Extremes*. Economically, politically and culturally, the country that has for better or worse overwhelmingly dominated the span of history it recounts, to the point where the short twentieth century is often simply called after it, is the United States. One would expect it to have roughly similar salience in the book. But in fact, there is no head-on treatment of the US at all. America features at relevant points in the narrative – First and Second World Wars, Great Depression, Cold War, Crisis Decades, and so forth – in passages that are nearly always sharp-eyed, but there is no consolidated reflection of any kind. The contrast with the Russia is striking. The index logs twice as many entries for the USSR as for the USA, but the disparity of attention is actually more marked than this. The Soviet Union receives three full-dress analyses: at the moment of Bolshevik foundation, of the high Stalinist system, and then of Brezhnevite decline and implosion under Gorbachev and Yeltsin. No one would want less of the October Revolution and its consequences. But this centrality of the loser makes the relative marginalization of the winner all the more pointed.

If *Interesting Times* sheds biographical light on the sources of an underlying discomfort with America, the reasons why its entrances are sporadic in *Age of Extremes* – as if for much of the time it really belonged off-stage – are likely to be more structural: an effect of composition as much as of alienation. For the United States has participated in only the most mitigated sense in the triptych into which Hobsbawm divides the century. Of the time of catastrophe, it knew only the depression – deep enough, but quickly sublimated into sentimental legends of the New Deal and America's most successful President, against which Hobsbawm himself is not entirely proof (FDR's regime 'became a government for the poor and the unions').[55] The two world wars were, relatively speaking, so many canters abroad, bringing prosperity rather than distress to an untouched homeland. The 'golden age', as Hobsbawm notes in *Interesting Times*, was continuous with the experience of the wartime boom. The 'landslide' has lofted the country to an all-time pinnacle of power. If China is never quite integrated into one side of the picture, America does not readily fit it on the other. The disappearance from

---

55. *IT*, p. 388.

Age of Extremes of the class of masters tracked by the earlier books may have something to do with this slippage of focus.

For, whatever its vicissitudes in Europe, in the United States there can be no shadow of doubt that the bourgeoisie, *haute* or *moyenne*, was in command throughout the first half of the century. We need only think of such different figures as Taft and Wilson, Coolidge and Mellon, Stimson and Cordell Hull, Acheson and the Dulles brothers, not to speak of the two Roosevelts themselves. Not, of course, that Europe was without their equivalents – Adenauer, Pinay or Scelba – even after the war. But certainly America was *par excellence* the land of the species at its most robust. Fifty years later, can we speak in the same sense of bourgeoisies in the West? Dropping them from the cast of his characters, Hobsbawm is unlikely to have been moved by the now unseasonable connotations of the term. It is more probable that he was, understandably enough, perplexed as to what had happened to them. For certainly among the effects of the 'social revolution' set in train from the sixties onwards were mutations in what Marx called the character-masks of capital itself. A certain plebeian marination of styles and personnel has undoubtedly occurred. But the more significant change is one not of tone but of scale. Never since the Gilded Age have financial buccaneers and industrial magnates stalked the earth with such giant strides, trampling over labour and swaggering through culture, from heights of power and wealth Gould or Morgan could scarcely have imagined. A glance at press or television is reminder enough of the ubiquity of this tribe. Omitting it, *Age of Extremes* offers a decapitated portrait of contemporary society.

What has been the political upshot of the social and cultural upheavals depicted in *Age of Extremes*? Certainly no matching revolution. If anything, the effect of its abbreviation of the landscape of wealth and power is to conjure up a world close to the dictum coined, though not endorsed, by Lutz Niethammer: the rulers have ceased to rule, but the slaves remain slaves.[56] Such a verdict is not Hobsbawm's way of putting things, but it poses the relevant question: what is his view of twentieth-century democracy? For here, of course, is the final – and from any mainstream standpoint, obviously most conclusive – argument against his contrast of the Golden Age and the Landslide. How could he have overlooked the greatest human progress of all, that has spread across the world in the latter rather than former

---

56. *Posthistoire*, Hamburg 1989, p. 156.

period? According to Freedom House (headquarters: Washington DC) the number of certified democracies on the planet increased from 22 in 1950 to a mere 31 in 1972; but between 1973 and 2000 it saw a leap to 85. No longer confined to Western Europe and its overseas extensions in the New World and the South Pacific, it has now conquered virtually all of Latin America; South Africa; Eastern Europe and most of the former Soviet Union; Thailand and Indonesia; Taiwan and South Korea; with new candidates lining up for admission annually. Isn't this enough to show that all that has really been crashing down the slopes are tyrannies of one kind or another? On this reading, the last twenty-five years have seen, not so much a period whose gains and losses might be roughly comparable to those of its predecessor, but an immeasurably freer and better world.

That Hobsbawm would be an unlikely adept of this vision can be seen already from the trilogy, whose treatment of the emergence of mass electoral politics in the late nineteenth century is consistently cool. *The Age of Empire* observes that Lenin's famous statement that 'the democratic republic is the best possible shell of capitalism' – which would have startled an earlier generation of revolutionaries – was a plausible conclusion in the years before the First World War, when the ruling classes of Europe 'discovered that parliamentary democracy, in spite of their fears, proved itself to be quite compatible with the political and economic stability of capitalist regimes'. After the war, however, the connection between the two proved highly fragile, and as Fascism spread, Communists argued the opposite case, that 'capitalism must inevitably abandon bourgeois democracy'. This proved equally wrong, as experience after 1945 was to show.[57] But, though democracy then re-emerged as the favourite system of prosperous and cohesive capitalist societies, it was a reality in very few of the more than 150 states around the world. Such was Hobsbawm's position in 1987, two years before the fall of the Berlin Wall.

How does democracy feature in *Age of Extremes*? Hobsbawm confines his discussion of it to two blocs of reflection, towards the beginning and at the end of the book. The first forms part of a more general analysis of 'The Fall of Liberalism' in the Age of Catastrophe, the core of which is a brilliant analysis of the rise of various types of right-wing authoritarianism, of which the most extreme was Fascism, in the inter-war period. Democracies fell like ninepins, he argues,

---

57. *The Age of Empire*, pp. 110–111.

because they require conditions of prosperity, consensual legitimacy, social harmony and low policy demands on government, that rarely obtained amidst massive economic dislocation and social tension. By 1940, out of some twenty-seven European states, only five survived as democracies. The whole chapter is a *tour de force* of terse diagnosis. But when the narrative moves to the post-war period, there is no equivalent account of the reconstruction of democracy in Europe and Japan, typically on broader suffrage bases than before: instead we move straight into the Cold War, with scarcely a mention of the fact that the 'Free World' was the banner under which the West fought it. Where democracy enters the story, it gets brusque treatment. Commenting on the rival super-powers, Hobsbawm writes: 'Like the USSR, the USA was a power representing an ideology, which most Americans sincerely believed to be the model for the world. Unlike the USSR, the USA was a democracy. Unfortunately, it must be said that the second of these was probably the more dangerous.'[58]

The absence of any particular attention to the spread of democracy as a modal political order during the Landslide is thus of a piece with the way it is handled in the Golden Age. But at the end of *Age of Extremes*, Hobsbawm returns to the theme, with a set of memorable remarks on the present. 'No serious observer in the early 1990s', he opens, 'could be as sanguine about liberal democracy as about capitalism.'[59] For the nation-state was being steadily weakened by the globalization of financial and product markets, in a world economy that was becoming increasingly uncontrollable by any public authorities, or combination of them. Democracies were now systems in which governments exercised ever less power, yet had to take more decisions – typically of technical complexity beyond the understanding of their citizens – while under perpetual siege from media that had become a more important part of the political system than parties or voting arrangements. Today peoples cannot in any realistic sense govern themselves; but nor can they be ignored by governments, that can themselves no longer fully govern. The result of this impasse is inevitably a politics of official evasion, obfuscation or plebiscitary manipulation. In much of the West, contemporary elections have become little more than 'contests in fiscal perjury'. Historically, in truth, 'representative democracy is rarely a convincing way of running states'.[60]

---

58. *Age of Extremes*, p. 234.
59. *Age of Extremes*, p. 575.
60. *Age of Extremes*, pp. 578–583, 138.

Amidst the reigning gabble of non-stop – bureaucratic, academic, journalistic – democratese, such astringency is a bracing corrective. If any testimony were needed of just how unassimilable Hobsbawm's work is to any comfortable consensus, these acrid verdicts would be enough. Descriptively, they correspond to the steady loss of substance of parliamentary and electoral systems, at a time of their greatest diffusion, that is certainly one of the hallmarks of the age. Analytically, however, they also signal a shift from the way in which democracy is conceived in the trilogy. *The Age of Empire* linked the function of democratic systems to the structures of class society, and the needs of capital, in the epoch of European domination of the world. If the democracy that existed then was to be criticized, it was in the name of a popular sovereignty and equality it thwarted. That was the point of Lenin's maxim. The thrust of *Age of Extremes* differs. A century later, it is not the inequality of postmodern democracies that is the focus of critique, but their governability. The class character of the representative order, as a structure of systematically skewed power, is no longer at stake. Bourgeois democracy has exited along with the bourgeoisie. In its place is something more like a radical version of a normally conservative discourse. For, of course, 'the crisis of governability' was the watchword of the Trilateral Commission itself, set up by David Rockefeller and Zbigniew Brzezinski in 1973 to bring together 'top politicians and businessmen' from the US, Europe and Japan, to ponder problems of jointly running the world. Just as the insistence in *Age of Extremes* that the main problem of the world economy is not so much slow growth as 'uncontrollability' echoes a motif of the same milieu. Brzezinski entitled one of his works (cited in another context by Hobsbawm) *Out of Control*.

It is not that the problems to which *Age of Extremes* points in such passages are fictive. The endemic instability of international financial markets and the scientific complexity of many environmental issues pose the difficulties to existing regimes that Hobsbawm indicates. But a survey of democratic dysfunctions that remains too close to a technocratic critique misses the ideological force of the present order. There is little sense of the indispensable role played by democracy as a winning card in the outcome of the Cold War: not the ace in the stronger hand always held by the West, which was the appeal of higher consumption, but an essential knave or queen all the same. In keeping with the logic of the trilogy, *Age of Extremes* considers in detail the fall of liberalism between the wars. But the story of its recovery in the Golden Age, let alone of the potency of its mutation during the Landslide, is not told. Neo-liberalism, whose spread to all continents over the past two decades has made it perhaps the most universal ideology in world history, is dispatched virtually between commas, as a passing utopian fancy.

Such minimization points to a tell-tale gap in the fabric of this concluding volume. The trilogy follows a regular pattern – first treating economies, classes and states; then arts, sciences and ideologies. In this scheme, the amount of coverage of the arts and sciences remains constant across all three volumes, and duly reappears in *Age of Extremes*, which has (in different ways) arresting chapters on each, in the last part of the book. If we look at ideologies, on the other hand, there is an unmistakeable parabola. *The Age of Revolution* contains two chapters, one devoted to religious, and the other to secular ideologies: 42 pages. *The Age of Capital*, part of a chapter: 22 pages. *The Age of Empire* a chapter: 13 pages. When we arrive at *Age of Extremes*, which many people think of as the era *par excellence* of ideologies, there is nothing at all. Ideas have lost their place in the history of the race. How is this apparent decline of interest in what once figured so largely to be interpreted?

One explanation, of course, would lie in an underlying methodological *parti pris*: the tendency, so to speak, of any historical materialist to see intellectual systems as no more than ancillary to the interplay of deeper economic and social forces, where the movement of a period is really determined. But too many Marxists have specialized in the history of ideas for this to be a convincing line of thought. Hobsbawm's own original ambition, he tells us in *Interesting Times*, was to work out the connections between superstructure and base, not the development of the base itself, and there is an obvious sense in which he remained faithful to it. An alternative explanation might be found in the character of the ideas which the successive installments of his history confront. The first volume affords generous space to the great monuments of the Enlightenment and its sequels: the classical political economy of Smith and Ricardo, the radical legacy of Rousseau, the philosophical syntheses of Kant and Hegel, and the culmination of these traditions in Marx. The second gives short shrift to Comte and Spencer, pays wary but curt attention to marginalism, offers a low opinion of the beginnings of academic history, and dwells at length on different manifestations of mid-century racism. The third discusses the spread of Marxism, the declining popularity of evolutionary theories and, rather cursorily, the emergence of psychoanalysis and classical sociology.

The fourth, dealing with a period twice as long, contains a page on postmodernism, a phrase or two on neo-liberalism, and that's it.

Obviously, it is tempting to conclude that coverage is proportionate to the affinities of the historian, declining first gradually and then precipitously as we move towards an ungrateful present. There is certainly something in this: it is one of Hobsbawm's merits that he makes no secret of what he dislikes or disdains. But it cannot be the whole story, since the same logic does not apply to the arts. *Age of Extremes* contains a substantial chapter on the fate of these in the twentieth century, that is a blistering attack on the claims of modernism, and the futile and decadent projects of the avant-garde, from which Hobsbawm detects 'the smell of impending death' – a philippic expanded in his Neurath lecture 'The Decline and Fall of the Twentieth Century Avant-Gardes'.[61] Distaste is no bar to determined engagement on this front. The reason why ideas fall out of the frame must to some extent lie elsewhere.

Could adopted national reflexes be at work? In Hobsbawm's impatient dismissal of arcane doctrines or overly complicated figures of thought, a note of bluff Englishry can at times be heard – the lowering term 'guru' recurs all too frequently in *Interesting Times*, asssigned to thinkers like Raymond Williams or Antonio Gramsci. Perhaps there is an earlier strain of *plumpes Denken* too. These might help explain the curious absence of ideas from his self-portrait. Or more simply, setting aside any cultural factors, there could be a temperament in which a no-nonsense rationality, averse to what resists a straightforward logic, is a strong element. That certainly plays a role in the way so many central ideas and episodes of the twentieth century are consigned to a single category beyond the ken of the historian. In the First World War the aim of unconditional surrender was 'absurd and self-defeating'. In the thirties Stalin's terror was a 'murderous absurdity'. In the Second World War, 'there is no adequate explanation' of Hitler's folly in engaging hostilities with the United States. During the Cold War, Western belief in the Soviet menace was 'absurd', and the nuclear arms race of the Cold War a 'sinister absurdity'. The 'murderous absurdities' of Mao's Great Leap Forward were followed by the 'surrealist absurdities' of the Cultural Revolution. The American War in Vietnam is 'almost impossible to understand'. Reagan's rearmament was 'apparent insanity'. Today the right to national self-determination has been reduced to a 'savage and tragic absurdity'.[62]

---

61. *Behind the Times*, London 1998.
62. *Age of Extremes*, pp. 30, 391, 41, 230, 249, 469–470, 244, 247, 567.

Such notes are closer to Voltaire than Marx. Their echo at a crux of the argument of *Age of Extremes* suggests the ultimate reason for its avoidance of ideas. In the first pages of the book, Hobsbawm declares that the binary opposition between Western 'capitalism' and Soviet 'socialism' which dominated the short twentieth century was an arbitrary and artificial construction, and that the conflict between them is of limited historical interest: comparable in the long run to the wars of religion or the crusades.[63] Returning to this theme in his conclusion, Hobsbawm writes that the 'debate which confronted capitalism and socialism as mutually exclusive and polar opposites' may well 'turn out to be as irrelevant to the third millennium as the debate between Catholics and various reformers in the sixteenth and seventeenth centuries on what constituted true Christianity proved to be in the eighteenth and nineteenth'.[64]

This trope is not just a framing device. One particular chapter makes it a structural feature of the narrative. 'Against the Common Enemy', substantially longer than the account of Fascism itself, is devoted to the anti-Fascist alliances of 1935–45: the Popular Fronts before the War, the Resistances after 1941, and above all the military pact between the USSR, UK and USA that eventually defeated the Wehrmacht. Here, Hobsbawm argues, the lines were drawn not between capitalism and Communism but between the descendants of the Enlightenment and its opponents. The unity of the struggle against Fascism, mobilizing an extraordinary array of forces, was 'not negative but positive and, in certain respects, lasting' – based ideologically on shared values of progress, science and education, and practically, on active management of the economy by the state. In many respects the victory of this common front forms 'the hinge of the twentieth century'.[65]

The element of wishful projection in this idealized image of the partners of Yalta and Potsdam, their best selves secretly at one with each other, is plain enough. Historically, capitalist and Communist regimes viewed each other with cold instrumental distance throughout their coalition of necessity. For Stalin, his alliance with the USA meant no more, or less, than his earlier pact with Germany (he made the same miscalculation about both). For Truman, who had welcomed

---

63. *Age of Extremes*, pp. 4, 9.
64. *Age of Extremes*, p. 564.
65. *Age of Extremes*, p. 176; 'The Present as History', *On History*, New York 2000, p. 238.

the Nazi attack on the Soviet Union as weakening both powers, contingency plans for an atomic blitz on the USSR began within weeks of the end of the war. The 'lasting unity' of anti-Fascism lasted no longer than Fascism itself. Capitalism and Communism were mortally antagonistic systems, as both sides knew. The Cold War was no aberration. The scrambling of analogies in Hobsbawm's construction, turning eighteenth and seventeenth centuries upside down – five years of Enlightenment, followed by forty-five of religious wars – says enough. The ideas pitted against each other in the Cold War were terrestrial, not theological: schemes of social organization, tested against each other in this world, not credal niceties about a supernatural one beyond it. They cannot be waved away, after the event, as so many irrelevances.

That this is so, *Age of Extremes* brings starkly home itself. For, far from the end of the Cold War leaving a pacified world, relieved of outdated sectarian passions – cruising, as it were, into the calm waters of a contemporary settlement at Utrecht – it has, according to Hobsbawm's own account, tipped us into cataracts of unpredictable violence and social despair. This is, in fact, the scandalous message at the core of the book. The victory of the West over the Soviet Union was historically neither neutral – a mere removal of misleading labels of difference; nor beneficent – the arrival of freedom and the promise of prosperity in lands of shivering dictatorship. The dissolution of the USSR was, on the contrary, 'an unmitigated catastrophe', plunging Russia into a slump of inter-war proportions, and creating a vast zone of disorder, conflict and mortality crisis across Eurasia. In the world at large, the October Revolution had twice saved capitalism from itself – by defeating Nazism on the battlefield, and obliging Western societies to prophylactic reforms after the war. That check on its feral instincts is now, to everyone's detriment, gone.

Five years after the publication of *Age of Extremes*, in a synoptic interview that forms a coda to it, Hobsbawm says he actually underestimated the gravity of the disaster that the collapse of the Soviet Union has meant: 'The scale of the human catastrophe that has struck Russia is something we simply don't understand in the West. I don't believe there has been anything comparable in the twentieth century.'[66] The historical break of 1991, he argues, is of greater long-term consequence than that of either 1918 or 1945. In short, it would

---

66. *The New Century*, London 2000, pp. 45, 74. This wide-ranging postscript has not received the attention it deserves.

be difficult to overstate Hobsbawm's conviction of the seriousness of the setback represented by the destruction of Soviet socialism.

Here, however, lies the tension at the heart of *Age of Extremes*. Two incompatible visions of the short twentieth century are in conflict within it. For the first, the confrontation between two social systems which started in 1917 and ended in 1991 was ultimately a mare's nest: benign similarities were always deeper than hostile contrasts, which to a large extent were figments of two equally anachronistic metaphysics. For the second, the struggle between revolutionary socialism and capitalism was a fight whose disastrous end, in the death of one at the hands of the other, is the measure of all that has been lost with the elimination of the difference between them. There is no doubt which of these two constructions is more plausible, or has greater weight in the architecture of the book. Calamity, not reconciliation, is the dominant key. It is this vision of the way the century closed that governs the tripartite structure of the book. For if we ask why the Landslide is comprehensively counterposed to the Golden Age, despite so many indicators that apparently qualify or reverse the terms of each, the answer is clear: it is the initially gradual, and then hurtling descent of the Soviet experiment that sets the slope of the time.

Hobsbawm has explained, with characteristic directness, how the organization of *Age of Extremes* changed as he composed it. Originally, he explained in a lecture given a year before it appeared, the book was conceived as a diptych: first an Age of Catastrophe, from the outbreak of the World War I to the aftermath of World War II, and then from the late forties to the time of writing, 'the exact opposite' – the reform of capitalism and persistence of socialism amidst an unparalleled 'Great Leap Forward of the World Economy', in which Russians themselves lived better under Brezhnev than any previous generations had done.[67] Two developments, he says, transformed his perspective: the collapse of the Soviet bloc at the turn of the nineties, and the coincident severity of economic difficulties in the West. Of these, there can be little doubt which was decisive. The long downswing of the world capitalist economy was plain since at least the mid-seventies, as he himself notes: the end of the financial bubble in Japan, and the American recession of 1991–92 were only its latest episodes – as it were, factored in advance into the ongoing Kondratiev he says he already assumed in the diptych. It was the fall of the USSR which changed everything.

---

67. *On History*, pp. 234–235.

Stratigraphically, the evidence lies in the final composition itself. The placing and premises of 'Against the Common Enemy' only really make sense from the original standpoint of the diptych. Then indeed it would have operated as the hinge of the twentieth century, when history turned through the ordeals of Kursk and Bastogne from one extreme to another – unparalleled collective disaster to hitherto unimaginable common progress. Once the shift was made to the triptych, this earlier layer survives as an outcrop in another formation. Elsewhere, there has been a visible compacting of thematic plates that tells much the same story. Thus the long chapters within the Golden Age, on the Social and Cultural Revolutions of the post-war world, are actually not confined to the period 1950–73 at all, but run to the end of what would have been the diptych – the first even explicitly extends to the year 2000, beyond the confines of the book. Here the contrast of formal periodization that generates the triptych is plainly an overlay on the continuity of the deposits beneath it.

If the two visions of the century coexist in the final version of *Age of Extremes*, rather than the second altogether superseding the first, the reason is that they correspond to the two political souls of its author, as he has described them. The first is suffused with the nostalgia of the Popular Front, and its wish to believe that the lion and the lamb could lie down in peace together. The loyalty of the second is to the October Revolution, whose sword divided the world. The ways they inform the book, however, have something in common. In his lecture, Hobsbawm told the audience: 'Much of my life, probably most of my conscious life, was devoted to a hope which has plainly been disappointed, and to a cause which has plainly failed: the Communism initiated by the October Revolution. But there is nothing which can sharpen a historian's mind like defeat.'[68]

In support of this idea, he cites a striking passage from another historian who experienced defeat, Reinhart Koselleck, a veteran of Paulus's army at Stalingrad: 'The historian on the winning side is easily inclined to interpret short-term success in terms of a long-term ex-post teleology. Not so the defeated. Their primary experience is that everything happened otherwise than hoped or planned. They have a greater need to explain why something else occurred ... In the short run history may be made by the victors. In the long run the gains in historical understanding have come from

---

68. *On History*, p. 239.

the defeated'.[69] Of course, Hobsbawm notes, defeat alone does not necessarily guarantee insight: but from Thucycides onwards, it has been a sharp spur to it. He is entitled to place *Age of Extremes* in that line. It is certainly the most formidable contemporary illustration of it. But for all its force, Koselleck's argument is one-sided. In pointing to the epistemological advantages of the defeated, it overlooks their temptations. First among these are the lures of consolation. It is here that the two alternating visions of the 'short twentieth century' intersect.

For the underlying message of both is a way of turning defeat. The dream of the Popular Front retrospect is that there was no victory of one party over the other, since in reality we were all on the same side. The claim of the Landslide is that there was no victory, since in reality the other side lost too. The two strategies of consolation, one euphoric, the other minatory, are distinct. In the language of the street, each have their eponyms: Pollyanna, Cassandra. But if the upshot of 'no one lost' and 'they lost as well', is psychologically very close, they are quite different as historical arguments. The first has no legs; it is the second that gives shape and direction to *Age of Extremes*. Whatever the criticisms to be made of its over-extension, the idea of a Landslide can appeal at least to the long economic downswing in the OECD, and to the depth of the social crisis in the CIS. Neither advanced capitalism nor post-Communism is currently in the pink.

But, of course, that does not mean the hegemony of the order created at Malta and Paris is weak or unstable, so long as alternatives to it remain little more than glimmers of phosphorescence in a surrounding darkness. To think otherwise is political self-delusion. A symptomatic consequence is the persistent underestimation of neoliberalism as the dominant idiom of the period. *Age of Extremes* comforted itself with the notion that since no government has ever

---

69. *On History*, pp. 239–240. The source is Reinhart Koselleck, 'Erfahrungswandel und Methodenwechsel', in Christian Meier and Jörn Rüsen (eds), *Historische Methode*, Munich 1988, now included in Koselleck's *Zeitschichten*, Frankfurt 2000: p. 68. One of the intellectual origins of Koselleck's conception was Carl Schmitt, of whom he was a pupil and friend after the war, and whose reflections in *Ex Captivitate Salus* on Tocqueville as a figure of defeat he cites. His own list of historical thinkers whose greatness was born from an experience of defeat includes Thucydides, Polybius, Sallust, Tacitus, Commines, Machiavelli and Marx (the June days and the Commune). Strangely, it extends even to the Scottish political economists, but omits Clarendon.

really practised consistent laissez-faire, purist doctrines would prove short-lived fantasies. Indeed, 'neo-liberal triumphalism did not survive the world economic setbacks of the early 1990s'. Four years later, after the Asian financial crisis, Hobsbawm was again proclaiming 'The Death of Neo-Liberalism'. Today *Interesting Times* brings the same tidings, though the note is somewhat more faltering. We are now told that 'perhaps' the bursting of recent speculative bubbles spells the demise of market fundamentalism, this time with the rueful rider: 'The end of the hegemony of global neo-liberalism has been announced long enough – I have done so myself more than once.'[70]

One element in this inability to take the enemy seriously is the general tendency to intellectual down-sizing noticed earlier. In the *Marxism Today* of the eighties, there was always a difference between its two leading commentators. Both were committed to a critique of the traditional left, but for Stuart Hall, 'the road to renewal' passed through an acknowledgement of the ideological strength of Thatcherism, to whose construction of a new common sense for the British people he devoted a great deal of attention: only by taking the full measure of this hegemony, he argued, could a better one be developed. Hobsbawm, on the one hand, placed his emphasis not on Thatcher's cultural-political ascendancy – he insisted she was always electorally quite weak – but on the division of her opponents. The way to regain power, he argued, was to win back the middle classes who had been alienated by the Winter of Discontent and Bennery, and the key to that was pragmatic – a formal or informal Lib–Lab Pact.

The sequel delivered a verdict on each of these views. Blair won back the middle class, and came to power on a tacit Lib–Lab deal; but Thatcherism, far from being counter-attacked, was assimilated as the ideological condition of the come-back. The pragmatic route, that made light of ideas, merely produced a mutant of what its advocate had most detested. *Age of Extremes* takes the dismissal of economic theories yet further, maintaining that what divided Keynesians and neo-liberals was simply a 'war of incompatible ideologies', each rationalizing an apriori view of human society, from positions 'barely accessible to argument'[71] – a view of the discipline that would have raised eyebrows in the days when he was teaching it at King's.

---

70. See *Age of Extremes*, p. 412; 'The Death of Neo-Liberalism', *Marxism Today*, one-issue revenant, November–December 1998; *Interesting Times*, p. 227.

71. *Age of Extremes*, pp. 409–410.

But underestimation of the force of neo-liberal theories – one need only think of the scope and coherence of Hayek's work – answers to a more familiar political craving as well: the need for good news in bad times. It is possible that the system set in place in the heyday of Reagan and Thatcher will finally buckle under the pressure of a global slump, although were that to be the outcome of the present contraction, it would put paid to any Kondratiev – the downswing that started in 1973 now already touching its third decade, beyond the quarter-century it should have lasted. But without a conceptual alternative capable of being articulated across the same range, from the philosophical through the technical to the rawly political, the improvements Hobsbawm would wish for are unlikely to materialize. *Interesting Times* is reduced to clutching at the straws of Stiglitz and Sen, as if Nobel Prizes were a token of intellectual hope.

Age of Extremes treats the inter-state system in a not dissimilar way. For if neo-liberalism is still the hegemonic ideology of the time, the hegemonic power – in a quite new sense – is the United States. With the USSR out of the way, and the IMF and UN at its disposal, no state in history has ever enjoyed such a global supremacy. This unprecedented position was already clear when Hobsbawm completed the tetralogy, but it is not reflected in it. All that *Age of Extremes* has to say on the subject is that 'the only state that would have been recognized as a great power, in the sense the word had been used in 1914, was the USA. What this meant in practice was quite obscure'.[72] The world portrayed in the concluding pages of the work is a system without a master – less than ever before in anyone's control. *Interesting Times* has adjusted to the reality of a 'single global hyperpower', but still implausibly insists that 'the US empire does not know what it wants to do with its power'.[73] The notion that American purposes are impenetrable is another way of suggesting that there is no real steering in the international order.

The daily evidence is otherwise. All hegemonies have their limits, and no policies ever achieve just what they intend. But the salient feature of the present is not that the world at large is out of control, but that it has never been subject to such an extent of control by one power, acting to diffuse and enforce one system, as we see today. American purposes, amply ventilated by the strategists of the state, could not be clearer: general expansion of liberal capitalism to the

---

72. *Age of Extremes*, p. 559.
73. *IT*, p. 410.

ends of the earth, and its organization wherever possible in keeping
with the national norms and interests of the United States. There is
nothing irrational about these objectives, which go back to the time of
Cordell Hull and Acheson. They do not, of course, preclude miscal-
culations, then or now. The difference today is just that America
has a much freer hand in pursuing them. Hence the ongoing series of
effortless military expeditions to the Gulf, the Balkans, the Hindu
Kush, and no doubt now Mesopotamia.

About these Hobsbawm has been unwavering. In the domestic
politics of the West, his instincts are often far from radical: capable
of being disappointed in Clinton, judging Lafontaine too far to the
Left, and finding it surprising that financial markets do not regard
New Labour as much of a danger.[74] Here his instincts derive, as he
says, from the Popular Front. But in the international arena, it is typically the other side of his formation that comes to the fore. There the
past decade has shown little sign of Browderite leanings; classical
Leninist reflexes remain unaltered. He rejected the Gulf War, bluntly
told a *bien-pensant* Italian interviewer that the Balkan War was not a
humanitarian intervention, has compared the Afghan operation to
earlier bombardments of the region by British imperialism, and exco-
riated the war on terrorism and upcoming attack on Iraq.[75] It is
difficult to think of any British intellectual of comparable stature with
as staunch a record.

Given the far greater importance of the current open revival of
imperial pretensions than of mere domestic perjuries – as if Brown
mattered more than even a cipher like Hoon, as New Labour once
again gears for war – the value of the line Hobsbawm has drawn here
is clear-cut. But *Age of Extremes* offers a more general lesson.
Historic political defeat all but inevitably leads to a search for silver
linings. Worldwide, much of the Left has spent the better part of a
decade doing little else. The two most standard moves in the repertoire of such reactions are those to which Hobsbawm has given an
exceptional expression: renaming the victorious system to render it
more palatable, and exaggerating the fissures in its victory to imagine
it more vulnerable. In either case, the underlying impulse is the same:
a sense that any effective opposition to the existing order requires
proximate expectation of relief from it – that to take the measure of
its unmitigated identity and strength must somehow lead to acceptance

74. See *The New Century*, pp. 107, 109.
75. *The New Century*, pp. 17–20; *IT*, p. 414.

of it. That is a mistake. Accurate intelligence of the enemy is worth more than bulletins to boost doubtful morale. A resistance that dispenses with consolations is always stronger than one which relies on them.

Such reflections do not affect the grandeur of *Age of Extremes*. The book is like a palace whose architect altered his plans while building it, leaving structural inconsistencies that make it stranger, but not less splendid, than it appears at first sight, housing room after room of paintings, in different genres, each with moments of magic, many with masterpieces. As with any Hermitage, there is no way of appreciating so much all at once: repeated visits are needed. Least of all should they be peaceable. Art is living only if it provokes dispute. The enormous patrimony Hobsbawm has left us should be approached in his own spirit, with warmth, passion and acerbity.

2002

DEBTS

1

THE *LONDON REVIEW*

OF BOOKS

The *London Review of Books* occasionally advertises itself as 'Arguably the best literary magazine in the world'. This collection provides some materials for arguing about the claim – though no book-length selection of articles from a publication appearing every fortnight could hope to be adequately representative of it.[1] Inevitably, much that is most distinctive of the *LRB* is absent here. There are no Letters, of the sort Alan Bennett rightly takes to be central to the character of the paper. At their own request, with a single exception, there are no articles by members of its staff. There are no poems, and none of the longer pieces, in various genres, that appear from time to time. The selection is taken from the last decade only. Even within these limits, omissions that any publisher would regret outnumber inclusions. Still, some idea of the *London Review* comes through these pages.

Generalizations about any significant publication that produces around a million words a year are always liable to go somewhat wide of the mark. For any assertion (or speculation) that can be made, exceptions or contra-indications are all too likely to be found. This is especially true of a journal that relishes the unpredictable. The mysterious elegance of the *LRB* resists easy capture. Little pretence of explaining it will be made here. But some comparative remarks may help to situate the paper, although a contributor can only express a personal view, no better than that of any of the paper's readers, who – if its correspondence columns are any evidence – would have equally decided opinions about the matter.

The *London Review* belongs to a small class of periodicals, broadsheets based on critical book reviews for a general readership, which originated in England on the eve of the Great War. The first

---

1. *London Review of Books. An Anthology*, London 1996.

appearance of the *Times Literary Supplement* as a separate weekly dates from 1914. The form was consolidated in the inter-war period, when the *TLS* – however suspect of complaisance in the eyes of Leavis – was by continental standards a journal of notably independent judgement. After the war, under a series of gifted editors who gave it wider ambitions, the *TLS* came to occupy a unique position as a journal of critical record, probably reaching a peak of influence somewhere in the sixties. It was not until 1966 that the form spread to France, with the appearance of *La Quinzaine Littéraire*, and 1984 that it arrived in Italy, with the launching of *L'Indice*. But although increasingly emulated in Europe (a Hungarian version dates from the nineties), it still remains pre-eminently an Anglophone phenomenon. Continental versions tend to be less outspoken – their function on occasion coming closer to publicity than scrutiny – and less central to the local cultures.

The development beyond the classical English model came from America, when a prolonged strike at the *New York Times* in 1963, temporarily suppressing its book section, cleared a space for the launching of the *New York Review of Books*. Three innovations marked the *NYRB* from the outset. A fortnightly rather than a weekly, it allowed for substantially longer articles than the *TLS* ever afforded; while retaining the ostensible format of a reviewing periodical, it carried essays unconnected to any books published; and it displayed an overt political profile, picked out by the signatures of its authors. The success of this formula, with its much more sharply focused and topical identity, was immediate. By the early seventies the *NYRB* was clearly dominant, setting the terms for the field with a circulation far larger than that of the *TLS*, which had now adopted the signed contribution and self-standing article within its own, otherwise still largely traditional format.

At the end of the decade, the scenario in New York was repeated in London, when a lengthy lock-out at *The Times* – prior to Murdoch's purchase of it – took the *Literary Supplement* off the streets for several months in 1979. The opportunity of its absence created the *London Review of Books*, launched financially as an offshoot of the *New York Review of Books*, and initially distributed as a local insertion folded within the latter's pages. Within a year, when the new venture had yet to become profitable, the *NYRB* shed responsibility for the *London Review*. But the common origins of the two papers, and their close original connection, make comparisons between them more or less unavoidable for readers on either side of the Atlantic today – notwithstanding the obvious discrepancies of style and scale, as of battleship and schooner, between them.

The contrasts between the two papers are in part a natural function of their objective settings. The American market, five times the size of the British, supports a much larger and richer journal, endowed with ample revenues from a publishing industry accustomed to spending heavily on promotion to reach a continental readership. Flanked by thicker columns of advertisements, average articles are longer and issues more copious in the New York than in the London periodical. Besides such differences in the structure of the market, the relationship of culture to power is also quite distinct in the two societies. Since the Kennedy era no American administration has been without a substantial penumbra of intellectuals serving or aspiring to serve at the highest levels of government – advisers in office, or advisers in waiting, according to the incumbency in the White House.

The relationship of journalists and academics to government is consequently much closer than in Britain, where the UK state has never brigaded intellectuals on the same scale as the US state. Although the Thatcher years did see the first signs of a Downing Street entourage, the parliamentary system in Britain leaves less space for this phenomenon than a presidential one. The difference of working environment is visible in the two *Reviews*. Articles in the *NYRB* tend to have a 'policy' tone, implying potential counsel to officialdom, that is generally absent from the *LRB*, which is much more detached from the worlds of Whitehall and Westminster.

There is also, of course, a subjective opposition between the journals. At the time the *New York Review* was launched, the war in Vietnam and ghetto riots in the US had created a radical opposition to the bipartisan estabishment in America which found lively expression in its pages. But once the war in South-East Asia was over, and domestic politics had reverted to normal routines, the *NYRB* gradually settled down to the role of a critical mentor of liberal opinion in the States – acutely conscious of social problems within America and hostile to the excesses of Reaganism, but supportive of the general direction of US diplomacy in the last years of the Cold War. Today, under a Democratic presidency, the result is a highly polished but increasingly predictable formula, in which besides the illustrious writers and scholars (many from this side of the Atlantic) on which the journal has traditionally relied, semi-authorized contributors of various kinds – former envoys, aides to the First Lady, bureau chiefs and the like – occupy more space than in the past.

Politically, the *London Review* started out from a position quite close to that of its progenitor. In the closing years of the Carter administration, the British equivalent was sympathy for the newly

minted Social Democratic Party. But the *LRB* soon moved in the other
direction – towards a more radical stance, with the result that today
the politics of the two periodicals have moved quite far apart. It
would not be difficult to contruct an index of the issues on which they
have taken opposite sides. Some of them are reflected in this collection. Simplifying greatly, it could be said that the principal contrast
lies in the unspoken aversion of the one to legacies of the Cold War
largely accepted by the other. This has not been just a matter of the
battle against Communism, but also of the role of the United States
in ancillary theatres of conflict around the world.

Victor Kiernan's contribution to the volume in hand, touching on
the USSR, is an indication of the width of the gap on the first. Paul
Foot and Edward Said on two Middle Eastern issues – the Gulf War
and the Palestinian Peace – suggest the contrast of attitudes to the
second. Similarly, Tom Nairn's reflections on nationalism give short
shrift to ordinary judgements in Washington or New York about the
Balkans. Above all, perhaps, Christopher Hitchens's indelible
portrait of Clinton is a commentary on the circumspection of the
NYRB.[2] In ways like these, the London journal stands well to the
Left of its counterpart in New York. It would be an error, however,
to take an instinct for a system. The contrariness prized by the *LRB*
can go the other way. Progressive pieties are rarely spared, as R.W.
Johnson's caustic survey of the new South Africa below makes clear.
Occasionally, there can even be a cross-over of transatlantic roles.
The *LRB*'s gifted correspondent in Russia upheld Yeltsin's brutish rule
long after the *NYRB* developed serious qualms about it: coverage of
Chechnya has been entirely to the credit of the American rather than
the British paper.

If this case is unusual, it is still a reminder that the *London
Review* can never be taken for granted. This holds true even of
domestic politics, where the pattern of its interventions has been
most consistent. The *LRB* was born under Thatcher, and has passed
all sixteen years of its life so far under a Conservative regime in
Britain. Very early on, it was a courageous opponent of the
Falklands War that entrenched the hegemony of the New Right, and
went on to become a savage critic of Thatcherism as a nostrum for

---

2. For a tremulous example, compare Gary Wills, 'The Clinton Scandals', in the
New York Review, 18 April 1996: 'Whitewater has been a scandal, but the clearest
proved wrong-doing has been by politicians, journalists and (well-paid) Clinton
critics. Clinton seems by comparison a paragon of virtue', etc.

national recovery. In fact, no other journal in the country published such lethal attacks on the callousness, futility and corruption of the Conservative system of power, and the ruins of British justice under it. The collection here gives little hint of this outstanding record.[3] The *LRB*'s attitude to the opposition, on the other hand, has always been less sharply defined. The paper lost patience with the SDP early on, and never showed much interest in either the leadership of the Labour Party, or its Left. Kinnock was viewed with brusque disdain, but given the remoteness of the Opposition from office, its vicissitudes never received over much attention. With New Labour now finally approaching government, however, a quite different political landscape lies ahead. The *London Review* has always shown innate resistance to *bien-pensant* outlooks of any kind: no paper could be further from a bandwagon mentality. It is unthinkable that it would become an ornament of the incoming regime. On the other hand, radical readers of the *LRB* would be unwise to assume they can forecast its attitude towards it.

The one article on Britain in this collection, by Ross McKibbin, is an example of the paper's ability to disconcert expectations on the Left. There are not many Labourists – let alone socialists – willing to express nostalgia for the era of Wilson and Callaghan; just as there are few civil libertarians who would dissent from Charter 88's call for a bill of rights – firmly rejected, however, by the paper's most regular contributor from the judiciary.[4] In different ways, both texts upset a certain consensus. Do they give comfort to another one? Perhaps the fact that Blair, when he was still an obscure back-bencher, first laid out his political wares in the *LRB*, is no more than a historical curiosity.[5] The first significant analysis in the paper of Blair's imprint as leader of his party has been scathing.[6] But the election of a Labour government will change the atmosphere in which the *London Review* has worked, and it is doubtful if anyone even inside the journal can be sure quite how it will react to the new dispensation.

There is a reason for such incalculability. The *LRB*, unlike the *New York Review*, is not an ideologically driven paper. Essentially,

---

3. See, *inter alia*, Ross McKibbin, 'Stormy and Prolonged Applause Transforming Itself into a Standing Ovation', 5 December 1992; Conor Gearty, 'The Party in Government' and 'Our Flexible Friends', 9 March 1995 and 18 April 1996; Ronan Bennett, 'Criminal Justice', 24 June 1993.

4. Stephen Sedley, 'Free Speech for Rupert Murdoch', 19 December 1991.

5. Tony Blair, 'Diary', 29 October 1987.

6. Seamus Milne, 'My Millbank', 18 April 1996.

its freshness of judgement comes from that. Even the main political contrast between the two journals suggests this asymmetry. Positive commitment to the broad lines on which the Cold War was fought to victory is a programme. Negative avoidance of them is not. The sources of the sensibility behind the *LRB*'s escape from the ruling conventions of international affairs are not easy to pin down. It seems probable that they include a generational element. The *NYRB*, based in the centre of the New World Order, is some two decades older than the *LRB*. Its principal writers were typically formed at the height of Containment – in the last couple of years, the average age of its most frequent contributors (three or more articles) was over sixty-five. For a younger age group, in what is now a minor power, the passions of that period matter less. The background of the editor may be relevant too. The *LRB* is possibly the leading journal in the West to be edited by a woman; with a deputy of the same sex. Politically incorrect to a fault, there has never been any feminist insistence in its pages, though the situation of women is often addressed in them. But it is reasonable to surmise that a certain indifference to the themes of the Free World may be connected to more contemporary concerns, related to gender. Whether, in the case of Mary-Kay Wilmers, Russian origins or Belgian schooling have anything to do with the matter is less obvious.

What is clear is that the most significant divergence between the way the two papers are run is a question not of personnel, but of editorial conception. Articles in both journals will be commissioned on a mixture of grounds, which include the reputation of the author, the urgency of the topic and the direction of the argument. But whereas for the *New York Review* the public salience of an issue is typically an imperative, in the *London Review* the style of a writer tends to come before the importance of a subject, or the affinity of a position. The latter enter into the editorial alchemy, but not at the expense of the former. The result is that the *LRB* is written to a higher standard, in a wider range of individual idioms – some of them of great brilliance – than its counterpart in New York, whose prose is often at best workmanlike, but it covers a narrower and more capricious range of current affairs. The *NYRB* – this is also true of the *TLS* today, under the capable hand of Ferdinand Mount – is much more sensitive to the scale of issues, and will always publish something moderately informative about the topics of the day, rarely failing to provide its readers with a substantial feature on any major development round the world. The *London Review* will ignore any country or a crisis if it cannot find a writer it likes about it. On occasion, it will be a question of means – payment is modest by American standards – that draws the blank; sometimes, no doubt, of knowledge; but much more often of taste.

The greater pleasures of reading the *LRB* are thus paid for in a more erratic and limited horizon. The patchiness of coverage may not be quite random. The Far East is the most striking gap. Suggestively, perhaps, the only text in this collection on Asia – the larger part of humanity – deals with a European missionary in India. Though the idea would be greeted by its staff with hilarity, to more outside eyes an unconscious outline, like a faint water-mark, of the Commonwealth can be traced in the distribution of the paper's attention. South Africa commands more space than all of Latin America combined. Australia has been generously represented in pages that scarcely register the existence of Japan. The Middle East features strongly; the Maghreb not at all. Even in Western Europe, the only country that can be counted on to figure in the *LRB* is Ireland: the steeples of Fermanagh and Tyrone are rarely out of sight, while the Continent more often than not remains fog-bound.

In these respects, Manhattan is a superior vantage-point to Bloomsbury. The global reach of the American empire leaves no part of the world beyond potential scrutiny, and the *New York Review*'s coverage reflects a sense of this responsibility. But talent is indeed not spread so evenly, and the products of a dutiful journalism that is invariably *à la page* risk being dull and conventional in a way that the *LRB* never is. Nor are its own interests merely wayward. If Ireland looms so much larger than Germany or France, the reason lies in a war that most of England prefers to forget. The *London Review*'s record of publication, on this least popular of all topics, puts to shame many journals to the Left of it. No paper can discuss everything; where it picks an issue, it oftens excels at it.

No particular line, other than abhorrence of official cant, unites the various Irish writers the *LRB* has published, of whom Colm Tóibín offers an example here. This touches on a more general feature of the paper, which distingushes it from its American counterpart. Writers are never subject to editorial direction in the *London Review*. Texts can be rejected, but once they are accepted, firm punctilio over syntax or phrase is combined with all but complete liberty of opinion, however wayward. No contributor will ever find their conclusions rewritten. This lack of pressure, as an operating principle, may have some relation to the inner metabolism of the journal. Karl Miller and Mary-Kay Wilmers have been two remarkable editors of the *LRB*. But no disproportionate will sets its stamp on every page, and different members of staff – editorial, design and business – themselves write for the paper they help to produce.[7] Anyone who has worked on a periodical will know how unlike the dynamics of this kind of office are from a more conventional hierarchy.

Such considerations particularly affect treatment of political issues, of course. The *LRB*, however, is first and foremost – as it describes itself – a literary magazine. The sharpness of its political identity comes, in fact, largely from the absence of ideological reflexes customary in the politcal world. But the paper is also literary in the more obvious sense that most of it is concerned with what is traditionally described as life and letters. Its approach to these is very much its own. The arts proper are dominated, as one would expect, by fiction and poetry, but not to any great degree. Painting and music have occasioned some of the journal's finest pieces: characteristic here is Nicholas Spice's beautiful reverie on muzak.[8] It is puzzling that the cinema should remain so relatively marginal – in this volume, the heads of the Marx Brothers stare out like some incongruous ancestral totem. Recently architecture has started to feature. Geographically the focus is essentially Anglo-American, with the traditional side-glance at France; chronologically, the framework is twentieth century, with the occasional shanghai of earlier works along contemporary lines, as in the famous sapphic reading of Jane Austen by Terry Castle included here. The mixture is less cosmopolitan than in New York, but livelier.

Ideas trace a somewhat similar pattern. Philosophy and history are better represented than natural science, where the comparison is decidedly in favour of America – the paper has never been able to attract contributors of the calibre of Stephen Jay Gould or Richard Lewontin. The social sciences get more of an airing, but the most striking feature of the *LRB*'s interests is a reversal of national stereotypes. Psychoanalysis enjoys much greater salience, and playful respect, in its pages than those of the *New York Review*, which has given ample voice to sceptical dismissals of it. The contrast of

---

7. For examples see: Peter Campbell on Tiepolo, 12 January 1995; Jeremy Harding on Zaire, 8 June 1995; Paul Laity on Murdoch's *Sun*, 20 June 1996; John Lanchester on Auden, 16 November 1995; Jean McNicol on mental health care, 9 February 1995; Andrew O'Hagan on begging, 18 November 1993; Sarah Rigby on the Yeats sisters, 15 June 1996; John Sturrock on Camus, 8 September 1994; Mary-Kay Wilmers on meeting General Sudoplatov, 4 August 1994.

8. By the same author, see also: 'How to Play the Piano' (on Glenn Gould and Alfred Brendel) and 'Music Lessons' (Mozart), 26 March 1992 and 14 December 1995.

attitudes raises a wider issue. Without question politically radical, how far is the *London Review* culturally so?

That there is no necessary join between the two planes is a familiar fact of intellectual life in general. In Britain, the *New Statesman* of old was famous for the contrast between its front and back halves – vehemently socialist politics allied to blandly conservative letters. *Scrutiny* could be said to represent the opposite combination: literary attack with political regression. These examples are not ungermane. Karl Miller, the founder of the *London Review*, was trained by Leavis at Cambridge and became literary editor of the *New Statesman*, before taking over *The Listener*. But it is just such precedents that indicate the extent to which the *LRB* departs from this pattern. From the beginning, comparable impulses have been visible in the political and literary sides of the journal, which has never segregated them in any particular order – opening (or closing) articles representing either, according to occasion.

Coverage of fiction has thus never been conventional. An established name is no guarantee of notice in the *LRB*, which regularly ignores novels by fashionable authors, whose review is *de rigueur* elsewhere. On the other hand, a still unknown writer may have higher chances of attention than anywhere else in the press. Among its 'discoveries' was Salman Rushdie, whose *Midnight's Children* received its only solus review when it first appeared in the *LRB*; more recently Paddy Doyle or James Buchan. Less orthodox forms – Georges Pérec or Christine Brook Rose – gain equal hearing. A sense for the new, or overlooked, has from the outset been a noticeable thread in the journal. Unrepresented in this collection, contributors under the age of forty could well make up another one. Here the contrast with the *NYRB* is at its sharpest.

Nevertheless, it is fair to say that the quotient of iconoclasm in the *LRB*'s coverage of cultural life is less than in its commentary on public affairs. On the whole, articles about contemporary authors tend to sustain rather than question existing reputations. This is a question of a ratio, not a rule. Contrary examples are not hard to find. A famous critical piece on Brodsky would be a case in point:[9] here, however, the target is off-shore: toes closer to home are more rarely trodden on. There the subjects for demolition are more likely to be found in minor rather than major genres: as it were, P.D. James rather than V.S. Naipaul. There are a number of good reasons for this. A distaste

---

9. See Christopher Reid, 'Great American Disaster', 8 December 1994.

for facile derision is understandable. It is also true that the most difficult form of criticism is affirmative, and this the *London Review* at its best accomplishes extraordinarily well, as a glance at essays it has published on, let us say, Bishop or Nabokov reveals.[10]

Still, there remains a difference between the ways in which common editorial instincts work themselves out in the two fields principally covered by the paper. It is not altogether clear why this should be so. It might be thought that it has something to do with the necessarily closer proximity to the world of publishing than of politics of any literary review, in a metropolitan setting in the UK. This is a scene which has been transformed in the past fifteen years, as processes of concentration have enormously increased the levels of investment that publishers make in leading writers, from far larger advances to huge budgets for publicity, with promotional tours for selling books now an automatic accompaniment of literary success. The saturation of the field by big money has occurred during the period in which the *LRB* has risen – a time when the first lyric poet was transported by helicopter to public readings – and has changed the environment of letters, with deeply ambiguous effects for writers themselves, in ways that have yet to be fully understood.

It cannot be said the paper has so far done much to discuss them. But the reasons for its relatively pacific coexistence with this constellation do not lie in any institutional entanglement. The small grant it receives from the Arts Council regularly excites the indignation of pundits on the Right, just because the *LRB* has not conformed to established expectations – the *Sunday Times* recently calling for it to be taken away, since the journal did so little to support British writers. Far from participating in a current literary scene agog with vogue and hyperbole, the *LRB* has kept what is widely perceived as a mandarin aloofness from it. Complicity with the institutions of literature, whether patrons or advertisers, is scarcely a charge that can be made against the paper.

An alternative explanation would look to the readers rather than sponsors of the paper. Common observation suggests that the average book-buyer combines habitual cynicism about politicians, of any kind, with casual credence in literary reputations, however gained. It is enough to think of the relative faith accorded parliamentary debates and literary contests. It is *bon ton* to be caustic about Major or Blair,

---

10. See Helen Vendler, 'The Numinous Moose', 11 March 1993; John Lanchester, 'Unspeakability', 6 October 1994.

less so about Barnes or Brookner. The automatic sales of prize-winning novels speak for themselves. Are there any traces of this sensibility – which can, after all, appeal to the common-sense view that politics is always a realm of rhetorical deception, literature of imaginary truths – to be found in more sophisticated form in the paper itself?

There is no denying some connection between a stratum with this traditional outlook and the *LRB*. The journal aims at what might be called a common reader in an updated Woolfian sense: that is, neither 'academic' nor 'avant-garde'. Although many of its contributors come from universities, and its correspondence columns include many fencing-matches of high-spirited erudition, the paper goes out of its way to avoid anything that smacks of the chair. Symptomatically, footnotes – a normal and useful feature of the *New York Review* – are banished from the *LRB*, as the corns of pedantry. Likewise, while experimental writing finds a place in the journal's interests, in the other arts – where they are stronger – avant-garde forms lie beyond its range. One would no more expect to find a consideration of Godard or Beuys in the *London Review* than a recension of Parsons (though it always has the ability to surprise one). In ways like these the journal keeps close to the ideal of a cultivated lay readership, immune to the tics of common-room or coterie.

But this rapport does not depend on any indulgence to passing consumer taste. If the *London Review* on the whole affronts received literary opinion less than political wisdom, a better guess at the reason might be the different weight tacitly given each. The key to the contrast seems to lie in its respective strategies of rebuke. If the paper dislikes a literary work, it will typically ignore it. But if it takes exception to a political process, it will roundly attack it. What the difference suggests is a conviction that inferior – indeed even fraudulent – art, however deplorable, is not a major public nuisance. In the balance of things, the meretricious or pretentious matters less than the cruel and unjust. The belief that the moral welfare – and *a fortiori* political health – of a nation is ultimately in the keeping of its literature has a long history in English intellectual tradition, and has not gone away. This is the assumption that the practice of the *LRB* denies. Forgetting himself, in a gesture perhaps of over-compensation, a star political writer recently spoke of 'the transmutation of the base into gold that is the raw stuff of literature – our slight and sardonic hope'.[11] No flourish could be further from the

---

11. Christopher Hitchens, 'After-Time', 19 October 1995.

mind of the paper. What distingushes it, discreetly, is a sense of proportion.

This could also be described as a sort of realism. The term, however, has a deflationary ring at variance with a journal whose note is anything but down-beat. It might be better to speak of its idiosyncratic form of worldliness. As editors, the peculiar genius of Karl Miller and of Mary-Kay Wilmers has been to find a tone that combines the values of the smart and the unpretentious. Smartness always risks a vicinity to snobbery, what is exclusive: 'distinction' in Bourdieu's sense. Characteristically, the *LRB* averts this danger by making of style a kind of informal elegance attached to the most ordinary subjects or appurtenances of life. The kinds of writing that really mark out the journal are actually neither political nor literary-critical, but ones which reflect this ethos best. They include the curiosity about chequered individual lives, on display in this collection. Another genre, unrepresented here, are documentary reports from the nether-worlds of begging or mental disorder, written by younger members of the staff, which have no counterpart in the *NYRB*. Last and perhaps most significant – *pace* Bennett – is the transformation by the *LRB* of the traditionally humdrum journalistic form of the Diary into a vehicle of astonishing variety, for many of the most memorable pieces the paper has published. The selections here are, if anything, among the lighter contributions.

A wonderful range of writing is offered in these and other forms. Stylistically, there are unspoken limits. The delphic or serpentine are not part of the repertoire. No fear could be more foreign to the journal than of 'the mischief of premature clarification', against which Fredric Jameson – whose arrival in its pages is a welcome departure from consistency – once warned. The too vehement is likewise at some discount, suspect of 'rant'. Perhaps the best way of conveying the overall climate would be to say that the paper resists any trace of *l'esprit du sérieux*, in the Sartrean sense: that is, of the portentous, high-minded, hypocritical. Against all these, its playfulness finds expression on the largest as well as smallest of topics. Emblematic in this collection are the saturnine tones of Edward Luttwak, as a 'heavy-weight' contributor.[12] It is enough to think of the contributions of President Havel to the *New York Review* to understand their antithesis.

---

12. See also 'Screw You' (on Italian corruption), 19 August 1993; 'Programmed to Fail' (the US Presidency). 22 December 1994, 'Does the Russian Mafia Deserve the Nobel Prize for Economics?', 3 August 1995; 'Buchanan has it Right', 9 May 1996.

The visual images of each periodical may have the final word. Among the many successful features of the *NYRB*, David Levine's drawings stand out in public impact, like some serial logo endlessly fertile in reproducing the identity of the paper. These are illustrations which play off against the the text. Where the prose can be solemn or sententious, the pictures are knowing and cynical. Heroes and villains alike become so many faintly reptilian marionettes, twitching on the ends of derision. The watercolours that adorn the front of the *London Review* work in the opposite sense, vivifying rather than mortifying the sense of the writing. The nonchalant wit and beauty of Peter Campbell's typewriters and wash-basins, tousled bedspreads and tropical frondage, offer a *promesse de bonheur* of what lies within – not invariably kept, of course. But though from time to time the ideal they figure exceeds the reality of the issues that follow, the covers say more of this periodical than any other in the world.

1996

Postscript

The *London Review* has since passed its quarter-century. In doing so, it has become the leading intellectual periodical in Britain, having relegated the *Times Literary Supplement* – potentially in baulk at the time of writing, conglomerate ownership uncertain – to a clearly secondary status, not only in the quality and range of what it publishes, but also in sales. Indeed, with a home territory a fifth of the size of the American, the *LRB* now has a circulation of 45,000 as against 135,000 for the *NYRB* – nearly half of it abroad, where the the figure for the *New York Review* is less than a tenth. Both periodicals have increased circulation, the *LRB* more rapidly, since 2000. But each reflecting distinct environments, their development has in other ways shown a criss-crossing pattern.

In Britain, the *LRB* faced a more drastic alteration of its setting, once New Labour settled into power as a successor regime to Thatcherism, encountering even less opposition than had the Conservative order of the eighties. The journal, as predicted, never became a side-car on the Third Way. But nor, as also implied might be the case, did it put up a especially spirited opposition to it. For quite some time, the *LRB* published little on the local system in place, and when it did so, contributions were generally low-octane. In a period marked by the war on Yugoslavia, and a steep escalation in the bombing of Iraq, its coverage of Clinton and Blair did not greatly differ from that of the *NYRB*: supportive of Operation Allied Force in the Balkans, and protective of the President in his hour of legal tribulation at home, regardless of how many rockets fell on Khartoum or Baghdad in the same cause.[13]

With the election of Bush in 2000, however, the situation of the two periodicals diverged. Faced with a Republican administration, the *NYRB* automatically went into opposition, in a way that set it apart from the ambivalence of the *LRB* under New Labour. Yet for nearly two years, till the autumn of 2002, it published little on developments in Washington. But with the approach of the war in Iraq, anxieties that the White House was discarding tried and tested formulae for the exercise of American power through the Security Council began to mount – albeit initially without questioning the existence of weapons of mass destruction in Iraq or the urgent need to take action of some

13. Compare successive articles by Lars-Erik Nelson, Ronald Dworkin, and Anthony Lewis: *NYRB*, 20 January, 9 March, 13 April 2000, with Stephen Holmes, Martin Jay and David Simpson: *LRB*, 18 March 1999, 29 July 1999, 23 September 2004.

kind against Saddam Hussein.[14] When the war was launched, criticism of Bush's departure from US traditions of multilateralism increased. But it was only after Iraqi resistance had started to inflict serious damage on the occupation that the tone of its coverage sharply altered. From the autumn of 2003 onwards, the *NYRB* rediscovered a *tranchant* it had not known since the sixties, not only attacking the institutionalization of torture under Bush, but the Administration's policies across the board, to great effect.[15] Such a no-holds-barred assault on the Bush regime, unaccompanied by much sign of enthusiasm for Kerry's candidacy, did not in itself differ significantly from the *LRB*'s attitude towards the Administration. But in London, Bush could act as a lightning-conductor away from Blair, whose treatment by the *London Review* remained noticeably milder. By the time of the 2005 elections, the balance-sheet of Blair's rule was certainly found wanting; but in tones of disappointment more than disgust. Even after the invasion of Iraq, *LRB* contributors were still regularly praising the personality of Britain's new ruler before venturing to disagree with his policies, as if to indemnify themselves for disloyalty to Labour with a novel style of criticism, more in admiration than in anger.[16] Here too the rise of the Iraqi resistance, and collapse of the myth of weapons of mass destruction, produced a shift. But it was not until the autumn of 2003 that a writer, not from a Labour but SDP background, could be found to call timidly – after regulation bouquets – for Blair's resignation.[17] Even the paper's finest

14. See Michael Ignatieff, 'Bush's First Strike', 9 March 2001; Brian Urquhart, 'The Prospect of War', 15 November 2001; Michael Walzer, 'The Right Way', 13 March 2003. *LRB* coverage of the run-up to the war was much firmer than this: compare, in its pages, Charles Glass, 'Iraq Must Go!', 3 October 2002; Norman Dombey, 'What has he got?', 17 October 2002; Edward Said, 'The Academy of Lagado', 17 April 2003.

15. The most remarkable example has certainly been Chris Hedges, 'On War', 16 December 2004; the most persistent critic, Mark Danner: 'Torture and the Truth', 'The Logic of Torture', 'Abu Ghraib: The Hidden Story', 'The Secret Way to War', 10 June, 24 June and 7 October 2004, 9 June 2005.

16. Examples of this genre include: Conor Gearty, 'How did Blair get here?', Ross McKibbin, 'Why did he risk it?', John Lanchester, 'Unbelievable Blair': *LRB*, 20 February, 3 April, 10 July. The opening sentence of the first reads: 'Tony Blair is the most successful politician of his generation'; that of the second: 'Whether or not we agree with it, there was always a plausible argument for intervention in Iraq'; the third declares: 'I thought Blair was *au fond* a good thing'.

17. Peter Clarke, 'Blair Must Go': 11 September 2003, which begins: 'There is a very good case for Tony Blair's handling of the Iraq issue. His critics never sufficiently acknowledged his efforts to play a difficult hand in a difficult game. He is nobody's poodle. It was wise, rather than naïve, not to isolate the Americans ...'

pieces on domestic questions, such as Stefan Collini's landmark essay on the hypocrisies and confusions surrounding educational reform,[18] have approached the government itself rather gingerly. In no way an ornament of the regime, the *LRB* has to date not been much of a thorn in its flesh either. There is no mistaking the contrast with its role under Thatcher.

In part, the reasons are clear enough, and have lain less in the journal itself than in its setting. In British political conditions, the reflexes of a two-party system run deep. Disaffection with Labourism is readily checked by apprehension at Conservatism, in a spirit of clinging to nurse for fear of something worse, even should the former enact legislation to which the latter dared not proceed. The parochialism of much local writing on politics, more at home with tax brackets or gambling laws in the UK than with Balkan or Middle Eastern affairs, reinforces such tribal instincts, in which parties often command a life-time allegiance no matter what they do, as if they were football clubs rather political organizations. To these circumstances can be added the captivation of much liberal opinion in Britain with the boyish figure of Blair, who long attracted the same kind of *Schwärmerei* that surrounded Kennedy in the USA – in both cases, a crush capable of surviving even political disillusion. Such humours undoubtedly made it difficult for the *LRB* to find political writing of greater mordancy or distinction than it succeeded in mustering; whether impossible is more moot. What is clear is that, paradoxically, one of its greatest virtues – its reluctance to interfere with the opinions of an author – also made it likely to reflect rather than contest the prevailing moods among the British intelligentsia, once New Labour was entrenched. Even now, the severest verdicts to be found in leading articles of the journal continue to be tempered by hope of better to come – social reforms under Brown as consolation for military adventures under Blair: as if after Kennedy, relief will come from a cleaner Johnson.[19] The paper has so far desisted from any reconsideration of Labourism as a political culture, in its old or new guises.

That this pattern has occurred more by default than intention is suggested by the contrast between the *LRB*'s own editorial voice, rarely heard and discreetly used, and the tones surrounding it in the liberal media at large. There, Blair was fawned on by political com-

---

18. 'HiEdBiz', 6 November 2003.

19. 'Most of the achievements of this government have been Brown's. Most of the mistakes have been Blair's. All in all, it is Brown I would like to vote for': David Runciman, 21 April 2005.

mentators and editorialists with a lack of restraint that has no precedent in post-war British politics.[20] With this degree of abasement, the *LRB* had no truck. Little is more revealing of the period atmosphere than the outcry when it declined to publish a specimen of this literature. [21] This gesture by Mary-Kay Wilmers, setting a political limit, in due course found its counterpart in a series of savage interjections on the war regime of New Labour by its consulting editor, John Sturrock, inconspicuously situated in a box reserved for personal commentaries.[22] Moreover, on occasions where there has been the chance of more radical publication than the run of domestic articles, the *LRB* has known how to take it. Its famous symposium on September 11, breaking away from the avalanche of piety and hysteria that rapidly covered the attacks on the World Trade Centre and the Pentagon, was a notable act of audacity and imagination that could only have been performed by the *London Review*.[23] Likewise, Eliot

---

20. For a florilegium, see Susan Watkins, 'A Weightless Hegemony', *New Left Review* No 25, January–February 2004, the best comparative analysis of New Labour to date.

21. The piece in question, 'The Liberal Nation' written by David Marquand, was gratefully published in *Prospect,* February 2002: Typical passages: 'Blair's handling of the post-11th September crisis was impeccable. His speech to the Labour conference was the most impressive delivered by a serving British Prime since Winston Churchill ... He was not, of course, the main architect of the anti-Bin-Laden coalition but it is hard to believe it could have been built without him... He showed that a British prime minister with the right mixture of courage, grace and forensic skill could still play a significant, outward-looking, internationalist geopolitical role ... His first big test will come over the euro. The signs are that he thinks he can win an early (or fairly early) referendum. I think he is right, but victory will not come by fudging. To win, Blair will have to play the same liberal-patriotic card that he played at the Labour Party conference ... If he succeeds, and the odds on his doing so are better than even, he will dominate politics at home as no prime minister has done since Mrs Thatcher in her glory days. For good measure, he will also be the strongest head of government in the EU ...' Two years later, the same author was writing of the same paragon, in the same venue: 'It was Blair who led Britain into war, not the joint intelligence committee. He helped inflict dreadful damage on the UN, poisoned our relations with the two core states of the EU, and split the Labour party' (*Prospect*, February 2004). Today, he might well be ruefully reflecting that he would have done better to accept the verdict of the *LRB* and hold his tongue.

22. See 'Short-Cuts', 17 April, 19 June, 7 August 2003, 6 November 2003; 21 July 2005.

23. 'Reflections on 9/11', 4 October 2001. The *New York Review* rarely acknowledges the existence of the *London Review*, but on this occasion it was moved to deprecate the most powerful of the contributions to this symposium: see Tony Judt, 'America and the War', 15 November 2001. Its own symposium on the US elections of 2004, the nearest equivalent in New York, was certainly oppositional, but otherwise quite conventional: 'The Election and America's Future', 4 November 2004.

Weinberger's 'What I heard about Iraq' in the spirit of Karl Kraus, Ed Harriman's 'On the Take in Iraq', exposing the scale of the looting of the country by the Coalition Provisional Authority, Patrick Cockburn's successive dispatches on the American occupation zone, have been interventions whose tenor stands out sharply in the now extensive critical literature on today's Mesopotamian campaign.[24] It is difficult to imagine any of these particular forms appearing in the *New York Review*. Still less the consistency with which the *LRB* has refused to let standard euphemisms and evasions cover the realities of Israeli expropriations and expulsions in the West Bank, or the hypocrisies of successive 'road maps' to the final subjugation of Palestinian resistance. There the voice of Edward Said alone, heard time after time in the *London Review* as nowhere else in the West, made the journal irreplaceable. Israeli dissidents and Palestinian activists have made their own signal contributions too. It is fair to say that the *LRB*'s record in this uniquely explosive area is without parallel in the Atlantic world. That its commitment to the cause of Palestinian Arabs has never been separated from remembrance of the fate of European Jews ought to go without saying. Thomas Laqueur's 'Sound of Voices Intoning Names',[25] on the children deported from France, is one of the most haunting reflections on their annihilation ever written.

In these years the geographical range of the paper widened considerably, earlier watermarks fading in a stronger international light. Japan, Nigeria, Guatemala, Syria, Nepal, Sudan, North Korea, Haiti – articles on these would have been less likely in the past; often, too, less sharp-eyed. There is still a major difference between the *NYRB* and *LRB* here, coverage in the former continuing to be more driven by topicality of the region, in the latter by quality of the report. The outlook of pieces in the *London Review* typically remains less conventional, although as before this is not guaranteed: aberrations – praise for American counter-insurgency in Colombia, blame for Chechen separatism from Russia – now and then still crop up. But overall, readers of the *LRB* can expect tarter fare, from a global menu that is more variegated, than a decade ago.

The electric international setting of the last few years has put the political record of journals like the *LRB* or *NYRB* in unusually high relief. But these remain journals in which public affairs, traditionally

---

24. Respectively, 3 February 2005, 7 July 2005, and from 24 July 2003 onwards.
25. 5 June 1997.

understood, occupy less space than arts and letters: perhaps a fifth of contributions to the *LRB*, under a third for the *NYRB*. What of the cultural record over the same period? Taking the Thatcher years as a base-line, literary articles in the *London Review* could be said to have moved in the opposite direction to those on domestic politics. Where the latter lost edge under New Labour, the former gained it. In the hands of James Wood, Christopher Tayler and Theo Tait, treatment of contemporary fiction became noticeably brisker. Writing by headline names like Amis, Barnes or Boyd, not to speak of younger camp-followers of ethnic or multi-cultural fashion, has come to enjoy less immunity than elsewhere in literary London. By more stringent standards, it is true, such criticism still remains quite circumspect. Older gargoyles of the prize circuit – Naipaul, Roth, Bellow – continue to be overpraised, and punches are frequently pulled at the end of even the most damaging notices of less venerable figures. Where pieces on domestic politics offer propitiatory compliments to the rulers of the country, before lodging temperate complaints against them, reviews of fashionable fiction tend to reverse the procedure, delivering judgements apparently ruinous to the work in hand, only to back-track with some *pro forma* bowing and scraping in the final paragraph.

The pressure of a too close milieu of metropolitan letters, in which ambitions and favours are continually forced together, can often be sensed in such sheepish retractions. The *NYRB* remains, of course, for the most part much kinder than this to the fiction it reviews, often by writers who appear in its own pages. But the liberation that distance can bring has on occasion allowed it to produce the kind of criticism of English fiction that continues to be missing in the *LRB*. A comparison of the reception given by the two journals to such a prime confection as Ian McEwan's latest novel should make Little Russell Street blush.[26] It is true that assessing contemporary literature is always the least grateful, and least disinterested, task of criticism. Where classical texts of the past are concerned, the *London Review* operates at a different level. There, essays like those of Michael Wood on James or Neruda speak for themselves.

In the other arts, the palette has broadened. Cinema, freed from studio releases, can now accommodate Godard – twice, even – and Kiarostami, alongside Stroheim, Welles, Buñuel. The architectural scene has been opened up to the wonderful dry eye of Hal Foster, a

---

26. See Christopher Tayler: *LRB*, 3 March 2005 vs John Banville: *NYRB*, 26 May 2005.

critic not just of buildings, but of contemporary visual arts, currently without equal for wit and range. Music remains notably under-represented, in contrast to the *NYRB*. In compensation, readers can find more poetry, by a less consecrated range of names, than in New York. Theory? A dutiful diet of analytical philosophy, and its bland political side-dishes, in an Anglo-American continuum from Yale to Cambridge, in both journals. In the *LRB*, however, there is far less closure. Where else could one find such alternative delights as Slavoj Žižek on Habermas's fear of cloning, Malcolm Bull on Agamben's state of exception, or T.J. Clark on the passion of Walter Benjamin – 'the Fabrizio del Dongo of Marxism' – for the Parisian arcades?[27]

In the sciences, where a decade ago the superiority of the *NYRB* was enormous, today the advantage, if anything, lies with the *LRB*. No change in the journal has been so impressive as this. Debates in evolutionary biology, in the history of earth, over the genome, the ice-cap, nuclear technology, the new pandemics: on all of these it has published compelling contributions, in which technical authority and personal expression sit easily together, without the rank-pulling of laureates or the bravado of performance artists in popularization. In this quiet widening of its intellectual span lies a major transformation of the paper.

But what perhaps in the end best defines the *LRB* of this period is the extraordinary sequence of autobiographical writing it has pub-lished these years. Typically longer than the average article, these star-bursts of life and memory have given the journal a register pecu-liarly its own. By what alchemy it has attracted them – such texts are beyond commission – is inscrutable. One can only say that their appearance in its pages is an objective homage to the spirit of the paper. David Sylvester's recapture of a Jewish childhood in Hackney; Richard Wollheim's strange *pointillisme* of his younger self; Wynne Godley's sensational switchback of mother and analyst; Jeremy Harding's deadpan tale of adoption[28] – the list of such *tours de force* could be extended. Here, one might say, can be found something like the core sensibility of the journal, from which everything else indirectly radiates.

2005

27. Respectively 22 May 2003, 16 December 2004 and 22 June 2000.

28. 5 July 2001; 15 April and 20 May 2004; 22 February 2001; 31 March 2005. Some would add Terry Castle, 'Desperately Seeking Susan', 17 March 2005.

2

AN ANGLO-IRISHMAN IN CHINA:
J.C. O'G. Anderson

The range of emotions parents can arouse in their children – affection, rebellion, indifference, fear, adulation, their disturbing combinations – suggest a repertory of subjective universals, cutting in each individual case at random across cultures. What children know – as opposed to feel – about their parents, on the other hand, is likely to be a function of objective constraints that vary more systematically: tradition, place, life-span. Is there an unalterable core, of *pudeur* or incomprehension, even here? That is less clear. In the American tropics, gaps of scarcely more than a dozen years between generations, not uncommon, can create an easy sibling intimacy between mother and child, grown up, difficult to imagine in the North.

At the opposite pole, my father was forty-three when his first child, my brother Benedict, was born. He died ten years later, when I was eight. But in his last years he was sufficiently ill for my mother to think it best to get us away to boarding school. Here the brevity of biological overlap was further reduced by social decision. My mother's motive was compassion, but her solution suggests a filter that might in any event have dropped between father and children, had he survived. The distance in years, and the scission of death, were sealed by a culture anyway marked by reticence. There was nothing unusual in such circumstances. A child of them was bound to know little of their father.

In our family, however, a further shutter fell across his memory. He had passed his life thousands of miles away from Ireland, where he ended and we grew up, in a China that ceased to exist as soon as he was gone. We knew he had worked there as a Customs Commissioner, but had little idea of what that might mean. In his last months, sitting by the fire in the damp Irish nights, he liked to tell us boys – my sister

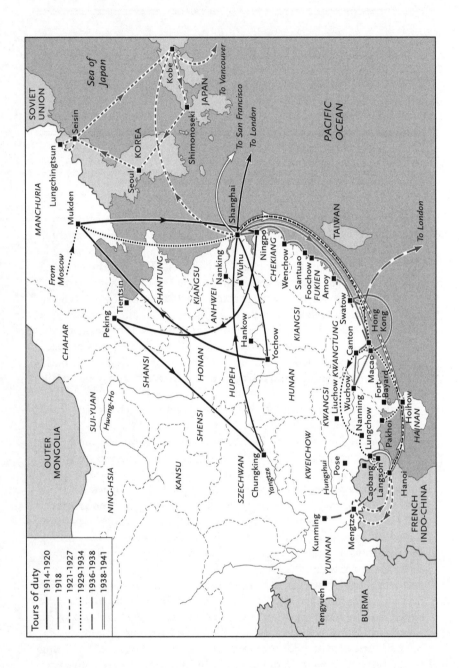

Tours of duty
1914–1920
1918
1921–1927
1929–1934
1936–1938
1938–1941

SOVIET UNION

Sea of Japan

MANCHURIA

Lungchingtsun

Mukden

From Moscow

OUTER MONGOLIA

CHAHAR

SUI-YUAN

Hwang-Ho

NING-HSIA

KANSU

SHENSI

SHANSI

HONAN

SHANTUNG

KIANGSU

Nanking

ANHWEI

Wuhu

HUPEH

Hankow

Yochow

HUNAN

KIANGSI

CHEKIANG

Wenchow

Santuao

Foochow

FUKIEN

Amoy

Swatow

KWANGTUNG

Canton

Macao

Hong Kong

Fort Bayard

Hoihow

HAINAN

Pakhoi

Lungchow

Nanning

KWANGSI

Liuchow

Wuchow

KWEICHOW

Pose

Hungshui

YUNNAN

Kunming

Tengyueh

BURMA

Mengtze

Hanoi

FRENCH INDO-CHINA

Langson

Caobang

Yangtze

SZECHWAN

Chungking

Peking

Tientsin

Seisin

Seoul

KOREA

Shimonoseki

Kobe

JAPAN

To Vancouver

To San Francisco

To London

Shanghai

Ningpo

TAIWAN

PACIFIC OCEAN

To London

Hanoi

was too young to listen – anecdotes about Parnell, whom he admired; and tales of junks and pirates, in which he escaped from brigands or captured prizes. Such images were too vivid to last, their over-bright tints fading into the dimness of nursery-stories that adolescents, with more impatience than condescension, put behind them – rather like the revolver I briefly discovered in a drawer one idle afternoon, whose weight surprised me, before my mother caught me and got rid of it.

Once these legends had receded, we were left with a world of objects, familiar and incomprehensible, recalling a past to which we otherwise had no relation: large buff tea chests, stamped with ideograms, still lined – is this a trick of memory? – with Chinese newspapers; dusty books and papers, with Chinese characters on the back, in the glass-case in the hall; a celadon lamp, yellow rug, small dark teapot; blue saddle-cloths my mother used to veil her television set; framed paintings of black-hatted sages, silk scrolls of ladies under parasols, a horse rolling on its back by a stream. As a resolutely philistine teenager, I had no time for any of these. Even the great broad-shouldered tiger, glowering magnificently down on us in the dining-room – a copy of a well-known Ming original, so one was later led to believe – made scarcely any conscious impression on me. Only the *Ch'ing Ping M'ei*, a domesticated version of the original, but at fifteen sexually electric enough, in an azure Shanghai binding of the thirties, caught my imagination. By the time I got out of university, associations with China were like faded scraps of wallpaper in a house one wished to forget, the Ireland of the Meet and the Mass of that time. 'Customs' conjured up only the local caitiffs of a seedy clericalism, peering at books on the quay-side to see if they were on a blacklist based on the Papal Index.

My mother, of course, could have told us more. But even as adults, something held us back from asking. She once commented on our lack of curiosity, but was too tactful ever to impose the topic. There were the family photograph albums of Kunming, where my brother was born, Swatow where I was conceived, later our house in Shanghai.* But there was little reference to all this. Why did she not volunteer more? In part, because of her own attitude to life – she had an unusual gift for making the best of the present: I often thought she became younger and more lively, the older she got. Her marriage to

---

* All place and proper names in what follows are in the Wade-Giles transcription, standard in documents of the time, not in contemporary pinyin. Swatow is today's Shantou.

my father had been a success. Then she had nursed him in his long illness. By temperament she had little inclination to look back, unless we invited her to. There was perhaps another element as well. She lived three years with my father in China before the Pacific War. But he had already lived there over twenty, and been married for a decade to another woman, the writer Stella Benson, whose novels stood preserved and largely unread on our bookshelves. My mother would have been aware of the limits to her knowledge of this other Chinese life.

After her death in 1933, my father deposited Stella's diaries in the University Library in Cambridge, not to be read for fifty years. When they became available, a fine biography of her was quickly produced, based on them.[1] My mother told the biographer, Joy Grant, what she knew of her husband's earlier life; but she, and we, learnt far more from it. The biography offers a sympathetic portrait of my father. But, drawn from the diaries of a writer who was remarkably honest, but also unusually introspective, it is confined essentially to the marital relationship – which is certainly striking enough. The journals, revealing in many other ways, are notably incurious about my father's work, while his experience in China before they met in 1920 remains a blank.

About this time, at the turn of the nineties, my attitude changed. No one teaching in Los Angeles could fail to feel the force of the Italian adage of the sixties: *la Cina é vicina*. With some of the best historians of China in the world on campus, and students from every part of the Far East, it was difficult not to wonder more about the family connection. By now a substantial amount of scholarship had appeared on the mysterious organization for which my father had worked, the Chinese Maritime Customs. But this work, much of it from the distinguished hand of John Fairbank, was mostly concerned with the nineteenth-century origins of the institution, shedding less light on modern times. For its more recent history, it was not even very clear where the records lay: the best contemporary guide to Chinese archives, produced in 1996, gives no indication.[2]

Last summer, enquiries through my brother established that the files I was looking for would be held in Nanking, though permission to consult them was by no means certain. The chance of a conference taking me to China, in due course I made my way to Nanking. The

1. Joy Grant, *Stella Benson. A Biography*, London 1987.
2. See Ye Wa and Joseph Esherick, *Chinese Archives: An Introductory Guide*, Berkeley 1996.

Second National Archive, which in principle covers central documentation of the Republican period (1911–49), is housed in a large
structure set back from the road, fronted by a traditional gaudily-
painted gate and a tilted-roof mansion put up by the Kuomintang not
long before the city was stormed by the Japanese in 1937. Nanking is
famous as one of the 'four furnaces' of China, and in that season the
reading room was largely deserted. Filial respect is understood in
China, and the staff were friendly and willing to help. But they were
not sanguine. The Customs archive, they pointed out, contained
57,000 volumes, and there was no detailed catalogue: where were they
to start? I suggested looking for reports from the province of Yunnan
for 1936, when my father was Commissioner there.

Within half a hour, I had his dispatches from Kunming in front of
me. The sensation of belated encounter was overwhelming, mixed
with a kind of awe. For I was looking, not only at the workings of the
life that lay behind mine, but at one of the most immaculate set of
records in the world. I don't know what I had expected to find, but
not quite this. Communications between the field stations – 'ports',
including inland as well as coastal cities – and headquarters of the
Customs were bound in red or black leather volumes, with gold-block
lettering, every year. Inside, dispatches and correspondence, in meticulous sequence, are as crisp and clear as when first typed; in their
margins, the handwritten comments of an indefatigable Inspector-
General and his assistants, or instructions for reply. Three separate
categories of communications were transmitted each month, and filed
and bound in different formats: Official Correspondence, covering
regular administrative business; Semi-Official, reporting political and
military developments in the area; and Confidential, for the most sensitive material to do with leaders, powers, wars.[3] These were, in
effect, the memorials of a state within a state. Across two decades, I
could follow my father's path within it, as he moved in orbit round
China.

Back in Europe, a few months later my sister mentioned that cousins
in Ireland had some old photographs and possibly documents about
our grandfather, who died in 1920 – known to be in charge of Army
cryptography at the beginning of the First World War, but otherwise a
shadowy figure – in the attic of a disused mill. Mildly intrigued by the
idea, I went to see them. There, instead, to my astonishment I was

---

3. The latter appear to have started in 1939, if the indications of a still approximate catalogue are to be accepted.

shown a suitcase of letters from his son, covering the entire span from his departure to China to his death in Ireland over forty years later. Addressed to his mother, aunt and sister, they must have been casually stuffed in drawers, without order or afterthought, many no less casually mislaid or thrown aside. Though no sequence is complete, no major period is missing; with all the reservations that attach to family correspondence of this kind – the immemorial censorship of sons writing to mothers – a more or less continuous frieze of my father's life, especially revealing of his early years, can be pieced together. The letters near Cahir could be regarded as a fourth series of reports – Personal – complementing, or offsetting, the three stored in Nanking.

They start on 19 July 1914, three days before my father's twenty-first birthday, as a passenger on the S.S. *Morea*, passing Stromboli in eruption en route to Suez. By the time he reached Colombo on 2 August, England was on the brink of war – 'two battleships in harbour and 25-mile searchlights playing'.[4] Hostilities broke out before he got to Penang, where he found 'the Straits are afraid of a Chinese rising' and the grounds of the colonial club already fortified.[5] Travelling without lights at night, the *Morea* made its way to Hong Kong, where after a few days he sailed north again on a mail-boat. Arriving in Shanghai in the last week of August, he was sent at a few hours' notice eight hundred miles up the Yangtze to a port deep in Hunan, to begin his career in the Customs. Why had he come to China? After a year as classical exhibitioner in Cambridge, neglecting or scorning his curriculum, he had failed his first-years exams. Outraged by this nonchalance, his father, a martinet, refused to let him sit them again, cutting off financial support. His uncle, another and more senior general, who had once commanded the garrison in Hong Kong, no doubt recommended him for service in the Maritime Customs. Academic grief was actuarial good luck. Gazetted into his future employment just before the outbreak of war, and issued with an 'outfit allowance' of £100, he was contractually bound to five years service in China. Unable to secure his release to participate in the slaughter in Europe, he escaped the fate of his younger brother, the apple of his parents' eye, killed in the last months of fighting. This death finished off his father. He had punished the wrong son.

The institution in which the young J.C. O'G. Anderson took up his post in 1914 had been in existence for nearly fifty years. By then it had

---

4. Letters: 3 August 1914. Henceforward L.
5. L: 7 August 1914.

no parallel anywhere else in the world. Its origins lay in the crisis of the Ch'ing Empire in the mid-nineteenth century, when the Taiping Rebellion gave a Western coalition, led by Britain, the chance to force a 'Treaty system' on the beleaguered dynasty, subjecting China to full commercial penetration. The immediate background to the creation of the Imperial Chinese Maritime Customs Service was the Anglo-French expedition to Peking, culminating in the burning of the Summer Palace, of 1860. Once brought to heel by force of arms, the recalcitrant Ch'ing state needed to be propped up against the threat of the Taiping insurrection in the Yangtze delta, with its menacing attitudes to private property and the opium trade. A new Customs Inspectorate, answerable to Peking but staffed by foreigners, would enforce the remarkably advantageous tariff system imposed on the dynasty, fixing a ceiling on import dues at 5 per cent *ad valorem*, and provide it with the steady revenues required to pay off the Anglo-French indemnity and finance military victory over the Taiping.[6]

From these beginnings, an extraordinary financial and quasi-political realm was built. Its architect, Robert Hart, was just twenty-eight when he became Inspector-General in 1863. Rapidly winning the confidence of the Chi'ng court, he gradually created the first modern administrative system in China. Its core was a fiscal bureaucracy that assured the late imperial state of a third of its revenue, and whose probity and efficiency extended into many other operations besides tax collection. It ran the postal service, managed waterways, improved harbours and planted lighthouses, established statistical services. Hart, a close confidante of the Empress Dowager, organized overseas missions, advised on diplomatic affairs, mediated in international conflicts. Theoretically, he owed his position to Britain's leading position in China's trade; in practice to its all-round imperial leverage in the region. Eventually London pressed him to become the British Ambassador in Peking.

But this was a role Hart rejected. Far from being any mere majordomo for foreign interests, he regarded himself as a loyal servant of the Chinese government, and was quite capable of cracking down on malpractices by Western merchants, pursuing law-suits against the British

---

6. For Fairbank, the creation of the Inspectorate fell into a long tradition, from Northern Wei through to Ch'ing times, of 'synarchy' – Chinese submission to, or employment of, foreigners for administration of the country,: a notion first mooted in *Trade and Diplomacy on the China Coast, 1842–1854*, Cambridge, Mass., 1953, pp. 464–468, and then developed in 'Synarchy under the Treaties', in John Fairbank (ed.), *Chinese Thought and Institutions*, Chicago 1957, pp. 204–231.

government, and crossing the Foreign Office when he saw fit. Imperial China remained an independent state, and he was committed to a conservative modernization of it, even if he ultimately came to fear that the dynasty might prove unreformable. His insistence on the autonomy of the Customs from the Western powers that had brought it into being, and the integrity of its allegiance to China was not simply disinterested, however. Hart's personal position depended crucially on dissociation from his parent state. He could never have wielded the same influence in the Forbidden City had he been a catspaw of Disraeli or Salisbury. But this sovereign role depended in turn on the extraordinary character of the organization under his control.

For the Chinese Maritime Customs was recruited, not just from candidates from Britain, but from all the major external powers of the day: French, Germans, Austrians, Italians, Russians, Americans, Japanese – not to speak of the lesser European states: Portuguese, Spaniards, Dutch, Belgians, Danes, Swedes, Norwegians. The stately Service Lists of the CMC, denominating the country of origin, as well as rank and posting, of every member of the organization – veritable works of bureaucratic art – offer a regular tableau of this international composition. If the British easily predominated, with over half the executive 'indoor staff', and English was the working language, Hart was always careful to balance his countrymen with other nationalities, whose education and talent he on occasion claimed were superior.

In effect, the Customs was an inter-imperialist consortium – comparable only to the Ottoman Public Debt Administration, set up as a tax-collecting apparatus run by foreigners for the Porte a couple of decades later. Both owed their form to a stand-off between predators. The rival Great Powers, jealously watching each other's manoeuvres, could not agree on a carve-up of either the Turkish or Chinese empires, settling instead for an indirect collective instrument to secure at least assorted indemnities and loans. The Ottoman institution, however, was not only more short-lived (1881–1918), but never employed so many Europeans, because it could rely on Greek or Armenian subjects of the Sultan for key posts.[7] Perched atop a more cosmopolitan pyramid, Hart had wide freedom of action to conduct affairs as he wished, and shape the Customs in his image. He had come from a modest background in Ulster, straight from Queen's to

---

7. For particulars, see Donald Quataert, 'The Employment Policies of the Ottoman Public Debt Administration 1881–1909', Festschrift für Andreas Tietze, *Wiener Zeitschrift für die Kunde des Morgenlandes*, Bd 76, 1986, pp. 233–237.

China. In power, he would not neglect kith and kin. He favoured his brother to succeed him, and when the latter died prematurely, plumped for his brother-in-law, Robert Bredon, another Ulsterman.

But here the Foreign Office was not keen, and he had to settle for Francis Aglen, the son of his best friend at school, whom he had installed as Commissioner in Canton – the port where he had himself started. Even from the grave, his nepotism lived on. Aglen was briefly succeeded by another Irishman, Arthur Edwardes, who was followed in turn by Hart's nephew, naturally also from Ulster, Frederick Maze. For the eighty years of its splendour, the Customs – forcing-house of administrative modernity – was in this respect run as a patrimonial bureaucracy. There were no formal criteria for recruitment, no real rules of promotion, no regularity or predictability of postings. The Inspector-General was an autocrat within his realm, answerable to no one. The indoor staff were rotated round the country at will, with a rhythm more rapid than Chinese magistrates had ever been, even under those dynasties most determined to prevent them forming local connections (a traditional preoccupation). Over time, this mobility intensified. In the twentieth century, it is doubtful how many CCP cadres, at the height of the party's mobilizing power, had careers of quite such geographical range.

The contrast with the stability of provincial assignments in the Indian Civil Service, with which contemporaries often compared the Customs, is striking. This had something to do with the diversity of Indian languages, which discouraged transfers once a local idiom was acquired, as opposed to the territorial uniformity of written Chinese; but also with more conventional forms of hierarchy. On the other hand, the Customs indoor corps was an elite with salaries and accoutrements not unlike those of their Indian counterparts: aspects impressing the young Maurice Bowra, on a visit to his father – Chief Secretary of the CMC – in 1916 ('life in Peking afforded comforts such as I had never known before and have never known since').[8] In 1914 there were only 321 foreigners on the indoor staff, out of a total personnel of some 7,600; new recruits got a starting salary of 1,500 haekwan taels a year – equivalent to about $2,250.

In 1911, with admirable timing, Hart died. Three months later, the Ch'ing Empire collapsed. But the Revolution of 1911 proved quite unable to create a unitary republic, disintegrating into a checkerboard of warlord regimes instead. In these conditions of endemic confusion

---

8. Maurice Bowra, *Memories 1898–1939*, London 1967, p. 49.

and division, Aglen – who personally never enjoyed anything approaching Hart's authority with any Chinese government – paradoxically gained even greater institutional power in Peking than his predecessor. Whereas in Hart's day, the foreign inspectorate had assessed customs dues that were actually collected by Chinese superintendents, for transmission to the central state and provincial authorities, from 1912 onwards revenues were directly collected by the CMC itself, and deposited in three 'custodian' banks – British, Russian and German – which held them for the CMC as security against foreign loans, only disbursing funds to regimes in Peking on the nod of the Inspector-General and the Diplomatic Corps. With this fiscal strangehold on the cliques competing for power in North China, the Customs would indeed become, as Aglen himself confidentially put it, an *imperium in imperio*.[9] Since 1913, the foreign powers had been backing the bid of the former Ch'ing commander Yuan Shih-k'ai to establish himself as China's new strongman against opponents, mostly associated with Sun Yat-sen's Kuomintang, whose strongholds lay in the south of the country.

Such was the scene when my father arrived in China, with only the sketchiest idea of what was in store for him. Making his way down the Yangtse – at a stop-off in Hankow, the Russian consul took him to the races – he arrived a week later at the small customs station outside Yochow in northern Hunan, where the Siang river, flowing through the vast Tung-ting lake joins the Yangtse.[10] Here, extremely lonely, he learnt basic procedures, and got his first lessons in Chinese. At this isolated outpost, futile shooting expeditions in the marshes on the opposite bank and dinners on a stranded French gunboat were virtually the only distraction.[11] But from the hill-tops above the river, the customs detachment overlooked an encampment of soldiers dis-

---

9. Aglen to Acheson, 28 February 1922: Aglen Papers. The potential risks involved in the shift from assessment to collection of revenues were noted by Leonard Lyall, a senior official in the Customs under Hart, in his reflective *China*, London 1934, pp. 280–286.

10. Yochow, today's Yuehyang, was picked by Hart in 1899 to be the first example of a 'self-opened' port – i.e. one that China, in theory, voluntarily made available to foreigners. His intention was to promote the commercial penetration of Hunan. But since there was little need for river traffic between Hankow and Changsha to stop at Yochow, his choice was ill-judged. For the way the CMC station was set up, see: John Fairbank, Martha Coolidge and Richard Smith, *H.B. Morse. Customs Commissioner and Historian of China*, Lexington 1995, pp. 145–161.

11. 'No pony no piano no dog and in the summer no ice! Swish!' L: undated, spring 1915.

patched by Yuan Shih-k'ai to hold the province – '15,000 men to keep down revolutionists in Hunan'. After dark, he reported home, 'unless you carry a light, the soldiers are liable to shoot you at sight, as they afraid of a rebel force entering the province, and the place is full of patrols and pickets'.[12] On the river itself, troop transports were on the move in both directions. It was an introduction to warlord China. Apparently quiet and studious, he earned the liking of the local Commissioner, a red-beared Scot, who regretted losing him when nine months later orders came for his transfer.[13] In April 1915, he was instructed to travel to Mukden for intensive instruction in Chinese at the Customs School set up to train new recruits in the language. Under Aglen, for the first time, advancement in the service above a certain level depended on passing a series of examinations in written and spoken Chinese, that stretched over nearly a decade.

Situated in a hamlet outside the city, the school itself was dull in setting. But here at least a twenty-one-year-old was among contemporaries, in company preferable to the solitude of Yochow. Manchuria, then falling under the control of Chang Tso-lin, the former bandit who would become the ruler of the region soon afterwards, was much quieter than Hunan. Even so, shock-waves from the rest of the country could be felt. My father arrived in Mukden just as the news of Yuan Shih-k'ai's surrender to Japanese pressure for sweeping territorial and economic concessions in China – the famous Twenty-One Demands – led to uproar across the country. 'No real trouble over the Sino-Japanese question', he wrote to his sister, 'though both Chinese and Japs here had fortified their respective parts of the village.'[14] In the school, instruction was from nine to three every day, exams every month. Once winter arrived, the main recreation was ice-hockey, to which he took with enthusiasm.[15]

---

12. L: Undated, September 1914; 22 January 1915. For the scale of Yuan's repressions in the province, see Ernest P. Young, *The Presidency of Yuan Shih-K'ai*, Ann Arbor 1977.

13. CMC 32130: R.A. Currie to Aglen, 9 September 1914, 12 April and 27 April 1915 – dispatches ending: 'Twenty-nine junks full of soldiers have gone down to Lin-hsiang during the month, from Changsha and other places above Yochow, and a similar number have passed up from Hankow to Changsha.'

14. L: 29 May 1915.

15. 'I do nothing except work, read and ice-hockey, which is a great game ... The last time we played mixed I had really got a move on with the puck when I collided into a Miss Moorhead, sat on her, and slid at least ten yards sitting on her!' L: 20 February 1916.

A group photograph of the period shows him reclining at the bottom of a pyramid of young trainees, dashing with monocle, moustache and cigarette. But he was evidently diligent. By October, the Commissioner in charge of the school, after describing a dinner with the Governor of the province and Chang Tso-lin – 'the latter has lost none of his ambition while he has added nothing to his education so defective from the Chinese standard' – was reporting to Aglen that 'there has been no student at the school yet whose capacity, aptitude for work, and progress have equalled Mr Anderson's'.[16]

After just under a year in Mukden, his course completed, my father was posted south in the spring of 1916, to the river port of Ningpo, fourteen miles inland from the coast in Chekiang, close to Chiang Kai-shek's birthplace. The inter-imperial character of the Customs was still untouched by the European conflict, and nationals from belligerent countries continued to work side by side. While his brother was fighting the Imperial Army in Picardy, he found himself filing reports to a German chief, whose only drawback was a touch of amiable *Schlamperei*. The small foreign community – forty-five strong – all lived on the miniature Bund along the river: 'from my verandah I can see ships and junks passing sometimes only 20 yards away'. The summer was sweltering, but trips up-river by houseboat made pleasant weekends. By now Yuan Shih-k'ai, after an abortive attempt to enthrone himself as Emperor, abandoned in the face of widespread revolt, was tottering. Within a week of arriving in Ningpo, my father was writing: 'The province we are in, Chekiang, has joined the revolutionary party and there has been a little fighting inland, but we are quite safe here as we have guarantees from both sides. I have just come back from Shanghai where I went at Service expense to carry dispatches as the rebels are opening all Chinese mail.'[17] Six weeks later, Yuan – about to seek refuge in the American legation – was dead. In Ningpo, my father went down with successive bouts of dengue fever, but still passed his critical Chinese exams in the autumn. In the spring of 1917, when China was finally cajoled into breaking off diplomatic relations with the Central Powers, German and Austrian staff of the CMC were sent home. There was little time to settle down under a new commissioner. In the first week of June, he was transferred to the CMC headquarters in Peking.

---

16. CMC 31910: Moorhead to Aglen, 23 October 1915. Six months later: 'As regards getting a real grip on the language he showed I think more power than any previous student': 12 April 1916.

17. L: 20 April 1916.

He had scarcely settled into his new post, in the Staffing Department, before the political kaleidoscope was shaken again. In the first week of July, the pig-tailed General Chang Hsun, a long-time Ch'ing loyalist, seized the city in a bid to restore the Manchu monarchy. Under artillery bombardment from rival militarists outside the walls, and after extensive bribery from within, the coup collapsed a few days later. 'All firing stopped at 10 am. Chang, the monarchist leader, is a refugee in the Dutch legation. The only thing to remind one there has been fighting is that a lot of glass has been smashed. There are bullet holes in our office windows, and in the Club.'[18] Though short-lived, the coup had lasting effects, leading to the secession of Kuomintang delegates from the Parliament, and the consolidation of an alternative power-centre animated by Sun Yat-sen in Canton. In the New Year, a drive to reconquer the South failed, splitting the regime in Peking.[19] Working in the Inspectorate-General under Aglen and Bowra, my father spent long hours decoding telegram traffic into the night, as the CMC – eventually taking control not just of customs revenues to fund foreign debts, but of the surplus beyond these obligations, for direction by the diplomatic corps – became an increasingly central player in the capital. 'The Customs have gained a great deal in influence since the war and up here in Peking we are more than half a political force', my father wrote home, 'we are taking over the government banks practically'.[20] From the Inspectorate, located in the middle of the Legation Quarter, on the eastern edge of today's Tienanmen Square, the cockpit of warlord conflicts in the capital was in constant view. In the summer of 1918 he was writing: 'reason is the religion of China and a very good religion too', except that it made for detachment: 'it is only the unscrupulous who go into politics, hence the present futile government'.[21] His attitude to warlord conflicts, like that of most foreigners at the time, was dismissive. But when the awaken-

18. L: undated, probably 12 July 1917.

19. 'There are about five separate rebellions going on with every prospect of a combined revolution financed by Japan, but business goes on much as usual. Yochow and Ningpo are both in it. Yochow was pretty well burnt out but the Ningpo merchants paid the revolutionary soldiers a sum of £10,000 to pass by without looting. Consequently they went on and looted the next town. The President of China is expected to make a run for it very soon and there are abut 3 ministers in charge of about 8 Ministries, all the others having made for the French Concession in Tientsin' – L: 16 January 1918. The evolution of the crisis is described in Hsi-Sheng Ch'i, *Warlord Politics in China 1916–1928*, Stanford 1976, pp. 18–23ff.

20. L: 27 January 1918.

21. L: 19 July 1918.

ing of 4 May 1919 came, with the student protests that marked the birth of modern politics in China, his response was briefly enthusiastic. 'All China is on strike! It is most impressive', he reported, 'all business is at standstill and the students, who are running the movement, are masters of the situation. There is a sort of epidemic of resignations from President down to Parliament.'[22]

Aglen evidently appreciated his work, taking him as private secretary on a tour of inspection by cruiser round ports in South China later that year, calling in at Canton, Wuchow, Amoy, Foochow, Wenchow, Macao and elsewhere. He came back with mixed feelings about Aglen himself. 'Sir F. Aglen is English', he informed his mother, 'big, heavy, good looking, rather awkward and shy, naturally lazy but now very hard working, very conscientious and absolutely "straight", clever at Customs work with a wonderful Customs memory: but rather selfish and inclined to bluster, quite stupid as far as the Chinese and political side of his job goes.'[23] His own prospects must have appeared good. Back in Peking, completing a translation for Kishimoto Hirokichi, the Commissioner in charge of Chinese negotiations in the Inspectorate, 'who is a Japanese and whose job I have my eye on twenty years hence',[24] his career seemed well on track. But ambition is not the dominant note in his correspondence of the time. He was in his twenties, and the pleasures of an out-door life – riding, skating, tennis, swimming – when office pressures slackened, figure more largely. The beauty of Peking, commented on all by foreigners of the period – 'a wonderful city', even when 'the high walls, dust, the dry harsh look of things' were oppressive in the hot season – and of the countryside of the Western Hills, where he tramped on foot at weekends, were natural attractions.[25] On the coast the Customs kept bungalows in Peitaiho, the resort where today Communist leaders gather in seclusion every summer.

But another concern was predictably uppermost, 'the incompleteness of bachelor life'.[26] Sexually, young European men in China usually

22. L: 13 June 1919.

23. 'This is my impression which may or may not be a just one' – L: 9 April 1919. Specifying Aglen as English to his mother suggests a shared sense of cultural distance. Years later, he would write of the ability to remain on amiable terms with people without ever getting intimate with them: 'This is an English quality. We Irishry can't do it.' L: 16 April 1933.

24. L: 23 July 1919.

25. L: 30 March 1918.

26. L: 4 July 1918, sent to his brother Sainthill, killed near Bucquoy on 25 August, who may never have received it. The death of his brother, to whom he was deeply attached, was a terrible blow. The news reached him in Peking only in mid-October.

found solace with local tea-girls or concubines. Hart, a devout Wesleyan, had three children by a mistress in Amoy before marrying a cousin from Portadown. My father, who found the typical 'China girl' in the Western community insufferably spoilt by the gender ratio, no doubt at some point followed suit. But in his last year in Peking, he fell under the spell of the wife of an Embassy official, Florence Harding, of unusual boldness (many years later, my mother noted with amusement that 'she apparently opened operations by slipping her hand in his pocket'). A turbulent affair ensued. It would have had to be highly clandestine. Even courtship of a single girl, if regarded as a unsuitable by parents or superiors, might result in an abrupt transfer to the remotest outpost the I-G could find – the fate of his best friend at the time, exiled to a fever-ridden hole on the Burmese frontier for this transgression.[27] In such conditions, the intensification of feeling generated by even ordinary secrecy is likely to have heightened.

In early 1920 my father was transferred to Chungking, 1,500 miles up the Yangtze, in Szechwan. This was a posting he had wanted, for reasons that are lost. Perhaps it was the attraction of further turmoil. The province had been an epicentre of revolt both in the overthrow of the Chi'ng dynasty in 1911 and the downfall of Yuan Shih-K'ai in 1916, when troops from Yunnan and Kweichow had taken it from the south, linking up with local insurgents. Four years later, it remained in a highly unsettled condition, as local Szechwan militarists sought to oust the Yunnan-Kweichow forces still in control of much of the province, including Chungking.[28] Besides continual marauding between warlord troops, piracy was rife on the Upper Yangtse. My father arrived at his new post in the first week of March 1920. The assistant he replaced, travelling in the opposite direction towards Ichang, was ambushed a few days later. 'Conditions down river are getting steadily worse', the station chief informed Peking. 'I had a letter from Mr Nordstrom, who left here on the 8th by wupan, telling me he had been attacked by robbers about 10 li above Yunyang who fired on his boat, killed the laodah, and took all his own valuables. Wires have come in during the

---

27. For having dallied with a dim but pretty sixteen-year-old, 'Black is transferred to Teng-yueh and I am sick as mud … it is a regular graveyard … I think her people asked for Black's transfer because the girl was getting too fond of him, and they were afraid she was making herself conspicuous' – L: 12 April 1918.

28. For the scene in Szechwan in these years, see *Sir Meyrick Hewlett: Forty Years in China*, London 1943, pp. 84–145, British Consul-General in Chengtu at the time; and Robert Kapp, *Szechwan and the Chinese Republic. Provincial Militarism and Central Power 1911–1938*, New Haven 1973, pp. 13–17.

last few days that three other boats with foreigners on board have been cleaned out in a similar manner and two gunboats have gone down river post haste.'[29]

By the summer, fighting between the rival armies was approaching the city. 'The Yunnan men are retreating. They levy contributions as they retire under threat of destruction of towns and villages ... It is possible the Ssuch'uan troops will be under the walls or in the city in three days. It appears evident that the Kueichou men have little hope of holding their own for they are still moving their impedimenta and today, as I came down the hill, I met many wounded men on their way south.' The economic situation gave small leeway to the Customs. 'Unfortunately business is at a standstill. Cargo cannot come down with all these military movements in progress. Junks will not move above Wanhsien without escort on account of brigandage and there are not enough soldiers to supply escorts. A week and more ago there were over 300 junks gathered at Wanhsien and this crowd, coupled with the military consumption, is causing the price of food to rise seriously.' As for the city itself: 'Whichever side is here it is pretty certain that Chungking will have to pay; it has always paid.'[30]

These were circumstances enough to absorb the energies of any young assistant. But his mind must also have been on his amour in Peking, and letters no doubt passing between them. In September, at all events, Florence arrived to stay with him, bringing – no doubt for the sake of decorum – two women friends along with her. One of these was Stella Benson, then travelling in Asia as a freelance writer and journalist. Shrouded in torrential rain, high above the city which lay on a ledge amid the swirling river below, the party quickly became an emotional hot-bed. Stella fell violently in love with my father, while he strove mightily to detach Florence from her marriage, freely regaling the first with confessions of his passion for the second. Arguments about Ireland – the Black and Tans had just arrived: my father sympathized with Sinn Fein – heightened the atmospherics. Below, pitched battles raged between Yunnan and Szechwan troops, in the last round of their struggle for control of the province: bullets flying in the streets, bodies floating down the river, as the agitated trio

---

29. Acting Deputy Commissioner C.F. Johnston to C.A.V. Bowra (Aglen was on leave): CMC 32045, S/O No. 210, 31 March 1929. A wupan was a somewhat larger sampan – literally, 'five planks' as against 'three planks'; a laodah was the boatman.

30. Johnston to Bowra: CMC 32045, S/O No. 215, 24 June 1920.

prepared to leave by boat for Shanghai.[31] Painful *mises-au-point* punctuated the route. Florence made her way back to Peking. Stella went
on to Calcutta. My father was left for the final months of his tour of
duty in Shanghai – a city he detested, where 'the Chinese are only tol-
erated to be kicked and sworn at'.[32] In the spring of 1921, at the age
of twenty-seven, he sailed home on his first leave.

What had he made of China? In all probability, my father would
have been hard put to give a focused answer, so closely must the particular encounter with a foreign world have been entwined, and
overlaid, by the general ordeal of growing up. For example, after
seven years, how proficient was his Chinese? Good enough to earn
special mention in a circular from the I-G, but what this meant in
practice is difficult to know. There are some indications he could read
classical poetry; but they may be misleading. Certainly, by the time he
left Peking, he was contemptuous of the attitude of most of his contemporaries. 'Europeans in China are so stupid', he wrote, 'if they
would take a little interest in the country they are living in, they
would enjoy life more. But they expect Chungking to be like Leeds
and regret the petty luxuries of a third-rate English town.'[33] Pride in
the variety of landscapes and cities he had already known, and the
scale of the organization of which he was part, are clear.[34] In his last
letter to his brother, he had written: 'I don't want to chuck China, in
a way I love the country, and I am so far from pining for "the fresh
green lap of fair King Richard's land" that I feel as if I couldn't stand

---

31. 'At 2, Chungking fell to the Szechwanese troops. We saw this like a movie-
show, there was firing from both ends of the city and the bullets splashed up and
down the quiet swift water. Directly the firing began, a sort of explosion of junks
escaping swept down the river, probably with escaping Yunnanese on board, dozens
of junks. All day there had been a more or less continuous succession of drowned
men floating down past us ... Towards evening the foreigners in the city got across,
some of them under fire, and Schjoth and Palmer came on board to tell us of the
Customs House barricaded, of heaps of dead men in the streets, of a fleeing Chinese
shopkeeper dropping his burst bag of silver dollars and leaving them in the street and
of the scramble by civilians and fighters alike to pick up the dollars. We had rather
an unfortunate farewell dinner for Shamus ...' Benson Diaries, Add 6782: 15
October 1920. On board there was stabbing and shooting by soldiers over supplies
of opium.
   32. L: 5 February 1920.
   33. L: 29 May 1920.
   34. To his mother: 'you will understand that after working here in an administration which extends over thousands of miles, I am not likely to be satisfied with a
parochial job at home' – L: 7 March 1919.

living at home'.[35] The second expression of feeling is stronger than the
first, without denying it all force. Of deeper attachment it is difficult
to speak. Claudel, a French consul in China for fifteen years, who
knew the Western community there well, wrote – echoing an opinion
of Stevenson – on the eve of the First World War: 'If a man becomes
an expatriate, it is not generally from a taste for adventure or an
energy impatient with constraints, it is simply because he did not
belong and is as if unfastened from himself [*comme de lui-même
décroché*]. Ask him: it is always *circumstances* that determined his
departure. You will never find in an expatriate that ecstatic faith in
the things of this world, the tenacity of purpose, the ferocious
appetite for power and money we admire in Balzac's heroes. The
expatriate always has something "loose", badly attached, about him:
some basic indifference of soul and body'.[36] Whatever the general
validity of the description, there are reasons for thinking it might have
particular truth in an Anglo-Irish case.

Back in London, within three months my father had married Stella.
When he took her home to meet his family in Waterford, roads were
criss-crossed with trenches, barracks detonated, bridges pock-marked
by ambushes. The locals, seeing her London flapper's hair-cut,
assumed she had been cropped for collaboration by the Sinn Fein.
While Griffith and Collins negotiated, the couple sailed off for an
American honeymoon. Motoring across the States, from Pennsylvania
to California, they arrived back in Ireland during the Civil War. Free
State forces, colluding with the British, were closing in on
Republican-held Waterford. It must have seemed a bit like Szechuan.
At the family dinner table, when my father continued to defend Irish
independence, the atmosphere became explosive – ascendancy houses
were being burnt, and his uncle was to be driven out of the country.
The newly-weds left for China the day after Collins met retribution in
Cork.

On arriving in Hong Kong, my father was posted to Mengtze in
Yunnan, on the Indochinese border. Rebuffing attempts by local
Intelligence to recruit him as a British agent – he was scornful of their
stupidity – he took his bride down to Hanoi, and then via the French
railway along the Upper Red River to Mengtze. Yunnan, famous for
its natural beauty and hospitable climate, was a province of China

---

35. L: 4 July 1918.
36. Paul Claudel, *Œuvres Complètes*, Vol. IV, *Extrême Orient*, Paris 1952,
pp. 92–93: written in 1909.

whose remoteness and ethnic diversity made its warlords virtually independent rulers. Economically, however, the region fell within the French sphere of influence – communications, concessions and trade flowing to Tonkin. Banditry was rife round Mengtze, where most of the hillspeople were Lolo. Riding in the countryside, Shaemas and Stella had some narrow brushes; but politically the area was quiet.

There, for two years, the young couple lived in a long adobe house 'on high stone foundations with a curling Chinese roof gaily painted underneath in faded blues and oranges and crimsons'[37] – part of the Customs compound that, fifteen years later, became the classrooms where William Empson taught English during the Sino-Japanese War, encountering his own brigands outside the city walls.[38] At Mengtze, wedlock all but crumbled. Stella fell violently out of love, my father into hurt brooding. They were physical antitheses. Suffering from acute ill-health – a chronically phthisic condition – throughout her life, she was spiritually passionate and carnally numb. Perhaps all her warmth was required for the effort just to survive. My father was emotionally steady but strongly and candidly sensual. Few marriages stand that strain. They talked of divorce. She buried herself in writing; he in studying Chinese. In the spring of 1925 he was ordered to Shanghai. She decided to take six months in Europe. At the quay, when the gangplank went up, she was vaguely surprised to miss him.

Meanwhile, China had been catching up with Ireland. Spreading through the big cities, modern nationalism had established a political base in Canton, where since early 1923 Sun Yat-sen headed a Kuomintang regime with Soviet advisers and Communist support. A bid to seize control of the local Customs had been thwarted by a flotilla of Great Power gunboats, but the Inspectorate in Peking was now facing a general rise in anti-foreign feeling in the South. At this juncture, just as my father left Shanghai, British sepoys in the city fired point-blank into a Chinese crowd demonstrating for the release of students held in a British police station. The massacre of 30 May 1925 set the country alight. A general strike was declared in Shanghai; anti-British rioting erupted and spread to other cities. Three weeks later, a major demonstration against the unequal treaties in Canton met with an Anglo-French fusillade that left many more casualties.[39]

---

37. L: 22 February 1923.

38. 'Moonlight Robbery: China 1938': *London Review of Books*, 5 October 1995.

39. The best account of the crisis and its context is Richard Rigby, *The May 30 Movement. Events and Themes*, Canberra 1980 – for the first week in Shanghai, pp. 34–43.

The result was a popular strike and boycott of English goods in Hong Kong and Canton that lasted for sixteen months – the setting of Malraux's memorable first novel *Les Conquérants*.

What was my father's view of these events? It seems probable he left the city around 3 June, having witnessed the initial explosion, and the strikes and repression that followed it, but no letter has survived from these weeks. All that is clear is that, instead of being assigned to an office job in the city, as he had expected, he was dispatched as Acting Commissioner – the youngest in the service – to the remote corner of China where Manchuria juts into a small gap between the northern-most tip of Korea and the frontier of Russia. Geographically, the nearest city to the settlement of Lungchingtsun, where he arrived on 10 June 1925, was Vladivostock. His first report started: 'LOCAL SITUATION: The Shanghai "affair" and the subsequent outbreaks, negotiations, etc are discussed and commented on by all classes of Chinese. In coming here I made the journey from the [Korean] frontier to Lungchingtsun on foot and found the country people in fairly remote villages talking over the situation. The Hunchun Chamber of Commerce is collecting money for the strikers' fund in Shanghai, there was a rather half-hearted demonstration at Yenchi, and the main shop of the B.A.T. dealer is boycotted'.[40]

He noted, however, that the political and ethnic balance in the region did not favour the national movement. In the ports of Central and South China, British power was still the main target of popular hostility. In the North-East, Japanese expansion represented a much more formidable force. Manchuria was the home territory of the dominant Northern warlord, Chang Tso-lin. But his regime was invigilated by Tokyo from positions of strength: Japanese military control of the Liaotung peninsula, cantonments in Mukden, armed guards along the South Manchurian Railway. The Chientao border zone where my father had been posted was of special concern to Japan, for the majority of its population were Korean immigrants, and it was the principal base area for underground nationalist activity against Japanese colonial rule in Korea. After its consulates were attacked in 1920, Japan had military police permanently stationed in the local towns.[41] Here, a few years later, Kim Il Sung would start his

---

40. CMC 31905: Lungchingtsun S/O No. 426, 4 August 1925.
41. See Gavan McCormack, *Chang Tso-lin in Northeast China, 1911–1928*, Stanford 1977, pp. 41–42; and for further background Chong-Sik Lee, *The Politics of Korean Nationalism*, Berkeley 1963 , pp. 158–163, 181–182ff.

career as a guerrilla in the communist movement. Today, the region forms the Yanbian autonomous Korean prefecture in the PRC. Then, a minority of Chinese settlers and a scattering of White Russians completed the scene. Though remote, the land was fertile and economic activity gathering pace. 'Lungchingtsun is developing fast and looks more like a prairie settlement in the Middle West of America than a treaty port of China. Builders' scaffoldings and new bald-looking foreign buildings are springing up amongst the adobe huts of the Korean settlers.'[42]

My father spent two years in this odd spur of Siberia. Winters were implacable, though not without elation. Reporting to Aglen on a '360 *li* inspection tour of the frontier barriers and patrol stations', he noted that for most of the journey, he could bowl along the frozen surface of the Tyumen river by car – 'a better road could hardly be found'.[43] Stella joined him, suffering from the bitter winds and isola-tion, but eventually making the local Russians into the material of her most successful novel. When she left for a six-month break in California, he took one to bed, and wrote – an impressive letter – for her consent. In a tizzy, she wired him the go-ahead; regretted it; on getting back, recriminated, let it go. By now she knew how strong was his attachment to her, and how little appeasement she gave him. Their strange disjointed existence – imagining, inspecting – resumed.

Meanwhile the Customs was overtaken by the political crisis in the country. In the summer of 1926 the KMT regime in Canton, now headed by Chiang Kai-shek, launched the Northern Expedition to oust the assorted warlords who ruled the rest of China. By the end of the year, Nationalist forces had advanced to the Yangtze and set up a government in Hankow. Aglen at the head of the CMC and Britain as hegemon of the Diplomatic Corps were now in a dilemma. Both had traditionally backed the warlord regimes in Peking. But Aglen, by channelling part of the Customs surplus to a domestic sinking fund, rather than hypothecating it all to foreign bondholders – a move that gave him greater leverage within Chinese politics – was regarded with reserve by the Foreign Office, as too independent. What line was now to be taken towards the Kuomintang? In the autumn Chiang Kai-shek cabled orders to suppress the long strike and boycott of British goods, hitherto supported by Canton. Delighted at the relief of Hong Kong, London in exchange made no fuss when the KMT imposed a surtax

---

42. CMC 31905: Lungchingtsun S/O No. 426, 4 August 1925.
43. CMC 31905: No. 444, 4 February 1926.

on foreign trade, technically in breach of the treaty system, and started to cultivate relations with Hankow.

Two months later, the Peking regime – now under the control of Chang Tso-lin, and formally claiming authority over all Chinese territory – responded by announcing its own surtax to the same amount, and instructed the Customs to collect it. Aglen, pleading diplomatic opposition, went south to discuss the delicate situation with the Hankow authorities. Before he could get back, the Peking government dismissed him for insubordination. London, whatever its feelings about Aglen, was determined to ensure that his successor was a British national – to which the Japanese Legation, after some hesitation, consented. In February 1927 the Northern regime duly appointed the current Chief Secretary, Arthur Edwardes, as Acting I-G. My father, who had known Aglen well, noted: 'Edwardes is a big fat Irishman with red hair who looks like a butcher, but is in fact a Butler on his mother's side, and related to the Irish dukedom of that name' – sociable enough, but 'not terribly hard-working' and 'likely to be kind to his friends at the expense of others'.[44]

Confronted with continuing territorial conflict, Edwardes opted for *de facto* cooperation with the North. Collection of the surtax was authorized – but by the Chinese superintendants, not foreign officials of the Service. Japan, now getting ready to abandon Chang Tso-lin, opposed the levy. In July, instructions for its collection reached Lungchingtsun. The Japanese headquarters there orchestrated a break-in of the Customs warehouse and a virulent press campaign against my father, threatening him with imminent bomb attacks from 'Korean gunmen' against which they could afford no protection – something more likely, he pointed out, to be directed against Japanese installations, since he had no quarrel with Korean independence. Stella noted: 'Machine-guns titupped about the streets, and peeped over the walls of the enormous fortified and bastioned new Consulate, built, so the Japanese say, as a "symbol of friendship between two great nations".'[45] In the event, the local Japanese establishment stayed its hand, but their last months in Manchuria were an increasingly tense time, as Chinese national sentiment – belatedly let off the leash by Chang Tso-lin – burst out in a campaign of popular demonstrations against Japan across the region. In the autumn, leave arrived, and Shaemas and Stella set off for Europe.

44. L: 8 March 1927.
45. Benson Diaries: Add. 13 July 1927; 'Storm in a Manchurian Teacup', *The Nation and Athenaeum*, 27 August 1927.

How far did the rhythm of absences from China, in theory a year in every five – a defining punctuation of this existence – intensify a sense of changes in the country, as each return took on something of an entry into the drama after missing an act, reconstructable only from indications in the scenes that followed, or furtive consultations of a programme in the dark? While my father was away, the political landscape of China shifted radically, and the position of the Customs with it. In the spring of 1928, the Northern Expedition was resumed. KMT armies, with assorted regional allies, advanced towards Peking. In early June Chang Tso-lin abandoned the capital, and was blown up on his luxury train back to Mukden by Japanese officers. In October a Nationalist government claiming control over the whole country was proclaimed in Nanking.

At the Customs Edwardes, who had never been accepted by the KMT, soon found his position impossible. From the start of his tenure, he had been threatened by a rival in the person of Hart's nephew, Frederick Maze, Commissioner in Shanghai. Maze, older and more skilled in manoeuvre, had cultivated good relations with the KMT ever since the 1911 Revolution, when he was Commissioner in Canton. When the Nationalist commander Pai Chung-hsi entered Shanghai in March 1927, Maze was on hand for secret talks with him, just prior to Chiang Kai-shek's massacre of Communists in the city, with Anglo-French complicity. Throughout the year Maze worked to win the favour of the KMT authorities and the backing of the Shanghai business community. He understood the requirements of the rising power, and had no hesitation in meeting them. In January 1929, Edwardes was ousted and Maze appointed Inspector-General.[46] The headquarters of the CMC were moved to Shanghai, and further recruitment of foreigners suspended. In the same month, China recovered tariff autonomy. The Nationalist Revolution seemed in full swing.

In reality, after turning on his Communist allies, Chiang Kai-shek had unified China only in name. Regional militarists, who lacked the same foreign and business connections, but were often better generals, controlled large territories and forces of their own, under the capacious ideological mantle of Sun Yat-sen's legacy. The direct authority of Nanking never extended much beyond central China, and was

---

46. Martyn Atkins, *Informal Empire in Crisis, British Diploamcy and the Chinese Customs Succession 1927–1929*, Ithaca 1995, offers an astringent, but admiring account of Maze's winning of the Inspectorate against Foreign Office opposition.

subject to frequent challenge even there. Over the next twenty years, Chiang's most formidable and persistent rivals came from the sub-tropical province of Kwangsi, a backward region along the Indochinese border with a large minority of Thai origin. Its leading generals, Li Tsung-jen and Pai Chung-hsi, had been more prominent in the actual fighting on the Northern Expedition than Chiang himself, ending it in control of a vast area that for a time included Hankow and Peking. Both commanders would distinguish themselves again in the war against Japan; and when Chiang finally had to step down after his disastrous failures in the civil war against the Communists, it was Li Tsung-jen who became the last President of Republican China in 1949, vainly trying to negotiate peace with the CCP. In old age he returned from exile, to die an honoured veteran in Peking.

In early 1929, however, Chiang suddenly gained the upper hand over the 'Kwangsi Clique', expelling them from the KMT and driving them into exile in Hong Kong.[47] There they plotted a come-back from their native province. To thwart them, Chiang inadvertently installed local officers with Left sympathies in office in Kwangsi. That spring my father travelled back to China alone, on the Trans-Siberian. The trip was bleak and his mind anxious: leave had been turbulent. Doctors had told him he couldn't have children, which Stella wanted. Roles reversed, he wrote to her from Hong Kong: 'If you really want a child, go ahead. I shouldn't mind so long as you didn't break with me.'[48] He assumed she couldn't join him. In considerable depression, he had just learnt that he was posted to Nanning, the capital of Kwangsi.

In fact, as he sailed up the water-way from the Pearl Delta and gradually saw the kind of country he was entering, his spirits lifted. Nanning lies just downstream from the fork between Right and Left Rivers, in a setting as far removed from the Tyumen as could be imagined. 'My house is on the river bank and looks across at neat clumps of feather bamboo and buffaloes, and Chinese washing their clothes, paddling, rigging up junk sails, etc. I have a charming garden, very much overgrown: hibiscus, frangipani, camelia, bougainvillea, tamarisk, flowering acacia, palms, bamboos, and various flowering

---

47. For these events, see Diana Lary, *Region and Nation. The Kwangsi Clique in Chinese Politics 1925–1937*, Cambridge 1974, pp. 13–145, one of the best studies of provincial politics in the Republican period.

48. L: 6 May 1929.

shrubs and trees of the kinds that are almost excessively fragrant.'[49] Trade was at a low ebb, and the workload was light. He settled in, waiting for Stella to join him. A few weeks later, an emissary from the CCP headquarters in Shanghai arrived secretly in Nanning. This was the entry into history of Teng Hsiao-p'ing, then a twenty-five-year-old not long returned from Europe – his knowledge of French perhaps selecting him for the mission, since he came up-river with Vietnamese Communist assistance through what my father called 'the back door' into Kwangsi, through the border town of Lungchow.[50]

Infiltrating the local government and garrison, Teng laid the groundwork for an uprising. In October, however, the officers in charge of the province – under whose protection the CCP had been working – declared prematurely against Chiang Kai-shek, in concert with other disaffected forces in the Nationalist camp, only to find their troops melting away, and clearing a path for a return to power of Kwangsi's famous militarists. Before they could reach Nanning, Teng ordered the detachments won to the Communist cause out of the city – one group towards Lungchow in the south-west, and the other to the Chuang minority zone in the north-west of the province, where he sailed up the Right River in a convoy of junks loaded with the city's arsenal to meet them. There, at the mountain town of Pose, controlling the passes to Yunnan, he proclaimed a soviet. Landlords were expropriated, Chuang villages mobilized, and soon an area with a population of about a million was under the control of the newly created Eighth Corps of the Red Army. My father reported to Maze: 'The whole of the Pose river is over-run by a force of communistic peasants who have lately captured P'ingma and Lungan, the latter town only 60 miles from here. At these places they have publicly burnt portraits of Dr Sun together with all title-deeds found in the hsien yamens!'[51]

A month later, in January 1930, the Kwangsi Clique was back in Nanning. 'POLITICAL: A great change in the situation since I last wrote ... Li Tsung-jen is here. Passing by the Customs House the other morning, he took shelter in my office from a sudden downpour of rain, and spoke freely and with seeming confidence of his plans.

---

49. L: 14 July 1929.

50. The fullest official version of Teng's activities in Kwangsi in 1930 is to be found in his daughter's account: Deng Maomao, *Deng Xiaoping. My Father*, New York 1995, pp. 162–191.

51. CMC 32519: No. 451, 9 January 1930.

He himself will direct operations from Nanning to clear the Lungchow and Pose rivers, at present infested with the remnants of Yü Tso-po's army and by the peasant communists. All is quiet locally and the Nanning Chamber of Commerce has paid over $70,000 to Li. The money was raised without much difficulty, as the merchants are interested in the reopening of communications with Pose, where opium stocks have been held up for a long time'.[52] In fact, Li and Pai could take no immediate action against the Communist forces in Kwangsi – where a few days later a second soviet was proclaimed on the Left River near the Indochinese border – because they found them-selves under assault from Canton, where an army had been mustered against them in the name of Chiang Kai-shek's government. Fighting spread in the east of the province, as they were joined by another leading commander of the Northern Expedition, Chang Fa-kuei, who brought the remnants of his 'Ironsides' into Nanning to block the Cantonese advance. 'Chang Fa-k'uei is now in charge of the defense of Nanning, and is setting about the task with great energy, digging trenches, putting up barricades, throwing out pickets, etc. I went to see him the other day and found to my surprise an undersized *chétif*-looking young man who might be taken for a rather elderly student ... His men throng the shops, tendering good Hongkong, Tonkin and Shanghai notes for their purchases. It is pleasant to hear the Peking burr so far south as this'.[53]

The atmosphere in Nanning became an uncertain mixture, perhaps not untypical of the time, of siege and diversion, vividly captured in Stella's diary. Cantonese aircraft would bomb the city one day; on the next the Kwangsi generals would be at their favourite sport. Stella noted in her diary: 'General Huang Shao-hsiang [the third member of the junta] ordered us by telephone to provide him with some tennis today – it seems there is a momentary lull in the fighting. He is a great man here and behaves as such. We hurriedly assembled tennis and tea out of doors, although a fine drizzle was falling. General Huang arrived with six soldiers with very long-nosed revolvers, as ever waving in the naked hand towards the eye of the host and hostess'.[54] Tournaments followed. At the dinner table, hot arguments were

---

52. CMC 32519: No. 353, 27 January 1930. For Li's own account of his move-ments after being expelled from Hong Kong by the colonial authorities, under pressure from Nanking, en route back to Kwangsi, see *The Memoirs of Li Tsung-jen* , Boulder 1979, dictated during his exile in the US, pp. 274–276.

53. CMC 32519: No. 358, 16 April 1930

54. Benson Diaries: Add 6798, 4 February 1930.

exchanged over the rights and wrongs of the current fighting with an Ironside staff officer to the LSE, in which Shaemas and Stella revealed common indignation at the plight of the Chinese peasantry at the hands of greedy warlords ('it was refreshing saying what one thought to a Chinese militarist'). Amid much European prejudice, this is a rare occasion where Stella lets slip evidence of what my father might have known of Chinese intellectual life: here she reports him as citing Hu Shih, the leading moderate of the May Fourth generation, as the most intelligent critic of the plagues of contemporary China – a voice to abash any retrograde warlord.[55]

In March the news arrived that the Left River soviet, under threat from French over-flights, had stormed foreign buildings in Lungchow. Teng Hsiao-ping was in the city when crowds assaulted and burned the French consulate, seizing weapons and funds, and then turned on the Customs House. The French Deputy Commissioner in charge – Comte O'Kelly – took refuge with local brigands, where he was held to ransom, before buying his way across the frontier to Indochina.[56] The timing of these events is unlikely to have been accidental. The Lungchow soviet was proclaimed on 1 February 1930. The first plantation strikes organized by the Communists in Vietnam broke out at Phu Rieng on 4 February. The Vietnamese Communist Party was founded in Hong Kong, where Ho Chi Minh was in exile, a meeting that lasted from 3 to 7 February. Teng arrived back in Lungchow from a trip to Hong Kong on 7 February. The first nationalist insurrection in Tonkin erupted with the mutiny at Yenbai on 9 February – a bolt from the blue to public opinion in France.[57]

This is a skein neither China nor Vietnam is anxious to draw attention to today, and which historians have yet to unravel. What is clear is that the colonial government in Hanoi was galvanized into action on both sides of the frontier. French aircraft bombed Lungchow – Teng later claimed his men shot down one during the attack. Soon afterwards Li Tsung-jen's troops recaptured the city. But no stable order was restored, and the region remained in bandit-ridden turmoil. At this juncture, my father received orders from Maze transferring him to Hong Kong. Nanning was still under siege from the east, so

---

55. Benson Diaries, Add. 6798, 10 April 1930.

56. O'Kelly to Maze: CMC 32578, S/O No. 474, 28 March 1930, for a breathless account of his adventures; he requested retirement soon afterwards.

57. On this sequence of events, see Daniel Hémery, 'Résistances, nationalismes, mouvements sociaux (1900–1939)', in Pierre Brocheux and Daniel Hémery, *Indochine, la colonisation ambiguë 1854–1954*, Paris 1994, pp. 303–306ff.

the only route out was down the Left River. With a morphine-addicted Swedish subordinate *in extremis* on board, my father and Stella set off in a motor launch, escorted by a gunboat dispatched by the Kwangsi generals.

Floating through wonderful, sometimes ominous, scenery for five days, Stella fell into a dream-like state, not unlike moods in a Chinese poetics of which she was unware: 'Lying down on my campbed this afternoon, I remembered that this was my childhood's ideal of travel – going along *very slowly, near the world*, lying down and head first – no effort – yet with a close world passing and a new thing to see every minute. It was beautiful at sunset and after – when the moon came out – sitting out on the bows of the ship – looking forward – the bows growling deliciously through the rapids. Living like this is like being exquisitely drowned in a sea of green non-thought – it is a real anti-climax to come to the surface – fireflies drifting like leaves from a pine-tree, across the beetling walls of an overhanging village – the darling nothingness of life'.[58] My father's version was less Taoist. 'The journey up river to a place called Lungchow was very good: "replete" with rapids, waterfalls, gorges, mountains and monkeys gibbering at us from the river bank. The monkeys were grey-whiskered gibbons, and the fact that the whiskering ceased in a careful black circle round their eyes gave them a very dissipated look. All this part of the country has been ravished (as you might say) by (a) brigands (b) communists a month before, and terrified run-away Chinese peasants peered down at our boat from caves high up in the mountains at the side of the river.'[59]

In the middle of this wildness, stopping at a hamlet one night, Stella was – unimaginably – brought a telegram from her publishers in London. At Lungchow, they inspected the sacked residence of the Commissioner ('We tied up at the foot of the Customs steps and went up to see the ruin left by the Reds', Stella noted: 'The Customs here must have been a beautiful property – two or three charming veranda-hed houses on a series of green wooded terraces falling to the river').[60] In the safety of French refuge across the border, they found Comte O'Kelly 'very much obsessed by his Communist and brigand experiences – a craving for *l'action décisif* everywhere – at Yenbai – in India – in France – at the Naval Conference – everywhere people should be

58. Benson Diaries, Add. 6798, May 6 1930.
59. L: 22 June 1930.
60. Benson Diaries, Add. 6798, May 10 1930.

put up against walls and shot'.[61] They made their way down to Hanoi, and back to Hong Kong.

In Kwangsi, the Right River soviet fell that autumn, after the CCP Centre instructed Teng and his colleagues to lead the Eighth Corps out of the Chuang base area on a disastrous march, theoretically towards Canton, from which only decimated remnants escaped to join Mao's fastness to the north. In Nanning, Li Tsung-jen and Pai Chung-hsi, now firmly in control again, set out to make Kwangsi a model region. Hu Shih, visiting the province a few years later, much approved their efforts to modernize the province. By then, Shaemas and Stella would have less to say for the Crown Colony.

* * *

In the third week of July 1998, a 'national anti-smuggling work conference' took place in Beijing. In sensational speeches, the rulers of the People's Republic revealed that China is currrently losing 12 billion dollars a year from a massive wave of contraband, involving public officials of every kind – not least the People's Liberation Army itself. To staunch this disastrous flow, President Jiang Zemin announced the establishment of a 'national special police force to crack down on rampant smuggling', to be rewarded from the proceeds of confiscations, and ordered the Army to withdraw from all its – multifarious – commercial enterprises. The issue has certain historical echoes.

In the spring of 1930, sixteen years into his service, My father was posted to Hong Kong. He remained there two years, technically assigned to Kowloon, but living on the Peak. He disliked the place. The setting might be 'carelessly beautiful', but the society was dreary and the town repellent. 'It is curious how out-of-date colonies are', he noted, 'Hongkong is just beginning to be Edwardian. Hanoi is almost entirely Jules Ferry. It is strange in Hongkong to meet young girls being girlish in the manner of 1900, and in Hanoi to hear Frenchmen airing ideas about colonial development etc which are audacious in the manner of Rudyard Kipling.' But whereas Hanoi was at least pretty, with streets radiating from a lake surrounded with trees at the centre, cafés with pink-and-white awnings, and flower baskets at every corner, 'Hongkong as a town is grotesquely ugly – the part which is intended to be dignified is simply terrible, a square with lawns all cluttered up with the most revolting statues of minor royalties'.[62] Stella took her

61. Benson Diaries, Add. 6798, 11 May 1930.
62. L: 17 July 1930; 12 February 1933.

aim at government licensing of forcible prostitution, in which teenage girls from the mainland were sold as virtual slaves to local brothels. Cutting through missionary pieties and realist hypocrisies alike, she made it clear the issue was not sexual morality but exploitation. ('To abolish brothels, and above all to withdraw even a semblance of government sanction from brothel-keepers, pimps, traffickers, "pocket-mothers" who exploit helpless girls is to establish the principle that a woman's body is her own, not to dispute it').[63] Against much official opposition, an effective campaign under League of Nations auspices forced a reluctant Governor to phase out the system.

This intervention naturally brought displeasure on her husband. But he was a servant of the Chinese rather than British government, and the Maritime Customs was at loggerheads with the Hong Kong authorities anyway. The colony was traditionally a smuggler's paradise, protected by British officials in collusion with local interests. Soon after my father arrived, Maze descended in person for a show-down with the colonial authorities over the facilities the Customs needed to crack down on contraband into China. 'We are busy quarrelling with the Hong Kong Govt and there is at the moment a prospect of our withdrawing from Hongkong and putting a cordon of cruisers round the island to annoy shipping', he wrote to Ireland. 'Last time negotiations were broken off and there was a good deal of ill-feeling. They don't like or trust Maze very much. But he is an able man and will get his way, I think. He doesn't care what people think of him as long as outward appearances are preserved.'[64]

Maze was indeed already giving a new dynamism to the CMC. The recovery of tariff autonomy by the Nanking government had increased import duties from semi-colonial levels, below even a nominal 5 per cent, to 15 per cent by 1931, now on a gold unit basis. The result was a big jump in customs revenues, which within three years virtually trebled. By 1932 the Maritime Customs was generating 60 per cent of central government revenues – far more than in Hart's day.[65] Since tighter fiscal pressure at the frontier made contraband much more profitable, smuggling soared. To combat its spread, Maze created a new Preventive Department within the Inspectorate, secured

---

63. Benson Diaries, Add. 8367: 370, 8–13 December 1931.

64. L: 2 August 1930; undated, *c.* September 1930.

65. Arthur Young, *China's Nation-Building Effort, 1927–1937. The Financial and Economic Record*, Stanford 1971, p. 73. Young, an American, was Financial Adviser to the KMT government from 1929 to 1947.

its own powers of armed interception for the CMC, and built up a modern fleet of fast cruisers, linked to a wireless network, for search-and-seize operations along the China coast. It was this kind of work to which my father was assigned, first as Deputy and then as Commissioner *ad interim* in Hong Kong, controlling the movement of small gunboats in the waters round the island. He was evidently good at the job ('we are choked up with seizures'), and enjoyed it.[66]

Contemptuous of the British authorities in Hong Kong ('an out-of-the-way silly government'),[67] he had also to finesse relations with the Chinese authorities he served. Canton was controlled by the Kwangtung warlord Chen Chi-t'ang, who had formed a regional bloc with Li and Pai in Kwangsi against Chiang Kai-Shek in Nanking. Each side naturally laid claim to the most valuable source of public funds available. My father's work was thus, as he put it, 'agreeably complicated by the fact that I serve two separate Governments', one in principle legitimate but distant, the other insurgent but much closer to hand. 'My chief card is *force majeure*. This word is very dear to all Chinese Govts, de jure or de facto (and in any case debilitated). An example. The Minister of Finance of the Central Govt instructs me in majestic terms to cease remitting certain revenues to the "rebellious dogs of the Canton faction" and to let him have them. This means I get a friend among the rebellious dogs to send an old steam tug, with five or six indifferently armed soldiers on board, to make an armed demonstration at one of my revenue stations outside Hongkong. We could perfectly easily blow up anything in the way of armed force the Cantonese could possibly send along, including their navy, which is very much less imposing than my own anti-smuggling flotilla. But instead of that I telegraph the Central Govt that I have been com-pelled to yield to force majeure. All is then well until the next crisis'.[68]

This insouciant note, no doubt coloured for effect, did not last long. In the autumn of 1931 Japan overran Manchuria, and six months later set up the puppet state of Manchukuo. At a stroke, the CMC was excluded from all Manchurian ports, a major revenue blow. In January 1932, Japanese forces in Shanghai launched an assault on KMT positions, which after severe fighting led to a further weakening of Chinese control around the city where the Inspectorate was now located. 'Though my personal position in the Customs is flourishing,'

---

66. CMC 32427, S/O No 595: 8 January 1932.
67. L: 30 June 1931.
68. L: 20 December 1931.

he told his mother, 'the position of the Customs is a little shaky in the view of the warfare at Shanghai.'[69] In the short run, the CMC survived well enough. But Japanese occupation of Manchuria, and gradual extension of territorial control below the Great Wall, affected the system of mobility within the Customs sharply. From now on, there would be steadily fewer ports available for postings to the north of the country, where the climate was better and conditions healthier. Stella, who loathed Hong Kong, left for Europe just before the Shanghai Incident, buoyed en route by a Femina Prize for her last novel. In April my father was transferred to Hainan.

He received his new post for a purpose. Hainan, a tropical island the size of Ireland, is the far southernmost extremity of China, lying on a latitude with Luzon in the Philippines, opposite northern Vietnam. Traditionally a place of remotest banishment for Tang literati, like Ovid's Black Sea exile, it was still quite wild, with non-Han tribal groups at large. In the interior, a CCP guerrilla was active: 'rank banditry cloaking itself in the garb of communism – a residue of the Borodin regime', as the Danish Commissioner who preceded my father saw it.[70] Its importance lay in its geographical position. All ocean-going junks from Bangkok, Singapore, Batavia or Saigon were required by an I-G directive to report to Hainan before proceeding to any mainland harbour in China. Across the narrow straits to the Luichow peninsula, however, lay the dormant French enclave of Kwangchow-wan, with its headquarters in Fort Bayard, some two-hundred square miles of lease extorted from the Ch'ing empire in 1898, and virtually forgotten thereafter. With the raising of Chinese tariffs in the early thirties, however, this shadow-zone suddenly became a magnet for large-scale contraband, landed in Fort Bayard and then nimbly shipped across to Hainan, or over the land frontier. 'Vast and powerful interests', the Danish memorandum warned, had given rise to a 'smugglers El Dorado'.[71]

This was why Maze had sent my father south, after drawing attention in a circular to the vigorous example set by his seizures in Hong Kong. The first instruction to him read: 'I consider that you hold one of the most interesting posts that the Service has to offer and that the problem of prevention in your district will afford you ample

---

69. L: 17 March 1932.
70. CMC 3250: 12 April 1932: official memorandum from K.E. Jordan, on handing over charge of the Kiungchow Customs. Kiungchow is today's Haikou.
71. Ibid. Fort Bayard is today's Zhanjiang.

opportunity to put the experience acquired in the Kowloon area to the best advantage'.[72] The CMC station in Fort Bayard was controlled from Hainan. His first task as Commissioner was to attack the illegal traffic from the French territory. My father proceeded to tours of inspection of creeks and bays on both sides of the straits, mobilization of cruisers, orders for more speedboats and armoured shields from Shanghai. Three months after he arrived, Hainan was the scene of a naval revolt against Canton, put down after a spectacular direct hit from the air – 'an enormous yellow flame and great columns of smoke' – sank the rebel flagship in Hoihow harbour, requiring him to telegraph warnings to mariners across South-East Asia.[73] He soon decided that it would be better to tackle the smuggling problem from the other side of the straits, and got colleagues to lobby the Inspectorate for the transfer of control over Fort Bayard to Pakhoi, the nearest port on the mainland, currently administered by a somnolent Dutch commissioner. Maze, seeing the sense of the proposal, appointed him to Pakhoi in the autumn of 1932.

Stella, after six months of literary success in London – prize-givings, *soirées* with the Woolfs, portrait by Wyndham Lewis, etc. – was meanwhile making her way back to China with foreboding. 'Now I am in danger again.'[74] Five days after she reached Hainan, she collapsed with a bronchial crisis, from which she only just pulled through – 'devotedly nursed day and night by a Chinese concubine (not James's) richer than we are'.[75] When they moved to Pakhoi a fortnight later, she had to be carried ashore. There she recovered a little, resumed writing. The Commissioner's house was 'almost palatial', set in a large compound filled with flowering trees and shrubs, looking down to the sea. My father, with his Russian deputy, criss-crossed the Luichow peninsula by car in pursuit of a tighter cordon round Fort Bayard. There, at any rate, society was less stuffy than in

---

72. 'The post calls for special qualifications and, as regards Kwangchow-wan, bristles with difficulties: you will have to display tact and patience with the French authorities and to act with circumspection on the land frontier until you have the support of sufficient guards, but the checking of smuggling by junk should afford you unlimited scope for action': Maze to Anderson, CMC 32358, 16 May 1932.

73. L: 14 July 1932. Suppression of the revolt was followed by an intensified campaign against the Communist movement on the island. 'Prisoners with captured red flags and red scarves are paraded through the streets of Hoihow at intervals. There have been a good many casualties on both sides, I think': CMC 32358, S/O No. 595, 15 September 1932.

74. Benson Diaries, Add. 6801, 25 August 1932.

75. *Some Letters of Stella Benson*, Hong Kong 1978, p. 38: 22 November 1932.

Hong Kong. The portly Administrateur – 'a bachelor and *impénitent*, which means he keeps two Annamite girls' – was fond of officially notifying him: '*Si quelqu'un me mord dans la derrière, je lui donne un coup de pied dans les roupettes*. This means there has been a "frontier incident".'[76] In this setting, manners were more diverting. 'At Kwangchouwan, I encountered a Chinese lesbian. A very curious woman, who is the wife of a Customs Clerk. She is called the "Conqueror", is tremendously bossy, and sends for sing-song girls to sleep with her.'[77] He seems to have enjoyed the challenge of this eccentric frontier, and confirmed the good opinion of his superiors, though the French authorities continued to turn a blind eye to forbidden traffic. For its part, the Kwangtung regime – which Hu Shih, after a brush with Chen Chi-t'ang, viewed as utterly benighted by comparison with Kwangsi – obstructed any effort to fortify the frontier on its side, viewing the Customs in Pakhoi as an agency of Nanking from which it stood to gain nothing.

By the late winter, Stella's health was worsening again. 'I am wondering now if I have not come to the end,' she noted: 'I do not really mind. I have come to my full stature, such as it is, and do not feel that anything very valuable would be cut off *untried*, by my death.'[78] In the summer, my father asked for a month's leave and they went on holiday to the Javanese uplands. She was still very weak. In the autumn they went to Tonkin, where he had Customs business. She stayed on after he went back for a few days in the Baie d'Along, famous for the allure of its mountainous islets. There she caught a last pneumonia, and died. My father buried her on an island in the bay. It had been one of those peculiar relationships – common enough, or a product of alien circumstances? – like a broken figure of eight. She had fallen passionately in love with him; he married her with his mind elsewhere. She frustrated him physically, he disappointed her emotionally. Attachment frayed, they twisted away from each other. Yet her company became essential to him, and she accepted displacement for it. Tender and insensible, he certainly ended by loving her more than she did him, yet practically she gave up more for him, with only intermittent regret. After her death, he wrote: 'it is difficult to put on paper the secret pride I have always had in her, even when we were angry with each other'.[79] There are no

---

76. L: 9 February 1933.
77. L: 4 June 1932.
78. Benson Diaries, Add. 6801, 12 March 1933.
79. L: 9 December 1933.

letters from his last months alone in Pakhoi. In April 1934 he left for Europe. Taking her journal to the University Library at Cambridge, he wrote in a small hand on the last page: 'This was a *magnificent* woman. Handing over these diaries is like burying her all over again. I can hardly bear it.'[80]

While he was away in Europe, the situation in China altered fundamentally once again. By mid-1934 Chiang Kai Shek's Fifth Extermination Campaign had made Mao's base in the Kiangsi-Fukien border area untenable. In October Communist forces broke through encirclement, and began the Long March. A year later, after tremendous losses, a small remnant arrived in Yenan. While the KMT and its warlord allies harried the CCP in its new base in the north-west of China, Japanese pressure escalated in the east. A month after Mao reached Shensi, the Japanese Army extended its grip round Peking, without serious resistance from the Nationalist regime. On 9 December 1935, student protests against Nanking's accommodation to Tokyo were broken up by police in Peking, with numerous arrests. In solidarity, patriotic demonstrations spread across the country, in which the Communist underground played a central role. After its military setbacks, the CCP was starting to recoup politically.

Arrived back in London, my father confessed he was still 'torn to bits with pain and remorse' about the death of his wife.[81] Unwilling to face China alone, he went to nightclubs, took up autogyros, considered alternative companions. Dining with my mother, he was taken with the way she waved her knife and fork about while talking. Eventually, he proposed to her. She was twelve years younger, in love with a guardsman whose family wanted no *mésalliance*. On country walks, in diary notes, she weighed up her choices. A trip to Ireland clinched it. In September 1935 they wed. Sometimes, an epoch later, she would speak of the marriage as almost arranged. Certainly China must have been a leap in the dark. But she was adventurous, and by current standards – then or now – the relationship must have worked. Maze cabled my father he was to proceed to Kunming. They set off in high spirits, missing one boat, catching another in Marseilles; my brother was conceived somewhere in the Indian Ocean.

In February 1936, they arrived in Yunnan. The new realities quickly made themselves felt. My father's first dispatch to Maze opened: 'THE COMMUNISTS: have entered the province in the north east

---

80. Benson Diaries, Add. 6802, note written on 4 December 1934.
81. L: 13 October 1934.

corner. Indications are that the Yunnan troops will not fight them, but steer them into Szechwan.'[82] Mao's forces had reached Shensi, but now a second column of the Red Army, whose base on the Hunan-Hupei border had held out longer, was making its way across China. Led by Ho Lung, a former commander in Chang Fa-kuei's Ironsides, it was eventually to reach Yenan in somewhat greater strength – about 20,000 soldiers – than the survivors of the Long March. In April Ho Lung's forces brushed so close to Kunming that that my father reported 'something very like a panic here ... last Friday the whole foreign population – and a good many Chinese – spent the night in trains with steam up, ready to leave at a minute's notice.'[83] In her diary, my mother gives a livelier description of midnight chaos at the railway station, and the opinion to be heard that the Communists would be an improvement for the local population if they did come. In fact, the Second and Sixth Red Armies did swerve west and north into Szechwan, without Yunnanese efforts to block them, as my father predicted.[84]

The alarm, however, brought Chiang Kai-shek to Kunming to review the situation. My father went out to the aerodrome with the official party for his arrival from Chengtu. 'He looked remarkably well, in contrast with his host General Lung Yun, who is, and looks, a heavy opium-smoker.'[85] Governor of Yunnan, the diminutive Lung Yun had ruled the province as a virtually independent state since 1928. A Lolo warlord from its north-eastern panhandle, he had never provoked the KMT regime as his opposite numbers in Kwangsi or Kwangtung had done, but he kept it if anything even more firmly out of his domain. Yunnan had its own silver currency, contact with the outside world through Indochina, tin mines to sustain revenue and – above all – the largest opium crop in China, filling its treasury and assuring the fortunes of its leading officials. Soon after his arrival, seizing a large consignment on its way to Tonkin 'bearing the labels of the Yunnan Opium Suppression Bureau', my father was obliged to relinquish it. Opium smuggling was, he reported to Maze, 'a very

---

82. CMC Mengtsze: 32611, S/O No. 863, Yunnanfu, 7 March 1936.

83. CMC 32611: Mengtsze, 13 April 1936.

84. For Ho Lung's passage through Yunnan, see Harrison Salisbury, *The Long March. The Untold Story*, New York 1985, pp. 306–310; for Nym Walers, 'Ho Lung was the most glamorous figure of all the Chinese Red leaders, as well as the most elusive': *The Chinese Communists: Sketches and Autobiographies of the Old Guard*, Westport 1972, p. 291.

85. CMC 32611: 25 April 1936.

important vested interest of the local Government. Unless I am authorized to close my eyes to the opium and salt traffic, and without strong Central government backing, I think it will be useless and dangerous to try to do anything. I would be grateful for a word of semi-official instruction in regard to this.'[86] He was tersely told to look away.

Even contraband that was less high-voltage was difficult to control, because of the sensitivity of Lung Yun's regime to any encroachment of central government authority on its prerogatives. My father's repeated requests for an armed guard to enforce Customs surveillance against ordinary smuggling along the railway line met with stiff resistance, and press attacks on the prospect. 'The Government views my attempt to recruit an armed guard and discovery of malpractice at Mapai as impertinent incursions in provincial affairs, whereas in fact I am attending strictly to my own business, revenue collection, which is the concern of the Central Government whose agent I am.' Over-impressed, as many educated Chinese were at the time, by Chiang Kai-shek's claims to be building a modern national state, he took a correspondingly low view of the Yunnanese authorities. 'The truth is that the Government is not only Provincial but also extremely provincial: it has very little knowledge or understanding of what goes on elsewhere in China, and is extremely suspicious and difficult to deal with. This is the opinion of every extra-provincial agency.'[87]

Such reservations could not impair the pleasures of Kunming, 'one of the most charming places in China'.[88] Set on a high plateau, under blue skies of a virtually perfect climate, the city was enclosed by massive russet walls, pierced by four ornamental gates, and surrounded by hills covered with camellia and fruit-blossom. The Liang river flowing past my father's office ran down to Lake Dian just south of the city, from whose western shore rose the steep escarpment of the Hsi Shan: temples and shrines on the mountain-side, sampans and islands in the water below. Such was the setting in which my brother was born. The family lived in a German-built villa owned by Lung Yun, next door to one of his residences. This was a golden age in family legend, which contemporary documents leave surprisingly intact: *fêtes champêtres* in the hills, midnight swimming in the lake,

---

86. CMC 32611: S/O No. 865, 30 March 1936.
87. CMC 32611: S/O No. 883, 10 November 1936.
88. CMC 32611: S/O No. 912, 8 October 1937. For Lung Yun and his regime, often under-estimated by foreigners, see John Hall, *The Yunnan Provincial Faction 1927–1937*, Canberra 1976, pp. 55–61ff.

the merits of the Lawrences (D.H. versus T.E.), children's parties in the garden, wives of the Governor or his cousin for tea. Perhaps there was too much entertaining; but when a transfer from the I-G subsequently came, it was the only time my father broke protocol with a protest.

During this idyll, the first major battles of what became the World War began, when in August 1937 Chiang Kai-Shek − having lost control of Peking − threw his best divisions against Japanese positions in Shanghai, in a botched assault that was eventually cut to pieces with a quarter of a million Chinese casualties, and headlong retreat to Nanking. In October, at the height of fighting, my father suddenly received orders for his departure from Kunming. In his last dispatches, he predicted that Yunnan would benefit economically from the conflagration: 'I now think something very like boom conditions are coming and will continue for the duration of the war. There is already an influx of Chinese refugees from other provinces. House rents are soaring'.[89] What he did not foresee was the cultural and political opening the war brought Kunming. Three months after he left, the transfer of the three leading universities of Peking and Tientsin to Yunnan, creating the famous joint Lianda campus, was to make Kunming the intellectual capital of wartime China. Lung Yun, who had every reason to be wary of KMT designs on the province, protected this ferment, while academic freedom was choked in Chiang's capital at Chungking. Inevitably, it led to increasingly lively political debate and opposition to the KMT. As soon as the war was over, Nationalist troops mounted a putsch, and gunned down students and intellectuals in a series of incidents that helped trigger the Civil War: events graphically recorded by Robert Payne, who was teaching at Lianda.[90] Lung Yun, arrested and deported to Chungking, later escaped to Hong Kong. He ended his days, like Li Tsung-jen, a honorific figure in the People's Republic.

In November 1937, as the Japanese swept the Nationalist armies from Shanghai, the family took the Michelin motor-rail − very advanced for its time − down to Hanoi, and thence by boat to Swatow, the port in Kwangtung to which my father had been directed. Known today principally as the birthplace of the richest of all Hong Kong's billionaires, the shipping magnate Li Ka-shung, who has liberally endowed it, Swatow has a sticky climate and granite hinterland. Neither of my parents liked it. Professionally, my father had some

---

89. CMC 32611: ibid.
90. *China Awake*, New York 1947, pp. 200–234, 417–419.

consolation: revenue collection was twice as large as in Yunnan, and staff more numerous. Here, the Superintendant – Chinese counterpart of the Commissioner, normally a figurehead – took an aggressive interest in Customs affairs. Calling on him immediately after arrival, my father 'found him, as I expected, out of humour and disagreeably inclined', and 'a fearful bore (in my experience an unusual quality in a Chinese official)'[91]: an aside significant not least for the implied comparison.

To this Maze replied in best colonial fashion: 'I trust that by your discreet handling of the situation the Superintendant can be made to realize his real position in the Customs.'[92] In fact, it became clear that the official in question was mainly concerned to tighten up measures against smuggling, an objective with which my father had every sympathy. Japanese warships were now patrolling along the South China coast to prevent military supplies reaching the Nationalist government, and Swatow was in the zone of blockade, a couple of destroyers lying a few miles outside the harbour. The effect was to confine Customs motor boats to the shore-line, increasing commercial smuggling at sea, where the standard practice was to dump contraband from steamers overboard in bales attached to buoys, to be picked up and landed by local junks. Norwegian vessels, travelling without anti-piracy guards, were the worst offenders. Planting undercover agents on one coming down from Hong Kong, and a speedboat in wait for junks in a nearby creek, my father netted a large haul of goods and runners – bringing dumping, temporarily at any rate, to a virtual halt. Looking at the handwritten annotations from the Inspectorate on this dispatch: 'a typical Anderson coup – well thought-out and planned',[93] faint images from childhood stirred.

A few days later, Japanese shells were falling on settlements near by and aircraft were flying overhead, though my father discounted an imminent landing. In March 1938, he was ordered inland to Wuchow on the West River. En route, he was told in Hong Kong that he needed an operation, and given six months leave for it. The family was back in London by May. That month, Japanese demands on the CMC came to a head. Japan had not formally declared war on China, and still had to reckon with the other imperialist powers in the region. Although Tokyo now controlled both Shanghai and Nanking, the

---

91. CMC Swatow 32374, 16 November 1937.
92. Annotation, ibid.
93. CMC 32375, 22 January 1938.

Customs could not be simply annexed or liquidated without provoking a conflict with Britain and the United States. Instead, the Japanese authorities demanded that all revenues collected in those parts of China under Japanese control be lodged in the Yokohama Specie Bank, and staff appointments to the service reflect Japanese preponderance. Under this pressure Maze, appealing for support from London and Washington, and understanding from Chungking, withheld accumulated balances in the Hongkong and Shanghai Bank, and refused wholesale staff changes, but otherwise conceded the first demand and went some way towards the second.

In the autumn, the Japanese seized Canton. Within another year, they controlled ports accounting for 90 per cent of revenue. Foreign commissioners – an American in Canton, a Briton in Tientsin, a Dane in Amoy, and so on – continued to operate under Japanese occupation, and Japanese authorities disbursed regular quotas to the Inspectorate for the expenses of the Service, while keeping the balances for themselves. Still legally a servant of the Chinese government in Chungking, the Inspectorate-General was now dependent on the remittances of a government at war with it. From his headquarters on Hart Road in the International Settlement, Maze sought to finesse the Customs predicament as best he could, flying to Hong Kong to secure unofficial tolerance of these arrangements from KMT Finance Minister H.H. Kung, coming in from Chungking. In a confidential letter to the London Secretary, he later wrote: 'my position was not merely difficult – it was impossible. An epigrammatist might describe it thus: 'Tokyo *required*, Chungking *objected*, and the Interested Powers *expected*'.[94] But whatever the pressure exercised from Japan, or information passed to Britain, his loyalty as an official remained to China.[95]

In October 1938, my father was recalled to Shanghai. My mother, protesting at his departure, remained behind. For six months, he led a becalmed life in the French Concession, in bureaucratic limbo. Nominally assigned as Commissioner to Wuhu, a Yangtze port in the Japanese war zone where no CMC station any longer operated, he lived in the Picardie Apartments, an Art Deco block on the Avenue Pétain, playing chess with Russian exiles, learning Italian, reading

94. Maze to Cubbon, 27 March 1943: Maze Confidential Papers, Vol. 15, 347.

95. For a good discussion of his role in these years, see Nicholas Clifford, 'Sir Frederick Maze and the Chinese Maritime Customs, 1937–1941', *Journal of Modern History*, March 1965, pp. 18–34; and *Retreat from China. British Foreign Policy in the Far East, 1937–1941*, Seattle 1967, pp. 56–61, 105–106.

Saint-Simon. When spring brought a post in the field, his relief was palpable. Of the dwindling number of ports under Chinese control, he was given Lungchow. The town itself had not changed much over the decade since the Left River soviet. But arriving via Hanoi, he found the scene on the Kwangsi–Tonkin border transformed. With the fall of Canton, this had suddenly become one of the only two overland routes left into Nationalist-held territory. On the narrow road from Hanoi to Nanning, the small examination parapet at the frontier was jammed with convoys of heavy trucks and other vehicles streaming from French into Chinese territory with military and civilian supplies. In the space of a few months, Customs revenues had increased over a hundredfold. Conditions in Lungchow, supposedly the unhealthiest port in China, were primitive and the volume of tasks enormous. But he was exhilarated to be there.

Meanwhile, the Japanese were turning Hainan into a major naval and air base, a hundred miles offshore. Soon, Japanese seaplanes started air raids over the area, bombing the road and strafing traffic along it. Cargo now had to be passed at night. By mid-August there were daily air attacks on Lungchow. Two of my father's assistants were wounded a few yards away, when a bomb hit his garden. A week later a squadron of heavy bombers, escorted by seaplanes, launched a much more savage assault, obliterating targets on both sides of the river, and smashing the Customs House. There was no anti-aircraft defence of any kind in Lungchow: 'the aeroplanes come down to low levels and habitually spend *an hour* here on every visit, bombing, circling round to look for dumps, bombing again, machine-gunning' – worse even than the din of the explosions was the murderous 'roar of the power-dive, which sounds as though a silken sky was being ripped open'.[96] When the alarm went, Customs personnel took refuge in deep caves in the nearby hills – though heading out was also hazardous: on one occasion the service car was riddled with bullets from planes coming in the opposite direction. In these conditions, my father moved his headquarters across the border to Langson – officially, the French Governor-General forbidding the move, in practice the Sûreté turning a blind eye. By day, and into darkness, the staff worked at Namkuan, 'Porte de Chine' – the *China Gate* of Samuel Fuller's movie; at night they slept in Vietnam. The European war was now two weeks away.

---

96. CMC 31607, Confidential Letters IGS, Lungchow 21 September 1939; L: 20 August 1939.

In between bulletins on the military situation, my father continued to file reports on the surreal customs problems of the region. 'There are five main kinds of smugglers of wood oil; the Kwangsi Syndicate, working to defeat the interests of the Trade Commission (which is to say the Central Government); the Syndicate's own staff, smuggling privately against the interests of both the Commission and the Syndicate; and local smuggling organizations working with the assistance and armed protection of local officials against the interests of the Commission, the Syndicate and the Syndicate's staff. (All this in time of war for China's national existence).'[97] Wood-oil was a hugely profitable export. But ordinary commodities were now so extortionately manipulated and taxed by Chungking that 'the exporter would have been less than human if he had complied docilely with Government requirements. He remained human and smuggled.'[98] In these conditions, far from pressing for further guards, he regarded them now as useless provocation.

For twenty-five years, my father had lived at a peculiar diagonal to Chinese society. The Maritime Customs was not a colonial elite, ruling a subject people. It was not a modern expatriate community, out for the take. It was not a diplomatic body, looking after national interests. The involvement it brought with China was more intimate than these. But, inevitably, it was still dissociated from the deeper fabric of Chinese life. In the imperial period, Western arrogance naturally permeated the Service. In the republican period, there was perhaps less of this, but the weakening of the state of which it was a semi-detached arm encouraged a certain ironic distance instead, capable of being no less indifferent to the human realities surrounding it. My father had seen a great deal of China, more than most educated contemporaries born in the country, but a basic remoteness remained. Now, perhaps, this gap lessened. Under Japanese attack, risks to life were shared, and my father's admiration for the fortitude and ingenuity of his subordinates came out of a common experience. The resourcefulness of ordinary Chinese, their extraordinary ability in time of war 'to get ten litres out of a litre bottle'[99] made a deep impression on him, and he became correspondingly more caustic about the authorities set over them.

---

97. CMC 31608, Confidential Letters IGS, Lungchow, 15 January 1940.
98. CMC 3326: Lungchow, Despatch No. 3405, Handing-Over-Charge Memorandum, 30 May 1940.
99. CMC 31608: Confidential Letters IGS, Lungchow 14 February 1940.

In November the Japanese navy landed an expeditionary force on the north shore of the Gulf of Tonkin, which rapidly crossed the mountains into central Kwangsi. An aircraft carrier supplied blitzes overhead.[100] By the end of the month Nanning had fallen, cutting the supply line to the interior – 'a severe blow', Maze wrote to London, since 'about one third of free China's imports of war materials passed along the Nanning road'.[101] Turning south-west, a flying column reached Lungchow in December and laid it waste. My father reported: 'four-fifths of the town has been razed to the ground, and the bridge over the river partly wrecked by dynamite'.[102] Namkuan was occupied a few days later. Customs staff were evacuated to Langson just in time. When Japanese troops moved on, they set up the frontier station again, and a detachment returned to Lungchow. In the midst of all this, my mother flew out from England, on a small French plane covering a few hundred miles a day, to join him in Langson. In the back country round Caobang, later scene of Sino-Vietnamese battles, she went along on inspection tours with him. In April Lungchow was heavily bombed from the sea again – 'I cannot conceive why. There is almost literally nothing worth attacking.'[103] In May he handed over charge to a successor. Within another couple of months, Japanese inspectors were stationed inside French territory, controlling all traffic to China.[104] In Nanjing, a collaborationist government had been set up under Chiang Kai-shek's vice-chairman, Wang Ching-wei, claiming legitimate KMT credentials.

Recalled to Shanghai, my father was promoted to Statistical Secretary, one of the grandest jobs in the Service – responsible for collation of returns, publication of results, maintaining of archives, running a printing-press, keeping a considerable library. In the summer of 1940 my aunt brought the children out across Canada. Probably, the family lived in some style – if with the discretion of the

---

100. For this campaign, see Frank Dorn, *The Sino-Japanese War, 1937–1941*, New York 1974, pp. 284–303.

101. Maze to Cubbon, 29 January 1940: Maze Confidential Papers, Vol. 14, 81.

102. CMC 31608, Confidential Letters IGS, Lungchow, 5 January 1940.

103. CMC 32583, Lungchow S/O No. 704, 20 April 1940.

104. For this development, see Minami Yoshizawa, 'The Nishihara Mission in Hanoi, July 1940', in Takashi Shiraishi and Motoo Furuta, *Indochina in the 1940s and 1950s*, Ithaca 1992, pp. 9–54; Hata Ikuhiko, 'The Army's Move into Northern Indochina', in James Morley, *The Fateful Choice: Japan's Advance into South-East Asia 1939–1941*, New York 1980, pp. 155–208. By September, the Japanese army was in occupation of Tonkin.

haut fonctionnaire, rather than the chromium opulence of Ballard's
business mileu in *Empire of the Sun*. Economic security and domestic
union were to hand; my father had badly wanted both. But he had
never liked Shanghai, symbol of everything Westerners made of
China; and he was bored by any desk job, however elevated – 'I like
moving about', he wrote from one of his wilder locations. Most
oppressive of all, of course, was the atmosphere in the International
Settlement, now surrounded by Japanese troops and warships on
every side, as the bad news from Europe came in. 'Shanghai life is
anything but gay', he wrote to Ireland in February 1941: 'it is quiet
and dull, and most of us prefer it that way in these times. Because the
alternative – tense and menacing – is never very remote.'[105] He wanted
a daughter, but could scarcely enlarge the family 'when there is always
the possibility of an evacuation scramble (to say nothing of a
Japanese concentration camp)'.[106] In April, twelve months leave came
due. Maze, reluctant to let staff go, tempted him with Tientsin, the
second largest port in the country. My mother put her foot down.
Europe was out of reach. We sailed in the *President Coolidge* for San
Francisco.

California in the summer of 1941 was in another time-capsule.
While the family settled at Los Gatos, the Japanese grip tightened in
Shanghai. Quotas from occupied ports for the expenses of the
Inspectorate were withheld until a Japanese Commissioner was
appointed in the city. Maze, citing his experience at Ichang during the
Boxer Rebellion of 1900, resisted any contingency planning for evacuation, keeping all Allied Commissioners at their posts.[107] Within hours
of Pearl Harbor, as my parents watched with astonishment mass panic
and exodus from the Bay Area, the Japanese took control of the
International Settlement. Two days later Maze was put under house
arrest, and dismissed by the Wang Ching-wei regime in Nanking.
Kishimoto, whom my father as a young man had dreamt of succeeding, took over as Inspector-General, and the service was purged of US
and British employees. In March the Kempetai, Japan's feared military
police, flung Maze into a felon's prison for lack of cooperation with
the new authorities. Nanking, however, had not yet declared war on
the Allies. After a month Maze was released, and in the summer of

---

105. L: 21 February 1941.
106. L: 28 January 1941.
107. Maze to Lockhart (American Consul-General in Shanghai), 29 April 1941:
Maze Papers, Confidential Letters, Vol. 14, US Section, Item 15.

1942 he and other Allied Customs staff were allowed – at the height of the Pacific War – to leave Shanghai for Mozambique.

The anomalous status of the Chinese Maritime Customs held good to the end. In the First World War, Germans and Austrians had been discharged, but not interned. Now the boot was on the other foot, and British and Americans were discharged. But the Nanking government in 1942 acted as the Peking government had done in 1917, treating them not as enemy nationals but merely as employees whose contract had come to an end. In Shanghai, bureaucratic continuity was meticulously kept up. Imperturbably, as the British were being routed in Malaya, the new Chinese Statistical Secretary was writing to the Inspector-General: 'S/O No. 224. Dear Mr Kishimoto, I beg to renew the suggestion made by my predecessor, Mr Anderson ...'[108]

From Lourenço Marques, Maze made his way at the end of 1942 back to Chungking to resume his position as Inspector-General in the KMT zone. He found everything changed. After the fall of Singapore and Hong Kong, the prestige of Britain was low; nationalist feeling against foreign officials was strong; and he was no longer shielded by distance from the Generalissimo, for whom he now developed an intense dislike ('it is noticeable that, while "Liberalism" and Communism are condemned, silence is maintained regarding Fascism and Nazism').[109] In May 1943 he threw in the sponge. The last years, he observed with a new-found candour, had seen 'the closing phases of the romantic story of the quasi-British control of the Chinese Maritime Customs Service'.[110] Now – it was useless to conceal some bitterness – the baton had to be handed over to America.[111] In June the Nationalist government, with the *agrément* of Washington, appointed Lester Little, long-time Commissioner in Canton, the last Western Inspector-General of the Chinese Customs.

In California my father, descending into long illness, was in no condition to go back to Chungking. Invalided out of the service in 1942,

---

108. CMC 30347: 10 January 1942.

109. Maze to Cubbon, London Secretary of the CMC, 'Secret', 3 May 1943: Maze Papers, Confidential Letters, Vol. 15, 403.

110. Dossier in Maze Confidential Papers, Vol. 15, 441.

111. See Maze to Cubbon, 7 May 1943: Maze Confidential Papers, Vol. 15, 414: 'When all is said and done, the appointment of an *American* to the office of I.G. (taking into consideration Hart's remarkable services to China and the world; and Aglen's outstanding administration of her financial affairs, etc, during the political confusion which for a time followed the overthrow of the Tsing Dynasty in 1911) is to some extent an affront to England – and, I am told, is meant to be so!'

he worked when he was able in the Office of Political Warfare in San Francisco, set up by London to collect information and broadcast propaganda to China. A film of pain obscures these years, in the few letters that survive. In 1945, the family boarded the *Queen Mary*, still a troop ship, for Greenock. On reaching Waterford, he assumed he had little time left. But his mind must have still turned to China. The last letter to be found is not by him. It is a reply from his Cantonese deputy at Lungchow, thanking my father for an enquiry about his fate that had taken six months to find its way round China in 1946. The letter, in tiny clear handwriting, told him without fuss the story of what had happened to his different assistants, scattered from Sinkiang to Kwangtung, and their children ('including the daughter who liked to dress as a boy'), during the war: hunger, captivity, escape, promotion, death. The author, now in charge of the customs in Hainan, ended: 'The Chinese people with the potential power of overcoming unbearable difficulties may set their house in order. It is very kind of you to think of us. If the people, especially those in power, of the world understand what is friendship and have in mind the farewell of others as you, an everlasting world peace would not be a dream. I hope I may be able to come over and see you some time in the future when the cost of an air passage will be reduced to an amount I can afford to pay, or at least I can talk with and see you in a television telephone. I have every reason to believe this is not a simple vision'.[112] The letter was sent in December. By the time it got to Ireland, my father was dead.

The Foreign Inspectorate of the Maritime Customs lasted until the PLA entered Canton in October 1949. Its final service fitted the American postscript. Well beforehand, on orders from Chiang Kai-Shek who did not trust his own navy, Little loaded up 200 tons of gold and silver in Customs cruisers – the whole bullion reserves of China – and shipped them off to Taiwan, to await the arrival of the Generalissimo.

1998–2005

---

112. Letter: Hui Sungkai, 14 November 1946.

INDEX OF NAMES